TEACHING FOR CREATIVE ENDEAVOR

Bold New Venture

ALREADY PUBLISHED IN THE

Bold New Venture *Series*

TEAM TEACHING
INDEPENDENT STUDY
FLEXIBLE SCHEDULING
NONGRADED SCHOOLS IN ACTION
TEACHING FOR CREATIVE ENDEAVOR

TEACHING FOR CREATIVE ENDEAVOR

Bold New Venture

EDITED BY

WILLIAM B. MICHAEL

INDIANA UNIVERSITY PRESS

BLOOMINGTON AND LONDON

Library of Congress catalog card number: 68–14607
Manufactured in the United States of America

TO MY FATHER
Whose Creative Impact as a Teacher
Is Exceeded Only by his Ingenuity
as a Dry-Fly Trout Fisherman

Preface

Bold New Venture Series

AMERICAN EDUCATION is emerging as a new frontier. Staggering challenges brought about by the contemporary demand for quality education for a bulging and diverse student population must be met. Old solutions for new problems will not suffice.

Pioneer educators are testing promising new programs and practices to effect fundamental improvement in the schools. Healthy dissatisfactions have led to the belief that if the schools are to be significantly better, they will have to be substantially different. Both the substance and the form of instruction are undergoing searching reappraisal. Exciting innovations have been instituted in schools scattered throughout the country. The *Bold New Venture* series is designed to inform educators and the interested public about these new developments and to assist in their evaluation.

The books in this series differ from much of the professional literature in education. The contributors, for the most part, are practitioners. Admittedly they are partial to their topics. Nevertheless, pitfalls are exposed and candid treatment is given to the issues. Emphasis has been put on reporting *how* as well as *why* new practices and programs were inaugurated. The volumes in this series are intended to be a stimulus to the conversation which must take place if fresh methods of teaching are to find their way into the schools.

Topics included in the *Bold New Venture* series include team teaching, flexible scheduling, independent study, the nongraded school, instructional materials centers, data processing, small group instruction, and technological aids.

While journalists criticize, scholars theorize about, and philosophers analyze education, the teachers of America must act. Educators must leap from theory to practice in individualizing instruction. More responsibility must be given and accepted by youngsters for their own learning. Intellectual inquiry must become full-time, leisure-time, and life-time pursuits.

Progress in education does not always come by the process of addition with more teachers, more books, more courses, and more money. Real improvement can come from original uses of scarce human talent, precious time, and new methods.

Because it is intended primarily for teachers and administrators, the *Bold New Venture* series focuses on the practical problems of teaching. What has been operationally successful for some teachers may have application for other teachers. If new practices or programs result from these books, then the series will have fulfilled its aim, for the *Bold New Venture* books are calls and guides to action.

Bloomington, Indiana

D.W.B.
E.G.B.

Contents

Introduction xi

PART I

THE DESCRIPTION, DEVELOPMENT, AND ASSESSMENT OF CREATIVE ABILITIES

Overview 1

1 Creative Abilities of Elementary School Children *E. Paul Torrance* 3

2 Implications of the Structure-of-Intellect Model for High School and College Students *J. P. Guilford and Mary L. Tenopyr* 25

PART II

CURRICULUM PLANNING AND INSTRUCTIONAL PROCEDURES FOR REALIZATION OF CREATIVE ENDEAVOR

Overview 47

3 Creativity in the Very Young *John A. R. Wilson and Mildred C. Robeck* 55

4 Creativity and the Curriculum *Louis J. Rubin* 74

5 Mathematics and Science in the Elementary School *Albert R. Hibbs* 90

6 The Natural Sciences *Abraham S. Fischler* 101

7 Secondary School Mathematics *Stephen S. Willoughby* 115

8 Language Arts in the Elementary School *Sara W. Lundsteen* 131

9 English Composition and Literature in the Secondary School *William Georgiades and Joan J. Michael* 162

10 Foreign Languages *Jesse O. Sawyer* 176

11 Elementary Social Studies *Mary Jo Woodfin* 191

12 Secondary Social Studies *Dale L. Brubaker* 203
13 Visual Arts *Jerome J. Hausman* 216
14 Performing Arts *John Edward Blankenchip* 230
15 The College and University *William B. Michael* 237

Part III

How Supervisors, Administrators, and Counselors Can Facilitate Expression of Creative Behavior

Overview 261
16 Supervisory Personnel *Mary Jo Woodfin* 266
17 The School Administrator
Irene S. Hophan and Mary M. Peters 282
18 Counseling and Creativity
Marcella R. Bonsall and Ernest F. Neumann 296

Part IV

Practice of Mental Health Principles at School and Home To Facilitate Creative Endeavor

Overview 313
19 Mental Health Principles at School
Donald A. Schwartz and Marcella R. Bonsall 316
20 How Parents Can Foster Creativity in Their Children
John Curtis Gowan 330
References and Selected Readings 342
Index 355

Introduction

DURING THE PAST TWENTY YEARS the teaching profession has been hearing much about creativity. Although considerable attention has been given to the description and measurement of creative abilities as well as to creativity in the teaching act, relatively little has been written regarding how school personnel—teachers, counselors, supervisors, and administrators—can bring about the expression and manifestation of creative endeavor on the part of the learner. Despite the fact that creative teaching and the observable creative behaviors in the learner are not and could not be completely separable experiences, the central purpose of this volume has been to suggest ways in which all people in the school community can help in the development of the creative abilities of children, adolescents, and adults. An effort has been made to demonstrate the application of existing knowledge and psychological principles of creative development to problems of school learning from kindergarten through college. Thus, the writers of many chapters have attempted to translate theories about creative behavior to school practice broadly conceived.

Despite the rather pragmatic direction of the volume, the two chapters in Part I are concerned with developing a largely theoretical base concerning the psychological development and nature of creative abilities. Nevertheless, the authors have made a conscious as well as conscientious attempt to suggest ways in which creative potentialities can be brought to fruition.

In Part II emphasis is placed on how curriculum planning and instructional procedures in a variety of subject-matter areas can be employed to facilitate the realization of creative endeavor. For the convenience of readers with specific subject-matter interests, an effort has been made to have several separate chapters in subject-matter areas at the elementary or secondary school levels. Setting the stage for this section are two chapters: Chapter 3, which is concerned with the development of creativity in the preschool and kindergarten child as viewed from the standpoint of learning principles with implications for instructional planning, curriculum development, and evaluation, and Chapter 4, which is devoted to general principles of curriculum development in relation to the manifestations of creative behavior largely in the secondary school and college settings. How teaching for creative endeavor in the elementary school may be realized is developed in Chapter 5 (Mathematics and Science), Chapter 8 (Language Arts), Chapter 11 (Social Studies), and Chapter 13 (Visual Arts). Relative to a principal emphasis on teaching for creative endeavor at the secondary level are five chapters: Chapter 6 (Natural Sciences), Chapter 7 (Mathematics), Chapter 9 (English Composition and Literature), Chapter 10 (Foreign Languages), and Chapter 12 (Social Studies). One chapter that seems to be almost as appropriate at the college level as at the secondary school level is that concerned with the Performing Arts (Chapter 14). Specifically prepared to emphasize teaching for creative outcomes for college and university students is Chapter 15.

In Part III attention is given to how key professional personnel in the school setting, whose major responsibility is not teaching in the classroom, can help to bring about creative behavior on the part of the learner. Thus separate chapters are included to reveal how supervisory personnel (Chapter 16), the school administrator (Chapter 17), and the school counselor (Chapter 18) can aid in the realization of creative endeavor in the learning situation.

Since a favorable state of mental health is hypothesized by many to facilitate the development of creatively oriented behavior, Part IV includes two chapters specifically concerned with this thesis. In the first chapter (Chapter 19) the writers direct their attention to how human needs and affective capacities of members of the school organization, as viewed within the framework of mental health principles, can influence students in developing and expressing their creative potentialities. In the second chapter the writer undertakes to show how parents can help to foster creative behavior in their children.

In the preparation of this volume the participants were given virtually complete freedom to develop their points of view and were encouraged not only to define creativity and related terms in a manner which to them was meaningful but also to implement theory in whatever way seemed most satisfactory to their particular orientation. The editor did indicate to each contributor his preference that relatively greater emphasis be placed on the means for the development and manifestation of creative behavior in the learner rather than on teaching activity itself as a creative process. Although, as implied previously, such a differentiation is somewhat artificial. Whenever they felt it to be appropriate, the authors were encouraged to cite research findings to substantiate positions taken, although it was clearly recognized that the existence of marked differences in the preferences of individual writers would lead to noticeable discrepancies in the amount of research cited from chapter to chapter. Moreover, the contributors were urged to draw on their own professional experiences and research backgrounds both in theorizing about creativity and in suggesting applications for school practice. Admittedly, some readers may be disturbed by the diversity in the definitions of creativity, by the differences in emphasis on product and process, as well as by some unevenness in relative stress placed on research, theory, and practice. However, the editor believed at the outset of this endeavor, as he believes now, that only by placement of minimal restraints on each author would there be a maximal opportunity for each writer to be creative in suggesting ways in which the learner can become creative in his own behavior and in his problem-solving capabilities. Thus it appeared that any major effort on the part of the editor to achieve a uniform style of presentation or to blend the presentations by any significant tampering with the text prepared by each contributor might seriously detract from the unique contribution which each contributor could make to the study of teaching for creative endeavor.

The editor would like to express his appreciation to the contributors for their prompt and enthusiastic response as well as for the innovative and creative nature of their chapters. The editor is grateful to the University of California for making available a one-semester sabbatical leave in residence during 1965-66 that permitted in large part the completion of this volume. Special thanks are extended to the late Dr. David Beggs for his encouragement and assistance in the preparation of this volume and to Jane Rodman and the editorial staff of the Indiana University Press for their helpful cooperation and numerous constructive suggestions.

San Marino, California WILLIAM B. MICHAEL

TEACHING FOR CREATIVE ENDEAVOR

Bold New Venture

PART I

THE DESCRIPTION, DEVELOPMENT, AND ASSESSMENT OF CREATIVE ABILITIES

Overview

As a prerequisite to the curricular and instructional concerns of the second major division of this volume, the two chapters of Part I furnish a foundation concerning the nature, development, and evaluation of creative thinking abilities. Whereas Torrance's chapter is primarily concerned with the development and assessment of creative abilities in elementary school children, the second chapter by Guilford and Tenopyr furnishes a theoretical structure within which the description and measurement of creative abilities may be viewed for the learner at almost any stage of his educational career.

With reference to the elementary school Torrance has suggested in the first portion of his chapter a workshop program that will develop teaching skills to elicit creative behavior in children. Some of the goals of such a program include the following: (1) showing respect for the questions and ideas of children, (2) asking provocative questions of children, (3) recognizing and valuing originality, (4) helping children to develop the ability to elaborate on their ideas, (5) giving time to children for unevaluated practice and experimentation in learning, (6) assisting children in their reading activities to become creative by heightening their expectations and by encouraging them to take an active part in reproducing imaginatively what is real, in elaborating upon what they have read, in transforming and rearranging what has been read, and by going beyond what has been read, (7) furnishing guided, planned sequences of learning experiences enabling task mastery and sustained motivation, (8) developing historiographic skills in "searching for the truth," in the process of which habits of reevaluating information and of proposing alternative interpretations of possible causes and consequents are developed, (9) having children participate in elementary descriptive research activities that involve answering questions about current observations, and (10) encouraging participation of children in simple experimentation that gives nearly immediate feedback.

In the second portion of this chapter Torrance turns his attention to ways in which creative abilities can be assessed. These methods include: (1) observation of children in their customary school activities, (2) observation of children in school activities that have been especially devised to assess creative abilities and associated motivational patterns, and (3) tests of creative thinking abilities. Specific illustrations of types of behaviors in observable situations as well as of testing procedures are cited.

Within the framework of the structure-of-intellect model Guilford and Tenopyr look at creativity as an intellectual process involving the generation of new information largely in a problem-solving context. To facilitate education for effective problem solving, they have suggested the need for (1) training students to develop basic abilities involved in productive performance and (2) furnishing them practice in solving a broad variety of problems for which environmental inputs can be monitored so that feedback can be provided to enrich the learning experience. Principles underlying use of auto-instructional techniques to facilitate realization of creative endeavor are cited. It is suggested that specific instructions regarding the nature of creative thinking activities can also be helpful in improving problem-solving capabilities in many fields of creative endeavor.

CHAPTER 1

Creative Abilities of Elementary School Children

by

E. PAUL TORRANCE

E. Paul Torrance has had a distinguished and varied career in education. He has been a high school counselor, teacher, and principal; director of research in support of U.S. Air Force Survival training; and director of the Bureau of Research and professor of Educational Psychology at the University of Minnesota. He is presently chairman and professor of Educational Psychology at the University of Georgia.

Dr. Torrance has won wide recognition for his studies of the psychology of stress and of creative thinking. He is the author of Guiding Creative Talent, Education and the Creative Potential, Gifted Children in the Classroom, Constructive Behavior: Stress, Personality, and Mental Health, *and* Rewarding Creative Behavior: Experiments in Classroom Creativity. *With B. F. Cunnington, he is the co-author of the Imagi/Craft Series, and with R. E. Myers,* Can You Imagine?, Invitations to Thinking and Doing, Invitations to Speaking and Writing Creatively, Teaching Gifted Elementary Children How To Do Research, *and* For Those Who Wonder. *He edited* Talent and Education, *and co-edited with Robert D. Strom,* Mental Health and Achievement: Increasing Potential and Reducing School Dropout. *He has also written several batteries of tests of creative thinking and motivation that have been widely used in research.*

Can Creative Abilities Be Developed?

AS AN ELEMENTARY SCHOOL TEACHER, supervisor, or principal you may have some misgivings about the development of creative abilities through formal educational experiences. You may even have doubts that creative abilities actually can be developed through school experiences. You may doubt that teachers who have been taught and have taught in traditional, authority-oriented ways can encourage their pupils to behave creatively and to learn in creative ways. You may be afraid that such teachers would feel psychologically uncomfortable if they did encourage their pupils to behave creatively.

These are old issues that have long been used to pour cold water on every bold venture designed to bring about a more creative kind of education. Alfred Binet, who was responsible for developing the basic pattern of intelligence testing throughout the world, spoke out quite strongly in 1909 and even earlier against the prevailing prejudice in his day against the "educability of intelligence." He clearly recognized that there are many important mental abilities not assessed by his measures and that all of them are susceptible of development. He saw that intelligence is not "a single function, individual and of a particular essence, but that it consists of all the little functions of discrimination, observation, retention, imagination, ingenuity, etc., which are plastic and extensible." In other words, Binet's concept of intelligence was bigger than the concept of mental functioning embodied in the test that has come to bear his name. He demonstrated that such abilities as he called "creative intelligence and ingenuity" can be developed through educational experiences, even among mentally retarded children (Binet, 1909).

If you are willing to examine the evidence available today (Taylor, 1964a; Torrance, 1962, 1965a), I do not see how you could have much doubt that it is possible to develop the creative abilities through educational experiences. Of course, you could argue that even if a child develops these abilities to a high degree, it does not guarantee that he will behave creatively or that he will make important creative contributions. This may be partly true, because creative achievement requires commitment, courage, hard work, honesty, and the like. The development of creative abilities certainly increases the chances that a person will behave creatively. In my own book, *Rewarding Creative Behavior* (1965a), and in *Creativity: Progress and Potential*, edited by Calvin W. Taylor (1964a, pp. 52-54), I have cited a great deal of the evidence that I believe shows that it is possible to provide educational experiences that will enhance the development of the creative abilities of elementary school children. Again, a number of experiments have shown that these abilities can be developed in children classified as mentally retarded and that growth can take place during the fourth grade period when a decrement in creative functioning usually occurs in schools in the United States.

I must admit that we do not yet have any massive amount of evidence to assure you that teachers who have been taught and have taught in traditional, authority-oriented ways can encourage children to behave creatively and to learn in creative ways. To make such a change requires considerable change in orientation and the development of a number of skills that have not heretofore been developed. Such changes require that the teacher be concerned about the effectiveness of his teaching and willing to expend some expensive energies in practicing and mastering these skills. He has to be prepared for some failures, discouragement, criticism, and hard work. If you are thinking about changing your teaching to encourage more creative development among your pupils, you might ask yourself how far you are willing to go to accomplish such a goal. Here are some of the specific questions you should ask yourself:

Would you be willing to let your pupils ask questions about whatever puzzles them?

Would you teach something outside your prepared lessons?

Would you teach something outside the curriculum approved by your school or school system?

Would you permit a child to work alone in the classroom?

Would you permit a child to continue an activity in which he is absorbed, even if he has to miss a planned activity?

Would you recognize and acknowledge some heretofore unrecognized potential and give it a chance to develop, even if the child misbehaves a great deal?

Would you allow the child to be successful in some way that is possible for him, even though it is not the way you had planned?

Would you withhold criticism or correction long enough to permit a child to discover and correct his own errors?

Would you give the unliked and unloved child a chance to make constructive contributions to the welfare of the group?

Would you sometimes carry out a child's ideas about a classroom activity?

Would you encourage, permit, and give credit for self-initiated learning inside and outside the classroom?

Would you use fantasies to help children get at real problems?

Would you support a child against peer pressures to conformity against his convictions?

Would you respect and acknowledge the potentialities of slow learners?

Would you plan a lesson specifically to help one child solve a problem?

To the teacher who has been taught and has taught in traditional, authority-oriented ways, these are nonhabitual ways of behaving and nonhabitual behavior takes deliberate effort and practice. Such a teacher has to give his own creative abilities a workout and develop them.

It is certainly natural to expect that teachers accustomed to teaching exclusively by authority will feel psychologically uncomfortable if they encourage their pupils to learn in creative ways. Some degree of success can give such a teacher courage and confidence. One way of getting started and achieving some success in creative ways of teaching is to use some of the already prepared, guided, planned experiences in creative teaching in the form of recordings, teacher guides, ideabooks, and the like. Success will not continue to come, however, unless you start using these to get new ideas and to use the experience yourself to develop creatively. What I have suggested to individual teachers and faculty groups is to undertake a year-long program of deliberate and systematic efforts or workshops to develop some of the skills needed for this kind of teaching (Torrance, 1964-65). I shall now outline quite briefly such a series of experiences that I have developed on the basis of the best that I have been able to find out about creative ways of teaching—or the kind of teaching most likely to result in the development of creative abilities.

Suggested Workshop Program

1. Being Respectful of Questions and Ideas

For the first deliberate effort or workshop, I propose that you work at developing the skills involved in being respectful of the questions and ideas of children. I believe that almost every elementary teacher could begin immediately to increase the total learning, as well as the creative development, of pupils by being more respectful of their questions and ideas.

One of the first requirements for creative behavior is the capacity to wonder, to be puzzled, and to respond constructively. Children have this capacity and their curiosity makes them ask questions and to seek answers, usually with energy and enthusiasm. This questioning can be irritating, threatening, and generally uncomfortable to teachers. There are temptations to discourage this curiosity in ways that are actually dishonest and damaging both to creative development and character development.

Being respectful of children's questions is not easy for teachers accustomed to teaching by authority. It requires that teachers respond with interest and curiosity rather than with threat and punishment. Poor questions should be used as an opportunity to teach skills in asking good questions. It requires helping children to find answers to questions and making the effort worthwhile. Perhaps the most important reward for the curious child is to find answers to his questions. This does not mean that the teacher has to answer immediately all the questions children ask. In some cases, the teacher need not answer questions at all. The teacher who uses creative ways of learning will learn how to enrich the period between the question and the answer. He seldom gives answers that can be discovered by the children themselves. He leads them to produce, consider, and evaluate a wide range of possibilities.

Children should be taught to test their ideas but this has to be done in a sympathetic and constructive atmosphere rather than in a hostile and punishing one. The teacher who respects children's ideas avoids making fun of the ideas expressed, the gadgets and inventions produced, and the songs and poems composed.

In this first month of skill development, I proposed that as an individual or as a workshop group that you test the ideas just reviewed. To do this, I suggest that you:

1. Think about what it really means to be respectful of the questions and ideas of children.
2. Try deliberately to be respectful of the questions and ideas of your pupils.
3. Write detailed descriptions of one incident in which you tried to

be respectful of an unusual or vexing question and one incident in which you tried to be respectful of an original idea proposed by a child.

4. Discuss your descriptions with someone else, trying to decide how well you succeeded in being respectful of the child's questions and ideas—not just appearing to be respectful. You should try then to produce a variety of other possible ways by which you could have been more respectful.

If you decide to do this in a workshop and this procedure is too threatening, you might discuss the description of one of the teachers who feels quite secure or incidents reported by other teachers. I have included a number of such incidents in *Rewarding Creative Behavior: Experiments in Classroom Creativity* (1965a). The most successful experimental attempt that I know about (Enochs, 1964) on developing these skills involved the use of videotapes of the teacher's classroom interaction. The teacher viewed the videotape with the experimenter and discussed it with him. This procedure produced greater changes in behavior and greater creative development of pupils than was found in control groups. I believe similar changes can be accomplished by any teacher or workshop group interested in examining their own behavior and trying deliberately to modify it.

As a first step, why not write out descriptions of incidents in which you tried to develop the skill of being respectful of unusual questions or ideas. The following questions can be used as a guide:

1. What was the question (idea)? Who asked (expressed) it? What were the general conditions under which it was asked (proposed)?
2. What was your own immediate reaction?
3. What was the immediate reaction of the class?
4. In what way was respect shown for the question (idea)?
5. What, if any, were the observable effects (immediate and/or long range)?

In faculty workshops, the success of this procedure will depend largely upon the degree to which the supervisor and other leaders create a situation in which members feel respected and are willing to expose their values and behavior patterns so that perceptions and reactions can be changed.

2. Asking Provocative Questions

Another sure way of improving classroom creativity immediately is to ask more provocative questions. By doing this, you would also increase excitement about learning, acquisition of information, ability to recall information in problem-solving, and depth of understanding.

Some surveys indicate that over 90 percent of the questions teachers ask call only for the reproduction of what is in the textbook. When I mentioned this fact in an article in *The Instructor* magazine (October, 1964), one teacher wrote the editor that she could "go me one better," that 100 percent of her questions called only for the recall of what is in the textbook. She wrote that in her opinion the first job of the teacher is to decide what students ought to know and that the second is to make sure that they learn it. I believe this teacher of thirty years' experience misunderstood what I was trying to say. I was not saying that there are not some things that are important enough to memorize. The important thing I was trying to say is that children ought to think about what they learn and be able to do something with it.

In a workshop aimed to improve ability to ask provocative questions, something has to be done to help teachers see what some of the different kinds of questions are, other than factual. A number of conceptual schemes are useful in generating ideas for questions that call into play different kinds of abilities and skills. Those of you who are familiar with Benjamin Bloom's (1956) *Taxonomy of Educational Objectives* might want to follow the categories used in this classification scheme—such categories as knowledge, comprehension, application, analysis, synthesis, and evaluation. One workshop project might involve a deliberate attempt on the part of teachers to think of questions that fall into each of the categories in this taxonomy.

Since many children have become so accustomed to the idea that all questions asked in school have a single correct answer, it is important to help teachers develop the skills of asking questions that call for divergent thinking (Guilford, 1959). By this, I mean questions that call for:

Fluency: the production of as many ideas as possible, not bothering at first about quality.

Flexibility: shifting to a variety of approaches or categories.

Originality: unusual or uncommon ideas, away from the obvious.

Elaboration: working out the details of an idea or planning the steps.

In some of the workshops I conduct, I ask participants to think of as many provocative questions as they can about "ice." I try to communicate what I mean by provocative questions, using "apple" as an example. I tell them that I am not interested in simple factual questions such as "What colors do apples come in?" "How many seeds do apples have?" and the like. I want them to ask provocative questions such as "What was there about the apple that caused God to use it rather than some other fruit to tempt Eve?" After this, I give them a list of questions about ice and ask them to pick out the five questions that they consider most provocative. Following these two exercises, we score both the questions they produced and the questions they selected, using Burkhart's (Burkhart and Bernheim, 1963) criteria for evaluating unusual questions. They recognize then that many of the questions they asked are purely factual, and not self-involving, and do not call for thinking, especially divergent thinking. They begin also to sense what a provocative question is and the potential these have for developing creative thinking abilities.

After a teacher has worked for a few days trying to ask more provocative questions, it is useful for him to check his progress. Teachers in the upper elementary and high school grades can do this by having a child record a list of all the questions asked. Primary teachers would have to have a parent, supervisor, or student teacher record questions.

Or, teachers might just try to recall all of the questions they asked as soon afterwards as possible. Questions can then be analyzed in various ways and changes can be charted and evaluated. In a workshop teachers can analyze one another's questions and discuss possible alternatives.

3. Recognizing and Valuing Originality

A separate workshop on recognizing and valuing original ideas is proposed because I believe firmly that all teachers should be on the lookout for original ideas and place as much value on original work as on the acquisition of information. Such a workshop might be opened with an exercise to determine how well participants are able to produce and judge original responses. One of the items from the Incomplete Figures Test (Torrance, 1965a) is good for this purpose. Participants are asked first to produce what they consider an original response and then to judge a set of ten responses for originality. The originality score of the ten responses can be given and each participant can evaluate his judgments. A list of the most common responses can also be given so that participants can find out whether their own response falls in this category. In the process, they can be shown why certain responses are obvious and commonplace, being produced by most primitive and easy type of closure before the mind has paused long enough to make the mental leap necessary for an original response. Such responses, which are not surprising, do not indicate a break from the safe and easy.

Practice may be given with other sets of criteria, depending upon the interests of the working group. Some might like to work with the criteria proposed by Hans Selye (1962). He says that to be creative an idea must be true, generalizable, and surprising in the light of what is known at the time. Others (such as the U. S. Patent Office) require that original ideas also be useful, represent a step forward, and require creative intellectual energy.

Whatever criteria of originality you choose, I would suggest that you try deliberately to recognize and encourage originality for about a month. You must recognize, however, that your love for the one correct answer may stand in the way of your progress. One way of pulling yourself out of this rut is to write out detailed descriptions of some of these attempts and get someone else to analyze them. In writing these descriptions, the following questions are suggested as guides:

1. In what form did original ideas by the pupil occur?
2. What was your immediate reaction?
3. What were the reactions of the other pupils?
4. How did you show respect for the original idea?
5. What were the immediate and long-range effects of this incident?

4. Developing Ability to Elaborate

Any successful creative thinker has to be able to elaborate his ideas and work out the details. Many very original thinkers never receive credit for important breakthroughs because they fail to produce the details to complete the basic idea they produce.

Even people who are not very original in their thinking can make important contributions by elaborating a commonplace idea or helping an original thinker elaborate his ideas. Some people do not think very highly of this kind of creativity, but our society needs people who can work out the details of ideas and make them practical and attractive. They are sometimes called "embroiderers" because they make ideas "fancy." You can, of course, be too fancy and your work will lose some of its meaning and worth as a result. Yet a certain level of ability to elaborate seems necessary even for adequate adjustment to life. In one study (Will, 1964), it was found that the most characteristic feature of a group of delinquent girls was their extreme inability to elaborate. On the other hand, in a group of home economists in the Peace Corps (Hanson, 1964), all of whom were unusually high on elaboration ability, ability to elaborate was negatively related to effectiveness as a Peace Corps worker. What happened here was that all of them were adequate elaborators but some of them tended to become so lost in their elaboration and made things so fancy that the effectiveness of their work suffered in underdeveloped countries. A person can be a compulsive elaborator rather than being free to elaborate or not elaborate, depending upon what will be effective.

In the in-service workshop, it is suggested that ability to elaborate be explored in much the same way that originality was explored. In fact, responses produced in the Incomplete Figures Test can be evaluated for elaboration.

In the classroom, the teacher might want to focus on encouraging elaboration in some particular subject such as reading. Reading is a good candidate since some reading experts (Durrell and Chambers, 1958) believe that well-developed exercises in elaborative thinking in reading will produce higher permanent retention and greater availability of information in new situations. One of the most common methods of elaborating what is read is to have children illustrate the poems and stories that they read. Other media, such as music, songs, rhythmic movement, and dramatics can also be used in elaborating what is read. Having children write different endings for stories or change a character in some specific way to see what else this would change, and asking them to expand upon a certain episode in a story or poem are other ideas for elaborating what is read.

A teacher might want to select some pupil who is having unusual difficulty in learning to read and to give him experience in elaborating what he reads. This procedure has been known to "unlock" some students having this difficulty and serve as the key to their learning to read.

A workshop group might see how many ideas it can produce for encouraging elaboration in connection with some particular area of the curriculum, such as reading instruction.

5. Unevaluated Practice and Experimentation

The use of the idea of giving time for unevaluated practice and experimentation has changed tremendously what happens in my own teaching. I do not grade the work of my students during the first half of the course. I want them to be free to read, think, and experiment. I want them to explore possible applications of the ideas they read and discuss. Prior to my adoption of this practice, few of my students made imaginative attempts to apply knowledge gained from the course in solving professional or personal problems. They now make far greater progress than formerly and the experience is much more likely to make a difference in their teaching.

With our bookkeeping system of credits and grades, it is difficult to realize that you do not have to evaluate everything a child does. Considerable theory and research, however, support the desirability of giving time for unevaluated practice and experimentation. External evaluation is almost always a threat and creates a need for defensiveness. This results in the denial of awareness to some portion of our experiencing or sensing. Then we lack the openness necessary in creative thinking. If a child is not free to test things out and to learn how to identify and correct his own errors, he will have no way of determining his own limits and potentialities.

To cultivate the skills needed in using unevaluated practice, you might try at least once each week for a month to arrange deliberately a time for unevaluated practice or experimentation. It is suggested that you record your experiences. You might describe the initial assignment, tell how you communicated to the children that they are free to experiment and that "it doesn't count on the record," detail what happened during the practice session and the nature of the later test activities, and evaluate the results. At the end of the month, you might compare the description of the first experience with the most recent one.

6. Developing Creative Readers

It is easier to remember and apply something read creatively than things read passively or even critically. When a child reads creatively, he is sensitive to problems and possibilities. To resolve this tension, he sees new relationships and possibilities, synthesizes unrelated elements, redefines known information into new uses, and builds onto what he knows. Thus, he produces multiple possibilities, looks at information in greater depth, and fills gaps to make ideas more useful, attractive, and exciting.

It takes effort to change from a passive or critical reader to a creative one. Teachers can help children become creative readers in two general ways: heightening their expectations and anticipations and encouraging them to do something with what they read. I have discussed these approaches elsewhere in some detail (Torrance, 1965b).

Heightening expectation involves some creation of tension or warming up. Doing something with what is read can occur at any one of four different levels:

1. Reproducing with imagination what is read, making things sound like the thing happening.
2. Elaborating what is read.
3. Transforming and rearranging what is read, as illustrated by Shakespeare's creativity.
4. Going beyond what is read.

In your workshop, teachers might work at the job of becoming more creative readers themselves. They should practice heightening their own expectations and anticipations when they read; try guessing what a story or book will be like, what its character will be like, and the experiences they will have. They should stop at various points and try to guess the outcomes and try to do something with what they read. They should try to read or tell stories with imagination, making them sound like the thing happening; elaborate what is read; transform and rearrange something read; and let their imaginations take them beyond what they read. It is anticipated that teachers who apply these ideas imaginatively to their own reading will be so excited about the experience that they will be unable to wait until the second week to begin teaching their pupils to become creative readers.

7. Guided, Planned Experiences

Creative thinking is unlikely to occur unless one thing can lead to another. Thus, the concept of guided, planned learning experiences is readily applied to classroom creativity. Investigators (Ojemann, 1948; Ojemann and Pritchett, 1963) are finding that mental development is quite different when children are provided planned, guided learning experiences than when they encounter only what the environment happens to provide. In a sense, I suppose this is the basic idea behind such projects as Head Start.

Guided, planned experiences represent a deliberate attempt to assist a child to learn by developing from an analysis of the learning task and the nature of the learner, a planned sequence of experiences for mastering the learning task and by motivating him to participate in these experiences. The instructional materials developed by Myers, Cunnington, and me (1965) during the past four years represent an attempt to translate this concept into concrete form, insofar as creative development is concerned. The ideabooks and teacher guides developed by Myers and me (1965) represent one kind of application, emphasizing warm-up experiences, producing ideas, and then doing something with these ideas. The recorded dramatizations of great moments of discovery and fantasies, recorded exercises in creative thinking, and supplementary exercises and activities in teacher guides represent another such attempt. All of these materials, which have fared rather well in field tests, are now available for more general use.

An in-service workshop might be built around the experimental use of the ideabooks or the recordings or around the construction of guided, planned experiences in creative thinking. To pursue the latter, teachers might be asked to examine their learning goals for the next month and to see which ones might be achieved with bonus dividends through guided, planned experiences in creative thinking. I would suggest the following steps:

1. Analyze the learning task and its nature. What are the possible ways or processes for achieving them? What are the alternatives? What conditions will help or hinder?

2. What is the level of development of the relevant skills and concepts of pupils? How well developed are the required abilities (such as memory, logical reasoning, and originality)? What are the pupils' preferred ways of learning? What are their potentialities?

3. What sequence of experiences will satisfy these requirements? How can pupils be motivated to participate in their sequence of experiences?

8. Historiography and the Search for the Truth

Since the very essence of creativity is "searching for the truth," it seems fitting that three workshop sessions be devoted to the development of skills required in the search for truth. The way will have been paved by the work on being respectful of the questions and ideas of children, asking provocative questions, recognizing and encouraging originality, encouraging elaboration, giving time for unevaluated practice and experimentation, developing creative readers, and the construction of guided, planned experiences in creative thinking.

Teachers should recognize that no subject—not even history—is a body of precise, memorizable facts. Historical interpretations change when we examine events at different times and places. An idea or event may be ignored at the time it occurred but take on much significance at a different time. Children should cultivate the habit of reevaluating information and considering alternative possibilities concerning causes and consequences. This calls for the skills and spirit of historiography.

If you are conducting a group workshop, you should familiarize the participants with the nature of the thinking processes and methods involved in historiography and give examples of how these methods can be applied to different subjects at all grade levels. Even children in the primary grades can study the changes that have taken place on their block during their lives or in their school building since they entered school. Children in the intermediate grades can use primary sources to try to determine which of several pictures of Christopher Columbus or of the Battle of Lexington tell the truth (Rogers, 1962).

In a short course on research methods, I teach sixth graders some of the skills of historiography through constructing from various witnesses and records their own growth curves, from kindergarten through sixth grade, for such things as height, weight, reading speed, vocabulary size, and curiosity. They immediately become involved in such problems as units of measurement, bias, conflicting information, inaccurate information, and the critical and creative processes of synthesizing information and getting at the truth.

As a workshop exercise, each teacher might create and test at least one lesson through which he attempts deliberately to develop some of the skills of historiography. Such a lesson might be about what happened in school or at home yesterday or last week, the changes in the school building during the past year, or an event in local or world history. It should involve the collection, evaluation, and synthesis of several different kinds of information.

9. Descriptive Research and the Search for the Truth

Methods of descriptive research enable us to tell more accurately and truthfully what is. Historiography helps us tell more truthfully what was and experimental methods permit us to predict what will be if certain factors are carefully controlled. Methods of descriptive research capture the results of experiments conducted by nature and society, while historiography helps discover the results of experiments conducted by time. A third method, experimental research, determines the effects of possible changes, procedures, and kinds of organization.

Focus in descriptive research is on existing conditions, or on how a person, group, or thing behaves in the present. It often involves comparisons or contrasts, such as differences between boys and girls or between children in Malaya and children in California.

As a workshop idea, I have suggested that teachers make visual aids of the following five ideas from Karl G. Anderson's unpublished "Creativity Is" (1964) that I think capture the spirit of descriptive research:

1. Wanting to know.
2. Looking twice.
3. Listening for smells.
4. Digging deeper.
5. Cutting holes to see through.

These five ideas can be applied in searching for the truth about almost anything. For example, select some object in the room, some event in history, some place in geography, some creative writing assignment, or the like. The teacher can then inquire: What do we want to know in order to describe it accurately? What can we find out by looking twice? How do we look twice? What do we do in listening for smells (using all of our being)? How can we dig deeper? How can we cut holes to see through (to keep from being deceived, to bring out something that is hidden)?

Children at least as early as the fifth and sixth grades can generate and collect quantitative data and apply many of the concepts of descriptive statistics, such as the mean, median, mode, range, and variability. Primary children can master simple methods of quantification and graphical representation as ways of describing something. They can construct models, illustrate, photograph, and develop other ways of comparing objects, events, and performances. All can begin developing the skills for finding out what they want to know, how to look twice, how to listen for smells, how to dig deeper, and how to cut holes to see through.

10. Experimental Research and the Search for the Truth

The workshop on experimental research should by all means involve participants in some kind of experiment. Special attention should be given to controlling as many variables as possible, the use of randomization, and careful delineation of the experimental conditions or treatments. There are a number of such experiments that are so simple that children in the fifth and sixth grades can conduct them by using children in the lower grades as subjects. If possible, the experiments should be planned to find out something that your teachers and pupils want to know. The experiments should be kept simple enough so that almost immediate results can be obtained and communicated through graphs, simple statistical tests, or the like.

Assessment of Creative Abilities

Can Creativity Be Developed If It Is Not There?

Teachers sometimes dismiss what we know about the development of creative abilities in elementary school children by saying, "You can't develop creativity if it isn't there!" I simply do not believe that there is any human being that does not have some creative potential—certainly not among the essentially normal human beings that populate our schools. Yes, I have seen some children who were so disturbed, so frightened and cowed, and so estranged that one would doubt that there was any creative potential there. I remember a tiny six-year-old girl named Penny. I did everything that I could think of to establish a relationship with her. I was unable to elicit any creative response. School had been in session for two months and the teacher had not yet been able to get her to say her name. She seemed frightened of everything. When I learned about her pathological family situation, I could understand her unresponsiveness. Later, when given an opportunity to express her ideas in figural form, she gave evidence of some traces of creativity. With much help and understanding, Penny finally manifested a reasonable degree of creativity, even in verbal areas. Kip, a six-year-old boy, was silent and unresponsive. No one could see much evidence of creativity. It was not until he started working with clay that he became alive. With clay as his medium, he was even able to loosen up and talk. I have known children who, through creative movement or dance, manifested the first evidence of creativity in school. This seemed to help unlock their minds and spirits, however, and they began showing creativity in other ways.

It may be that you have some youngsters who are so sick that you see no trace of creativity in their behavior. They may be beyond the help of the classroom teacher or the special area teachers. Psychotherapy may be necessary, but I believe that each individual has creative possibilities to some degree. Some children, however, do not prefer to learn in creative ways. They learn faster and more effectively when taught by authority. They become more creative when there are authorities upon whom they can depend.

There are a number of misconceptions, however, that blind us and keep us from seeing creative potentialities in some youngsters. One of these is the false belief that anyone who possesses a spark of creativity will somehow show it in spite of neglect, punishment, and coercive pressures. In our longitudinal studies I have seen children sacrificing needlessly what had seemed earlier to be a great creative potential. It is true that some of these youngsters will regain their creativity when they learn how to cope with the coercive pressures. Some of them, however, will never regain their creativity. They will choose instead the path of delinquency, crime, and mental illness—or, at best, a life of mediocrity and unrealized potential.

We are frequently blinded to creative potentialities by our emotional reactions to certain kinds of socially disapproved behavior. The child who is unsophisticated, quiet, strongly emotional, critical of others, stubborn, perhaps even negativistic, unwilling to accept things on the say-so of teachers, timid, and perhaps even fearful may be seen as totally lacking in creativity. Yet these are characteristics that actually describe many of the most highly creative people of the past.

We may also be blinded to creative potentialities in youngsters who swear, fight, or cheat. Yet I have known outstanding creative potentialities to be recognized through just such acts as these. This does not mean that we have to approve or condone such behavior. I believe, however, that teachers and counselors are capable of offering a kind of guidance that has important consequences for the realization of potentialities for constructive, creative behavior. If you believe this, you will not be willing to limit your concern to those potentialities that will flourish in spite of all efforts to thwart them. We should be concerned about all of those potentialities that can be realized with intelligent guidance, the provision of more favorable conditions, and opportunities for creative achievements.

We may also fail to see creative possibilities in youngsters who lack verbal skills. We tend to believe that a person who cannot express his ideas in words is not capable of producing ideas of genuine merit. The truth is that a person can be creative in an infinite number of ways and that many important ideas are expressed in media other than words.

We may also fail to identify creative potentialities when we place too high a premium on speed in tests and other indicators of ability and achievement. This is true of many youngsters from economically and culturally disadvantaged homes. Some of them are capable of a high level of thinking and will learn well, if not placed under time pressures. They learn by experimentation, testing alternatives, and examining various possibilities, and this kind of achievement takes time.

Methods of assessing or identifying creative potentialities may be approached from at least three levels: (1) the observation of children in their usual school activities, (2) the observation of children in school activities especially created to assess creative abilities and motivations, and (3) tests of creative thinking abilities.

Observations of Usual School Activities

There are times when a teacher is able to so involve an entire class that the general atmosphere is a creative one. Usually, however, different levels of creative functioning can be observed among the pupils of any particular classroom unless creative behavior is severely repressed. From a list of 230 different signs of creative classroom behavior compiled by the 200 students in one of my classes in "Creative Ways of Teaching," I offer below an abbreviated checklist that you may find useful in assessing the creative involvement and, perhaps to some extent, creative abilities of children:

Intense absorption in listening, observing, and doing
Intense animation
Use of analogies in speech and writing

Bodily involvement in writing, reading, and drawing
Tendency to burst out to complete teacher's sentence
Tendency to challenge ideas of authorities
Habit of checking many sources
Tendency to take a closer look at things
Eagerness to tell others about discoveries
Continued creative work after "time is up" (bell or deadline)
Tendency to show relationships among apparently unrelated ideas
Follow-up at home or in community of ideas generated at school
Manifestations of curiosity
Spontaneous use of experimentation and discovery approaches
Imaginative play
Excitement in voice about discoveries
Habit of guessing outcomes and checking accuracy
Honesty and intense search for the truth
Low distractability
Manipulation of objects and ideas to obtain new combinations
Tendency to lose awareness of time
Penetrating observations and questions
Self-initiated learning projects
Tendency to seek alternatives and explore possibilities
Willingness to consider or toy with novel ideas

Observations in Activities Created to Assess Creative Abilities

Taylor (1964b) has offered a number of illustrations of how teachers can create situations to identify creatively gifted individuals. The following are a few of them:

1. At times, let students do most of the planning on their own and make most of their own decisions and observe which ones are most dependent and which ones have the least need for training and experience in self-guidance.
2. Develop exercises through which children report their inner feelings and impulses and then have them see how well they can intuitively anticipate a correct course of action.
3. Pose complex issues and see which children take a hopeful attitude rather than a position that things are in an impossible state of affairs and nothing can be done about them.
4. Have idea-generating sessions to see who comes up with the

most ideas, whose ideas bring out the strongest negative reactions from their classmates, and who tends to lead in expressing strong negative reactions. Observe who has the most courage to hold his ground or even move ahead, instead of retreating or giving up in the face of negative reactions.

5. Ask students to do a task which they have done before, but take away most of the facilities previously available to see who will be the most resourceful in improvising or in accomplishing the task without the usual facilities.

6. Structure some classroom task where those who tolerate uncertainty and ambiguity do better than those who are unable to do so—in other words, a situation in which the rewards go to those who keep the problem open and keep working on it with their own resources until they eventually attain a solution.

These are examples of the countless opportunities teachers can create in evoking and identifying behavior that will reveal glimpses of creative potentialities. Teachers who have used the ideabooks or exercises created by Myers and me (1965) often remark that almost any of these exercises can be used as tests of creative thinking abilities. In a sense this is true, although we have generally discouraged any kind of scoring or grading of these exercises. Teachers have made the same kinds of remarks about the Imagi/Craft materials (Cunnington and Torrance, 1965b). It may be discovered eventually that such activities as these provide more valid assessments of creative abilities than will carefully designed and scored tests of creative thinking abilities. The tests devised by Wallach and Kogan (1965), in fact, are quite similar in many ways to these activities. They tried deliberately to create a non-evaluative, game-like atmosphere and did not use the term test. They also avoided group-testing situations.

Test Ways of Assessment

In many situations, tests of the creative thinking abilities are useful in making teachers aware of creative potentialities that might otherwise go unnoticed, even though they may not be able to predict every possible kind of creative performance. To me, this is an important enough use of any test. I am convinced that teachers continue to be ineffective in working with creative youngsters until they identify in them some kind of creative potentiality.

The history of the development of tests of creative thinking is a long and interesting one. There have been many promising developments but there has been a lack of sustained effort. Thus, there is not yet on the market a standardized test of the creative thinking abilities for use with children. After about eight years of sustained work, I believe we are approaching a point in our own work where a general purpose battery for research purposes can be offered commercially. This battery will fall far short of what would be desirable, but we are confident that its use will help teachers, psychologists, and counselors to see potentialities that would otherwise remain unnoticed.

The basic battery now in use consists of three non-verbal, figural tasks (Picture Construction, Incomplete Figures, and Closed Figures) and six verbal tasks (Ask Questions, Guess Causes, Guess Consequences, Product Improvement, Unusual Uses, Just Suppose, and Unusual Questions). This battery yields scores for fluency, flexibility, originality, and elaboration separately for both the figural and verbal tasks.

We have tended in the direction of fairly complex tasks that have features that make use of what we know about the nature of the creative thinking processes, the qualities of creative products, the creative personality, and conditions that facilitate or inhibit creative behavior. We then examine the products and seek to determine the extent to which they reflect sensitivity to problems, ability to redefine or restructure, fluency, flexibility, originality, and elaboration. We are continuing to experiment with new kinds of tasks that make use of excerpts from films, tape recordings, and the like. One of these procedures, *Sounds and Images* (Cunnington and Torrance, 1965a), is built upon a recording of a series of sound effects. It makes use of the progressive warm-up, both verbal and figural responses, and other built-in features based on research findings.

This continued experimentation is necessary because we do not know what range of tasks and response patterns are going to be necessary to obtain a reasonably adequate picture of a child's creative functioning. Some individuals respond more creatively to things that they hear, while others rise to greater heights in response to visual stimuli. Some children are free, spontaneous, and bold in their thinking when permitted to express their ideas in some non-verbal form, but are paralyzed and impoverished if they have to express their ideas in words. For others, the reverse is true.

In general, test-retest reliabilities after two weeks or two or three years have been reasonably satisfactory. Battery totals have in general been quite satisfactory for the intermediate grades and above (reliability coefficients largely in the .80's). In the primary grades, reliability coefficients have generally ranged from about .35 to .70. Personally, I have been less concerned about the lack of reliability over time in the primary grades than I have about the conditions that cause this low reliability in performance.

During the past eight years we have accumulated a variety of evidence concerning the validity of these measures. Most of this evidence has been summarized in a variety of open sources (Torrance, 1962, 1965a). In general, it can be said that persons identified as high or low on the measures can be differentiated in terms of behavior that can be regarded as creative and children so identified have been found to possess characteristics similar to those reportedly displayed by eminent creative people at the time they were children. It can also be said at least for a variety of groups that individuals identified as being creative on some criterion can be differentiated on the basis of these measures from individuals not so identified but similar in other ways. Long-range prediction studies are underway but by necessity several years must elapse before appropriate data become available.

Conclusion

No attempt has been made in this chapter to document what is known about the development and assessment of creative abilities in elementary school children. This documentation has been presented elsewhere in sources open to all who seek it. What I have tried to do is to present one of my own syntheses of some of the things that can be done by elementary school teachers, supervisors, principals, and others to improve their effectiveness in the development and assessment of the creative abilities of elementary school children. There is a great deal more that we should know, but in my opinion we know enough to provide some useful guides to our behavior in working with elementary school children—in fact, we know enough to do a far better job of encouraging creative growth than we are now doing.

CHAPTER 2

Implications of the Structure-of-Intellect Model for High School and College Students

by

J. P. GUILFORD AND
MARY L. TENOPYR

Emeritus Professor of Psychology and Director of the Aptitudes Research Project at the University of Southern California, J. P. Guilford received the A.B. and A.M. from the University of Nebraska and the Ph.D. in Psychology from Cornell University. He has taught at the Universities of Illinois, Kansas, Nebraska, and Southern California. He is the author of a number of books, including Psychometric Methods, General Psychology, Fundamental Statistics in Psychology and Education, Personality, *and* The Nature of Human Intelligence.

Dr. Guilford is recognized for his contributions to psychophysics, scaling, and test methods. He has been active in other research concerned with analyses aimed at the discovery of basic traits of personality. He is best known for analysis of intelligence into component abilities and for the development of the theory known as the "structure of intellect" and its three-dimensional morphological model. This theory has led to general psychological theory and to a point of view described as "operational-informational."

Mary L. Tenopyr holds degrees from Ohio University and a Ph.D. in Psychology from the University of Southern California. She has worked at the Ohio University Testing Bureau and has spent several years in a civilian capacity conducting research and constructing tests for the U.S. Air Force testing programs. For the past eleven years she has been employed by

North American Aviation, Inc., where her present position is corporate manager of employee evaluation.

The past decade and a half has seen a revolution in the study of creativity and the abilities involved in productive endeavors. Many of the early writings in this area were anecdotal or introspective and often posed more questions than they answered. Certainly, many a school child has pointed out to a bewildered parent that Thomas Alva Edison was considered a dull student by his grammar school teachers. Whereas such anecdotes have probably not aided materially in explaining away bad report cards, they have formed at least part of the basis for research on the role of abilities relative to creative performance. In an era in which little was known about the nature of human abilities, evidences of creativity such as those shown by Edison were considered to be merely annoying habits (Guthridge, 1959; Josephson, 1959).

We were still very much in the dark about the nature of creative thinking until the early 1950's when the senior author of this chapter (Guilford, 1950) called attention to the dearth of research in this area and presented several hypotheses for research. In the ensuing years, considerable progress concerning our knowledge of the nature of creativity and the conditions making for productive behavior has been made.

One of the greatest deterrents to understanding creativity has been the theory of intellectual functioning centered about a concept commonly called "general intelligence." Although this theory still has its adherents even today (McNemar, 1964), the ever-expanding body of knowledge concerning differences in abilities within individuals makes such a theory highly open to question. There is now considerable evidence of zero correlations between many tests of intellectual abilities (Guilford, 1964c). Students with considerable ability in one area may have little ability in other areas.

Structure-of-Intellect Model

A multi-ability theory of intellect is necessary to account not only for the creative abilities, but also the many other abilities which have been discovered. The structure-of-intellect model (Guilford, 1959) offers just such a theory. It provides a means for understanding the nature and organization of human abilities, and it can be used as a conceptual basis for education in various areas such as creativity.

The structure-of-intellect (SI) model has been developed on the basis of factor-analytic studies of the intellectual abilities. The model is based on the premise that abilities can be organized in the form of a rectangular solid as shown in Figure One. Each little cube within the solid represents a known or hypothesized ability. To date, more than 80 abilities have been shown to exist (Guilford and Hoepfner, 1963; Guilford, 1965).

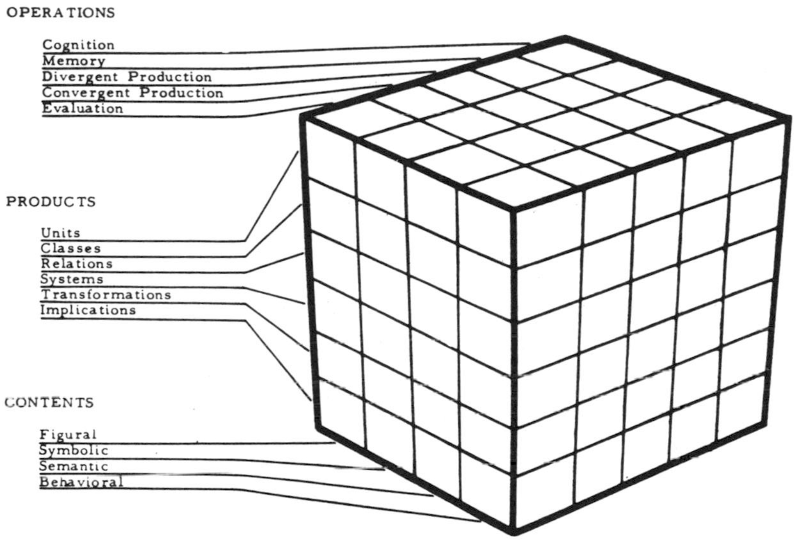

MODEL OF STRUCTURE-OF-INTELLECT
FIGURE ONE

The SI model implies the view that the individual is a processor of information, for 10 of the 15 categories of the SI model pertain to information. The concept of information has some parallels with information in communication engineering, but is used in a different sense than in that field. Information for our purposes is that which the organism discriminates.

The five operations of the SI model are the major kinds of intellectual activities or processes that the individual goes through with information. Cognition is the immediate discovery, awareness, rediscovery of information in various forms. The process may be equated with comprehension or understanding. Memory is the retention or storage, with some degree of availability, of information in the same form in which it was committed to storage. The operation is indicated by the information being given in response to the same cues in connection with which it was learned. Divergent production is generation of information from given information, where emphasis is on variety and quantity of output from the same source. Convergent production is generation of information from given information, where emphasis is upon achieving unique or conventionally accepted best outcomes. Evaluation involves reaching decisions or making judgments concerning the adequacy of information in terms of logical criteria such as identity, consistency, and similarity.

Contents in the SI model are broad classes of information upon which the individual performs the various operations. Figural content is information in concrete form as perceived or as recalled as an image. Implied in the term "figural" is some degree of structure or organization. Different sense modalities may be involved. Symbolic content involves information in the form of signs, having no significance in and of themselves. Included are "code" elements, such as letters, numbers, and musical notations. Semantic content is information in the form of meanings to which words commonly become attached and is, hence, most notable in verbal thinking and in verbal communication. Behavioral content is information important in the area of human interactions, dealing with awareness of the attitudes, needs, desires, moods, intentions, perceptions, and thoughts of other persons and of ourselves.

The final set of categories, products, in the SI model is that dealing with forms that information takes in the individual's processing of it. Units are relatively segregated or circumscribed items of information having "thing" character. Classes are recognized sets of items or units of information, grouped or categorized by virtue of their common properties. In the relations category are recognized connections between units of information, based upon various variables or points of contact which may apply. Systems may involve organized or structured aggregates of items of information; these are complexes of interrelated or interacting parts. Transformations are changes of various kinds of known information or changes in the use of such information. Implications involve extrapolation of information in th expectancies, predictions, known or suspected antecedents, tants, or consequences.

The Creative Processes

Relative to use of the SI model in teaching for creative endeavor, we must first define creativity and decide what it is we want the student to learn. For our purposes creativity is any mental process or interrelated set of processes in which an individual generates information he did not have before. Generated information may be in one of many forms; developing new strategies or thinking of a new use for information previously stored, for example, could be considered as generating new information. There is nothing in this definition to preclude the individual's use of information either from his memory store or from the environment at some stage in the process; however, the end product must be more than repetition of information from these two sources. The word "generates" in the definition carries the implication that the individual must do more than recognize things such as structure or similarities in the information with which he starts. That is not to say, however, that recognition or understanding ("cognition" in SI terms) does not play a significant role in creativity. A further point about the definition is the requirement that the end product be new to the individual. There is no requirement that the end product be new to others. Teachers should not become impatient with training for creativity if such training does not result in astounding new ideas on the parts of students. Many students may do little more than "invent the wheel again"; however, if a student's end product is something he never thought of before, that person has exhibited creative behavior.

At first glance, it might seem that only a limited number of SI abilities is involved in the creative processes; however, this is not the case; as we develop the relationships between creativity and problem solving, it should become apparent that creativity may involve any or all of the individual's abilities, depending upon the nature of the situation. It might also seem that training for creativity as it is defined here would necessarily be narrow, but we shall show later that this is not the case.

Creativity as Problem Solving

The senior author has proposed elsewhere that creative thinking and problem solving are essentially the same mental phenomenon (Guilford, 1964b). We defined creativity as any mental process or set of processes in which an individual generates information he did not have before. Now, let us look at problem solving in light of this definition. If a person recognizes a situation as a problem, it can be inferred that he has no readily available information for coping with the situation—otherwise it would not be a problem. To solve a genuine problem requires the person to generate information he did not have before. Hence, in solving a problem, a person has demonstrated creative behavior, no matter how slight.

The reader may well question whether all creativity is problem solving. It is easy to equate the two in connection with science, invention, writing, and planning; however, it is not so clear whether they should be equated in music and in the visual arts. In the latter two instances, however, we may follow a psychoanalytic point of view and suggest that artists' problems many times arise from within themselves; these problems are of such a nature that they require artistic expression for solution.

Before presenting a new view on problem solving, we might say a word about previous models developed to account for related situations. Dewey's (1910) model for problem solving, Wallas' (1945) model for creative production, Rossman's (1931) model for invention, Polya's (1945) and Johnson's (1955) problem-solving models have all been essentially linear in form. Each writer described in steps the succession of events believed to take place in time between the origin of the problem and an accepted solution. All of these models are strikingly similar, so one will suffice as an example. The typical arrangement of steps is indicated by Dewey's model as follows: (1) a difficulty is felt, (2) the difficulty is located and defined, (3) possible solutions are suggested, (4) consequences are considered, (5) a solution is accepted.

To cover the wide range of possibilities in problem solving we need a broader and more comprehensive model such as that developed by the senior author (Guilford 1964a, 1965) and presented in Figure Two. This structure-of-intellect problem-solving model (SIPS) is based on a number of dynamically interrelated processes.

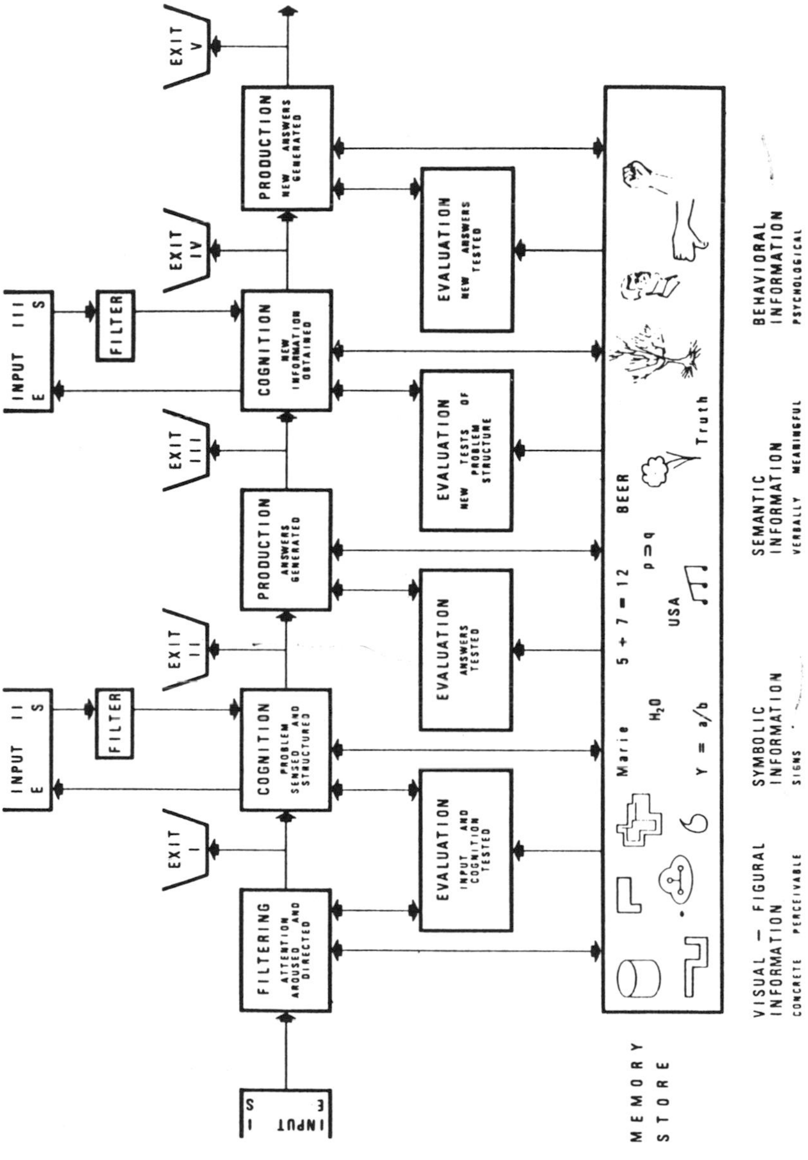

STRUCTURE-OF-INTELLECT PROBLEM-SOLVING MODEL
FIGURE TWO

Essentially what is involved is that the individual recognizes a problem, sets up a "search model," delves into his memory store and the environment, as necessary, and finally produces answers for the problem. The process is to a large extent self-regulatory, as evaluations are made at all stages of problem solving.

A search model is an item of information which has certain form and other characteristics. One specification for the model should be that it falls within one of the six SI product categories. Beyond this requirement, other properties must be added to give the search model its unique character.

The SIPS model is based upon some of the principles of cybernetics in which human mental processes are presented in relation to similar processes in a computer. The arrows in the figure represent possible ways information may flow in the system. It is possible for information at one point in the system to cycle back to earlier phases of the system, and in some cases, information may flow in either direction.

Our problem-solving episode begins with a set of inputs, mostly by way of the senses. These inputs are represented at "Input I" in the model. The "E" and the "S" stand for environmental and somatic sources of input, respectively. These inputs may be quite complex in nature and represent any form of information. The inputs must be such that the individual has no readily available means of coping with them; otherwise, there is no problem. The somatic inputs, which may include both motivational and emotional components, are quite important at this point, for these inputs may play a significant role in determining how much effort the individual puts into attempting to solve the problem and what approaches he takes.

"Input I" involves a process of filtering, which determines just how much and what kind of information will affect the behavior of the individual. Filtering is akin to attention, which, as we know, may be highly selective. It is at this point that the memory store comes into play. The double arrow between filtering and the memory store indicates that information may flow in either direction. What is attended to affects what is drawn from the memory store, and, in turn, what is in the memory store affects what is attended to. Note that both memory and evaluation have to be taken into account throughout the whole problem-solving sequence. Evaluation or testing is not left to the final stage of the process as is common in many other models. The present model, in its emphasis on evaluation, is similar to the TOTE model of Miller, Galanter, and Pribram (1960), where TOTE stands for "test, operate, test, and exit."

After filtering, modified through memory and evaluation, comes cognition. At this stage, there is awareness that a problem exists and structuring of the problem. Again there is dependence upon memory and evaluation. In attempting to cognize the problem there may be searching for outside information, as at "Input II." Filtering of this second input occurs, as well as evaluation.

With the problem cognized, there is a search for answers or information from which answers can be developed. If answers constructed at the production stage are found acceptable through the process of evaluation, there is an exit from the problem-solving situation at Exit III, and the problem is considered solved. Using Exit I would have indicated a dodging of the problem. Using Exit II might represent giving up or being distracted before the productive operation got started.

If no good solutions to the problem are produced, and if there are doubts about the interpretation of the problem, a new major cycle begins as is shown at the second cognition block. To reinterpret the problem, new inputs may be sought, and steps similar to those described before may be carried out. A number of these cycles may take place in what has often been described as trial-and-error learning. The general flow of information is from left to right; however, exactly which paths are followed in the system depends upon the exact nature of the situation. In any case, there is not direct progression from input to cognition to production. There is always dependence on the memory; there is always evaluation of input, cognition, and information tentatively selected from the memory store. When tentative answers are generated, they are always evaluated in some sense.

A period of incubation, such as that emphasized by Wallas (1945), is indicated by a temporary cessation of active problem solving without a complete exit from the system. In a problem-solving method like brainstorming (Osborn, 1963) in which many possible solutions to a problem are considered regardless of their merits, there is, in effect, a bypassing or relaxing of the evaluative process relative to testing answers.

Brainstorming and its counterparts are based on the notion that in many people the evaluative process is too strong, and often potentially good ideas are rejected. The optimal strength of the evaluative process depends upon the nature of the problem. If the problem is well structured and there is a unique solution, a strong evaluative process to screen out all of the possible wrong solutions is required.

However, if the problem is less structured, and there are a number of possible solutions, a very strong evaluative operation may be a deterrent because of the rejection of too many acceptable solutions.

The relation of this problem-solving model to SI should be obvious. The operations of cognition, memory, and evaluation are all represented in problem solving. One distinction is that in the SIPS model, both divergent production and convergent production are subsumed under the simple heading "production." Which kind of production occurs in problem solving depends upon the nature of the problem and the way it is cognized. If the problem is understood as one requiring a single correct answer, convergent production is necessary. If the problem, however, is not well-structured, or there is not enough information to arrive at one right answer, and there may be a number of acceptable solutions, divergent production is the operation required.

The broad information categories, contents, are represented in Figure Two by the objects drawn in the memory store. The four types of content are segregated only for illustrative purposes. Examples of most of the products, e.g., units and classes, are shown. Transformations, being changes, are not so easy to show in pictorial form, but a modification of either equation would be an example; inversion or rotation of one of the figures would be another.

Education for Problem Solving

As was emphasized previously, although there is a general trend in the flow of information in problem solving and the same general operations are involved for all problems, each problem-solving situation is to some extent unique. Different information may be involved; different paths, including the retracings of previous steps, may be followed; different search models may be required. Drill in the various types of problem solving would be an endless task and probably far less effective than other approaches to training. Problem solving is about as broad as behavior itself; consequently, training for more effective productive behavior must be general.

There seem to be two general categories into which education for effective problem solving might fall. First, there should be training to develop the basic abilities involved in productive performance. Second, there should be practice in solving a wide variety of problems;

environmental inputs can be monitored to provide feedback and a richer learning experience for the student.

Development of Basic Abilities

The development of basic abilities may be included within the context of almost any course of instruction; all teachers can contribute to the potential for creative performance of their students. Ability development should be considered as important a function of the history teacher as it is of the mathematics teacher. If the student is to develop the capabilities for coping with all the problems he may face in his lifetime, all of his abilities must receive attention. He must have training relative to his mental operations: cognition, memory, convergent production, divergent production, and evaluation. In addition, he must have experience with all types of information

We know little now about how amenable to training the basic abilities are. Some are likely to be more easily developed than others, but it is almost a certainty that all abilities can be developed at least to some extent by the processes of education.

Many of our suggestions for methods the teacher may use for training in the basic abilities are not particularly novel; yet the methods may take on new meaning when they are viewed with respect to the problem-solving model.

The development of cognition, one of the first operations in the problem-solving sequence, may be fostered by teaching with emphasis on understanding. When units of information are taught, stress should be placed on relations between units. Habits of forming classes of information and relations between classes should be developed. When a unit of information falls within a system of information, the place and function of the unit within the pertinent system or systems should be considered in teaching. The student's becoming aware of implications is the basis for developing foresight. The student cannot be expected to solve a problem effectively unless his cognitive abilities are developed to the point at which he understands the situation surrounding the problem. Recognition and correct definition of problems is crucial and often quite difficult. Everyone certainly has seen someone who has failed to note what seemed to be an obvious problem or has "spun his wheels" trying to solve the wrong problem.

As we have seen, the memory store is involved throughout the whole problem-solving sequence. Unless the student has a good supply of information of all kinds in his memory store, he cannot be expected to solve problems. Teaching of facts, then, should not be belittled, provided that this teaching is geared also to promote understanding.

One of the peculiarities of problem solving is that much of it depends on transfer recall. A simple demonstration of transfer recall is finding a new use for a brick or tin can. Unfortunately, as important as transfer recall is, there have been surprisingly few studies on the subject. Some of the principles governing non-transfer recall may also apply to transfer recall, but others may not have so much generality, and perhaps new ones will have to be discovered.

Some of the traditional conditions favoring non-transfer recall are (1) completeness of cues; (2) overlearning; (3) recency of practice; and (4) a state of relaxation. We might speculate on how these conditions would affect transfer recall, particularly when divergent production of ideas is involved.

Completeness of cues pertains more directly to non-transfer recall, involving the cues in connection with which the information was acquired. However, there is a parallel in connection with transfer recall, if we substitute the concept "search model" for cues.

Overlearning deserves consideration in connection with transfer recall, but as to its effects, we can only speculate. Overlearning in connection with non-transfer recall has the function of reducing interferences or, in this context, confusion of information. Relative to the given definition of information, it might be said that overlearning has the effect of sharpening discriminations and better encoding of the data. The danger of negative transfer is thereby lessened and the chances for positive transfer are increased. It is possible that the probability of transfer in recall is also enhanced by overlearning; however, this remains to be demonstrated.

A powerful condition in recalling particular information is recency of practice, but this condition may be too powerful when the more recent information is not the information we need. Recall of recently practiced information may set up interference which prevents us from recalling the information we do want. This may be the basis for the presumed effectiveness of an incubation period in problem solving. During this period, the strength of the unwanted information will decrease, and the chances of recall of the wanted information will thereby be enhanced. There does not seem to be an obvious way to suggest how recency of practice could be of advantage to the problem solver who will ordinarily not know in advance what particular information he is going to need to solve the problem. In practice, however, the person teaching problem solving will know at least some of the information which most students will require to solve the problem and can effect practice on the information shortly in advance of the actual problem solving task.

The condition of relaxation may mean several things. One effect of relaxation may be lowered muscular tonicity. Another effect is related to the amount of effort directed toward recalling the particular information we want. Perhaps we often try too hard for our own good. In making a search for something in the memory store we do something akin to dispatching a messenger to bring back certain information. Having dispatched him, we can do little except wait, expectantly, of course. It is possible that our confidence of correct recall has much to do with the success of the memory-scanning process. A third interpretation of relaxation in the recall process may be a form of what Osborn (1963) calls "suspended judgment." We have said previously, in connection with divergent production, that the evaluation process may be too strong and that by being overly critical of our ideas, we may fail to find a solution to our problem. Suspended judgment is essentially a relaxation of the evaluation process. There appears to be ample evidence that this form of relaxation is quite effective when divergent production is in order.

With reference to the subject of transfer recall, there are at least two other conditions that merit attention. We have made reference before to the search model, which serves as a cue or collection of cues in the instigation of transfer recall. The more clearly defined our conception of the goal or of what kind of end product is wanted, the better should be the chances of retrieving the right kind of information. With a good idea of what is wanted, we can scan our memory stores quite selectively and set the evaluative filter to exclude competitors to the needed information. This kind of selectivity can be very useful in mathematics, logics, and the sciences, where only one or, at the most, a few alternative items of information are acceptable. It should also be useful in the solution of everyday problems, and, to some extent, in the arts where somewhat greater latitude in solutions can be acceptable. Even in the arts, the creator has some general idea in advance concerning what kind of eventual end product is wanted. Some idea of what criteria the end product must meet can also be an aid in divergent production. For example, it might be specified that the title for a play must be different and "catchy." The problem solver could gear his memory-scanning processes to be less selective and cover a broader range of information, but he could also set his evaluative filter to reject most common and trite titles.

In order that information in the memory store be easily sought out by a well-specified search model, the information must be well-coded and labeled or, as some would say, "put in neat little compartments." Classes and subclasses and their organization into larger systems are aids in giving the information its properties of identification.

Again, the importance of teaching for understanding cannot be overemphasized. There is far too much learning that limits the information to unit form, as in learning concepts with minimal definitional information. The practice of rote learning of isolated facts, although often condemned, cannot be criticized strongly enough. Teaching with emphasis on relations between items of information, classes and systems of information, and implications of information can be an aid not only in understanding and recognition of important aspects of problems but also in encoding information so that it may readily be retrieved in solving problems.

Whenever possible, the learner should be encouraged to take the initiative in discovering and explaining things for himself. That which a person discovers for himself is seldom forgotten. In addition, much attention should be devoted to teaching principles, which are more easily remembered than most isolated facts. Principles are likely to serve an important function in encoding information for easy retrieval.

Teaching for convergent production also has its roots in teaching for understanding. A memory store with information encoded well is also basic to the production process. However, one of the most important features of both convergent and divergent production abilities is transfer recall.

To promote convergent production within a given field we cannot rely solely on the operations described earlier, nor can we rely on effective teaching of the subject matter. We must do more in order to ensure that there is transfer recall. The student must become experienced in attempting to produce the unique answers required in convergent thinking.

A teacher should not rely solely on true-false or multiple-choice examinations and quizzes which are very much confined to cognition and memory and do not allow the student to practice or to demonstrate convergent or divergent production. This is not to say that the objective test on subject matter does not fulfill some imporant functions in the educational process.

One alternate or supplementary technique which may be employed in examining is a test of short completion questions which require at least some transfer recall. This coupled with carefully formulated feedback to the student is likely to be quite useful in developing convergent thinking. Essay examinations requiring convergent production should probably be used more frequently. A subsidiary benefit from employing such methods might be a change in the study habits of the student. It is well known that pupils gear their study habits to the teacher's examination practices. The suggested revision of testing practices could effect significant alterations in the strategies students use in preparing for their class. In any case, at least part of the evaluation of a student's degree of mastery of a course should be his ability to apply the subject matter in new ways.

The opportunity for transfer recall can also be afforded by carefully planned classroom discussion on problems within the subject-matter field. In such discussions it is important that all students be given the opportunity to participate. For this purpose, it might be wise to divide the class into small groups.

None of the preceding methods discussed with respect to developing the basic abilities has been greatly different from the good teaching practices in vogue today. However, the matter of teaching for development of divergent production abilities is a somewhat different situation. In most disciplines the past emphasis has been on producing "correct" answers whether in response to questions calling for facts or as a result of problems which have only one or two acceptable solutions. To a large extent, divergent production has been neglected except in areas such as art and composition.

It is undoubtedly easier to foster divergent production in some areas than in others; however, the ability can probably be developed at least to some extent in many subject-matter areas in which the ability is practically untouched now. Science and social science classes are likely to be fruitful ground for training in divergent production. A simple problem which could be used in history classes would be, "What would our lives be like now if . . . ." There are, of course, many other types of problems which could be used.

Training for improved divergent production should not be limited to a selected few or directed only toward the students with high verbal intelligence. As Covington (1965) has shown, the productive abilities of even students with low I.Q.'s can be improved through appropriate training.

The typical method of determining the relationship between intelligence and creative abilities has been to correlate scores on tests of divergent production with those on general-intelligence tests. It might be noted that the SI ability most involved in the typical intelligence test is cognition of semantic units. To get a relatively pure measure of this ability, one can use a vocabulary test. The linear relationships between intelligence scores and divergent production scores have generally been low and, at the most, moderate (Guilford and Hoepfner, 1963).

It has been suggested (Getzels and Jackson, 1962; Stein and Meer, 1955; Guilford, 1964a) that a relatively high I.Q. is a necessary but not sufficient condition for high-level productive performance. It has been argued that a person with low "verbal intelligence" cannot be very creative; whereas a person with high "verbal intelligence" may or may not be highly creative. This would suggest a non-linear relation between the two types of ability.

Even though it appears to be unlikely that a person of low "verbal intelligence" can be very creative, there is still the strong possibility that his creative abilities can be improved at least to some extent. A further point which should be noted is that much of the information we have now is based on the relationships between verbal intelligence tests and verbal divergent production tests. There is still the possibility that the student low in verbal intelligence may be creative in non-verbal ways. It can be hypothesized that these students might be very creative in fields such as music, art, or mathematics. At present, there is no reason to believe that training for divergent production cannot be carried on effectively even in trade-oriented courses. Girls in home economics classes could be encouraged to try to develop new recipes or dress designs. Industrial arts courses could be used as an avenue for developing creative performance in invention or design.

Training for improved divergent production can be effective even in the lower grades (Covington, 1965). There is no reason to reserve such training for older students. Of course, there must be special efforts to maintain the motivational level of younger children.

One of the most difficult tasks for the educational administrator is the development of climate in which divergent production is accepted and encouraged. Perhaps the first step would be to encourage divergent production among the teachers themselves and a favorable attitude toward the activity.

Very little is known now about training relative to the evaluation abilities; on the basis of the problem-solving model, however, it would seem that these are some of the abilities for which it would be most difficult to establish effective training. As has been pointed out, evaluation of one type or another underlies the whole problem-solving process, but we must remember that there are likely to be a number of separate evaluative abilities involved in any given problem. Of particular difficulty when we think of training is the likelihood that the optimum strength of some of the evaluative filters depends on whether the problem calls for divergent or convergent production. Nevertheless, there seem to be some teaching approaches which can be useful as bases for improving evaluative abilities.

Training to improve abilities in the area of evaluation should, it appears, have more than one aspect. Evaluation involves determining whether information meets certain criteria. The criteria may be as simple as identity, or they may, as is often the case in solving difficult problems, be quite complex and numerous.

In any given problem-solving situation, the criteria upon which evaluation is based are determined at least in part by the manner in which the individual cognizes the problem and the kind of search model he constructs. If a person cognizes a problem incorrectly, he is likely to set up the wrong search model and the wrong criteria for evaluating information produced from the memory store.

Another possible difficulty is in the evaluation of inputs from environment and soma. Let us assume that a student is told to develop something "novel." Evaluation processes throughout the whole problem-solving sequence will depend upon the criteria the student sets up for "novelty." These criteria, in turn, depend upon the conception of "novel" in the student's memory store.

Again, we come back to the basic teaching processes so important for developing cognition and memory. Unless concepts are taught in such a way that their relations with other classes and their places or functions within the systems of which they are a part are cognized by the student, the student may experience difficulty in using these concepts when needed as criteria in evaluation.

William James (1890) suggested that in everyday situations we learn to make discriminations through the attachment of a unique set of associations to each of the things we discriminate. For example, we are able to discriminate a sheep from a horse, because we have a unique set of associations with each. Unfortunately, there is little research related to James' early suggestion. There are some parallels, however, between what James has proposed and the process of teaching for understanding we have suggested here. Cognition, which is related to James' concept of discrimination, is achieved not just through a process of making associations, but through a process involving many of the SI categories.

Another aspect of the evaluation process which deserves attention is the fact that in problem solving we are often dealing with criteria which are not discrete, but are continuously distributed. For example, "pertinent" and "not pertinent" are not two distinct categories. There are all degrees of pertinence. Where relative judgments must be made, the crux of the evaluation process is where the individual chooses to "draw the line" between the two extremes for a given criterion.

Although negative examples are probably not so useful as positive examples in concept formation (Hovland and Weiss, 1953), the student probably needs to be presented with some negative examples so that he can cognize the whole continuum related to the concept. Only if the student cognizes the whole continuum with respect to a given criterion can he set and make the changes in the position of his cutting point on the continuum, as is required in evaluation in a dynamic problem-solving situation. For example, a student cannot effectively decide what is novel and what is not novel, unless he can cognize degrees of novelty.

Another line of endeavor which may be fruitful is teaching relative to evaluation of inputs and to cognition of problems. Sensitivity to various kinds of problems is highly important in almost any area. The student must learn to pay attention to problems not only in academic areas but also in everyday life.

Instructional Devices for Facilitating Problem Solving

Auto-instructional techniques, used widely for the teaching of concepts, have not until recently seemed very promising candidates for training for such a dynamic process as problem solving. Some of the characteristics of programmed instruction usually considered noteworthy, have seemed almost antithetical to the objective of teaching for creative endeavor.

As Crutchfield and Covington (1965) have pointed out, programmed instruction for creative performance can only be effective if the programming itself is a result of creative action. Some of the principles used by these authors in developing programmed-instruction methods for use with grade school children were as follows: (1) to allow for transfer, specific skills should not be practiced separately, but within the global context of whole and relatively complex problems; (2) in the early part of the program, problems should be kept simple; (3) instruction in principles of creative thinking and practice in evaluation should be given early in the program; (4) steps in the program should be large enough to encourage the student to exert a genuine creative effort at each stage; and (5) feedback should be relevant and reinforcing for all students regardless of the diversity of responses given by them. The type of feedback designed by Covington and Crutchfield (1965) consisted of things such as giving a list of questions which might have been asked or providing a number of ideas the student might have produced at the particular stage of the process.

The preliminary results from employing these techniques have been very promising (Crutchfield and Covington, 1965; Covington, 1965). Use of the techniques has resulted in substantial gains in both divergent production and convergent production for students at various intelligence levels. There may be some question, however, as to whether gains are a result of increased learning or of sensitization of students to relatively dormant abilities. In line with what we have said before, it is important to note that these techniques have emphasized general problem solving and involved use of a number of abilities by the students.

Another example of general and broadening training is illustrated by the workbook, "Creative Analysis" (Upton and Sampson, 1963). The authors claim that training of college students with the aid of this book in a course yields an average increase of 10 points in I.Q. These findings were independently supported in a study by Brunelle (1964), who also found marked improvement in tests of divergent-production abilities.

There appear to be distinct advantages to teaching students about the nature of thinking, as well as giving them drill in problem solving. In learning to play a game such as tennis or golf, it would certainly be worthwhile to learn something about the principles of the game; we should not rely solely upon drilling in the physical aspects of the game. Forehand and Libby (1962) found that employees in governmental administrative positions improved in their degrees of innovative performances if they had had instruction in the nature of creative thinking along with drills in such activity, but others who had only drills did not improve. Apparently a high degree of maturity is not necessary for learning at least some of the principles of thinking, for Torrance (1963) found that providing elementary school children with only minutes of instruction on the nature of divergent thinking seemed to give them an advantage in tests of divergent-production abilities. On a more extensive scale, it should be of considerable value to give instruction to all students, as soon as they are ready for it, concerning all of their different intellectual resources. It might also be well to show students how their mental functions work in interrelated ways in problem solving.

A number of special techniques for training for creative production have been developed. Some of these methods can probably be adapted for use in the classroom. Two of those which are particularly related to the SIPS model presented are brainstorming (Osborn, 1963) which has already been discussed in relation to the evaluation process, and attribute listing (Crawford, 1954), which places emphasis upon classes, which are so important in encoding of information in the memory store.

The number of systems developed for training for productive performance is so large that we cannot discuss all of them here. In almost any of these systems, however, one can find at least some of the concepts we have stressed in connection with the SIPS model.

The subject of motivation is not within the scope of this paper; needless to say, however, without some degree of appropriate motivation, the student cannot be expected to progress very far in problem solving. We still need to know much more about the optimal levels of motivation at various stages of the problem-solving process. Perhaps some stages require a high level of motivation; whereas other stages are handled better if the problem solver is less tense.

Summary

Creative processes and problem solving have been defined as involving identical operations which can be represented as a dynamic interrelated set of operations based on the structure-of-intellect model.

It has been shown how all of an individual's abilities are involved in problem solving or creative performance. The suggestion has been made that many of the teaching principles which can result in improved problem solving are not very different from contemporarily accepted rules for good teaching; relative to divergent production, however, some new teaching methodology seems necessary. There has been emphasis on the need for general training for problem solving and on the applicability of such training in many fields of endeavor. Evidence has been presented to indicate that all students can profit by problem-solving training. Several techniques designed specially to improve problem solving or productive behavior have been mentioned.

PART II

CURRICULUM PLANNING AND INSTRUCTIONAL PROCEDURES FOR REALIZATION OF CREATIVE ENDEAVOR

Overview

For the preschool and kindergarten child Wilson and Robeck state in Chapter 3 three basic assumptions: (1) creativity is present to some degree in all individuals, (2) creative behavior can be learned and facilitated by the teaching process, and (3) creative expression in children can be built on the foundation of accumulated mental, emotional, and aesthetic patterns of behavior. To help one to understand the development of creative potentialities, the writers have proposed a learning-motivation model that involves sequential steps of the formulation of associations and conceptualizations leading to creative self-direction. Underlying classroom approaches to the realization of creative endeavor in the young child are suggestions that efforts be taken to (1) teach children to live richly, (2) reinforce divergent behavior, (3) value unique production, (4) schedule a regular choice period, (5) provide a variety of materials, (6) present techniques of instruction that will assure a satisfying experience (for both the child and teacher), (7) help children to identify areas for conformity and adherence to meaningful conventions (e.g., the development of self-discipline in conventional mechanics of communication frees the child's time for creative endeavor in other areas of learning), (8) extend original behavior to all feasible activities, (9) separate temporally and spatially "idea generating" from "critical judgment" situations, and (10) develop a climate that nurtures creative activity. Wilson and Robeck conclude that the most significant creative approaches are those of teachers who reward and encourage the self-directing experiences of children—the very same kinds of self-discovery and self-actualizing activities underlying the method of inquiry which is developed by Rubin in the subsequent chapter.

In setting forth in Chapter 4 the thesis that the ferment and upheaval in teaching methodology during the past decade should closely follow teaching implications from research on creativity, Rubin stresses the importance of the method of inquiry in which a student actively uses his accumulation of information and knowledge to solve problems. In such self-discovery activities he gains on his own initiative new rational insights, gives meaning to recently generated information, and develops capabilities of ordering his conceptual understandings into patterns of meaningful relationships. For most new curricula, Rubin believes that the method of inquiry which involves a number of different ways of thinking in a self-discovery context is an essential approach to learning in a creative fashion. Thus the basis of the curriculum has shifted from a static view involving mastery of content for its own sake to a dynamic activity concerned with how one acquires and uses knowledge. Rubin suggests that accumulating evidence on the nature of creativity shows a marked similarity not only to the mainstream of current curriculum theory but also to the psychological propositions of the learning process. In his view curricular experiences need to be arranged so that there are provisions for the student to (1) develop transfer capabilities, (2) expand his capacity to solve problems in alternative ways, (3) develop abilities to select appropriate ways to think about specific tasks and thus (by minimizing adherence to fixed psychological sets) to learn more effectively, and (4) augment creative resources through acquisition of alternative styles of thinking.

In Chapter 5, Hibbs points out that the developments in mathematics and science are so rapid that much of what the elementary and secondary school child may learn will be out of date by the time he is ready to apply what he has acquired during his period of formal schooling. In addition, practical difficulties arise in finding either teachers in science and mathematics who are qualified or textbooks that are suitable. Besides stressing the importance of acquisition of skills in reading, written and oral communication, and mathematics, Hibbs emphasizes the importance of developing a scholarly attitude—

an attitude which with its characteristics of curiosity, self-confidence in one's own ideas, competitiveness, and skepticism underlies teaching for realization of creative endeavor. In giving an illustration of an elementary science demonstration which he had observed, Hibbs emphasizes how much more exciting and thus creative the experience could have been had the elementary teacher allowed pupils to pursue a line of inquiry suggested by one class member instead of her insisting upon their discovery of the scientific principle she had intended that the class group derive from the experiment. Reiterating in his own way Rubin's position concerning the value of the method of inquiry, Hibbs urges that internal intellectual directions be allowed to guide a pupil in self-discovery learning. In short, the process of learning and discovery with its concomitant enjoyment is far more important than is the correct answer expected by the teacher. Thus the pupil teaches the teacher about the nature of science, and the teacher gives a helping hand in showing children about the process of learning.

Echoing, for both the elementary and secondary school level, many of the points suggested by Rubin and Hibbs—particularly the notion of active self-discovery, Fischler elaborates in Chapter 6 on the whole dynamic nature of scientific enterprise with particular emphasis on the discrepant event, an observation that does not fit the expectation or paradigm of the scientists. The resulting frustration forces the scientist to reexamine his model and to search for a resolution of the problem that has been generated. Basically the same kind of discrepant event is the key to creative problem solving by pupils who when faced with a problem situation actively collect their own data, draw their own inferences, formulate their own predictions, and then test them against the realities of the environment. Fischler also gives considerable weight to the importance of behaviorally stated objectives that can furnish direction to science teaching as well as to the description of the types of creative activities that may be expected of pupils provided that they are given appropriate opportunities and encouragement. To illustrate ways in which elementary and junior high school pupils may do original thinking involving divergent production, Fischler has included several examples of curricular experiences from the biological sciences.

The same basic theme of permitting students in secondary mathematics the opportunity to discover and to think for themselves underlies Chapter 7. In pointing out that the school has traditionally rewarded the child who can learn and synthesize the thoughts of others rather than the one who can produce significant thoughts both of and on his own, Willoughby urges that the teacher encourage independence of thought and creative endeavor even though he may be compulsively driven to pass on the vast accumulation of knowledge in mathematics. In essence the teacher who can effect creative behavior in his students is highly flexible and sensitive to how much information need be given to the learner in his self-discovery of the solution of problems in mathematics. Neither complete freedom in classroom activities nor the complete structuring of the problem situation is customarily desirable in teaching for creative endeavor. Willoughby has provided numerous examples to illustrate how the teacher in secondary mathematics can bring about the fruition of the creative potentialities of the learner. Perhaps most important, by rewarding creative acts, by permitting children to think and to talk about problems without expecting them to give the correct solution or without furnishing them the right answer, and by being poised, happy, and supportive, the teacher can avoid repulsing those from education who already are highly creative in their behaviors.

Although problem-solving activities would obviously be basic to creative endeavor in mathematics and the sciences, Lundsteen argues in Chapter 8 that the problem-solving process itself is probably the most effective way to teach language arts in the elementary school. Preferring to use the term creative problem solving (rather than problem solving) she indicates that this process involves (1) clarification of the problem, (2) formulation of hypotheses of an original and free-flowing nature, (3) planned procedures with built-in flexibility and elaboration, and (4) evaluation, which may be delayed to encourage the outpouring of new ideas (fluency). The focus on creative problem solving is intended to encourage transfer within the whole spectrum of language arts areas from the receptive side—reading and listening—to the expressive modes of writing and speaking. Numerous examples and anecdotes are presented to illustrate how creative potentialities of children can be realized and how autonomy in learning by the pupil can be achieved.

In Chapter 9 Georgiades and Michael have undertaken to define conditions conducive to producing a creative environment for teaching English composition and literature in the secondary school. In directing attention to the size and structure of the classroom, they have described three types of units—conventional-size classes, assembly groups, and inquiry groups—and have given specific examples of how creative outcomes can be accomplished. They also have illustrated how independent study can play a vital role in encouraging and in bringing to fruition the creative potentialities of the English student. Particularly important is the stress which they have placed on a meaningful system of evaluation to determine whether cognitive as well as affective objectives in creative programs can be attained and whether any transfer effects can be achieved relative to other areas of the curriculum. In terms of their experience with team teaching, flexible scheduling, and paraprofessional aides, they speculate that the generalist in the teaching of English in 1968 will be replaced in another ten or fifteen years by numbers of specialists. Such a development, they anticipate, could encourage a higher level of creative endeavor on the part of the English teacher. The implication is that the high school student could also display an augmented level of creativity brought about by the specialized skills and inspiration of the highly competent English teacher.

Despite the protestations of a few idealists among the foreign language teachers, it appears that the teaching of oral and written skills in foreign languages is less likely to result in the manifestation of student behaviors that can be judged as creative than is teaching in almost any other subject-matter area. Although recent emphasis on teaching the speaking of a language represents somewhat of a revolution in methodology that may be viewed as offering numerous opportunities for creative teaching, the fruition of creative potentialities on the part of the learner is admittedly difficult to conceptualize. In Chapter 10, Sawyer points out that the modern language laboratory offers not only a variety of visual and sound media but also numerous models such as tape recordings for student imitation. The key to creative endeavor in foreign language learning, Sawyer suggests, is the provision of an exciting school atmosphere with interesting teachers, books, and materials—an atmosphere in which the student is encouraged to be innovative in finding ways of learning on his own. The language laboratory can provide an environment of books and other instructional materials that do not irritate the learner but involve him psychologically in reaching realistic goals that he is encouraged to set for himself.

In her consideration of the elementary social studies in Chapter 11, Woodfin injects content, process, and product components of Guilford's structure of intellect into a unified problem-solving approach.

Believing that the teacher needs to observe children at work in order to answer questions concerning conditions under which they learn, she describes areas of diagnosis, outlines conditions for diagnosis, indicates how diagnosis may be utilized for evaluating behavioral changes in each child as well as in the group as a whole, and emphasizes the importance of diagnosis in identifying teacher preferences within the instructional process. To help children become increasingly adept at creative thinking, Woodfin suggests that the teacher needs to (1) interrelate content, process, and product, (2) improve question asking, (3) recognize the value of varying answers, (4) avoid seeking closure too soon, (5) provide alternative activities, (6) encourage both creative producers and consumers, (7) devise ways for the child to teach himself, (8) involve children in evaluation procedures, (9) try to overcome some sex role handicaps to learning, (10) provide time for individual study projects, and (11) provide practice and help in the group learning process. As have many of the other contributors, Woodfin has stressed the need for creative problem-solving experiences in the classroom and has urged that teachers try out new strategies for improving their own creative problem-solving capabilities.

Although giving incidental attention to the process and product concerns of productivity in social studies at the secondary level, Brubaker, in Chapter 12, gives major consideration to how the classroom experiences and the activities outside the classroom may facilitate the expression of the student's creative potentialities. He believes that the key to such expression is the example which the teacher himself sets as a creative person. Essential points of this argument include: (1) the selection of teachers who understand the historiography and methodology of history, (2) an honest communication by the administrative staff of the school system to the teacher regarding what they consider to be teaching qualities that foster creativity, (3) joint participation by teachers and administrative staff in the selection of textbooks and instructional materials that will foster creative endeavor, and (4) opportunity for the students to have informal visitation privileges and access to their instructors. Two helpful examples which are included to show how teaching and learning atmosphere can bring about creative expression illustrate the author's thesis that what students learn is caught rather than taught.

To set the stage concerning the problems involved in teaching art in the elementary school, Hausman states in Chapter 13 ten key propositions. Particularly pertinent to the development of creative potentialities are such points as the following: (1) the creative artist's act can have either positive or negative values, (2) the pupil can begin to approach creativeness in art when he engages in his own exploration of reality, (3) teachers need to take care in finding an appropriate balance for their pupils between "sufficient latitude" to allow uniqueness of expression and "sufficient structure" to permit the student to progress confidently, (4) generation of conditions in which pupils can come to learn the joy and thrill of searching for visual ideas and of investing their own ideas and feelings toward realizing new forms. Subsequent to stating the hypothesis that a teacher who is informed about the large number of parameters involved in his own decision-making activities is likely to render qualitatively superior decisions, Hausman enumerates what he believes to be three key factors of which the art teacher must be aware and then goes on to cite certain basic steps that the teacher can take in relation to helping pupils to become creative in their artistic endeavors. These three factors include the teacher's awareness of (1) the medium or media used, (2) the dynamic relationship between the medium employed and the ideas being formed, and (3) creativity in art as not involving the creation of a form from nothing. Teachers may help pupils in the classroom by (1) accepting and valuing them as being creative (2) consciously relating the inventions of one person to what others are accomplishing, (3) recognizing the importance of feedback, invention, and intuition, and (4) encouraging them to make visual judgments. As children become more sensitive to and better informed about the visual world as an activity and emotionally rewarding experience, the quality and meaningfulness of their creative experiences can reach a high level that will give new vision to the place of art education in the curriculum.

In Chapter 14, which is concerned with ways in which creative behavior may be brought to fruition in the performing arts, Blankenchip suggests that the key is the development of imagination, the facilitation of which is a major responsibility of the teacher. Stressing that the student must become aware of the possibility of numerous correct answers to the interpretation of a role or to a specific production in the performing arts, the writer notes that successful creative endeavor is dependent upon the performer's conveying the intent of the author or composer as well as upon a selective blending and integration of the key elements in the medium. To encourage both the creator and the interpreter in the arts, opportunities for imaginative preparation in a permissive environment need to be provided.

In Chapter 15, which concludes Part II of this volume, Michael considers how creative endeavor in the college and university setting may be facilitated in terms of five major courses of action: (1) a flexible admissions policy in which allowance is made for accepting a certain proportion of highly creative students despite their relatively low level of performance on conventional tests of scholastic aptitude or in their high school grade point averages; (2) modifications in curricula and in patterns of course requirements that would allow for (a) fewer courses with relatively larger numbers of credit hours per course, (b) assignment of credit or of a mark of passing to at least on independent study course each semester, (c) acceleration of gifted and creative students whenever feasible; (3) placement of creatively oriented students in those college and university environments in which creative endeavor is encouraged and rewarded; (4) adaptation of teaching procedures and of course requirements to the particular cognitive and affective needs of the creative student; and (5) the development and use of a variety of meaningful criterion measures such as the open book test and the research project that are oriented toward operationally stated objectives for the purposes of evaluating student performance, of gaining evidence regarding the effectiveness of the total educational program, and of making appropriate modifications both in the curriculum and in instructional procedures. It is pointed out that although the faculty and the administration of an institution of higher education can cooperatively do much to foster creative endeavor the final responsibility rests upon the student himself who must exhibit sufficient discipline to carry out the hard but rewarding work of creative learning.

CHAPTER 3

Creativity in the Very Young

by

JOHN A. R. WILSON AND
MILDRED C. ROBECK

A native of Western Canada, John A. R. Wilson received two degrees from the University of British Columbia and has taught in elementary, junior and senior high schools. He has also worked in industry, railroading, and sales occupations. Upon receiving his Ed.D. from Oregon State University, he began his career as an educational psychologist at the University of California, Santa Barbara. His principal research interest has been the nature of human learning with particular concern for learning in young children. Dr. Wilson is best known as one of the authors of the Kindergarten Evaluation of Learning Potential. *Research, carried on jointly with Dr. Mildred C. Robeck, has led to a neurologically based Learning–Motivation Model that promises to be extremely useful to teachers at all levels of education and in many varied disciplines.*

Mildred C. Robeck is associate professor of Education at the University of Oregon. She has coordinated two NDEA Advanced Study Seminars in Early Childhood Education and was research consultant for California Project Talent. Before earning the Ph.D. degree at the University of Washington, she taught children from preschool ages through junior high school. She has nine grandchildren whom she regards as examples par excellence *of the uniqueness of each person.*

IN THE CONTEXT of the very young, we define creativity as the ability and the willingness to generate something that is new, at least for the child, in ideas or materials. This chapter develops three basic themes: (1) that creativity, like intelligence, exists to some degree in all people, (2) that creative behavior is learned and therefore can be taught, and (3) that children's creativity is built on the mental, aesthetic, and emotional patterns they have accumulated. We would like to describe procedures that kindergarten teachers use to identify creative abilities and to outline some approaches that primary schools find helpful in the development of creative self-direction in young children.

We hold that the uniqueness of expression that is characteristic of the spontaneous speech and play in young children results from the necessity to respond to situations which are new to the child; that is, situations for which no convention or cliché or stereotype has been learned. One three-year-old we know uses "yesterday" as any of the past thousand days—the time Santa Claus brought her baby, or Marky started school, or she waded on the beach. The psalmist reminded his Creator, "a thousand years in Thy sight are but as yesterday." Although the similarity in usage and in spontaneity is significant, the mature artist-poet will extend his conscious use of words to create a hundred psalms, but within a short time the child will learn to use yesterday in conventional ways. Can we who teach do anything to span the chasm between uninhibited and conscious self-expression?

Many adults believe that creativity is endemic to childhood; that a natural feeling for rhythm and design, if not inhibited, will find easy expression with paint or bells; that pupils gradually are stifled in their impulse to be creative. The apparent conflict between creative expression and the need to conform to the group has been discussed frequently. We see these two forms of behavior as potentially complimentary rather than as mutually exclusive—an idea which requires some explanation.

The need to develop cooperation and conformity is basic to productive learning of any kind in the school. Children need to learn the rules of living together in groups. The need to take turns in speaking and in playing is basic to survival of any group organization in which the patterns of interaction include all members. Learning to conform to the rules of the classroom makes life pleasanter for all the participants. However, if creativity is to be fostered, the child starting school must develop independence at the same time he learns a willingness to cooperate. Balancing these two facets of conformity and creativity requires sensitivity on our part as we help children work out productive roles as pupils.

Too often the fruit of acculturation is the gradual development of conformity at the expense of the impulse toward freedom or nonconformity. Some elements of creativity may need to be directed, but none should be eliminated or the whole potential for unique productivity is likely to be lost. If creativity is to be fostered it needs to be given recognition and to be valued, even as the conventions which are necessary to successful living together are valued. The creative person is neither a compulsive conformist nor a compulsive nonconformist. He chooses the appropriate mode for the situation.

Whoever is productive in school, or in life, must relate to the social group in ways which minimize friction so that individuality will not become distracting, disruptive, or destructive. The creative individual needs the feedback and the reinforcement which come from interaction with others if he is to build upon the cultural foundations which predate his efforts. On the other hand, a point of departure from the past is inherent in every creative act. At this point the learner is on his own. The essential aloneness of learning, the uniqueness in time or space of every moment of discovery, and the supremely personal nature of motivation in creative situations are familiar experiences to the kindergarten child, whether or not he ever grows up to reflect on the nature of creativity.

In a climate where all are worthy, teachers who reward children in their efforts to be original help them build tangible identities and pride in themselves. Strengthened in this way by the teacher, the child develops an eagerness to do the work of putting down or putting out or revealing himself in a product or an idea. "I am the only one who *can* do this in this way," may be the child's way of expressing his acceptance of the value we have in mind.

This expanding concept of self-worthiness and the selective reinforcement following his creative acts should comprise a consistent and significant part of the individual's early experience, if his creative potential is to flourish in the gradual but necessary social indoctrination. Creativity can be learned and it should find frequent expression before the acculturation, which, all too often stifles creativity, is accomplished.

If creativity can be taught, how does one go about it? The ideas and practices we would like to share have reinforced us in our attempt to be supportive of young children as they develop imagination, self-expression, and unique production.

When we as school people encourage the child to be spontaneous and imaginative, to show ingenuity and initiative, we are building him up as a creative person. The opportunities for individual expression in the kindergarten and primary classrooms are many, but this kind of learning is more likely to be promoted fully when we make it a conscious objective. Some schoolroom activities are more conducive than others to highly individual responses. When we initiate these opportunities—easel painting, role playing, inventing rhythms or musical themes, unstructured conversation—we see wide differences between individual children in spontaneity, abandon, and willingness to reveal the self. We found in our development of the *Kindergarten Evaluation of Learning Potential* (KELP, 1967) that creativity in children can be observed and encouraged.

Creativity, Like Intelligence, Exists in All

After sixty years the measurement of intelligence has become sophisticated; many instruments have become available and a wealth of experience has accumulated about the pitfalls and problems inherent in using these instruments. Creativity, on the other hand, has been a much more elusive characteristic. Certain periods of time, certain communities, even certain families have contributed disproportionately to creative pools of individuals. A thread that seems common in all of these manifestations of creativity is one of a willingness to value and reward the expressions of creative endeavor (Goertzel and Goertzel, 1962).

During the research phase of the development of the KELP we found many ways in which the teacher could encourage and reward children for creative behavior so that their productive abilities could expand and grow. Each separate area of expression requires its own development; the child has to come to want to create in a particular sphere. We found that both the basic learnings and the basic motivations could be taught in comparatively simple stages. In our adult haste we sometimes overlook steps in either the development of ideas or skills or motivations that seem obvious if we pause and analyze the creative process.

The urge to create seems to be present, at least to some degree, in everyone. Often, especially as we get older, this impulse seems to be crusted over or hidden by seeming indifference, by the glaze of fear of trying anything new, or by the smug satisfaction of rolling along in deeply worn ruts. Too many hurts, too many rebuffs to venturesomeness of any kind result in a kind of death—death of the push to create. The very young have not had time to learn these painful lessons, so they still explore and try to interpret their private worlds. The reinforcement we can give them for the trying—even partially unsuccessful trying—can nourish and strengthen the flicker that comes and goes uncertainly.

Nothing we have said should be taken to mean that we believe the ability to respond creatively is shared equally by all people. Human traits are never given with equal beneficence to all but neither are talents distributed so that a few have all and many have none. The creative spark seems to be distributed in young children according to this same normal curve, which theoretically indicates the incidence of all human traits. Some children can be taught quickly and easily to be highly creative and others must learn more slowly. Some are able to progress only to the foothills rather than to scale the heights with their more agile peers.

Creative Behavior Is Learned

Our experience has shown a three-step learning model to be helpful in building both the intellectual skills and the motivational drives that are important in creative production. The interaction between the intellectual and motivational drives is shown in Figure One. Let us begin our discussion with the cognitive—or intellectual—aspect of creativity.

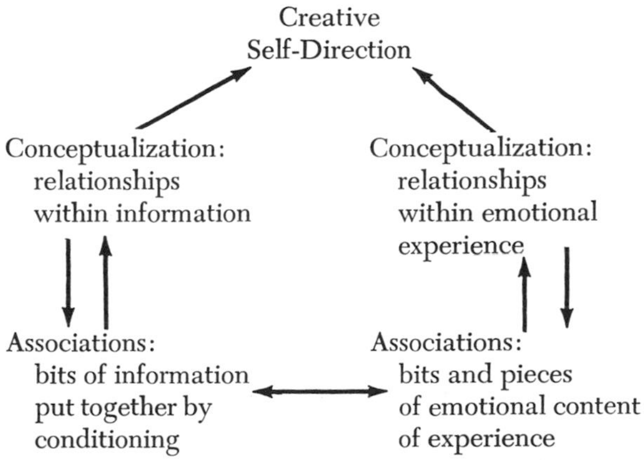

FIGURE ONE
LEARNING-MOTIVATION MODEL

Steps in the Intellectual Sequence

The first step to learning is the formation of associations, such as the names of objects or the awareness of differences in size, shape, color, tone, or mood. These associations are learned because they occur close together in time, as is often the case in classical conditioning, or they may be built up and strengthened as the child is reinforced for coming closer and closer to the discrimination of differences in sight, sound, or the like.

The child may be building a conditioned response when he comes to associate the words of the teacher announcing the nutrition break, "It's time to have our milk now." As the child learns the names of the colors and is able to discriminate and name the difference between red, brown, and pink, he will most likely have gone through a process by which someone has reinforced him for each step closer to the correct answer he has made.

To move to a higher level in our learning structure, certain kinds of learning are based on inherent meaning. After a minimum number of associations have been built, the relationship between them can become apparent to the learner. One explanation is that a series of associations form a loop or grid in the brain so that the parts form a larger whole. Some learning theorists refer to this learning event as closure. An example may be drawn from mathematics or arithmetic where adding "one more" generates the next highest number. Before a child can grasp this relationship as a conceptualization or a whole idea, he must have built numerous associations. The conceptualization of generating the next highest number by adding one more is preceded by associations such as numbers with size, numbers in sequence, and the experience of increasing a number by one. Once he has these bits of knowledge the child can grasp the relationship between numerical order and the addition of one more.

Often we are tempted to try to shorten the process and to tell the child the answer, but all this telling does is to build another association between the words that go together to make the answer rather than to achieve an understanding of the relationship. The meaning is missing. As we have watched both levels of learning occur, we have come to realize the necessity for patience as each child reaches for meaning on his own.

Some illustrations from language arts can be used to show the difference in the process of building associations and of generating a conceptualization. Many words such as "here," "on," or "run" have no inherent meaning. The word and its meaning are related by a series of discriminations that are reinforced for correct usage. The French say "sur" and the English say "on" to mean the same thing. One is not right and the other wrong; rather one is right in the milieu of a French culture and the other is right in the society of English-speaking people. The child must learn these lessons in a step-by-step series of associations.

In the following incident a child generated a concept by seeing the relationships in a series of vocabulary associations. Tammy, age 3, liked to take her aunt to the granary where a quiet wait would be rewarded by a visit from the squirrel. On one such visit she said, "Come and sit with me in my bin?"

"No that's barley and has barbs on it, I'm sitting in the wheat."

"This is barley and it's a grain. That's wheat and it's a grain. That bin has oats. Is it grain, too?" asked Tammy.

"Yes."

"Then they are all grain and that's why we call this a granary." At this point Tammy had grasped a concept of grain which now allowed her to classify rye and corn as grain.

Creative behavior, the theme of this book, proceeds from the associations and the conceptualizations which become building blocks available for the child's use in his creative self-direction. Each child will use the materials he has available in his own particular way. Individuality and uniqueness are characteristics of the creative product as is the drive that is characteristic of the creative process.

Steps in the Motivational Sequence

The three steps in learning described as association, conceptualization, and creative self-direction have a parallel sequence in the development of motivation. At the first level the basic associations are the simple enjoyment of the creative experience. At level two the child conceptualizes the cause-effect relationship of creative production and the pleasure he feels. At level three he internalizes these pleasures and ideas to the extent that his self-concept becomes one of a creative individual. We have called this the actualization step in the motivational process. Since this structure has not been published elsewhere, each of these steps will be elaborated.

When the child's early experiences in creative output are made pleasant by conveyed appreciation, not necessarily verbalized, the kinds of associations are built that lay the foundation for a highly motivated child. The simple enjoyment which comes from the parent's or teacher's attention to a painting or a rhyme is associated with the child's effort. It is less important at this stage that the painting have artistic value than that the painting occur in an atmosphere of delight. At level one the child need not be conscious that conditioning is occurring, but the essential role of self-motivation of any creative production demands that the child want to repeat the experience. The close relationship of pleasure and creative activity ties these together as fundamental associations.

As enough of these associations between pleasure and creative production accumulate the child may become aware of the tie between them. He need not verbalize but, like the hobbyist, he has become aware that he does these things because he likes to do them. They give him pleasure and he knows that they give him pleasure—the conceptualization level in motivation.

As primary teachers we frequently schedule a choice or free activity period when children may choose a medium with which to work—chalk, finger paints, clay, puzzles, or tone bells. To our dismay some children want to use the same medium day after day. This situation becomes more productive and the child's creative potential is extended if we understand why he wants to repeat a pleasant experience and help him to move from level one to level two in the motivational sequence. Essentially this is done by helping the child realize the possibility of getting similar satisfactions by working in other materials. The help given the child to see the possibility of similar pleasures in work with other media clarifies for him the relationship of pleasure with creation in the first experience. If this directed movement from one medium to another is repeated with satisfying results, the child may come to seek new modes of expression on his own initiative. If he does this, he has come to the place we call self-actualization. The distinguishing marks of the self-starter—who sees himself as one who engages in creative endeavors—include a venturesomeness and a willingness to struggle to express his ideas or his personal view of things. He has escaped from fear of the new, at least, in several areas. The child who has reached a self-actualization level in his cognitive and motivational sequences finds himself free to explore and to express himself in varied and different ways. His internal satisfactions are now often more powerful than the adulation of his peers even as his unique and untrammeled approaches sometimes are dismaying to those around him. His freedom is precious to him and he will guard it jealously.

Creativity Is Built on Previous Experience

Mention was made earlier of the fact that a person does not create out of nothing. The building blocks he uses as he creates his new structure are the mental, aesthetic, or emotional materials that are available to him—blocks that have been given to him by his previous experiences. When these experiences have been restricted, cabined, or confined, as is true for many of our disadvantaged youngsters, they have only meager resources with which to create.

We have found that many children start school with a wealth of background experiences. They have had parents who talk with them of birds, flowers, numbers, words, and persons. Other children need time to accumulate a body of associations, words that stand for experiences, and a chance to generate for themselves the relationships in a series of experiences. Some of them lack stimulating home backgrounds and others lack the intellectual maturity to profit from the opportunities they have had earlier for learning. Patience and tolerance help these less favored or more backward children develop the essential building blocks needed for creative production without, at the same time, developing the self-concepts of failure and worthlessness that are so easily generated when they compare themselves with their more favored peers.

Classroom Approaches to Creative Behavior

As we accept the idea that all original production in children is creative we are faced with a threefold challenge—to encourage and reinforce initiative and self-expression, to devise and initiate the steps that lead to these abilities, and to help the child develop the habits necessary for seeing his creative attempts completed. The overwhelming challenge to teachers comes when we try to anticipate unique responses from the thirty children who make up our class. Motivation and evaluation are always difficult, but in creative work the teacher's task is multiplied because creative work must be individualized. When the product is unique by our own intent, the criteria for evaluation must be suited to each child, his talents, his potential, and his level of development in both cognitive and motivational sequences. So when we set down some guidelines which have worked well in various situations, we do so with more than a little awe of the complexity of the task. Fortunately some of the most stimulating resources for creativity are inherent in the climate of whole class activities. The suggestions which follow were gleaned by observing our very young teachers—the kindergarten and primary children from whom we learn.

Teach Children to Live Richly

The stuff of which creative responses are built are the experiences of the individual. We have found that a rewarding first step is to help children reach out into their environments and to seek to interpret the sensory stimulations—the sights, smells, sounds, tastes, and touches of the world. A trip to the playground where the children sit on the grass can expand the sensory world in which they live. When the children are asked to close their eyes and to tell what they hear one will tell of a cricket in the tall grass; another, the bus stopping at the corner; a third may hear the custodian closing the incinerator; while a fourth hears his friend breathing. After they have discussed the world of sounds, another round of listening can demonstrate that each hears more and different things than he heard the first time. Children help each other live more fully as they try to find words to describe what they heard.

The "sounds under the horse chestnut" or "under the Chinese elm" can be put down in free verse which the class does together, like an ordinary experience story of less vital or poignant meaning. In this way the class explores the senses one by one—sights, smells, sounds—and then shares the struggle for the right words to express what different individuals experienced. Each child gradually becomes confident in probing and interpreting the environment and in realizing what he thinks about things is valued by others. Children begin to learn the pleasure that comes with bringing together the right words, or colors, or tones.

Anthologies of children's poems, such as *Very Young Verses* (1945) or *Told Under the Green Umbrella* (1962), are resources that, kept within arm's reach, can be used to provide an uncommon poem to illuminate a shared event. These poems help the children learn new words or new ways to use old words to express the feelings they hold in common. Used in this way at the appropriate moment, the poem about "Mrs. Peck Pigeon" may have more impact on a child's appreciation for poetry than lesson upon lesson of structured analysis and rhyme finding.

Similar sensory-expanding experiences can be brought into the classroom. A bag that contains different kinds of rocks, passed around the class, enables the children to describe the differences in texture they feel between sandstone and mica, limestone and obsidian, or granite and pumice. As the child increases his facility in verbal description and tactile discrimination the teacher increases the number of kinds of rocks.

One kindergarten teacher we know sharpens the sense of smell by bringing prescription bottles, lined with tissue paper which covers eucalyptus nuts, cedar shavings, gardenia petals, sage leaves, freshly ground coffee, tea leaves, cinnamon sticks, nasturtium petals or anything else that has a distinctive odor. As the children try to put into words a description of the various smells, this teacher records the efforts of the children in a free-verse book called "What Is a Smell?"

As the children participate in organized activities which enhance sensory awareness, they increasingly make their own individual discoveries and bring them to sharing periods on their own initiative. They tell of hearing the frogs on hot nights, the feel of damp grass on bare feet, the mustiness of fallen leaves after a storm, or the way the sun lights the edges of leaves against the sky. The shared joy of these experiences helps build vocabulary, sensory discrimination, and motivation to explore and to tell of the exploration. Families that produce artists tend to help their children develop these sensibilities, to help them interpret their environments aesthetically, and to help them screen out the sensations that are, at least for the moment, irrelevant. Teachers who help children to share another's joy in discovery are helping all to live more richly and are developing the elements of experience and motivation that creative people need.

Reinforce Divergent Behavior

As the children experience the world which comes to them through the senses, the teacher has opportunities to pick up and to reinforce any evidence of uniqueness and sensitivity expressed. Classroom materials are available that build for individual expression and are structured to reward evidence of divergent thinking. In the *Kindergarten Evaluation of Learning Potential* the bead-design item helps the child build associations between shape, color, order, and tactile sense as he copies different designs. It asks him to conceptualize the nature of design in order to reproduce from memory a string of beads that is too long for recall unless he has understood bead design as a repetition of a smaller pattern. Finally the child is asked to use this conceptualization of the nature of design to build a new design of his own. Small specific learning experiences such as bead and block design help develop an attitude that values the new, the divergent, and the different.

Value Unique Production

Uniqueness can be its own standard and the very fact that it is the child's own makes it good. This kind of interaction with the child needs to take cognizance of the child's level of ability to function in creative ways. What may be a major step in creation for one child, and therefore deserving praise and reinforcement, may very well pass unnoticed in the child who has progressed beyond this particular level of production. One six-year-old reflected the fact that unique productions were valued as she explained her bead design to a visitor, "In our room we don't have to do things all the time the way you are supposed to do them."

Teach the Techniques that Are Needed To Assure a Satisfying Experience

Considerable discussion transpires between those who would develop creative talent in an unstructured, undirected, highly permissive environment and those who would develop artistic production in pupils by the same steps once taken by the teacher, that is, to teach students the techniques of the art directly and in preordered sequence. To attempt the uncontrolled approach in the classroom is to preorder chaos and to foreordain little or no place in the school for these kinds of activities. On the other hand, to program the techniques evolved by an adult artist on a group of children, each being highly individual in the extent of his creativity and in his profile of aesthetic talents, is likely to suppress any flicker of aesthetic aspiration and to eliminate the potential for innovation and invention in the techniques themselves. We find the middle ground between these extremes offers potential to the teacher for an imaginative approach to teaching. Flexible, goal-oriented teaching provides the child with some help in the control of his media and some reinforcement through adult appreciation of his unique productions. We have discovered few if any absolutes in the teaching of techniques. The essential condition seems to be, at least in the beginning, that a climate of pleasure comes to be associated with attempts to create at school.

Some teachers have found watercolors too difficult for primary children to manage. We believe the teacher should have a satisfying experience with most lessons and see no reason why all teachers should be required to use watercolors in the classroom. At the same time the very young pupils of some other teachers do fabulous things with large brushes, absorbent paper, and soggy whole-pan watercolors. *C'est la vie!* We as teachers need freedom within the curriculum to use our own talents in creative ways. If there is no one path to creative productiveness in students, certainly the same is true for teachers. The sensible approach is to make new media available one by one and to make clear some ways to control and care for materials through discussions, or films, or demonstrations. In general we try to assure a successful experience. The teacher observes and anticipates when to support or help a child and when to put him on his own. For most children rhythm instruments provide a surer beginning than the clarinet; free verse is easier to write than a sonnet, and finger painting may be rewarding at an age when still life is not.

Teach Pupils to Identify the Essential Areas for Conformity and Adherence to Convention

At the beginning of this chapter it was pointed out that children must learn to conform to certain rules and regulations during the same period of time we want them to develop the freedom to express themselves creatively. An element of discipline is essential in all creativity, but overemphasis on conformity can stifle the freedom needed for the child to learn to express himself spontaneously. Certainly the rules and conventions must be learned for freedom to be meaningful. Creativity in spelling is frowned upon, grammatical constructions have been developed to ease the task of communication, handwriting needs to conform to certain conventions if others are to read what one writes. The acceptance of the editor's format for manuscripts—rules for titles, margins, names—can free the person to use the available decision-making energy in other more important areas. These conventions are accepted and taught as tools to facilitate creativity; rather than as ends in themselves, they stimulate rather than retard creativity.

In this same context—conformity to free energy for creative activity, the child can be helped to observe common courtesies, to take his turn, to listen while others are talking, and to respect another's views even while disagreeing with them. The penalties for neglect of these learnings are energy wasted in fighting, attention diverted from creation, and happiness clouded by his view of a world that seems forever cruel. We teach the conformities which free the child for unique and important pursuits.

Schedule a Regular Choice Period

One of the arrangements which encourages creative production within the classroom setting is the free time or choice period. To give children freedom to choose an individual activity or project provides them with an opportunity for constructive production in areas of interest or special talent. Unavoidably pupils are thus given the freedom to make less than optimal use of their time. Self-direction can then be taught by formulating standards with the class, by attending individually to children who need most to increase their independence, and by giving prompt attention to their products through regular and constructive evaluation.

When kindergartners first come to school, we need to begin with a manageable situation—a choice between easy alternatives such as pastels or crayons on newsprint. Gradually the choices are broadened to include collage, puzzles, blocks, paper sculpture, easel painting, listening post, rhythm instruments, finger painting, and number boards.

As children grow older the choices come to include imaginative writing, book making, science experiments, mathematical puzzles, and the like. The significant ingredients of the choice period regardless of the age of the child are (1) the opportunity for creative activity and (2) responsibility for completion of selected projects.

Provide a Variety of Materials

Some of the experiences described as ways to help the child live more richly depend on providing materials that increase his awareness of the physical environment. The different kinds of rocks hold opportunities for widening the touch sensations, the provision of medicine bottles with odors, the trips out of doors to see, hear, and smell the world all come into this category of providing materials to help the children generate the experiences basic to creative self-direction. Picture books, of which there are many available, all are valuable in helping children step from the direct world of the senses to the vicarious world of literature.

Structured-learning sequences have been designed during recent years to help teachers at crucial points as they seek to develop the creative facet of child personality. From the materials of the

Kindergarten Evaluation of Learning Potential, which build and test creative expression, we selected the number boards for a brief description of how creative self directed behavior is developed. The sense of wonder and excitement that is a part of the generation of motivation needs to be nourished as the child is first exposed to the magic world of number.

In the KELP numbers item, many of the associations and concepts are developed while the teacher works with the whole class around the flannel board. These associations and conceptualizations are then broadened and enlarged as selected children work with the individual plastic number-board sets. They associate the various sizes, the numerals, and the sequences with each other as they manipulate the pieces. When children develop the concept of the relationships within a number, of the systematic structure of a number they are in a position to go forward on their own. The discovery that four is made up of 1-1-1-1; 2-2; 3-1; 1-3 can lead naturally into exploration of the relationships inherent in number 7. The use of materials that make this exploration simple encourages the child to think beyond the program for the whole class. The elements that are essential for creativity in number seem to be basic associations, some basic concepts about relations, the motivations to explore further, and the materials that make the exploration possible, clear, and fruitful.

Materials are a help toward a goal; they are not ends in themselves. Children can be stimulated rather than frustrated, encouraged rather than discouraged, if the materials provided are suitable for creative exploration.

Extend Original Behavior to All Feasible Activities

Initiative and creative production have been accepted by all cultural groups in graphic arts, music, folklore, and literature. In school the temptation may be great to overdirect the child's participations in order to assure a product that can be understood and approved by the adult community, by assuring that the product resemble adult art. To help a child grow in the ability and the willingness to examine and interpret the world of people and things as he sees them, the adult must make the effort to understand what the child is revealing, or at least the adult must convey the desire to understand the child's view of things.

To us who teach young children this means that (1) we encourage pupil initiative in various school activities and (2) we postpone the use of adult standards in the arts until the children are approaching a time they can begin to see the physical or social or religious world through adult eyes. Parents need to be helped to react meaningfully and appreciatively to creative production, whether this be a hand puppet, or the discovery that counting by 2's can go on indefinitely. Easel paintings can then be sent home with the assurance that a rebuff or misinterpretation will not occur.

The essential point, if we are to extend creativity to all possible areas, is that art activities are not necessarily a creative experience for the child, and almost any school activity has the potential for the child's going beyond group work to what we have called "creative self-direction." When every clown must look like the adult image of a clown and every pony have four hoofs, probably we will duplicate an adult's clown and an adult's pony which children will be directed to color red or brown. A shocking premise of learning theory is that children learn to enjoy even this activity if we reward them. But have they moved "one mouse step" toward interpreting their world or ours?

On the other hand, such activities as making and keeping the rules can be a creative process. Of eleven items in KELP, nine include a third level – beyond association and conceptualization – creative self-direction, in activities as varied as bead design, calendar, and social interaction. The five-year-old who said, "My friends Jimmy and Frank and I relate well," was well on the way toward constructive social interrelationships. This talent was revealed in another way when he was observed mediating a quarrel between two peers and asked the intervening adult, "Please, would you give me a chance to see if I can settle this?" Whether an activity fosters or inhibits creative behavior depends upon the extent to which we encourage responsible freedom, the levels at which our pupils are able to function, and the eagerness with which creative activities are pursued.

Separate "Idea-Generating" from "Critical-Judgment" Situations in Time and Place

In creative activities the child produces an idea, a painting, or a new way of doing something. Even before he shares his effort with the teacher or other children there is usually a point at which he steps back to see how well his work has been done. Before children learn habits of being overly critical of themselves and others, they can start to learn an approach to criticism—an appreciative understanding of what the fellow artist was trying to say or do. If the child says, "I can't paint," or "I can't write," a supportive and encouraging conversation to help the child clarify what he wants to attempt is often all the help a hesitant child needs. "What would you like to paint? Where do you plan to put your clown? A good idea! How big do you plan to make him? Show me with your hands. Will the paper let you make him bigger? What color is his suit? His face? Where will his face be? Is he a happy clown or a sad clown? Very good! I see you have your picture all figured out."

The careless, often outgoing child, who slops something down and appears to think his first effort almost completely satisfactory poses a different problem. He may need specific guidance, immediately preceeding his next attempt at similar work to help him set higher but attainable goals. A child who is to learn to create must be taught to avoid both pitfalls—destructive self-criticism and self-acceptance of a mediocre product.

One technique for helping the child to grow in the process of evaluation is to place the emphasis on how to take the next step—whether he be the fearful inhibited child who does not complete his work or the careless child whose work is good enough for him in spite of severe scrutiny. The evaluation should be a shared experience, designed for growth toward greater maturity or more sensitive behavior. Evaluation should be positive and should be available at times when the child has reached a barrier—whether motivational, intellectual, or mechanical—in his control of the medium. The final stopping place in creative activity should be at the point of some pleasing outcome for the child so that the next day, the next week, or the next year a new attempt can be launched from a point of satisfaction with its attendant motivation.

We have said nothing to this point about the development of creative talent in the physical sciences and technological research. At least some of the innovators in these fields established childhood interests and abilities through manipulations of the environment and discoveries of relationships not shared by their peers. Valuable background knowledge which has implications for those who teach young children is contained in other chapters of this volume. We have no conclusive evidence to show that young children are suited to hypothesis generating or hypothesis testing, divergent thinking or convergent thinking, research or scholarship, creation or criticism. We think young children who are prepared for creative self-direction need to learn the roles of freedom and of discipline, of brainstorming and of critical analysis. In hypothesis-generating discussions we let the class know we are asking for all possible solutions, explanations, ideas, or approaches. The brainstorming group also should know that all new ideas, sincerely proposed, are valued. At a later time these many suggestions will be reexamined and one or several research designs will be selected for perusal. As teachers, we should distinguish and let the class know whether the common goal is one answer or process, or whether the premium is on divergence and fluency.

Develop a Climate Which Nurtures Creativity

All of the discussions of techniques for developing creativity stressed the need for joy, pleasure, and happiness in the activities that are creative or unique. The element of creativity that keeps the artist striving toward greater and greater perfection is another important component.

The exhilaration, which we all feel in situations where we are free to be ourselves, needs to be accompanied by selective reinforcement for creative accomplishments. Any response that is sensitive and honest and responsible should be rewarded. The exhilaration of freedom and the completion of the creative product are the foundations of discipline which are characteristic of every great creative artisan. This kind of climate is created by the adult who is sensitive to the responsibility a child can handle with security.

Summary

This chapter develops three basic themes: (1) that creativity, like intelligence, exists to some degree in all people, (2) that creative behavior is learned and therefore can be taught, and (3) that children's creativity is built on the mental, aesthetic, and emotional patterns they have accumulated.

A model of learning was presented that consisted of a cognitive sequence: (1) associations built on contiguity in space and time, or on reinforced discriminations and responses, (2) conceptualizations in which the meaning and relationships are understood, and (3) creative self-direction. The motivational sequence consisted of (1) simple associations between pleasure and creative activities, (2) a conceptualization of the relationship between creativity and pleasure, and (3) self-actualization, a fulfillment of self as a creative person.

These principles of learning are inherent in some suggested ways of working with a group of children to make explicit the creative potential in each individual. Basic principles for creative teaching are:

1. Teach children to live richly.
2. Reinforce divergent behavior.
3. Value unique production.
4. Teach the techniques that are needed to assure a satisfying experience.
5. Teach pupils to identify the essential areas for conformity and adherence to convention.
6. Schedule a regular choice period.
7. Provide a variety of materials.
8. Extend original behavior to all feasible activities.
9. Separate "idea-generating" from "critical-judgment situations" in time and place.
10. Develop a climate which nurtures creativity.

Most significant are the creative approaches of the teachers, who encourage and reward the self-directing activities of children. Their work ensures the expansion and enlargement of a pool of creative talent for tomorrow.

CHAPTER 4

Creativity and the Curriculum

by

LOUIS J. RUBIN

Louis J. Rubin has taught in elementary and secondary schools and has been a professor at San Fernando Valley State College, the University of California, Berkeley, and the University of California, Santa Barbara. He has served as a curriculum coordinator and as a consultant for many school systems. He has consulted extensively with the U.S. Office of Education in Title III and Title IV programs. Mr. Rubin is the co-author of Process and Product in Education, *and is chairman of the Editorial Board of the* Journal for Secondary Education *and chairman for the 1969 Yearbook Committee for ASCD. His interest in creativity results from a number of monographs produced for the Ventura County Schools office.*

When one considers in its length and in its breadth the importance of this question of the education of the young, the broken lives, the defeated homes, the national failures, which result from the frivolous inertia with which it is treated, it is difficult to restrain within oneself a savage rage.

ALFRED NORTH WHITEHEAD wrote these lines some years ago in his *The Aims of Education* (1929, p.25). Until recently, this frivolous inertia has characterized American education. The inertia was not attributable to a specific failure, nor was it always so frivolous. Rather, it resulted from several afflictions: provincial public attitudes toward education, a dearth of able, well-schooled teachers, disinterest of influential scholars, and inadequate provision for research.

In sharp contrast, the last decade has been a period of ferment and upheaval. Many restricting conditions have been altered, and a spectacular overhaul of the curriculum is in process. Dramatic departures from long-standing tradition have occurred in the sciences and in mathematics. Methods of teaching foreign languages have been recast, and newborn procedures for streamlining English teaching are in use. The transformation has heralded no minor content changes, but a pedagogical revolution. Curriculum makers, confronted by increasingly untidy accumulations of knowledge, have sought aid from scholars at the crest of research. Psychologists, fresh from a long due reappraisal of learning theory, have challenged several crucial assumptions at the bedrock of educational practice.

As a result, public education has been pressed by a series of arguments which—in their literal impact—condemn traditional teaching methods, require a reorganization of content, redefine the purpose of education, and generally demand a greater individualization of instruction. The fruits of this pedagogical revolution have found their most characteristic expression in the new curricula for physics, chemistry, biology, and mathematics which have been painstakingly designed by men of unquestioned ability. Additional efforts have already extended to curriculum reconstruction in history, English, and the foreign languages. One must now assume that the reform is no mere footnote but a foreword to future events in education.

This chapter maintains that in improving education, the rebellion from traditional methodology should closely follow teaching implications from research on creativity. These implications lead to teaching which exploits the student's creative capacities, and which at the same time result in an infinitely better style of learning.

The Method of Inquiry

Contemporary learning theory places a premium on the learning impetus which young children derive from their innate tendency to explore unknown situations, to seek challenges which tax their freshly won skills, deliberately to find problem situations at the edge of their potential, and generally to gain pleasure from the active pursuit of learning. The use of these principles in curriculum design suggests that the mature student should similarly be involved in intellectual activities which arouse his curiosity and force him to confront the challenging and the unknown. Psychologists hypothesize that man is motivated by a strong urge to understand things which stimulate his inquisitiveness and which test his power to control his circumstances.

In consequence, the testimony of recent research on learning argues that students, rather than carry on their work in situations free from tension, ought purposely to be thrust into a study environment with at least some built-in stress. Learning under limited stress does not mean a return to ferule-and-frown teaching, but it may mark a retreat from the completely permissive classroom. Spare the rod, but stress the child.

The heart of the method of inquiry lies in the notion that the student ought to procure significant information for himself by processes which are in their own right valuable acquisitions. The method is self-directed in the sense that the student performs whatever operations are required to gain the desired understanding. The crux of the method, at least from the standpoint of the curriculum, hinges upon selecting suitable questions for inquiry. Only a reasonably well-informed mind can perceive answers when they appear. Obviously, learning through inquiry does not imply that the student must acquire all his knowledge through self-discovery. What it does imply is something profoundly important in learning: that periodically the student ought to use his aggregation of data, however accumulated, in attacking problems so that he gives meaning to his information and order to his conceptual understanding and his rational insights. The benchmark of most new curricula is thus the provision for inquiring into phenomena, for experimenting with unknowns, and for utilizing one level of knowledge as a springboard to more knowledge at a higher level.

The use of inquiry as a teaching method permits student accomplishment that is largely prohibitive in expository teaching. Coincidentally, however, it places a greater strain on the artistry of the teacher and requires a different yardstick for judging student achievement.

Traditionally, knowledge has been compartmentalized into arbitrary sequences and transmitted to the student. The student was asked to "learn" the content and "prove" his mastery. Inasmuch as such proof, for the most part, consisted of performance on an objective examination of facts, the student's academic exercise was almost exclusively verbal. Even today, the student tends to accept a prefabricated gospel without regard to its logic or significance; he memorizes conclusions without questioning either their validity or their importance. Because he is judged to have learned when he can give back what he is fed, he gears himself for the rapid assimilation of whatever is set before him. While all teaching need not be this shallow, the unfortunate fact is that much of it is.

Theorists argue that it is precisely this reliance on accumulating odd bits of information which handicaps the student in applying his learning some useful way. In contrast, when he himself constructs patterns from the data he gathers, and searches out and verifies conclusions, functional learning is more likely to occur. During these moments of inquiry, the student has the exhilarating experience of being more than a mere sponge. In reduplicating the role of the inquirer, the student becomes a scientist, critic, or artist. In discovering for himself frames of reference, he is creating the most important and enduring frame of all—his own intellect.

Two related points are worth noting. First, several writers have suggested that the principal problem of human memory is not storage, but retrieval. The mind is capable of housing an enormous quantity of information but the difficulty lies in recalling desired information at will. These writers maintain that when the student engages in the intellectual processes necessary for establishing relationships and organizing information, he substantially enhances his ability to retrieve his knowledge upon demand. Information that has acquired a relationship is not only easier to recall, but because it has enjoyed some scrutiny and evaluation and because it has been processed into frames of reference, the student is able truly to integrate it into his conceptual framework. Second, skill in self-directed pursuit of knowledge does not evolve naturally but must be learned as specific processes involving a number of different ways of thinking. In his initial efforts, the student is likely to be easily dislodged from the right track. Gaining skill in efficiently directing one's efforts to achieve necessary information, therefore, is in itself a form of learning of exceptional worth. It is a classic case of the principle of transfer.

Aside from the modest innovations referred to earlier, heuristic learning is still in a developmental stage. The design of teaching patterns in which inquiry complements other useful methods of learning needs more experimentation. Curriculum reformers must, for example, find a more efficacious way of selecting, organizing, and presenting the most appropriate content. Because the intelligent use of verbal explanation, expository discourse, drill, and memorization still has a place in the classroom, a balance between inquiry and other kinds of learning needs to be established. More than anything else, inquiry provides the student an opportunity to connect various kinds of information into significant relationships, to invest available knowledge—as a sort of intellectual capital—in the accumulation of more knowledge, and to stimulate learning which comes more from authentic desire than from obligation.

Reorganization of Knowledge

The traditional curriculum is based on a fundamental assumption that knowledge is static. Moreover, it tends to labor only one of several kinds of knowledge: that typified by facts, principles, laws, and generalizations. It stresses the view that education is predominantly a systematic and logical process of adding new information to old. The traditional curriculum in history, as a case in point, evolved through this sequence: first, a compilation of available historical data; second, a selection of information which appeared to be of greatest consequence; third, the organization of the information into a chronological or some other orderly system; fourth, the development of logical procedures for transmitting the information to the student. Despite its logic, the approach poses a number of limitations. For example, as man's amassed knowledge expands, the selection process becomes increasingly critical; what has been accepted as true at one time may come to be regarded as false at another time. Most important, education is reduced to a simple matter of sponging up information.

As Whitehead suggested almost four decades ago, ideas do not remain static but either become more significant or grow obsolete. The often-referred-to explosion of knowledge testifies to the plastic nature of man's convictions. Even when existing beliefs are not superseded, they may, as a result of new interpretation, take on quite different meanings. Darwin's theory of evolution is a common example; it came out of a new interpretation of existing data rather than a discovery of new data. Human achievement is as much a tribute to man's continuous escape from earlier error as it is to his invention of new truth. Lawrence Frank (1960, p.18) puts the problem this way:

> Until pupils are aware of their preconceptions, their customary assumptions and expectations, the folk-wisdom and traditional beliefs from earlier stages in the history of thought, the once valid common sense, they cannot learn the new, they are handicapped by these older concepts, these familiar ways of thinking. Here we should rec-

ognize a crucial problem for education today, namely the problem of *unlearning*, or if you prefer, re-learning. It seems clear that if a child (or an adolescent, or an adult) is to learn new concepts, new ways of perceiving and thinking about the world, he must first become aware of his preconceptions, recognize his familiar habitual patterns, what he has previously learned from his family and his neighbors, what has been built into his frame of references, and so guides, directs, or even coercively controls what he learns. Without this cognitive self-awareness, he cannot ordinarily recognize that he must give up the old in order to learn the new.

Another impetus to the current curriculum reorganization stems from the supposition that forms of knowledge other than accepted facts, laws, and theories are pertinent to the school's purpose. A sense of what we do not know, for example, is also an important kind of knowledge. The student whose education is restricted to knowledge in current vogue suffers from intellectual malnutrition. He may often accept what is only a temporary notion as a permanent concept. In contrast, let the student gain a broad exposure to the history of man's riddles—to the critical questions yet unsolved—to the historical evolution of a concept through all of its inconstant states, and he will gather a more realistic perception of the intellectual world.

The Application of Information

A grasp of how to apply information is also important knowledge. The historian and the student conceivably may have the same information at their disposal; the difference lies in the historian's awareness of what can be done with it. To again use the history class as an example, a competent student may know seventy or eighty separate bits of information about the Civil War; but while his aggregate assortment of information allows him a reasonable picture of the war itself, he may still not understand the war's sociological impact or he may be unable to deploy his information in a useful application. Assuming, for the moment, that he had a similar fund of information on the Korean War, he ought to be able to perceive similarities and dissimilarities between the two. Further, he ought to understand connections between wars and postwar economics and comprehend the cause and effect link between war and industrialization.

The essence of a discipline lies not in the sum of its assembled data but in the particular data which define important relationships and give meaning to the major concepts. For example, an idea which explains a number of interesting facts, but which does not suggest further experimentation, is of less use to a scientist than an idea which establishes new unknowns and generates new paths of inquiry. This is not to imply that the student's function is the advancement of knowledge but to suggest that if the curriculum must judge the usefulness of various kinds of information a subject offers, the most fitting criterion may be the degree to which the information contributes to the learner's conceptual framework. Individuals tend to achieve maximum effectiveness by excluding the parts of their intellectual resources which are peripheral and irrelevant to the task at hand. By conjoining the principle of inquiry learning with a reexamination of the fundamental purpose of instruction, we can perhaps cope with the questions regarding the kind of knowledge that best breeds wisdom. The parallel between curriculum innovation and creativity research is most visible in their mutual concern for problem solving, for self-determined learning activity, and for dealing with unknowns.

As a preliminary summation, then, efforts to cover subject matter are giving way to an emphasis of significant concepts. The student is not only taught what to know, but how to know. He is not so much given a set of facts as encouraged to develop patterns and methods to assimilate and understand facts. The conceptual understanding gained serves as connective tissue in integrating different sorts of information for dealing with ideas of greater complexity. Information, once mastered, is put to functional use by engaging the student in investigatory learning—in laboratory experimentation, in the formulation and verification of hypotheses, and in the reconstruction of theories. Moreover, the student uses his knowledge in a self-directed quest for additional insight. He develops skill in establishing crucial questions, in selecting relevant data, and in drawing conclusions which again lead to the formulation of new questions. In developing a competence to use different learning processes, he engages in different forms of thinking. He learns how to isolate and clarify tasks, to order alternatives in their relative importance, and to analyze, infer from, test, and reformulate conclusions. Uppermost, the basis of the curriculum shifts from the mastery of content to techniques for acquiring and using knowledge. How something is learned, in brief becomes infinitely more important than what is learned.

Intellectual talent is a precious commodity; moreover, we have come to recognize that creativity, among other distinctive intellectual gifts, cannot flourish in the ordinary school milieu. In carrying on the routine of the school, we tend to ignore those matters which cannot be dealt with precisely, which are difficult to manage, or which run counter to custom. A creative child is usually the archetype of "those matters." As a case in point, there is reason to believe that the education of intellectually proficient students is perhaps best served by requiring them to work at the extreme brink of frustration. Assuming that the notion is valid, its implementation will demand a sharp departure from habit and create difficulties; its usefulness, nevertheless, will be lost unless a deliberate effort is made to overcome the problems. As in any other system, education is prodded from time to time by provocative new ideas. During these periods of stimulation a good deal of change is unavoidable, and the face of education is inevitably altered. The tragic folly we are courting is that we shall continue to test the worth of new ideas by determining whether the existing system can accommodate them. We must, in short, begin to display a far greater willingness to modify the system, to take calculated risks, and to accept occasional failure as an inevitable feature of progress, so that promising new ideas can be tested fairly.

Because creativity does not occur in a vacuum, efforts to nurture it in the classroom must deal with teaching tactics, with learning theory, and with the peculiarities of knowledge. The growing evidence on the nature of creativity bears a striking similarity not only to the mainline of contemporary curriculum theory but also to the propositions advanced by psychologists concerning the way learning occurs. For example, the student with a preference for working in isolation is customarily encouraged to relate more closely to his group. The student who is not well-rounded or square but who displays uneven contours and sharp edges is manipulated until he, almost in self-defense, resembles the psychological and intellectual topography of his more conventional peers. It is probable that such practices have stifled individuality and the creative potential of a gifted few as well as impaired the capacity of most students to learn efficiently.

Our concern is less with the fashioning of creative geniuses than with what Henry Murray calls "paralysis of the imagination." Arguments for classroom procedures which enhance, rather than inhibit, the development of creative abilities obviously are advanced in the hope that the rare, specially endowed youth will benefit from liberating experiences in the school. In the broader sense, however, there is a certain tragedy about all individuals who have lost the technique and the incentive to pit their creative power against their problems. We all have a measure of creativity in us, and its expression is enormously satisfying. The stunting and blocking of creativity lead to the deepest frustrations. Over a hundred years ago Henry David Thoreau observed that "the mass of men lead lives of quiet desperation." In our own time a good many social scientists have alluded to the desperation in our society and to the growing debilitation of man's sense of self-fulfillment. The suggestions for teaching which follow are thus oriented toward a twofold purpose: the betterment of the general majority and the nurture of the very talented minority.

Any implication for the classroom taken from research on creativity obviously must be qualified by the tentative conclusions of the research itself and by the circumstances of the particular classroom situation. Different classroom pursuits will afford different opportunities to exercise the student's creative capacities. Understandably, no segment of the curriculum can direct itself exclusively to creativity; the research evidence, however, indicates that all classes, at one point or another, can contribute to the promotion of creative behavior. The school's task demands many different objectives—the mastery of prescribed content, the development of specific skills and attitudes, the formation of particular habits—and the development of the creativeness of a few select students must be regarded as a part rather than as the whole game. Obviously, a public school cannot be the exclusive domain for the elite, nor can creativity be a surrogate for anything new or radical. It is of the utmost importance that procedures directed toward the exploitation of creativity be carefully assessed; simple permissiveness, the casual use of unstructured time, elimination of rules, the careless acceptance of disorganization, and many other things are easily confused with the truly creative situation. But research which results in understanding what constitutes creativity can invigorate the curriculum for all students. It can also separate the truly creative from the unorthodox and from that which is merely uncontrolled.

Creativity, unfortunately, has become a somewhat indiscriminate term in recent literature. It habitually has been employed as a synonym for any unformularized venture, many of its peripheral characteristics have been inflated into pseudo-prescriptions, and it has often been represented as no more than simple self-expression. Then, too, the putting to use of the research findings is itself difficult. In view of the existing structure of the schools and the public expectation of what learning ought to be, many of the implications of creativity cannot be employed without irritating the conservative position. Many patently foolish things have been suggested in professional writings: for example, the intimation that control should not occur in the classroom or that a course is creatively taught when there is no preorganized structure.

Aside from rare exceptions in the secondary school and sporadic incidents in the elementary school—centering for the most part on interpretive activities such as finger painting, improvised dramatics, and toy orchestras—creativity has escaped the curriculum. George Stoddard (1959, p.181) has written:

> Creativity came close to being a lost cause in American education. Progressive education, a phenomenon rarely observed in pure form, helped to revive its spirit. Education, frequently viewed as an aggregation of facts or the preparatory stages of a prosaic life, carried on the scholastic tradition. The urge to inquire, to invent, to perform was stifled in millions of school children, now grown up, who did not get above rote learning, or at least did not stay above it. Their final culture pattern is all about us.

The record of education, in regard to teaching method and content, points conclusively to a strong prejudice against self-directed student behavior. At the risk of laboring the obvious, it is worth noting that self-direction need not be unduly permissive. Properly controlled, the uninhibited student in the laboratory can function quite as efficiently as the scientist. The notion that we must train the child in the way we want him to be still colors public attitude. The curriculum, consequently, still reflects memorization, factual tests, and ancient half-truths. We take an intense satisfaction in having students demonstrate what we cherish and hold dear. This has led to a situation in which able students are motivated almost exclusively by the conditions for reward, that is, by doing whatever is required for good grades. Any successful student recognizes that success stems, not from being knowledgeable, but from being able to appear knowledgeable. Beyond this, a rather sizable segment of the population, including a representative sample of teachers, comfortable only with carefully closed minds and the unshakable convictions of conventionality, insist upon a similar pattern for the young. And the youth's innate curiosity is soon debilitated.

Modern psychology has indicated that humans are strongly motivated by a desire to explain questions dealing with their milieu; the drive, regrettably, is as well satisfied by a bad explanation as by a good one. Our compulsion for omniscient instruction has resulted, first, in an absolute unwillingness to deal with unknowns; second, in a nation of educated people who often espouse convictions which are hopelessly false; and third, when the only possible answers are unbecoming to our self-image, in a deliberate misrepresentation of fact.

Aside from a gesture toward intellectual honesty, a willingness to introduce unknowns into the curriculum will provide the student with a perspective on the creation of knowledge. Whether the answer is unknown to the teacher, or to mankind, the student becomes sensitive to the importance of questing for information. If he is distinctively creative, his appetite for both inquisitiveness and inventiveness may be stimulated. If he is relatively uncreative, his search for an answer can teach him much about the organization of knowledge and about efficient methods of finding solutions. The advantages of treating unknowns are so great that the teacher would even be well advised to fabricate a number of synthetic examples, if none existed, to stimulate learning. Unknowns seduce the curiosity, and curiosity can be a sublime form of motivation. Teaching by requiring students to seek answers to unknowns not only encourages intellectual divergency among students, it also permits them to attempt novel and difficult tasks. Further, it places value on nonverbal achievement and problem solving, thus helping students to define their own uniqueness.

While research has not yet provided us with a universally accepted catalogue of human thinking, we do know a number of thinking processes that differ from one another. Deductive thinking, for example, is easily contrasted with intuitive thinking. When an individual is endeavoring to find something out, he will not think in the same way as when he is interested in interpreting information he already has. Some problems require that we think analytically while others do not. Thus, we can arrange a curriculum in which the student engages repetitively in many kinds of thinking. In this way we shall in all probability: (a) provide him with a transferable capability of great worth; (b) expand his capacity to cope with phenomena in alternative ways; (c) develop his ability to select an appropriate way to think about the task at hand, thereby permitting him to learn more efficiently; and (d) enhance his creative resources by providing him with styles of thinking he might otherwise not have.

A further illustration of the parallel between teaching for creativeness and good teaching in general lies in psychological "set." The desire to solve a problem is a common point of departure in a creative effort and in learning. Research on failure in problem-solving suggests that besides inability or laziness, a persistence in following an erroneous pattern is often a common fault. Einstein once observed that the formulation of a problem was infinitely more important than its solution. But the individual who, through conditioning, is "set" for a specific way of looking at the problem, fails to explore approaches which might be more fruitful; his intellectual habits cause him to labor uselessly until he perceives that his approach is unworkable. Even where he is able ultimately to make his solution work, his rigidity has prevented him from finding a more effective method. In its extreme, psychological set may even cause the individual to distort the factors involved. To come at the matter another way, "set" tends to moor a person to the old and to prohibit his acceptance of the new. It would be relatively simple to introduce various sorts of exercises into the curriculum which stress selection procedures for attacking problems. When routine techniques are taught, a subsequent consideration of instances in which the techniques are not applicable would help to decrease dependence upon preconceived formulas. Freedom from habitual reactions is obviously important to creativeness.

The examples given typify an astonishingly large number of instances in which both creativity and education are enhanced by the same stimulus. The arguments advanced have not been intended as a plea for the involvement of all students in activities which stimulate creativity nor as a suggestion that the curriculum should serve as a springboard for creative students. The school's duties require that the nurture of creativity be regarded as accessory rather than as a mainspring. Nevertheless, as methods are refined for distinguishing the creative from the highly intelligent and from other forms of talent, there may be considerable benefit to designing specialized training experiences for students with very special capacity to produce original thought. As Toynbee has noted, a few creative minds can make an enormous difference to a civilization.

Curriculum and Instruction

Many of the points set forth in the subsequent chapters of Part II are reflected in the arguments of subject-matter specialists regarding the teaching of content. Hausman, for example, points out that the creative act can have either positive or negative value. He suggests that the student can begin to approach creativeness in art only when he engages in his own exploration of reality. In another of his propositions, he reiterates the principle that teachers must take care to strike a balance in their students between "sufficient structure" and "sufficient latitude"; in short, the student must have both an adequate supply of information and adequate freedom to play with the information before he can function creatively.

In their chapter on teaching English composition and literature, Georgiades and Michael also comment on "freedom to experiment." They contend that while the basic rules relating to our written language are indeed important, their mastery is something entirely separate from creative thought. While the teacher must indeed concern herself with punctuation and grammar, she must also take care occasionally to interrupt this concern in deference to the flow of creative thought. In their discussion of independent study, they reinforce many of the points made about self-directed learning. Since creativity is a highly idiosyncratic matter, a strong case is made for the use of independent study in English teaching programs.

In a particularly telling argument, they indicate that creativity is likely to continue to be a lost cause in education unless teachers and administrators themselves develop some creativeness in the matter of evaluating student efforts. Specifically, they urge that caution be exercised lest evaluative measures be based upon group norms alone, since the individual student's creativity may easily take him outside the normative range.

Willoughby, in discussing the teaching of mathematics, suggests that creative behavior can occur only when the student thinks. In the teaching of mathematics it is not uncommon to find the teacher controlling students with a prescriptive formula for solving problems and with predetermined stipulations about what is true and what is false, thus sparing them any obligation to think or to discover for themselves. In a related point, he maintains that the schools have traditionally rewarded the child who can learn and synthesize the thoughts of others rather than the one who can produce significant thoughts of his own. In his description of discovery learning in the classroom, he makes it abundantly clear that the creative learning situation is not synonymous with complete freedom for the child to do whatever he wishes: "Sometimes it will be necessary simply to tell the pupils certain things, while at other times it may be possible to start them out with a simple problem and let them play with it with almost no direction." Hibbs, in speaking about mathematics and science in the elementary school, emphasizes a point that is also made by Hausman, namely, that a scholarly attitude is typically characterized by a high degree of curiosity, and that it is this curiosity which must be carefully nurtured by the teacher.

Creativeness does not preclude conformity. It would be nonsensical to contend that the school does not have a responsibility for developing reasonable homogeneity with respect to fundamental attitudes and beliefs, and for that matter, with respect to a basic core of general education. The school, after all, represents in our society the primary agency for the socialization of the young. While education perhaps has allowed the matter of social adjustment occasionally to get out of focus, restricting the energy of individuality, the perpetuation of our society is in part dependent upon fashioning in the young at least some congruence regarding cultural values. It is well to remember that many of our most extraordinarily creative personalities behave in a highly conforming manner, and to remember also that everyone conforms upon occasion. The important thing, however, is that a student can be taught to conform in general without conforming in specific: in order to function in an original manner in a science class, it is not also necessary that he wear his pajamas in the street. What we wish to breed in our students is a habit of questioning accepted suppositions rather than an attitude of worshipping nonconformity.

Lundsteen maintains that while all problem solving is creative, not all creative thinking is problem solving. In defending this position, she argues that creative problem solving is essentially a process in which the child directs himself from a problem—as he perceives it—to what is for him an acceptable solution. With respect to the teaching of language arts, she suggests that not only are there many possibilities for interrelating the language arts so they focus on creative problem solving, but the problem-solving process itself is probably the most effective way to teach the language arts. In citing a great number of activities for creative problem solving, she places a considerable emphasis on the neglected area of listening, contending that creative listening is an effective stimulus to creative production. Blankenchip, in dealing with the performing arts, suggests that the development of imagination is a major responsibility of the teacher. Precisely the same sorts of things which inhibit the ability to think creatively inhibit also an openness to the fruits of someone else's creativeness.

The imaginative teacher can rekindle in the student the ability to wonder, so characteristic of the young child. It is perhaps tragic that the high school student no longer wonders—as does the child—why the sky is blue, or why whales are not fish. A teacher who can stimulate an appetite for the unknown, and who can develop a taste for learning, provides his students with a form of intellectual inquisitiveness that becomes a wellspring of future growth.

Brubaker suggests that the secondary student, if he understands social science and history properly, will not only be informed as to the methodologies of the various areas of social science, but also will be free to discover. He feels that the teacher contributes more to the development of creativeness in his students by providing an example of a creative mind than by artificial attempts to foster creativeness. He sees the total school as a sort of social system that can collectively foster or stifle creativity in the student. Beyond this, he maintains that many valuable things can take place outside the classroom in social studies activities which provide an opportunity for teacher and student to interact.

The research evidence unfortunately does not suggest that by using a prescribed scheme we can produce creativeness at will. What it suggests, rather, is that virtually everyone has more creativity than he makes use of, that different conditions flush it forth in different individuals, and that a given procedure tends to nurture a part, but not the whole, of one's creative capacity.

It often has been observed that creativeness begins when the individual poses a problem for himself. Fischler reinforces this notion, in his treatment of the scientific enterprise, by defining the function of the discrepant event. It is the discrepant event which creates the problem, raises frustration, and requires the scientist to reexamine the evidence in search of a solution. Fischler makes much, too, of the tentativeness of scientific inquiry. Much as the truly creative person continuously searches for more and more elegant solutions to the problem, the scientist continuously searches for a closer approximation to the "truth." Fischler wishes the science student to secure information in new ways, to process the information by engaging in a variety of activities, and ultimately to make his own inferences and predictions and test them against the reality of the world.

When the student is put to work excavating the underground stuff within an idea, an intellectual stage is set for image, for analogy, and, upon occasion, for the perception of a truly creative vision. It is perhaps our habit of conceiving of learning as the acquisition of information alone, instead of including in our concept a subsequent searching out of the consequences of knowledge, that moved Charles Kettering to observe that "the inventor is a fellow who doesn't take his education too seriously."

Woodfin argues that before the teacher can truly nurture the creative potential of her students, she needs to know which children prefer to work alone, which work better in groups, which work rapidly and which slowly, and which need teacher direction and which do not. In short, she suggests that a teacher must cope with individual differences before she can provide a learning climate that is truly appropriate for the divergent personalities in the classroom.

In carrying on the well-ordered work of the school it is difficult to conceive of adding still another burden to the already heavy responsibilities assigned to the teacher. There is much to suggest, however, that some aspects of creativity can be harnessed without undue stress, and can, additionally, contribute to the general improvement of learning. Immersed as we are in a particularly involved period of change, the arguments advanced are perhaps especially timely. The preoccupation of the contributors to this volume is less with the propagation of a nation of creators and more with coping with what Henry Murray has termed "a paralysis of the imagination."

CHAPTER 5

Mathematics and Science in the Elementary School

by

ALBERT R. HIBBS

Albert Hibbs, who holds a B.S. degree from the California Institute of Technology in physics, a M.S. degree from the University of Chicago in Mathematics, and a Ph.D. degree from Caltech in physics, is employed by the California Institute of Technology's Jet Propulsion Laboratory as a senior staff scientist. Under a Caltech contract with NASA, he has directed operations of research and development groups in mathematical analyses of spacecraft trajectories; the construction of spacecraft instrumentation; the direction of subcontracted work on development and manufacture of specialized electronic, optical, and structural components for space use; and a variety of research projects in both space technology engineering and the science of astronomy. He has acted as a consultant to other aerospace industries and is the author of some sixty papers in the field of space science and engineering.

Dr. Hibbs has also been a consultant to several local boards of education in the Southern California District and to the State Board of Education for curriculum planning, the gifted children program, and special training of science teachers. He was science editor of the National Broadcasting Company and has appeared regularly on his weekly NBC radio show, "World of Science," and the weekly NBC television show, "Exploring."

THE MODERN AVALANCHE of scientific developments presents both a challenge and an opportunity to educators interested in science teaching in the elementary grades. Certainly the new perceptions of the universe which science is offering to us must be given full consideration in planning the curriculum and creating and selecting textbooks, but equally important is the role of the classroom teacher and the problems which a teacher faces in attempting to teach science to elementary grade students. In this consideration, it may be that the possibilities and problems faced by the classroom teacher are more significant than the new developments of science.

One cannot help but be impressed by two characteristics of the elementary teachers today in their approach to science education. First is their remarkable enthusiasm for the subject—an enthusiasm that is usually shared by their students. Second is their almost constant feeling of insecurity in dealing with a subject in which they feel their training is inadequate.

To some extent, the insecurity of the classroom teacher is justified. She is faced with two frustrating questions: What to choose out of the vast material offered to her by modern science as a subject for teaching, and how to answer the typical (and usually complex) questions asked her by her students.

Suppose we try to approach these two questions from the point of view of professional science, setting aside for a moment the special problems of the educator. To begin, what can a classroom teacher teach? What subjects are so important to science that they must be learned in the elementary grades?

I have asked these questions of my scientific colleagues, and have gotten back a curious range of answers. In many cases, I have heard a reflection of the educational history of the particular scientist with whom I am talking. He usually starts out by cataloging the very subjects which were typical for his elementary grade experiences, such as electricity, how automobiles work, the nature of the public utilities, what a rocket is like, weather prediction, and so on. But a continuing conversation usually results in the conclusion that these subjects, fascinating as they are, are not really directed at the true nature of science, nor do they take advantage of the opportunities which science offers for elementary educational techniques.

In a sense, the subjects, such as those listed above, are more in the applied science or engineering field. Of course, this does not in any sense mean they should be neglected. Usually, children are more interested in the applications of science than in the theories and research results. But at the same time, one should not conclude that teaching of such things as methods of weather prediction has satisfied the need for scientific learning, or taken full advantage of the child's natural scientific curiosity. Furthermore, if a child should not be interested in such applications, it would be incorrect to conclude that that child is not interested in science.

It would be realistic to look upon these areas of applied science as sources of intellectual stimulation—valuable if they work in this role, but not of great importance if they fail. It really does not matter whether or not a child in the elementary grades learns how rockets work, or how weathermen manage to put out their predictions. In this regard, one factor must be brought out—a factor that is fundamental to all of this discussion. Scientific investigations are enabling us to change our concepts of the universe at a very rapid rate. Many of the ideas which we look upon today as valid scientific theories will be proven false within the next ten to fifteen years. It is this length of time—some ten or fifteen years—than an elementary school student must wait before he can take his place in adult society, either as a professional scientist, or as a citizen in a technological society. Therefore, it is not terribly important that he commit to memory either the ideas or the processes which are today considered proper scientific and engineering techniques.

Even though the applied sciences are not vitally important as scientific subjects, they do offer some important possibilities. After all, children are often fascinated with rockets, electricity, and so on. It may turn out that this interest can be exploited pedagogically in a number of directions. A book about rockets might help a slow reader much more effectively than a reading textbook. A study of the life habits of the mouse might teach proper dietary habits or give a better impression of the importance of public health program.

Some scientists, when answering the question about what should be taught in the elementary grades, come up with their own special fields—fields in which they themselves are so immersed that they tend simultaneously to exaggerate the importance of the field and to underestimate its difficulty. I have had my friends suggest stellar astrophysics as a proper subject for the elementary grades, since after all, it is the study of the largest and most important bodies in our universe. Biochemistry is another candidate, since it underlies all of our life processes. Of course, nuclear physics is a candidate, not only because of its current popularity, but also because of its obviously fundamental nature.

Two objections can be raised immediately to these ideas. The first is the objection already raised, namely, that it will be ten to fifteen years before these students have a chance to apply such knowledge in any meaningful way, and by that time, our understanding will have so evolved that the ideas we taught them when they were young will no longer be considered valid. The second objection is the practical difficulties of finding a teacher for these subjects, or a textbook suitable for such a grade level.

Scientists who think about these problems soon set aside such initial suggestions, and begin to think a little more deeply about the problem. Typically, the third area suggested is that of the fundamental laws of science, such as the law of the conservation of energy, or Newton's Laws of Motion. However, few scientists have any good suggestions as to how elementary teachers can really learn about these deep, basic laws of science. Even more difficult is the question of how this learning can be passed on, even from a well-educated teacher. It often turns out that a graduate student in physics being examined for the degree of Doctor of Philosophy finds himself unable to explain adequately such fundamental notions, but can only repeat from memory the mathematical expression of these laws. Perhaps such occurrences are a bad mark against the student, or perhaps against his professors. But in any case, it is clear that these fundamental ideas are not simple to understand, or to teach. After all, the reason they are fundamental is that generations of brilliant scientists have worked over these ideas for many decades, in some cases many centuries, in order to reduce them to the so-called "simple" form in which we now study them. Although one might be able to memorize the words which go with the law of the conservation of energy: "The sum total of mass and energy cannot be destroyed or created, but only changed from one form to another," it might well take a volume of scientific exposition to define each of the substantive words used in this expression, and still more volumes to describe what the sentence as a whole means.

Many professional scientists who have grappled with the problem of science teaching in the elementary grades have come to a very frustrating conclusion, which is to forget the whole thing, and wait until the students get into high school or college, where they can be taught science properly and contemporarily. The subjects which can be taught at the primary level are too often simply applications, rather than true science, whereas the subjects which a scientist would call science are much too deep to be taught to elementary students. A student could do little more than be amused and entertained by the applications on the one hand or memorize the wording of the fundamental laws on the other. In either case, he would end up with little more than a pedantic display of a technical vocabulary, rather than an understanding of the world he lives in. And yet, it is possible to go beyond this frustrating conclusion, and bring out those subjects which really are important for the elementary grades, from the point of view of a professional scientist. A thoughtful search turns up four categories:

1. Reading. The ability to assimilate information and ideas quickly and easily from the printed page, an ability so thoroughly engrained that the process is a pleasure rather than a burden.

2. Communication, Both Writing and Speaking. The ability to express ideas, and to formulate ideas in a manner that can be understood by others, and can, in fact, enable oneself to grasp better the idea at hand.

3. Mathematics. The basic tool of all scientific thought and much of general human thought, including arithmetic, geometry, and many other concepts of mathematics which can be grasped with surprising ease by elementary students. Mathematics should be looked upon as the ability to manipulate abstract concepts, whether expressed in terms of numbers, or in terms of any other sort of symbol.

4. A Scholarly Attitude. This is perhaps the most difficult to describe as a subject for instruction, but is at the same time one of the most important from the point of view of professional science, or professional anything else.

It is toward this last point that I will direct most of my remaining comments.

A person with a scholarly attitude displays a number of typical characteristics. He is curious, with that curiosity which is typical of children, but which seems to die between the first few years of school and the final years of college. He is courageous in standing up for his own ideas, and seeking out new ones, regardless of whether or not they happen to agree with what he reads or what he hears, or even what he has believed before. He is competitive, and willing to pit his thoughts and abilities against those of his co-workers. Honor and prestige are important parts of his professional success.

All of these traits are valuable in any professional field, not simply in science. But there is one characteristic which seems particularly characteristic of science, and in which the scientist is perhaps unique. This is the tendency to doubt. This is a particularly difficult tendency to come to grips with. Doubt without hope is useless, and customarily results in nothing but constant negation. But the doubt characterized by the small voice in the back of the mind that constantly asks "Is that really true? Isn't there maybe a better answer?" is not only healthy for a scientist, but an actual requirement. Without such feelings, a well-trained person might become a good technician, but never a scientist.

Of course, doubting is a typical characteristic of young people, and one which is typically hard to deal with on the part of their elders—whether teachers or parents. Nor do I have any magic words of counsel to offer as to what to do about it, except simply to do one's best not to kill it.

The process of elementary education seems particularly well versed on the techniques of teaching reading, the art of communication, and mathematics. Perhaps the major problem then, from the point of view of scientific education in the elementary grades is the last point, that of the teaching or encouraging the development of a scholarly attitude. In this regard, there may be a special use for the studies of the applied sciences. Here the natural interest and curiosity of the child can be exploited. Of course, it doesn't matter which particular subject is chosen for this purpose nor does it matter whether or not the student learns any so-called "facts." What does matter is the enthusiasm of the student for the process of learning. The question is how to capture and hold this enthusiasm, and the problem stems from the fact that the teacher cannot possibly know all of the subjects which her students might be interested in learning.

It is my intention now to suggest that it does not matter whether or not the teacher knows the facts of the subject—she can teach science in spite of that. For example, suppose a student is interested in rockets, and wants to know in particular how they are steered. A reference book available to the teacher in the third or fourth grade might say that modern rockets are equipped with a "guidance system."

If the student wishes to know what a guidance system is, perhaps that reference book will have a few more words about it, but perhaps it will now be necessary to go into more advanced books, or even turn to the library. If so, the student might come up with the statement, "There are two kinds of guidance systems used in modern rockets—inertial guidance and radio guidance. Inertial guidance systems use gyroscopes and radio guidance systems use radar."

It is perfectly clear that this is an unsatisfactory answer for an interested student. It simply opens up a host of new questions. One of them might very well be, "How does a gyroscope steer a rocket?"

This question probably demands knowledge beyond that available to the typical classroom teacher, and very likely also demands knowledge beyond that available in reference books accessible and understandable to that teacher, so the question is, what now?

At this point, there are two allies which the teacher can call into play. The first is the public library. It is possible that the student's interest in gyroscopes will lead him to learn how to use the card index system. If so, this is a major educational accomplishment. It is possible that his investigation of literature about gyroscopes will lead him off into another area, where his enthusiasm can be matched by understanding, all on his own. Or, of course, it is possible that he will simply become frustrated by the nonavailability of books about gyroscopes written at a level which he can understand.

We will say more about that last possibility in a moment, but first, we should mention the second ally, classroom demonstration equipment. It may be that the school has on hand a gyroscope demonstration kit, complete with instructions. It is possible of course that the teacher study the kit in detail, and its instructions, and then give a demonstration to the class, including the student who originally asked the question. On the other hand, it is also possible simply to turn the whole thing over to the student, and let him figure it out for himself. It may well be that he never quite assembles the kit properly, and never performs the demonstration which the manufacturer intended. But does this really matter? It is very likely that he will have a delightful time in fiddling around with all of the gadgets, and so long as he does not break anything valuable, he will get a better education by this process than he would have by watching a prepared demonstration according to the instructions.

An elementary grade teacher once told me of her own frustration in dealing with a prepared demonstration taken from the textbook. In this demonstration, she used a pan of water and an empty glass. The glass was turned upside down, and lowered down into the pan of water. In accordance with the instructions, the teacher then asked the students, "What do you see?"

One of the students replied, "I see waves."

"Well, that's right," said the teacher, "but what else do you see?" It was at this point that her frustration began. She, too, saw the waves, but the textbook hadn't said anything about them. The purpose of this demonstration was to show that air takes up space. The students were supposed to notice that the water did not come up into the open end of the glass as the teacher pushed it down into the pan of water. They were to be led to the conclusion that the air in the glass kept the water from coming in, and thus realize that air displaces volume.

But, unfortunately, the students noticed the waves, and the attention of the class was called to that phenomenon. What now?

The teacher felt constrained by the instructions in the textbook to proceed ahead, directing the attention of her class to the water levels in the pan and the glass, and away from the interesting wave pattern. And indeed, it is an interesting wave pattern. Waves develop both inside the glass and outside. They are circular waves, and if the glass is positioned close to the center of a round pan, the waves reflect nicely off the walls of the pan, return to the walls of the glass to reflect back again, and so on. Meanwhile, inside the glass, the waves reflect to the center and out again. The circular wave pattern is similar to that made by a pebble dropped in a pond, but now walls are present, and the reflection phenomena are fascinating to watch.

Of course, eventually the persistence of the teacher won out in its battle with the curiosity of the students, and they were led to the successful (but by now uninteresting) conclusion that air displaces volume.

How much more exciting it would have been for the teacher and her students to spend the rest of the allotted time watching the waves, perhaps drawing pictures of the patterns on the board. They might have seen what happened when the glass was raised and lowered near the side of the pan instead of in the center, or perhaps when a square pan was used instead of a round one—or they might simply have watched the waves they started with in more and more detail. Leonardo da Vinci, who began the whole idea of experimental science in the Renaissance, pointed out, "The secrets of nature lie in her detail."

If the teacher had felt she had the freedom to allow the students to pursue their interest in wave-making, both she and they would have had an honest, valuable, and exciting experience in scientific education. It is true that they might not have learned that air displaces volume on that particular day, and perhaps they would have had to skip it for that particular month, or even that particular year. But, after all, air has displaced volume for quite a number of years now, and is quite likely to do so for a number of years in the future.

This property of duration is characteristic of scientific phenomena, and so relieves us of the need to worry about maintaining any particular teaching schedule. Combined with the ephemeral nature of scientific ideas, it even suggests that we should put off the teaching of scientific theories as long as possible. In any case, it proves that we can let the enthusiasm of the students be our guide to subject matter, rather than the material in the particular textbook selected for the class.

A particular type of behavior of advanced students is worth noting in this regard. It is customary (though certainly not universal) for graduate students to ask their advisors to suggest subjects on which they might do research for a doctor's degree. Naturally, the advisors would prefer to find their students inspired with their own ideas, rather than waiting for an intellectual handout. It is sometimes suggested that this sort of behavior has been learned during the student's previous educational history, wherein a student was repeatedly shown that subjects for learning were not to be selected on the basis of his interests, but rather on the basis of the teacher's schedule and textbook material. Although this is clearly required in many portions of mathematics and reading education, for example, it would be worthwhile if some area were left freer—some area in which the student could indeed be guided by his own interior intellectual directives. In the elementary grades, science may fill that requirement very nicely.

But now back to our student and his gyroscope kit. We left him assembling it to his own satisfaction, and presumably learning more that way than he would by watching, or even participating in a carefully prepared demonstration.

Even though this may be a successful and enjoyable operation, the student may yet find his question about how gyroscopes steer rockets not answered to his satisfaction. This is the point at which we might mention the third ally which the teacher has on her side, and that is her own scholarly point of view. She can always remember that there was a time in human history when nobody knew how a gyroscope could steer a rocket. Someone had to learn first, and in the process, he had no teacher to guide him.

Perhaps with this point of view, a teacher might encourage a student to make up his own explanation of how a gyroscope steers a rocket—not in order to pass a test or answer a set of questions in a book, but rather to teach the teacher, who readily admits her own ignorance on the subject.

In attempting to lead a student through this process of discovery, there are clearly a number of difficulties, and to compensate for them, a few artificial burdens have to be cast side and left by the road. One of these burdens is the demand for correct facts. Clearly, it does not matter in the least if the student actually learns what rocket guidance experts might accept as the proper explanation. What does matter is that he pursue his investigation in a manner compatible with his educational level; that is, he must read and absorb information in accordance with his reading skills. He must put together whatever sort of arithmetical calculations are required in a manner consistent with his current mathematical skill, and beneath it all, he must go through a thought process of learning and discovery, which is appropriate for his educational level. If he does all of these things correctly, then no matter what answer he gets, it is right.

Far more important than a correct answer from such a process is the enjoyment of the process itself. Learning and discovery are exciting things, and this is the fundamental nature of science. It is easy to take an enjoyable experience, which is potentially educational and realize that potential. It is difficult to go in the opposite direction.

If the teacher were to adopt this point of view on science education, then she must make a point of always learning all of her science from her students, and never from reference books. This gives the students practice in arranging and expressing their thoughts and observations. The teacher must be critical of their analytic processes, but always remain uneducated—always judge the answers on the basis of the evidence presented by the student, and never on the basis of authoritarian textbooks. Of course, the teacher has the duty of warning the student of the role she is playing, and should avoid as much as possible the idea that her acceptance constitutes the stamp of authority.

(Of course, it is perfectly all right if the teacher does happen to know about some field of science. It may turn out that she is a gem stone collector, for example. In this case, she can certainly make a learning process much more exciting by introducing some of her own knowledge. But passing on facts about science to a student is not a scientific education. This is simply an education in history of science. Learning what has been discovered is not learning science.)

After a teacher has gone through a learning process with one student about, for example, gyroscopes, she must, of course, return to her original uneducated state, so that the next student who picks this subject can have the privilege of approaching her fresh mind.

Let us put the example one step further, and suppose that the student tries out a gyroscope in the demonstration equipment by putting weights on it at various places, or perhaps hooking two gyroscopes together in his own unique way; suppose he reads about ideas such as precession which he does not quite understand, and out of this, comes to the conclusion that if he could only make a combination of gyroscopes big enough, and start them spinning fast enough, they would take straight off into space, having canceled out the force of gravity. What a marvelous and exciting conclusion! Of course, its completely wrong, but does that matter? If a grade school student is so enthusiastic about gyroscopes that he manages to invent an anti-gravity machine, then surely this satisfies the objectives of a scientific education in the elementary grades. If only that enthusiasm can be maintained through the next eight years or so, until he gets into college, he will then have ample opportunity to learn all of the details about gyroscopic behavior in as pleasant a manner as possible, and then can go ahead to become an outstanding nuclear physicist, if that is his desire.

There are too many students dimly aware that anti-gravity machines are supposed to be impossible, but who don't really care one way or another—students who are in college just because their parents want them there. There are far too few students dedicated to the creation of an anti-gravity machine.

Of course, this is only a very specific example, and it is equally possible that the enthusiastic student will arrive at an idea much more in line with modern scientific notions. Or, it is also possible that the student will simply follow his investigation into frustration. Is this intolerable? After all, frustration is as much a part of the scientific profession as it is of any other human activity. It would be cheating the students a little bit to imply anything else.

To sum up these suggestions, a professional scientist looking upon elementary education is convinced that the fundamental educational tools are as invaluable for science as for anything else; that is, reading, communication arts, and mathematics. After that, and of equal importance, is the creation and maintenance of a scholarly attitude toward learning. Completely unimportant is the objective of learning any specific set of facts, laws, or rules.

As a pedagogical technique for accomplishing this objective, I suggest that the teacher allow her children to teach her science, while she teaches them the process of learning. In so doing, she makes the very best use of her own special skills and of theirs. After all, as a trained educator, the process of learning is her own domain, and conversely, it often turns out that the matter of science is the domain of children.

This joint teaching arrangement might turn out to be much more enjoyable for both the teacher and the student, and certainly, much more productive. And as for what they learn, if they learn only that it is fun to learn, their lamp of knowledge will be self-refueling.

CHAPTER 6

The Natural Sciences

by

ABRAHAM S. FISCHLER

Abraham S. Fischler, who holds a B.S. degree from the College of the City of New York, a M.A. degree from New York University, and an Ed.D. degree from Columbia University, is the James Donn Professor of Education and Dean of the Education Center at Nova University, Fort Lauderdale, Florida. As an assistant professor at Harvard, he became actively involved in team teaching programs of various types. Also interested in innovations and experimentation in all phases of the public school curriculum, Dr. Fischler helped to develop new curricula at Lexington, Massachusetts, and Colorado Springs, Colorado. While a professor at the University of California, Berkeley, he worked on problems in curriculum with the Carmel and Palo Alto, California, school districts.

Dean Fischler is the co-author of Modern Science, Grades 7, 8 and 9, Science: A Modern Approach, *and a new elementary series entitled* Sciences: A Modern Approach. *He is also a consultant to the Ford Foundation in the development of modern science programs for the schools of Chile and Argentina.*

THERE IS A DILEMMA which we face in teaching the natural sciences. Most individuals would agree that in order for a scientist to be creative, he must have amassed a great deal of what is already known. Yet, it is important also to admit that an education in science must give him much more. The scientist must be ready to work in areas where no solution to his problem is known. He must be ready to judge the importance of his work in relation to existing theories and models. He also must have developed the intellectual tools and techniques to approach problems which he might encounter in the future. The major breakthroughs in science do not occur in a vacuum; they occur when existing lines of research seem to provide problems which current theories cannot explain. Thus, the breakthrough occurs when lines of research can be brought together by the invention of a new theory.

Given the above dilemma, the writer will attempt in this chapter (1) to elaborate on the dynamics of the scientific enterprise, (2) to consider the problems of learning in relation to manifestation of creative endeavor on the part of pupils, and (3) to set forth appropriate illustrations from the biological sciences in the public schools.

The Scientific Enterprise

At one time, science was looked upon solely as the systematic accumulation of information. Although teaching primarily from textbooks, instructors did undertake some demonstrations to illustrate that what was written in the text was true. Students were taught the taxonomical and morphological aspects of biology. In chemistry, they memorized the symbols of the periodic table, valences of each element, and then the balancing of equations. Information was given, memorized, but little thought was given to "how we know what we know," and "how well we know it."

Today the emphasis is changing. The nature of science is better understood. Moreover, one finds that "science" is treated as a verb instead of as a noun. For the first time, education in the natural sciences "has assigned the acquisition of scientific information and concepts a place of lesser importance than the understanding of the nature of scientific enquiry and of the scientific enterprise in which modern man is embarked" (Glass, 1962).

In order to be more specific, let us immerse ourselves into the scientific enterprise. Its dynamic nature is illustrated in Figure One. For the sake of clarity, let us begin with a scientist making an observation of a phenomenon which raises a question in his mind. This observation, which does not fit the paradigm, sets the problem. We refer to this event as a "discrepant event." It produces some frustration; it forces the scientist to re-examine the paradigm and to search for resolution. If the observation fits his intellectual construct, then there is no problem. He only has a problem when the observation is discrepant.

Having been confronted with this event, the scientist gathers information from various sources and tries to formulate possible explanations or hypotheses. He looks for many alternatives and ulti-

STEPS IN SCIENTIFIC ENTERPRISE

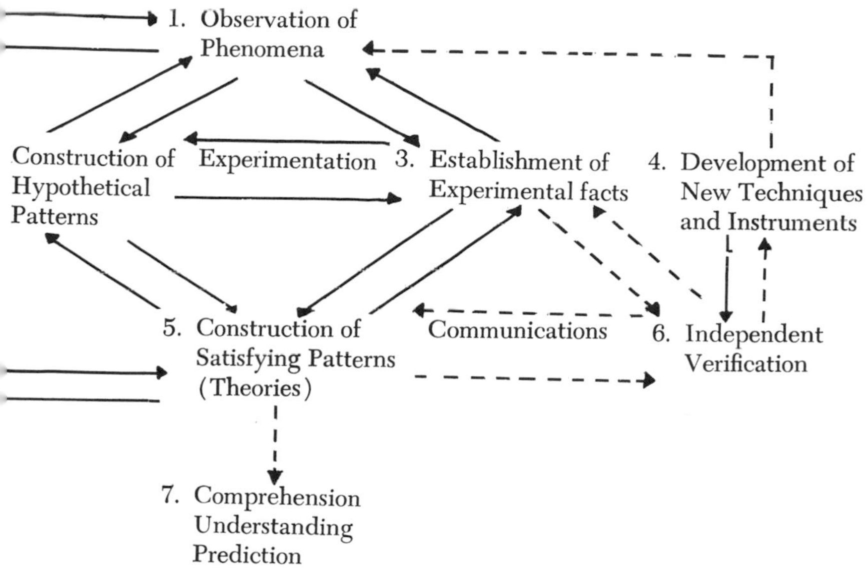

FIGURE ONE

mately settles on the one which seems most logical and is testable. He then proceeds to perform an experiment which leads to an experimental fact. The "experimental" is very important. It defines the parameters associated with the fact. The data affirm that under conditions A, B, and C, we observe D. If we change A to A_1 and keep conditions B and C constant, we might not get D. If A represents the acidity of the soil, B the amount of water, and C the temperature, then we observe D. If, however, we change A from acid to an alkaline soil, then D might be different. Thus, when we teach a scientific fact, it is important that we also associate the parameters of the fact.

The nature of the enterprise encourages a scientist to publish. He does this not only to gain recognition among his colleagues, but also to add his new knowledge to the accumulation of other experimental facts in the hope of formulating a concept, generalization, or theory. In his writing, he utilizes precise language, so that other scientists have an opportunity to verify his results. Thus, an important aspect of the scientific enterprise is the reproducibility of results. The avoidance of vague language is necessary in order to ensure reproducibility.

If others verify the scientist's results, this adds to the reliability of the original result. However, if a second scientist obtains different results, he too publishes and others begin to experiment to try to clear up the differences in their findings. It is this aspect of the scientific enterprise that keeps scientists "honest." In science, frauds are usually discovered rather quickly.

To digress for a moment, the writer might point out that in education we tend to lack the precision associated with the pure sciences. We tend to word our objectives in rather vague terms which then become difficult to measure. Most of our "educational experiments" either end up with no significant differences, or just fade away. Since education is a social science, it is much more difficult to identify and to control all the variables than it is in the instance of the physical sciences. However, we must continue to make strides in this direction.

Within science, there is a constant attempt to develop new techniques and new instruments to enable the scientist to make new observations and to refine further the paradigms. For example, new techniques in genetics have changed our knowledge of the way hereditary traits are transferred from parent to offspring. Fifteen years ago, we were teaching that genes were the units of heredity. Today we speak about D.N.A. and R.N.A. In chemistry, we had a rather fixed model of the atom (Bohr Model), but today we have a dust-cloud model and we speak of energy levels and probability. In physics, because of the development of the large accelerators, we have discovered many new particles in the nucleus of the atom. In fact, nuclear physicists are now speaking of families of particles in the nucleus. Depending upon the definition of particle, there are as many as 65. In astronomy, we are now "listening" to the heavens instead of just looking at the heavens. Information derived through the field of radio-astronomy will add greatly to our knowledge of the universe. The use of satellites and landings on the moon will also aid us in this process.

The information derived from all these experiments enables the scientist to construct concepts, generalizations, and theories. These theories enable the scientist to look at the world and to make predictions. Scientists do not give up theories easily. It takes more than one discrepant event—or one experimental fact. For example, when scientists first studied the decay of the neutron into a proton and electron, they found that not all the energy was accounted for in the above reaction. The mass was conserved, but the energy was not equal to the theoretical calculations. Since the scientists held to their belief in the conservation of energy, they had to "invent" a particle called the neutrino (little neutron) which has a mass of zero, no electric charge, but contains energy. This invented particle would account for the difference between the theoretical reaction and the experimental result. It was not until approximately twenty years later that Reines and Cowan actually observed the particle in the laboratory. Thus, generalizations and theories have associated with them some degree of longevity. It is an understanding of these generalizations and theories, as well as the dynamic nature of the enterprise, which produces a scientifically literate individual. This is one of the goals we must strive to achieve for all children in our schools.

To summarize, within the enterprise, the tentativeness of the results of scientific inquiry must be stressed. "Truth," as such, in science does not really exist. The search is for closer and closer approximations to the "truth." It is the search for even higher probability than that previously attained without expecting certainty. The willingness to regard all scientific statements as subject to possible modifications, corrections, or rejections has had highly useful consequences for scientific inquiry. The usefulness of scientific inquiry may be measured by the extent to which the results facilitate explanation, prediction, and, on occasion, the control of events.

The Student

If we return to the observation of the discrepant event, we can see the relationship between the scientist in the enterprise and the pupil in the science classroom. In his discussion of Piaget's work Ripple (1964) wrote of Piaget's exposition of four factors contributing to intellectual development—nervous maturation, experience, social transmission, and equilibration. In the first three, something is done to the learner; the fourth, the learner must do for himself. It calls for the learner to become active; it calls for intellectual transformation—a series of accommodations, followed by assimilation, followed by equilibration. When equilibration has occurred, we must then introduce another discrepant event.

Nervous maturation is physiological but experience is the school's concern. Pupils in the elementary grades must be given a great deal of experience with concrete objects, through which they develop language for social transmission. In order for this process to take place within the learner, adequate time must be allotted.

Jan Smedslund (1961) of Sweden did an interesting experiment which illustrates the importance of experience and time. He worked with eleven children (ages 5-7) who had acquired conservation of weight by training with clay on a balance through observing demonstrations performed by him. He also took thirteen children (ages 5-7) who had acquired conservation previous to this experiment through experience and maturation. Smedslund attempted to extinguish the principle of conservation of weight by cheating the subjects. When he changed the shape of the clay from a ball to a rod, he took away a piece of clay without the subjects' knowledge. When he asked them to predict what would happen when he placed the changed shaped clay on the balance scale, they said it would balance. On observing that the scale did not balance, he was interested in the type of argument which the subjects would offer. The results showed that all subjects who had acquired the nature of conservation by training on the balance had learned only a relatively arbitrary empirical law. They did not seem concerned that their observations were contrary to what they had been taught. They remarked that it was interesting, and readily modified their explanations and predictions. However, six of the subjects who acquired conservation of weight through experience and maturation resisted the extinction process. This group thought that either some material was stolen or that the scale was wrong. They were not about to change their explanations or to make different predictions.

Many times the author has gone into a fourth grade class and offered the geocentric model of the universe. In addition, he would present a model of the earth with edges. Very few arguments were offered by pupils that would not be refuted. Although pupils did not accept the geocentric theory, they could not devise any arguments against it. This outcome should not surprise anyone, since it took man approximately 2,000 years to arrive at the heliocentric point of view and an additional 200 years for it to be accepted. In teaching this concept to children in the fourth grade, we do not realize how difficult this abstract concept is to grasp. Do *you* realize that this earth is rotating at 1,000 miles per hour and at the same time revolving around the sun?

Thus, for the manifestation of creative endeavor on the part of pupils in their discovering, understanding, and applying scientific principles, the previous arguments suggest that due allowance must be made for individual differences in level of maturation, general state of readiness, and amount of previous incidental and formal experience. Creative behaviors cannot be expected to emerge prior to a pupil's having had enough time to be exposed to and to be stimulated by his environment.

Also dependent upon the maturational process and an appropriate state of readiness is concept of development, which may be described in simple terms as consisting of differentiating properties of objects or events, of abstracting certain common characteristics, and of placing the proper label on the characteristics. It enables the pupil to include or to exclude an object from the "class." Children learn rather early that objects or events can be classified in many different ways depending upon the frame of reference.

If we are to connect concepts, in order to evolve generalizations and principles, then students must collect concrete data, and must formulate inferences from the data. Then, they can test their inferences by applying them to known principles, or through making testable predictions—as in the if-then type of sequence.

Such active participation would appear to be an almost necessary condition or prerequisite for the development of problem-solving capabilities of pupils in their classroom, laboratory, and field experiences in the science curriculum. Opportunities for inductive learning seem almost essential for the development of creative solutions of problems posed by teachers interested in having their pupils learn how to think in terms of the steps involved in the scientific method.

Space does not permit a detailed explanation of learning theory; however, utilizing Cassidy's (1962) terminology, we find three sets of operational processes: (1) the process of analysis, which might consist of accumulating data, and classifying data; (2) the process of synthesis, which establishes connections between data, formulates hypotheses and generalizations from data, carries out inductive and deductive analyses, and creates new technological devices; (3) the process of reduction to practice, which consists of utilizing the new devices, of determining their effectiveness, and of redesigning these new devices.

Finally, a few words should be spoken regarding the clear expression of key objectives in science teaching. Such outcomes are usually most effectively stated as activities written in the form of verbs. If the science teacher is to think clearly regarding what he would like to see evolve in the behaviors of his pupils, he can be aided by a set of operationally expressed activities. At a meeting held at Cornell University under the sponsorship of the American Association for the Advancement of Science, a group of scientists and educators tried to write in behavioral terms, what was meant by certain objectives. The list presented in Table One evolved. Of course, this list is not definitive, nor is it offered as the perfect answer. However, it attempts to indicate behaviors which might be associated with educational objectives through the teaching of science and with the sort of activities that the pupil with varying degrees of creative potentialities may be anticipated to exhibit if given the appropriate opportunities and encouragement.

TABLE ONE

LIST OF BEHAVIORALLY STATED OBJECTIVES IN THE TEACHING OF SCIENCE

Classified Verb and Verb-Object Combinations

I. Knowing that . . .		
Observes	Gathers	Looks
Identifies	Accumulates	Sees
Describes	Counts	
II. Manipulating . . .		
Measures	Computes	Demonstrates
Selects instruments	Reads scales	Balances
	Uses instruments	Weighs
III. Applying . . .		
Classifies	Identifies	Transforms
Interrelates	Rejects	Experiments
Structures	Reorganizes	Controls
Assigns	Gathers	Selects
Defines	Estimates	Discriminates
Quantifies	Equates	Segregates
Associates	Sorts	Abstracts
Dissociates	Prefers	Orders
Arranges	Rearranges	Ponders
Re-centers	Plans	Utilizes
Plays	Organizes	Groups
Re-casts	Compares	Re-groups
Distinguishes	Concludes	Decides

IV. Creating . . .

Hypothesizes
Generates ideas
Interrelates
Re-centers
Induces
Deduces
Formulates possibilities
Analyzes
Selects strategy
Gathers data
Designs experiments
Re-casts
Plans
Structures
Organizes
Re-organizes
Compares
Concludes
Classifies
Transforms
Arranges
Re-arranges
Reflects
Guesses
Conceives
Reduces
Invents
Comprehends
Speculates
Doubts
Appreciates
Maximizes
Infers
Incubates
Abstracts
Synthesizes
Formulates
Controls variables
Utilizes
Proposes
Predicts
Criticizes
Estimates
Generalizes
Forecasts
Extrapolates
Interpolates
Explains

V. Evaluating . . .

Ponders
Controls variables
Applies generalizations
Generalizes
Insists on reproducibility
Pools data
Estimates
Recognizes errors
Compares
Strives for mastery
Classifies
Collates
Questions
Doubts
Verifies
Decides
Interrogates
Isolates
Selects
Transposes
Equates
Distinguishes
Categorizes
Averages
Interprets
Criticizes

VI. Communicating . . .

Tabulates
Graphs
Writes
Speaks
Reports
Explains
Uses references
Teaches
Informs
Reads pictures
Charts
Formulates
Questions
Debates
Argues
Expresses
Describes
Demonstrates
Compares
Interrogates
Instructs
Plots

AAAS Conference on Elementary School Science, Cornell University: Report of Group 1.

Illustrations in the Teaching of Science for Generation of Creative Behaviors

Examples will be drawn from various projects being supported by the National Science Foundation. The reason for doing this is simple:

it gives more authenticity to the argument that we must select what we teach more carefully and give students more opportunity to engage in science as a "verb" if they are to develop problem-solving skills and novel ways of conceptualizing scientific principles. It will also enable the reader to see the similarity of tasks being performed by pupils in the elementary grades to those in the secondary grades. Lastly, it will allow the reader to see that content can be defined as the systematic sequencing of discrepant events. Such sequencing encourages the pupils to go through the processes of accommodation and assimilation. From these processes is derived knowledge which then becomes a tool for the acquisition of new knowledge and for discovery of scientific principles. More simply stated, it is the sequencing of activities which encourages children to observe, describe, categorize, quantify, hypothesize, infer, and predict. From such activities they derive information which, when fitted together, leads to concepts, generalizations, and theories. When pupils can pursue these activities of observation, description, categorization, hypothesis making, inference, and prediction in new problem settings under a minimum of guidance, the stage is set for expression of problem-solving behaviors that may be deemed creative.

In the Science Curriculum Improvement Study (SCIS), which has been under the guidance of Robert Karplus of the Physics Department of the University of California, Berkeley, children in the first grade are given a box containing various objects. They are taught, through games and various teaching techniques, to describe objects by utilizing their properties. Although the term "property" is invented by the teacher, pupils have a great deal of opportunity to use the teacher's invention. Given a handful of buttons they are asked to see how many different ways in which they can group their buttons. The teacher is to look for internal consistency. One child may group them by their size; another, by color; a third, by their composition; and a fourth, by the number of holes. Although each solution may be correct, each one can be different. Pupils learn that it is possible for two people to have different results, and yet that both solutions are correct.

Variation, another unit, is introduced in the second grade of the SCIS program. Children are given pea pods and are asked to count the number of peas in each pod. Having completed this task, they are then asked to see whether there is any variation in the number of peas in the pods. The histogram is "invented" by the teacher as a way of organizing the data. Gradually, the children, through various exercises utilizing raisin bread, vinyl tile, ash leaflets, and other objects, learn to make predictions and to develop an intuitive understanding of probability. They realize that it is safer to give a range of numbers than to answer by guessing 5 or 6. Children respond by saying, between 6 and 9, or between 5 and 7.

Classes make histograms utilizing height and frequency, or weight and frequency. In order to determine whether children understand, the teacher can ask how the histogram might change if they did the same activity in the other second grade class. A more difficult question is how they expect the histogram to look when they get to the third grade.

Animals and plants are introduced into the classroom. Children are asked to observe the animals. How do they move? How do they get their food?

In this particular project, the invention of a "system" is introduced in the second grade and pupils utilize the concept as they look for evidence of interaction within the system. This applies to physical as well as biological systems.

The Elementary School Science Project, which has been under the guidance of Chester O'Konski of the Department of Botany, University of California, Berkeley, utilizes the same overall approach. In a unit on animal coloration written by Professor Robert Stebbins, children are given an opportunity to develop insights into the theory of natural selection. Children paint toothpicks various colors, and then the teacher and class go outside the room into a grass area. The students turn their backs while the teacher throws the toothpicks into the air allowing them to fall freely on the grass. Playing the role of hawks, the children are given thirty seconds to find as many toothpicks as they can. After this time, they stop and pool their data. Soon they infer that certain colors are more difficult to see, and therefore more difficult to find.

Dioramics are built in the classroom out of cardboard. The insides are painted in various ways to resemble many of the natural habitats—water, desert, grasslands, or forests. Given various animal shapes made of paper, the children must color them in such a manner that they blend in with the background. From this, they learn protective coloration, countershading, and many other important ideas related to natural selection.

Elementary Science Study of Educational Services, Inc. (ESS), in

Watertown, Massachusetts, produced a unit dealing with animal behavior. Given goldfish, pupils are asked numerous questions which can be answered by observation of the goldfish under various conditions. Do the goldfish swim backwards? What effect does light have on their behavior? Do the fish hear? How can we find out? What effect does warming the water have on the gulping rate of the fish? How does a fish orient itself? These and other questions lead the students to perform experiments, to observe the environment, to collect data, to record these data, and to draw inferences from data. They also realize the necessity of pooling their data in order to increase the probability of making correct inferences.

In Blanc, Fischler, and Olcott's (1967) *Modern Science, Book I* for junior high school students, various habitats are explored. Students are encouraged to collect samples of specimens living in ponds. One group studies organisms on the bottom of the pond, another large water plants, and still another the larger animals. They collect their specimens in jars and return to the classroom for laboratory work. They have "keys" which help them identify the various organisms. They study animal and plant adaptation. They study the food pyramid, and the consumers and producers, which they can relate to the energy cycle.

This study can be followed by several others—involving salt-water organisms, organisms in streams and/or lakes. Students are free to investigate, observe, describe, categorize, infer, and predict. They are able to see what happens when a salt-water organism is placed in fresh water or vice versa.

The members of the Biological Science Curriculum Study Committee (BSCS) under the direction of William Mayer of the University of Colorado, Boulder, Colorado, have prepared courses in biology in which the same approach was used. They have built five courses: three regular (blue, green, and yellow), a course for slow learners and an advanced course. In addition, they have produced twelve laboratory blocks for use in either the regular courses or the advanced course. These blocks take the place of similar sections in the texts. The nine themes woven through the regular courses are worth listing

1. The change of living things through time evolution.
2. The diversity of type and unity of pattern in living things.
3. The genetic continuity of life.
4. The complementarity of organisms and environment.

5. The biological roots of behavior.
6. The complementarity of structure and function.
7. Regulation and homeostasis: preservation of life in the face of change.
8. Science as inquiry.
9. The history of biological conceptions.

Each version gives a different emphasis to each of the themes: Green—ecological approach (Biological Sciences Curriculum Study, 1963c), Blue—bio-molecular approach (Biological Sciences Curriculum Study, 1963b), and Yellow—the cellular or physiological approach (Biological Sciences Curriculum Study, 1963a). The laboratory is an important part of all the courses (Biological Sciences Curriculum Study, 1964).

The more advanced course goes further in laboratory interaction. In fact, the title of the course is "Biological Science: Interaction of Experiments and Ideas." The course consists of thirty-eight investigations, although students are not expected to finish all of them.

Our thread in this chapter, which was introduced in grade one of the elementary school, is continued as high school students study the blowfly. First, a careful description of the behavior is studied. What does the animal do? Is there a sequence or pattern of acts? Is this sequence invariably maintained, or is there variation in the order of the actions of the pattern? How does the expression of the pattern vary with the time of day? With the season? With the life cycle of the animal? (Biological Sciences Curriculum Study, 1965.)

Although at the high school level in comparison with the elementary school level the questions are more difficult and the investigations require more technical skill, more nearly accurate measurement, and more nearly precise observation, yet the intellectual operations are essentially the same. The creative child will see many opportunities in this approach. Creative thinking requires a classroom atmosphere where divergent thought is encouraged; yet evidence to support and reinforce one's ideas is expected. The various curricular experiences show how the learner can develop solutions on his own and can experience the excitement of discovery of scientific concepts and generalizations. Such school experiences thus afford needed opportunities for the realization of divergent production which itself is such an essential component of the creative process involved in problem-solving activities of the science curriculum.

Summary

Progress in science comes from original thinking. This is built by securing information in new ways, looking at information in new ways, and challenging the basic assumptions upon which present investigations are formulated. The more a student collects his own data (as undigested as possible), the more opportunity he has for creating his own ideas. Instruction could be improved by a substantial factor if the teachers could read the chapters in textbooks in advance and would allow pupils to perform the activities suggested, to collect their own data, to draw their own inferences, to make their own predictions, to test their own predictions against the reality of the world, and then to allow them to read the chapter to see whether the authors agree with what the children themselves have found on their own initiative. Thus, the stage would be set for future innovation, experimentation, and creative endeavor for these same pupils throughout their remaining school years and during their adult lives as responsible citizens who have acquired a curiosity to keep abreast of rapid changes in the fields of natural science and related technology.

CHAPTER 7

Secondary School Mathematics

by

STEPHEN S. WILLOUGHBY

Stephen S. Willoughby received his formal schooling in the Madison, Wisconsin, public schools, Harvard College, Harvard Graduate School of Education, and Teachers College, Columbia. He has taught in the Newton, Massachusetts, and Greenwich, Connecticut, public schools, at the University of Wisconsin and at New York University, where he is chairman of the Mathematics Education Department. He is the author of books on the teaching of mathematics and pre-calculus probability and statistical inference, and the co-author of two high school textbooks. He is on the editorial board of a forthcoming NSSE Yearbook on the teaching of mathematics and has served as consultant to various school systems, textbook publishers, and a film company.

Although he holds a doctor's degree (a clear indication of a lack of creativity), he believes that the experience of having his major professor recommend his expulsion from Harvard for "resisting authority" gives him some insight into the problems of the truly creative individual.

CREATIVE TEACHING is not particularly common. Unfortunately, however, creative teaching is more common than is teaching which encourages creative endeavor on the part of pupils. Interestingly enough, it is sometimes the case that the most creative teacher is so creative that he allows little opportunity for his students to be creative. On the other hand, there are examples of teachers who seem to be very poor, but who produce surprisingly good results.

Poor Teacher—Good Education

For instance, the physics department of a large university noticed that a great proportion of its best graduate students came from an otherwise mediocre, small liberal arts college. They investigated and found that the physics professor at the college had a heavy load but was quite lazy. Therefore, he had his best juniors and seniors teaching the freshman and sophomore physics courses. The experience was so good for the juniors and seniors that it made up for the harm that might have occurred in the first two years. The only creative thing the professor had done was to discover a method of avoiding work, but the graduates of the system had learned to be quite creative.

Another professor, known throughout the university for his lucid and brilliant lectures, found himself teaching two sections of freshman mathematics. In order to avoid boredom for himself, he decided to do the worst possible job of teaching in one of the sections, while maintaining his usual high level of pedagogy in the other. He mumbled. His explanations were confusing. He was disorganized. He strayed from the subject. He refused to give the students appropriate help. He wrote illegibly on the blackboard. In short, his teaching in the one section was all we think of as typical of the pedagogically incompetent college instructor. He was so bad that the dean received several complaints from students in that section. When the final examination was graded, it turned out that the students in the section in which he had been a "poor" teacher did significantly better than those from the other section. Presumably, they had learned to do mathematics independently of the instructor, and therefore found it easier to produce results when they could not depend on his aid.*

These are not isolated examples. Many teachers who believe themselves to be very good at their chosen profession can find such examples from their own experience—if they are not too embarrassed to mention them. For example, the author was once teaching a very difficult experimental course in algebraic geometry to a class of tenth graders. When the regular teacher was absent for several days, a substitute who knew almost no mathematics was brought in. She let the pupils take turns teaching the class. On the next examination, the

* These two stories were told (and vouched for) by Dr. Alvin Eurich, vice president of the Fund for the Advancement of Education.

pupils did better on the proof of the Pythagorean theorem, which had been taught to them by a fellow pupil, than on several easier theorems which they had learned from their peerless teacher. This experience was both embarrassing and educational to the teacher.

From the above examples, it would be easy to jump to the conclusion that the laziest, most incompetent, least educated teacher is the most effective. Needless to say, that is not the conclusion that will be drawn here. Rather, the conclusion to be drawn from the three examples is that spoon-feeding knowledge is not necessarily the best way to assure the intellectual well-being of the pupil. It is true that in some cases clear explanations will be needed. Surely the pupil cannot be expected to acquire all his knowledge without any guidance, and in order to avoid too much frustration and waste of time, pupils must be helped over very difficult spots.

On the other hand, in entirely too many classes, it is common to find the teacher telling the pupils what is "true," how to work the problems, how to avoid making errors, and so on, without really giving the children an opportunity to think. Then the teacher wonders why the pupils are not able to handle new and different problems when they arise.

I.Q. vs. C.Q.

Psychologists have been working with methods of testing a child's creativity lately, and it has become reasonably clear that there is a creativity factor which is somewhat independent of what is called intelligence. No doubt, we will soon have a creativity quotient (C.Q.) as well as an intelligence quotient. When this occurs, I predict that experimenters will find that the creativity quotient is inversely related to success in school. In particular, the child who is most successful in school is the one with high I.Q. but low C.Q., while the one who is least successful is the one with low I.Q. and high C.Q. For centuries, schools and schoolteachers have put high priority on the child who can learn and synthesize the thoughts of others without having any significant thoughts of his own. If a creative child seriously questions the statements of his teachers, he is thought to be a troublemaker, and is usually penalized by getting a lower grade or by being made to stay after school. In fact, if a child has an average or below average I.Q. and is very creative, he is almost certain to wind up in a remedial class because he cannot (or will not) learn the "correct" way of doing things.

In secondary school mathematics, there are several common places where creativity on the part of pupils is frowned upon, while docility is highly prized. One such example is in the solving of linear equations. Give the beginning algebra pupil the problem $3x + 5 = 20$, with instructions to determine the value of x, and he will tell you almost instantly that the answer is 5. The fact that he gets the answer so quickly is the tip-off. He is not doing it the "right" way—if he were, he could not get the answer so quickly. So after long, hard (and often very creative) work, the teacher convinces most of the pupils that they should do this problem by subtracting 5 from each member of the equation and then dividing each member by 3. However, the truly creative pupil is likely to have found a different method of solving such problems (even when they become difficult). Some teachers reward such creativity by marking the pupil wrong each time he uses his method (he must show all his work, and he has to take the steps in the "right" order). Some teachers simply ignore his attempts at creativity (in the hope that they will go away). Unfortunately, it seldom occurs to the teacher to reward such creativity—either with praise or with something more tangible, such as grades.

The method most commonly discovered by beginning algebra pupils for solving difficult linear equations is the following: To solve $ax + b = c$, guess some number, g, as your answer. Try it: $ag + b = d$. If d happens to equal c, g is the right answer, and you are finished. If d is less than c, the answer can be found by adding $(c-d)/a$ to g.* That is, the answer is $g + (c-d)/a$. That this procedure will, in fact, always produce the correct answer can be demonstrated by anybody who knows a little algebra. Of course, the pupils convince themselves that the procedure will work by simply thinking about it.

A specific example may be of some help: to solve $3x - 5 = 11$, guess that the correct answer is 2. $3(2) - 5 = 6 - 5 = 1$. Since 1 is 10 less than the desired result (11), the guess of 2 was too small. Since the coefficient of x is 3, whenever the value of x is increased by 1, the value of the entire left member will be increased by 3. So the guess must be increased by 10/3 or $3\frac{1}{3}$ in order to increase the result by 10. Thus, the answer must be $2 + 3\frac{1}{3}$ or $5\frac{1}{3}$.

Another time at which it is tempting for teachers to squelch

* If d is greater than c, a slight variation is necessary.

budding creativity involves the trisection of angles. Now, every mathematics teacher knows that it is impossible to trisect a general angle (that is, any angle other than certain special ones, such as a 90° angle, or a 45° angle). Teachers know this even if they have never seen a proof of the fact. When they tell this to their pupils, most pupils accept the fact and go on about the business of learning geometry. However, there are always a few who, upon hearing that angles cannot be trisected, set out to trisect the angle. Most geometry teachers think of angle trisectors in the same general category with the plague. Some teachers simply refuse to look at the "proofs" because they could not be right. Of course, the teacher cannot be expected to spend all of his time looking at angle trisections, but he should encourage the pupil to try to create a careful proof and look for errors himself. He might agree to look at no more than one angle trisection a week from the pupil, so that the pupil will be careful to submit only his best efforts. But the teacher should not discourage the entire enterprise. Many good mathematicians learned a great deal of geometry and quite a bit about proof by trying to trisect angles.

Encourage Independence

One of the hardest things for any adult to do is to encourage independence in those for whom he feels responsible. This is true of parents and others who have contact with children as well as teachers. We would all like to help children to know the things we know, to avoid the mistakes we made (and the mistakes we did not make), and generally to become more perfect (that is, more like us) as rapidly as possible. And, it is true that one of the great advantages that the human race has had over other animals is the ability to pass along to each new generation the accumulated wisdom of previous generations. However, we can never hope to pass on all the accumulated wisdom of the ages to each new generation; so if this were our only goal, we could expect a gradual reduction in the total knowledge available. Actually, it is well known that the amount of knowledge available is increasing rapidly—in fact, exponentially. This is at least as true in mathematics as in any other field of human thought. Thus, it seems the creators are very important people in our society. With this in mind, it is desirable that teachers not get so wrapped up in the process of passing on information that they neglect the encouragement of independent thought and creative endeavor.

On the other hand, we cannot expect each child to create all, or even any substantial part, of the wisdom which has been discovered before his time. To expect such a thing would be to deny him the wisdom of others, and would be a colossal waste of his energies—he would almost certainly never learn enough to be able to consider problems that had never been solved. Thus, we must compromise between an environment which requires complete creativity on the part of the child, and one which allows no creativity.

Do not do all the work for the pupils, only what is necessary to keep them from being completely lost and undirected. With a large class, this may be more difficult than with just one individual. In such a situation, it is usually desirable to choose one individual to represent the class. This should not be the brightest child in the class, in general, but rather an average pupil. Give the entire class time to think before asking for a response, and then allow all of the children the opportunity to raise questions and argue—even when you believe that the answer given is the correct one. If you only encourage questions when you believe the answer to be wrong, the children will soon become very good at reading your mind, but will not necessarily improve their own minds.

Oftentimes it is desirable for the teacher himself to question the pupil and make him defend his conclusions—even when the teacher believes the answer given is correct. This will keep the children from guessing that when the teacher asks a question about a pupil's conclusion, this necessarily means that the teacher thinks the child has the wrong answer.

In order to carry on discussions such as those described above, it will be necessary for the teacher to have a very good background in his subject. Otherwise, he will not know the reasons for various things, and may find it difficult to get the class to arrive at desirable conclusions after the appropriate amount of discussion. For example, why do we always have to rationalize fractions? Would it not be just as well to leave the radicals in the denominator? (After all, the roots of trees are always on the bottom.) The answer is that, in general, there is no reason to rationalize $3/\sqrt{2}$. The representation "$3\sqrt{2}$ / 2" is no better a representation of the number in question than is $3/\sqrt{2}$, for most purposes. However, in one specific case—the case in which you would like to determine a decimal approximation for the number

—it is nice to have it in rationalized form. The way to convince children that this is true is to let them try finding a decimal approximation starting with each representation, and let them decide for themselves which they prefer. However, it will still be true that when a decimal approximation is not wanted, rationalization is often a waste of effort.

There are many other examples of this sort throughout mathematics. It is important to remember that there are generally reasons for the things we do in mathematics. Sometimes, they are simply conventions. Sometimes there are logical reasons. But do not get upset when the pupils fight for what they think is right—even if you are convinced that it is not. The times this is likely to be most upsetting is when you know what the right answer is but do not know why. Constantly learning more mathematics will help to avoid some of these cases, but you will still find some. In such cases, think about the other possibility—could it lead to trouble? If so, what kind of trouble? Why is it better to do it the usual way than the way suggested by the pupil? If you cannot find a good argument for doing it the usual way, you might try consulting somebody who knows more mathematics than you do, or you might even try it the other way to see what happens. Of course, in some such cases, you may have to simply announce that that is the way it is done and, therefore, we shall do it that way. But try not to do this more than is absolutely necessary.

One example of a situation in which pupils may question the usual way of doing things involves the use of "i" to stand for the square root of -1. Why not use "$\sqrt{-1}$" instead? If, rather than just saying that this is a convention, the teacher tries experimenting without the use of i, he (and the class) will quickly learn that there is a good reason for the introduction of a special symbol.

Consider $\sqrt{-2} \times \sqrt{-2}$. By definition, $\sqrt{a} \times \sqrt{a} = a$, and therefore $\sqrt{-2} \times \sqrt{-2}$ must be -2. However, if we carry out the usual manipulations, we can show that $\sqrt{-2} \times \sqrt{-2} = \sqrt{(-2) \times (-2)} = \sqrt{4} = 2$.* Of course, the reason for this paradox is that $\sqrt{a} \times \sqrt{b}$ does not necessarily equal $\sqrt{ab}$ for complex numbers as it does for real numbers. In particular, if both a and b

* Pupils nowadays will already know that the radical symbol without a sign in front means, by convention, the principle (in this case, positive) root. Therefore, this problem cannot be resolved by pretending that the radical symbol has a built in "plus or minus" sign. If it did, it would never be necessary to annex one.

are negative, the rule for reals does not happen to be true. Incidentally, this fact may help the teacher to sympathize with pupils who do not understand why the rule is true for real numbers. It is not, and should not be, immediately obvious.

Discovery

There are many kinds of activities in the classroom that go under the name of "discovery." One of the most commonly used forms of discovery is the Socratic method of teaching. This is exemplified in "Socrates and the Slave" by Plato (Fadiman, 1958, pp. 49-57). In this demonstration, Socrates starts with an ignorant slave boy and, by asking him the right questions, shows that the boy knew the Pythagorean theorem all along—he just had to be encouraged to remember it. Socrates asks questions in such a way that it is almost impossible for the boy to make a mistake. When the boy does answer a question incorrectly, he is asked several more questions which show, beyond a doubt, that he must have made a mistake—so he corrects his mistake and continues.

It is very impressive to watch such demonstrations, and there can be no doubt that creative teaching is involved in this process. However, it is very doubtful that there is any creative endeavor involved on the part of the pupil.

Some months ago I was using the discovery method to demonstrate to a young lady that the proper formula for determining how many permutations there are of the letters of the word "Mississippi" is $\frac{11!}{4! \times 4! \times 2! \times 1!}$. I started out with simple problems, and broke them down into small questions to which the answers were obvious. As we proceeded through the lesson, she got the right answer to each question. Then, as we got to the final formula (for the general case), I asked her the question and, while waiting for the answer, beamed at the small group of mathematicians and educators who had been watching the process. The student said, "I know what the answer is but I have no idea how I got it, and could never do anything like that again without you there to ask me the right questions."

In fact, I, like Socrates, had trapped my pupil. This is not teaching for creativity—it is creative debate. Although it may be impressive, it is not good education. In fact this process has essentially the same defects as a very well-programmed teaching machine would have.

Another kind of teaching, which some people have referred to as the discovery method, is a radically distorted version of "Progressive Education." In this process, the child is given complete freedom to do whatever he wants to do. This is not what Dewey had in mind, nor is it good educational procedure. There is a great deal to learn in the world, and we owe it to our children to give them an opportunity to learn it in a reasonably structured and efficient manner. There is a delightful entry in the notes kept by one of the science teachers in Dewey's experimental school at Chicago. It goes like this: "We asked the children what they would like to do today. They didn't know. So we told them." This is as it should be.

The type of discovery that encourages creative thinking on the part of the pupils, but still gets information into their store of knowledge in a reasonably efficient manner is somewhere between the highly structured approach of Socrates and the complete laissez-faire of the radical progressive. Sometimes it will be necessary simply to tell the pupils certain things, while at other times it may be possible to start them out with a general problem and let them play with it with almost no direction. In the latter cases, you will probably find that they are not exposed to as many facts in as short a period of time, but they will almost certainly be learning more about creative thinking and self-reliance.

An Example of Discovery

One case of this third type of discovery can be seen in the following example (Willoughby, 1963): In a class of reasonably bright sixteen- and seventeen-year-olds who did not like mathematics (and were not very good at it), the old "twelve-coin" problem was posed. The problem is: Given 12 coins, one of which is a counterfeit, find the counterfeit coin in 3 weighings with a balance scale and tell whether the counterfeit is heavier or lighter than the others. You know that all the good coins have the same weight and that the counterfeit is either heavier or lighter than the others (but you do not know which).

The pupils were allowed to make several attempts at solving the problem in class, and then given the assignment to continue trying it as a homework assignment. Although nobody was able to solve the problem before the next class period, the pupils were able to pool their information (and misinformation) in such a way that by the end of the second period one boy was finally able to come up with the usual solution to this problem.

Then the teacher suggested that perhaps they could figure out a way to generalize the problem. Could they discover a similar problem with a similar solution? One pupil suggested that if there were more coins, more weighings would probably be necessary, and it might be interesting to find out how many weighings would be needed for, say, 20 coins or 25 coins. Another pupil suggested that it would be more efficient to determine the maximum number of coins that could be used for a given number of weighings. Finally, as the period ended, a third pupil suggested that the next step ought to be to determine the number of coins possible with four weighings, and this was taken as the homework assignment for the weekend.

Interestingly enough, although nobody had solved the problem correctly, that Monday was the first time during the year that every pupil had clearly made a really serious effort to do the assigned homework. These pupils had grown accustomed over the years to not liking mathematics, and to thinking up imaginative excuses for not doing their mathematics homework. In this case, however, every pupil had an answer which he was ready to defend, and almost every answer was different from all of the others.

The largest number proposed was 48. This pupil had decided that he could apply a discussion about looking for patterns (carried on earlier in the year) to this problem. He tried the problem with two weighings and found that three was the maximum number of coins possible. Multiplying by 4, he got 12, so he assumed that he would get the right answer for four weighings by multiplying by 4 again. Neither he nor anybody else was able actually to produce a method of finding one counterfeit coin in 48, and it was finally decided that although it seemed to be a good idea, he must have generalized from too small a sample.

The next largest number proposed was 36. The girl who proposed it had a method of actually carrying out the weighings which she described to the class. Before she had completed her explanation, one of her fellow pupils had noticed a way to improve on it. He found a way to do the problem with 38 coins. After considerable discussion, the class was about ready to accept this as the answer when another boy found still another variation which allowed a solution with 39 coins. As soon as this suggestion was made, and before it had been worked out in detail, the boy who had originally predicted 48 agreed that 39 must be the right answer, and further predicted that with five weighings the number of coins possible would be 120. While the rest of the class had been working on the problem with precisely four weighings, he had continued looking for a general pattern. The results he now had in front of him were:

1 weighing	0 coins
2 weighings	3 coins
3 weighings	12 coins
4 weighings	coins

After looking at this for some time, he decided that in order to determine the number of coins possible with n weighings, he could take the number possible with n-1 weighings, add one, and multiply by three. After more consideration, the pupils were able to show that there is always a general method of solving the problem for the number of coins indicated in this formula.

Although the mathematics discovered in these lessons was admittedly trivial, the children had learned it in a manner that was significant. They had learned to make and test conjectures. They had learned to generalize a problem. They had learned to look for patterns. And, they had learned that they could create mathematics themselves—without being led by the hand. The pupils in this class were thinking like mathematicians and really doing mathematics—not just memorizing theorems, proofs, and facts created by others. This was teaching for creativity.

Other Examples

There are many other examples of teaching for creative endeavor which are worth considering. One of the most impressive of these is the work of R. L. Moore at the University of Texas, which has also been carried on by some of his former students, most notably R. H. Bing at the University of Wisconsin. In their topology classes, these professors do not use textbooks, and do not allow the students to look up proofs in published books. Rather, the student is given a list of theorems to prove, and is expected to go ahead and prove them on his own. There is a system of records through which the professor can tell which theorems the student thinks he knows how to prove. Then, when the time comes for a particular theorem, the professor can call on anyone of the students who knows a proof to demonstrate it to the entire class. The theorems become more and more sophisticated, until, near the end of a full year course, the problems might include some which have not yet been solved. When the student gets finished with one of these, he has a doctoral dissertation. Several students at the University of Wisconsin have been known to complain that, having taken R. H. Bing's course in topology, they had spent so much time and energy on topology that they could not afford to get their degree in any branch of mathematics except topology. However, the training is clearly good. A surprisingly high percentage of the topologists in this country are either students of Moore's, or second generation students of his (that is, students of his students).

Interestingly enough, many mathematicians believe that students coming out of this system do not know as much mathematics as they ought to know, in spite of the fact that they are topnotch research mathematicians and excellent teachers. However, as one mathematician put it, "they may not know much, but they have guts—they don't think there's anything they can't do." In today's world, if a university has to take a choice between a professor who knows a great deal but cannot do original work and a professor who knows relatively little but has created a considerable amount of new mathematics, it will choose the latter every time. It would be nice to have both, but the premium is on creativity. This is true, not only in higher mathematics, but in essentially all fields of endeavor in the modern world. Therefore, if we must err, let us err on the side of creativity, not on the side of large quantities of factual information.

Difficulties

Trying to teach for creativity is not easy. Even if you learn how to do it, there will be many problems which you must face. The most common problem faced by today's teacher who is trying to teach for creativity is the fact that the pupils are not accustomed to being creative.

Early in my teaching career, I was asked to substitute for a social science teacher one day. During the class discussion, one of the pupils raised a question relating to science, "Why does the siren on a fire engine sound higher when it's coming than when it's going?" Since the answer was one which I felt the childern could find for themselves with a little encouragement, I said, "Well, let's see if we can figure it out." Promptly, one of the better pupils inquired, "Would you like me to run next door and ask Mr. Jones (the science teacher)?" Through further discussion, it became clear that every child in the class thought that the way to find out the answer to a question in science was to ask the nearest authority. The thought of "figuring something out" for themselves had never really occurred to them—at least, not as it pertains to academic subjects, such as science. Furthermore, they were convinced that I did not know anything about science, since I would never have suggested trying to figure out the answer to a question if I already knew it.

Of course, if you have the same group of pupils for a long period of time, the number of such ego-damaging events will probably be reduced, but you can expect to face other problems. One of the most serious of these involves other teachers. If, by teaching children to be creative, you end up making life more difficult for other teachers (and you almost certainly will), you can expect some bitter complaints.

For example, there is the case of the eighth grade mathematics teacher who gave his pupils the following problem:

ABCD is a parallelogram with $\overline{EF} \perp \overline{CD}$, and $\overline{GH} \perp \overline{BC}$. If DC = 10″, EF = 4″, and BC = 5″, how long is $\overline{GH}$?

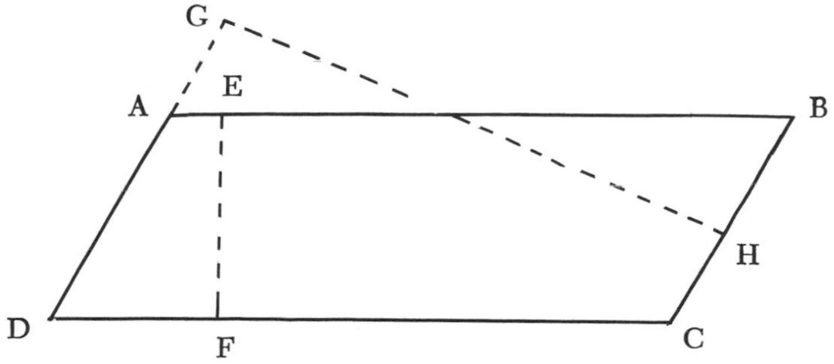

At the next faculty meeting, a teacher rose to bitterly denounce the teaching of trigonometry in the eighth grade. It turned out that the second teacher had been hired as a tutor for a child in the first teacher's class, and had been unable to do the problem in question. He was not appeased when he was approached later by teacher number one and told that knowledge of the formula for the area of a parallelogram was sufficient to solve the problem. Nor did it help him to find out that a small amount of information about similar triangles would also have led to the solution. He was not used to looking at parallelograms that way (on their sides), and he did not much like the idea of teaching children to look at them that way.

Although the sort of problem mentioned above is probably not unusual, a far more common problem occurs when a whole class of pupils leaves one teacher and goes to another. If the children have been encouraged to create, to think, to question, and to resist intellectual authoritarianism, and the second teacher believes that education consists of stuffing the cerebrum full of as many facts as possible in as short a time as possible, there is almost certain to be a conflict. The first teacher will probably find himself accused of doing all sorts of damage to the children—or, at the very least, he will be accused of rocking the boat.

There is no simple answer to the question posed by the noncreative teacher. The fact is that many teachers are not particularly creative, and are not likely to become creative in the near future. It is not surprising that these teachers feel that their security is being endangered when other teachers are trying to encourage different kinds of intellectual behavior. Perhaps the best answer to such a situation is to try to live and let live. Do not try to make the other teacher conform to your way of doing things any more than you should be willing to conform to his way. He is likely to be under enough pressure from pupils and others (parents, administrators, etc.) without your going out of your way to add to the pressures. Hopefully, in time, a majority, or at least a large minority, of teachers will encourage creative behavior in their pupils. When that time comes, the teacher who is teaching for creativity will find his job somewhat easier.

Still another problem which results from the large number of uninspired teachers is the resistant pupil. Most very young children are creative. Probably some of this creativity wears off through the normal process of growing up. However, the teachers they meet in school undoubtedly hasten the process. If a child has been rewarded for many years for regurgitating facts and doing problems in the "right" way, he is likely to find it difficult to accept the idea that he is now going to be rewarded for thinking. Furthermore, there are many children who are better at repeating what they have seen others do than they are at being creative. What do you tell the child (or parent) who says that he has always been good at mathematics, but cannot do it your way? What can you do with the child who wants answers and correct methods to memorize? Again, this is not an easy problem to solve. You will have to get used to the idea that the child whose grade improves will assume that it is because of him (which will probably be true) while the child whose grade gets worse will be certain that it is all your fault (which also may be true). However, seeing the creative children become more creative, more intelligent, and more interested should be sufficient reward for an excellent teacher. Of course, the teacher should still try to encourage creativity on the part of the less creative pupils, and help them learn what they can.

One final problem that often arises in classes where the teacher is trying to teach for creative endeavor has to do with discipline. There is always the danger that if the pupils are taught to be intellectually independent, they will decide to be independent about their social activities also. The important thing for the teacher to remember is to distinguish carefully between intellectual independence and creativity and the type of social behavior which will tend to limit the intellectual freedom of all. A chaotic classroom is not conducive to intellectual activity—independent or otherwise. In this respect, the role of the teacher is quite similar to that of a democratic government—and it is not always easy for either the teacher or the government to distinguish between antisocial behavior and intellectual freedom. But it is important for each to make this distinction.

Must We Teach for Creativity?

If the schools have done such a bad job of teaching for creativity in the past, why is it that there are so many creative people in the world? Is it, in fact, possible to teach for creativity, or must we simply teach for knowledge? These questions have occurred to many teachers, and there is some evidence to support the view that the most stultifying of school systems can produce highly creative individuals. There is also considerable doubt that the schools are doing a very bad job—in fact, they are probably doing a better job than ever before. However, the fact still remains that some very creative individuals have come out of the most unpromising situations. Why?

It is probably true that a person who is highly creative at the age of five will remain creative no matter what the world does to him (within reasonable bounds) over the next ten or twenty years. In fact, by trying to kill the creativity in him, it is entirely possible that the system may be making him even more creative. In order to survive in the system and struggle against the inequities he feels are present, he may become far more creative than he would have been otherwise. Making life easy for a creative individual is not necessarily the best way to make him more creative.

On the other hand, if the creative individual finds that he must constantly fight the educational system in order to be creative, he may lose his desire to learn. He may decide that if this is education, he wants no part of it. A constant source of embarrassment to the University of Wisconsin is the fact that "the two University of Wisconsin engineering students whose names are more widely known the world over than any others never graduated. The name of the first is Charles A. Lindbergh; of the other, Frank Lloyd Wright" (Cass, 1965, p.35).

This is not a unique situation. It is far too common to find creative dropouts. Yet there is always the nagging feeling that if formal education is really worth anything, these creative people would have been even greater if they had been able to stand their formal schooling longer.

So, to some extent, it may not be so important that we teach for creative endeavor—if we can just avoid repulsing those who are already creative—and give them an education without turning them against learning, and without reducing their creativity. We can do this by rewarding creativity; by allowing the children to think and discuss without constantly telling them the right answer; and by remaining calm, happy, and encouraging, even when they question facts which we know to be true, but for which we have no good reason.

CHAPTER 8

Language Arts in the Elementary School

by

SARA W. LUNDSTEEN

Currently associate professor of Education at the University of Texas, Sara W. Lundsteen was formerly assistant professor of Education at the University of California, Santa Barbara. She received her Ph.D. at the University of California, Berkeley, after earning her B.A. and M.A. from Southern Methodist University in Dallas. She also studied at the Sorbonne in Paris and at the University of Copenhagen.

Recently, Dr. Lundsteen received a substantial research grant (the Thinking Improvement Project) from the Charles F. Kettering Foundation to study children's thinking in the language arts. This study involved 29 schools and 900 pupils in Santa Barbara and Ventura counties, California. Perhaps best known for her work in listening, she has designed and produced a television series and four-track experimental curriculum lessons and tests in connection with the Thinking Improvement Project.

WHY TEACH FOR CREATIVE ENDEAVOR in the language arts? Is this kind of teaching needed because it fits the context of democracy? Should this nation advertise democracy to the world but educate as if it believed in authoritarianism? If teaching is to be consistent with democratic values, then is a key point enhancement of the individual? It has been said that the alternative to teaching for individual development is the production of blind, conforming "sheep."

If a key point is individual enhancement rather than an alternative of suppression, are communication skills central to the individual's progress? Can teachers look into a pupil's head to determine his readiness to operate creatively? Can teachers look into a pupil's head to receive feedback once they have attempted a stimulating activity? If verbalization is a major window to a child's thinking, if verbalization influences behavior, if language arts occupy at least three fourths of the school day, can teachers fail to be concerned with communication skills?

Assuming, then, that the task of teaching for creative endeavor is important, how can the teacher accomplish it? What kind of teaching fosters creative endeavor? Is the alternative to creative teaching, "tell, tell, tell," with a continual and relentless loss as specific facts are eroded by the ravages of time on pupil rote memory?

How do instructors teach for creative endeavor in an already overcrowded curriculum? Indeed, what is it? Moreover, what, specifically, can the teacher do in areas of listening, speaking, reading, and writing?

If these questions make a need apparent, if they kindle a vision, if they give promise of action, then this chapter proposes to throw light on the following understandings:

1. A defense against the "cookie-cut mind" (generally, what teaching for creative endeavor is and what to do about it).
2. A focus, an interrelating thread, running through the language arts versus a "barrel of snakes" (how to do it most economically).
3. Activities for creative problem solving in the areas of listening, speaking, reading, and writing (specifically what to do).
4. A sampling of what research says to the teacher about each of the above areas (some evidence for doing it).

The "cookie-cut mind" means an imposed mental conformity, and the "barrel of snakes" means the unstructured slippery conglomerate that is the unfortunate reality of most programs in elementary English.

What Is Teaching for Creative Endeavor in the Language Arts?

If the problem of how to go about teaching for creative endeavor is to be solved, it seems that the first step is to define the terms in the problem. First, what is creativity in the language arts? Perhaps it is actually creative thinking and perhaps creative thinking can be classified as creative problem solving. Second, is the best way to "get the most mileage" out of learning experiences to focus teaching on creative problem solving? Third, what is teaching for creative endeavor? Perhaps such teaching is maintaining an open system. Perhaps such teaching is giving children a defense against the cookie-cut mind.

What follows is an attempt to answer these questions or to define the parts of this problem: "What is teaching for creative endeavor in the language arts?"

What Is Creative Thinking?

Thinking is a process rather than a fixed state. It involves a sequence of ideas moving from some beginning to some goal. It moves through a pattern of relationships, varying from relatively undirected to highly directed organized activity. Russell (1956) has identified six processes of thinking, two of which are of major concern here.

These two processes, creative thinking and problem solving, appear to possess certain similarities and differences. The contrast between them, while often not extensive, may lie in the greater part played in creative thinking by novel, original insights, the stage of illumination, and the insinuation of less conscious fringe thoughts. The creative process has been described, in perhaps a narrow way, as more personal, less fixed, ranging close to fantasy, playlike, free rising, and dreamlike. But the ability at will to make creative thinking coordinate with more logical reasoning may make the difference between lunacy and creativity.

What Is Creative Problem Solving?

In contrast, problem solving depends more on careful preparation, conscious organization, direction, and verification as a basis for action. Problem solving is more factual and coincides more often with previously determined conditions and consequences.

Bloom (1956) stressed "application" as an important part of problem solving. Given a problem new to the pupil, he will, not merely can, apply the appropriate abstraction or principle without having to be prompted. Getzels (1964), however, criticized the work of Bloom as dealing only with "presented problems" rather than with "discovered problems."

Getzels classified problems as to what is known and what is unknown. When there are "knowns" to all aspects of a problem for a pupil, as is often the case in school, the task verges on uncreative drill. He concluded that (a) there is a neglected group in which the problem is not given but is discovered and (b) there is a range of problems with various degrees of what is known and unknown, requiring various amounts of innovation and creativity for solution. He pleaded for more problems in school with more unknowns, at least for the child, for here is the genuine challenge to the learner.

For example, children may listen to an unfinished problem-story about a girl and a new school. They could be told the problem (integration into a new peer group) or the problem could be inferred, more creatively, by the children themselves. The solution could be told to them, or the solution could be unknown. If the answer is unknown, the children themselves could think creatively to a solution. In the language of Guilford (1961), the problem-solving process would have moved along the continuum toward divergent (creative) thinking, away from convergent (restricted) thinking.

When the term "problem solving" is used in its most creative sense, with emphasis on unknowns, with flexibility of categorization, with suspension of evaluation until a free flow of ideas has been completed, with elaboration, with information recalled in new connections, in revised or novel form—then the following statement is reasonable. All problem solving is creative, though not all creative thinking is problem solving (Guilford, 1964).

Creative problem solving is the process by which the child directs himself from the problem or goal as he sees it to a solution which, for him, is the product meeting the demands of the problem. This process includes (a) clarification of the problem, (b) creative formulation of hypotheses (original, free flowing), (c) highly conscious planned procedure or organization (flexible, elaborated), and (d) planned evaluation (highly conscious).

These four aspects or steps in the problem-solving process may occur in the order just described, in no fixed order, in repetition, or even simultaneously. The only restriction is that, generally, when teaching for creative problem solving, the evaluation steps should be suspended in favor of encouraging fluency of ideas first. (See Figure One.)

But what about elaborative and appreciative thinking? It seems that these operations can be included in both creative thinking and problem solving. Russell (1961) suggests that the child who appreciates what he hears and reads and who elaborates "between the lines" is being creative, too. For example, the child may think creatively when he appreciates beautiful language found in *Miracles on Maple Hill*, or identifies with a character, such as Johnny Tremain.

Images, identification, and projection have emotional overtones which support the relationship between creative thinking and appreciation.

CONCEPTS FOR A CREATIVE PROBLEM-SOLVING PROCESS
(Not necessarily in left-to-right order at all times, and including possible periods of incubation)

Goal or Problem	*Hypotheses*	*Planned Procedure*	*Planned Evaluation*
Sensed, analyzed, structured Categorized with flexibility, even novelty Subdivided Defined	Generated with fluency, originality	Elaborated with flexible categorization Constructed with search strategy for needed data (unknowns) and application of principles	of input, of hypotheses, of consequences, of criteria

FIGURE ONE

Moreover, subcapabilities involving other thinking processes (that is, perceptual thinking, associative thinking, concept formation, critical thinking, creative thinking) may well support creative problem solving, the broadest and most inclusive of the thinking processes (Russell, 1956).

A FOCUS FOR INTERRELATIONSHIP

Consequently, if the focus for teaching in the language arts is creative problem solving, then all other processes of thinking can be meaningfully interrelated within this broad process. Thus, as far as thinking processes are concerned, it is possible to effect the most economical mileage or transfer within the whole spectrum of language arts areas.

Furthermore, a focus on the concepts in problem solving may solve another problem. This generic process can give some meaningful structure to each area in that barrel of snakes. Parenthetically, the term for the language arts, "barrel of snakes," means simply that no structure, as advocated by Bruner (1960), or no possibility of transfer from one facet to another is present. Instead of possessing a core of ideas amenable to teaching for creative endeavor, the language arts resemble a seething, fragmented mess. But through the creative problem-solving process some structure can be present.

The following examples are given as an overview to the sections which follow:

1. The large concepts in a problem-solving approach can be transferred from the pupil functioning as listener to the pupil functioning as speaker and as reader.

2. The abilities or principles in story writing can be grasped as a problem-solving situation. Furthermore, the content of certain types of stories has been patterned by the author into problem situations to be solved by his characters. In thinking as a writer, the pupil may use this pattern.

3. Moreover, the content of problem solving in children's literature may organize experience or serve as bibliotherapy. As a result of such exposure, a child may gain insight into solving his own personal problems.

4. A generic problem-solving process might be applied autonomously by a pupil to his own spelling problems or might help him think as a maker of language, a grammarian.

The possibilities for interrelationship of the language arts through a focus on the creative problem-solving process are numerous. This focus will be further detailed in sections for each language arts area. Figure Two gives some indication of interrelationships that can be effected by a creative problem-solving focus. The problem-solving process in Figure Two is the same as in Figure One.

The Teaching-Learning Act—An Open System

After leaving an explanation of creative problem solving as an economical means of approaching creativity in the language arts, the next step is to think in terms of teaching. But how do instructors actually teach for creative problem solving? What do they do? Bernard Shaw once said that if you teach a man anything, he will never learn. Creative teaching is not telling. What is it then?

Some authorities have defined teaching creatively as follows:

1. Generally, creative teaching is experience providing (Russell, 1956; Torrance, 1963). Hypothetically, it is providing a friendly,

INTERRELATIONSHIPS EFFECTED BY A CREATIVE PROBLEM-SOLVING FOCUS IN THE LANGUAGE ARTS

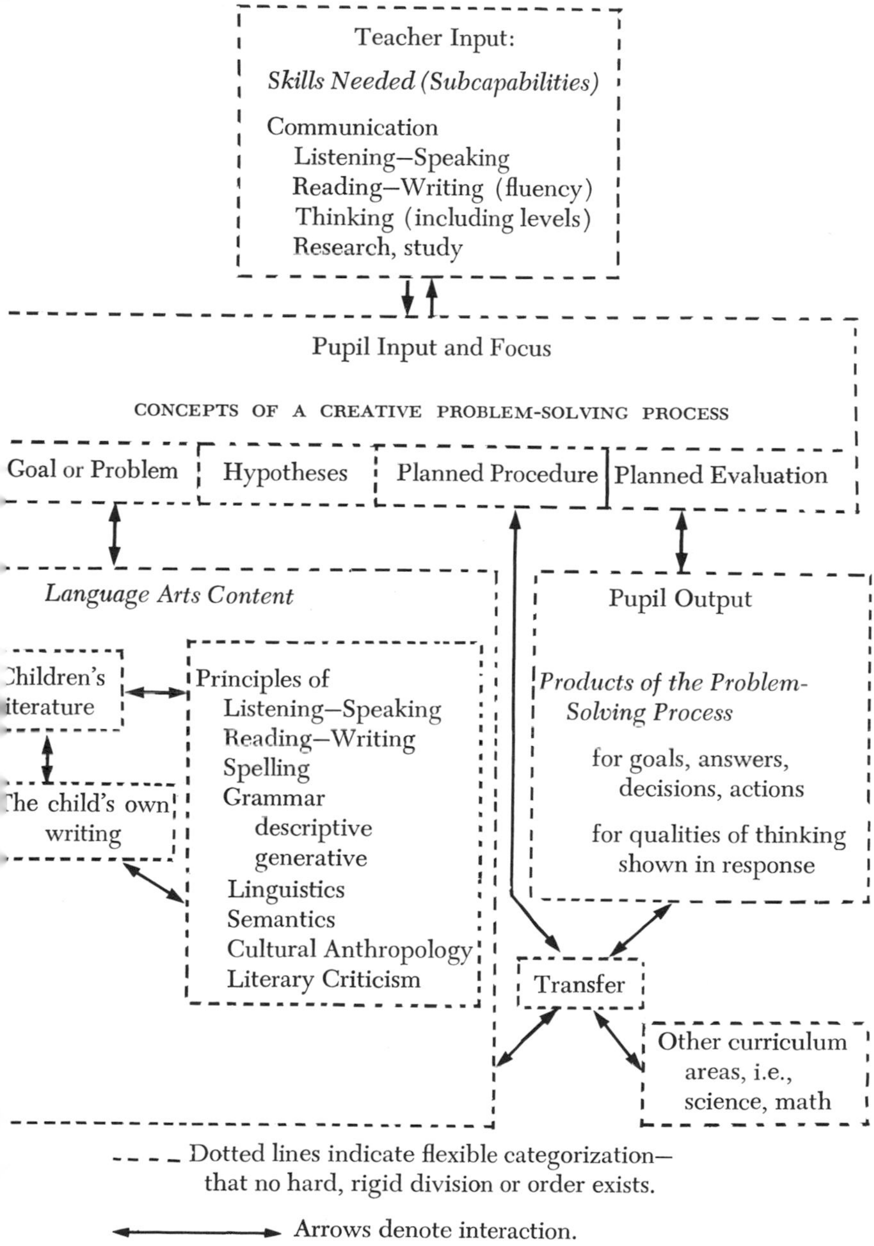

FIGURE TWO

informal, nonthreatening, accepting, yet motivating atmosphere or environment.

2. It is working with pupil or group characteristics, such as motivations, emotions, thinking styles, and attitudes (Russell, 1956). It is providing an open set—a tolerance for ambiguity, for probability, for multiple causation, and for increased sensitivity (Carroll, 1964; Taylor and Barron, 1963).

3. It is fostering needed subcapabilities or skills of verbal fluency or communication, flexibility, originality, elaboration, knowledge, thinking processes, and research (Taylor and Barron, 1963).

4. It is an attitude. This attitude may include being respectful of children's questions and ideas. It is realizing the need for ideas to incubate (Torrance, 1962; Wallas, 1926).

5. It is adopting certain teaching strategies. It is turning yourself into a "question asker," not an "answer giver." It is using questions to pace thought and to lift thought to higher, more complex levels when pupils are ready (Taba, 1964). It is using questions that open up rather than narrow down thought: "What did you notice about this story?" or "What do you think Betty's trouble was in this story?" not "What color did Betty say her socks were?" It is getting pupils to ask questions that take them some place: "How might I test this idea?"

6. It is helping pupils to think abstractly enough to go beyond the data (Bruner, 1960): "What does this mean?" It is helping pupils to reflect on consequences and evaluation: "What would happen if you solved the problem this way?" It is developing powers of symbolic thought.

7. Finally, it is fostering pupil autonomy or freedom to act independently. It is withholding correction long enough to permit a child to discover and correct his own errors (Suchman, 1962).

In sum, instructors teach for creative endeavor by fostering an open system. This kind of teaching is difficult; it demands thought. But this kind of teaching is important as never before. Mass media, such as television, and outside pressures common in our society induce children to conform, to be in one mold. In a journal for television advertisements it was stated smugly that children are living, talking records of what advertisers tell them every day (Packard, 1957). Moreover, peer groups as well as parents and teachers exert pressure to conform. It has been said that all these forces take on the aspect of a giant cookie cutter, molding children's minds all in one pattern. Teaching creatively may give children a defense against the "cookie-cut mind."

A final word on teaching: any of the activities listed in this chapter which are designed to develop problem solving in the language arts could be presented in an uncreative way yielding uncreative results. To keep the creative teaching-learning act in mind, activities will be subdivided in the following way: (1) motivational or readiness activities to build subcapabilities, (2) activities for creative problem solving in the specific area, and (3) evaluative activities. Whenever possible, transfer to other areas will be indicated. In addition, each major area of the language arts will include a section on what research says to the teacher.

The Language Arts

The final term to be defined in the problem—"What can be done to teach language arts in a creative way?"—is the phrase, "language arts." Since the language arts deal with ideas—their impression and expression in words—the following analogy may be made. A course in painting is like the language arts: In the study of painting the student examines great works and actually uses the paintbrush in self-expression; similarly, in the language arts, dealing in the medium of words, the student listens to and reads the best that has been recorded, and at the same time he is helped to express his own thinking. In effect, the language arts, the arts of understanding, interpret the world to him and him to the world (Applegate, 1963).

A Creative Problem for the Reader

The question for this section, "What is teaching for creative endeavor in the language arts?" becomes for the reader a creative problem itself. This section of the chapter has presented some tentative definitions for parts of this problem. Growing out of these efforts, one broad definition could be the following: Teaching for creative endeavor in the language arts is a focus on creative thinking and creative problem solving. This focus leads to economy rather than to waste, leads to structure rather than to chaos, leads to autonomy in learning for the pupil rather than to the cookie-cut mind.

But the reader himself must actually, autonomously define this problem, seek hypotheses, and elaborate his planning. Some possible answers are given, some attempts along the way are offered, but the reader will find out that there are many unknowns yet to challenge him, many unknowns pleading for discovery.

Activities for Creative Problem Solving in the Area of Listening-Speaking

Much of the world's work is being done through oral language. How much of the day does a child listen? How much of the day does the child talk? How much talking can he do? Teachers need to give time for children to talk about problems. Oral language is the foundation of the whole language arts program. Although no carefully controlled experiments give evidence of the validity of the following activities, all have appeared to foster growth in oral language during actual classroom trials.

Motivational or Readiness Activities to Build Subcapabilities

1. Taking a Test. Questions measuring creative and critical listening can be found in the *Sequential Tests of Educational Progress: Listening* (Educational Testing Service, 1956-59a), and may be adapted from sections of the tests that accompany the Ginn Basic Readers. Or the teacher can develop tests by looking in the index of workbooks or manuals under the topic, "creative reading." The selections can then be given orally. The following is a test selection adapted for listening from *Tom Sawyer.*

> Tom Sawyer was in the act of "mending the health" of a crack in the living room floor with some new medicine that his Aunt Polly had left for him to take. She, strictly an angel of healing, she thought, loved to try out the newest fake cure-alls—on others. The medicine tasted something like bottled fire. Suddenly his aunt's yellow cat came along, purring, eyeing the teaspoon of medicine greedily and begging for a taste. "I want to be fair," Tom said to the cat. "Don't ask for it unless you want it." But the cat was sure he wanted it. "I won't keep it from you then," said Tom as he pried the cat's mouth open and poured down the pain-killer medicine meant for Tom. One teaspoon was enough. The cat sprang a couple of yards into the air, delivered a war whoop and set off round and round the room, telling the world of his ecstasy and knocking over every flowerpot in his path. Tom's aunt entered in time to see the cat turn a few double somersaults, deliver a final hurrah and sail through the open window, carrying the rest of the flowerpots with him.

The following are sample test questions from which to pick and choose. The function of the question, or the operation that the question is designed to provoke, is given in parentheses. The questions, which ask for more than one answer, represent samples from experimental tests under construction by the author.

Question 1: What clever title could you give to this story? Or, what unusual, "way out" uses can you think of for the pain-killer medicine? (Warm-up)

Question 2: What kind of person would you say Tom's aunt was? What kind of person would you say Tom was? (Facts and conditions)

Question 3: What was Tom's problem? Were there any smaller problems or parts to this problem? What type of problem is this? (Problem definition)

Question 4: Why do you think Tom gave the medicine to the cat? (Causes)

Question 5: How do you imagine Tom felt about the way the cat acted after the cat took the medicine? How do you think Aunt Polly probably felt when she entered the room? How do you think she felt about Tom? (Appreciation, inference)

Question 6: Is there anything else you would need to know to solve this problem? How would you go about finding it out? (Missing data and search strategy)

Question 7: How would you have solved Tom's problem about the bad-tasting medicine? (Hypotheses)

Question 8: What would happen if you solved the problem that way? (Evaluation)

Question 9: What do you think will happen next? (Elaboration, prediction, evaluation, consequences)

Question 10: Does this selection remind you of another story or scene that you have heard before? Were the two authors' purposes the same? (Comparison, contrast, generalization, and transfer)

Question 11: If you could talk back to these authors what would you say? (Projective technique, elaboration)

This activity, just described, is designed to help the child put something of his own experience and thinking into listening. The child is encouraged to listen beyond the literal ideas in the passage and to voice fresh, original ideas not explicitly stated in the selection. In gathering material for a creative listening test, the teachers should probably include at least two or more of the following ingredients:

1. For comparison, two or more characters with hints of relationship, feelings, motives, problems, and descriptive states.
2. Situations with possibilities for elaboration, conducive to comparison, inference, prediction, and relationship.
3. Clues for inferences from conversations, actions, and other suggestive details.
4. Ethical values to stimulate appreciation, inferences, prediction, or analysis of relationship.
5. Literary elements for appreciation, such as, mood, symbolism, imagery, and analogy.
6. Hints as to the author's attitudes, preferences, and opinions.

The reader can elaborate this beginning list and think of other ingredients. This activity may apply to reading as well as to listening.

2. Keeping a Listening Log. Serving the purposes of motivation and readiness, another activity follows. Approach this activity as a descriptive experiment for the class, and as a way to do research other than from books. This activity may be used flexibly as a long term project or as a short term project.

Ask the pupils to make a record for a day or so of the amount of time they listen (and the amount of time they read). Encourage them to classify their listening (and reading) activities into different levels or types of listening. These levels may include marginal, purposive, creative, and critical classifications. Allow pupils the autonomy of arriving at some of their own classifications. Pupils can compare the relative amount of time they employ the two modes of language reception, listening and reading. They might compare the differing purposes, situations, and advantages of listening and reading. Through self-diagnosis, pupils may discover some individual needs, and may develop a desire for improvement of listening skill and sensitivity.

A composite look at the total class results will usually stress the importance of listening for obtaining information simply because of the sheer number of hours spent. In addition, results may point to the need for increasing opportunity and the inclination to listen creatively. (Speaking logs, reading logs, and writing logs are also revealing and could be compared.)

3. Ways to Encourage Discussion. Many teachers voice this concern, "But how do I know whether many of my pupils are listening creatively or not, when I cannot get them to open their mouths during discussion." After the prerequisite of a friendly, accepting and nonthreatening atmosphere has been established, some of the following activities to encourage verbal fluency may be tried:

1. Some children may be helped by having the safety of hiding behind a puppet theatre while they make the "puppet talk."

2. Next, an accordion-style book can be set up on a table with a hole cut out large enough for the pupil to place his face there. Around the hole can be pasted, for example, appropriate hair, hat, elephant ears, and whiskers, to fit the character that the child is presenting.

3. Next, the comfort of small, informal groups rather than the total class setting may help pupils to start verbalizing. Picking objects such as a corncob holder from a box and saying anything they like about it in a given amount of time may help. If pupils cannot think of anything to say, they may repeat the last sentence until they think of something else. (This same timed technique for fluency may be also used in creative writing.) Shy children could fill the box with "something you made all by yourself" or something "tiny-tiny." The same technique could be used in talking about a child's hobbies, or a common field trip. Children will know what they would enjoy talking about.

4. Or, given a 9″ × 12″ paper, folded so that it will stand on his desk, the child can draw a picture of something he especially likes or dislikes. He can then hold up his picture and explain it to the group.

5. Sensory expression may be the springboard to discussion stimulated by such questions as, "If you were a raindrop where would you like to fall?" or "If you were an ant, where would you like to crawl?" Pupils might describe the place, how it feels to be there, and what their reasons are for their choice.

Or the problem may be the basic need of a rich vocabulary. If a rich meaning vocabulary is being developed, pupils will feel adequate, feel a sense of power. Being "word-ready" comes from a mental closet well-stocked with words. Some of the following activities deal with quality of meaning. Other ways to encourage verbalization are given by Applegate (1963, pp.179-90).*

4. Concept-Building Anecdotes. It has been said that ability to think with an abstract quality will help children to reach beyond the concrete details of data. When children think beyond the data, they can find more lasting, more transferable, more creative solutions to their problems. The following activities are designed to help children gain facility on various levels of thought. This facility makes possible a broader representation of the world, which is helpful to creative problem solving.

Tell the pupils a story or relate an anecdote concerning some famous person who typifies the meaning of an abstract word. Give concrete, sensory details, as well as actions or functions of the person. Most children give attention to a storyteller. Moreover, when children are far removed from the listening circle, the word picture will still linger in their minds. They will remember the meaning of the devotion of Clara Barton, the versatility of Paul Revere, the ambition of Napoleon, and the persistence of Louis Pasteur. The quality of the meaning of the word will be enhanced if pupils note and group (1) the sensory details, (2) the doing or the actions, and then (3) try to think of a word or a group of words that takes in many cases, details, or instances. Taking into account many cases helps pupils achieve the symbolic or the abstract quality of thinking. Encourage a pupil committee or individual pupils to prepare these anecdotes.

5. Stupid Puppet. Puppets may be used to carry on a conversation or inquiry about a word. Children enter the world of the abstract through the door of the concrete. Through a series of comments or questions, the puppet can reveal ignorances and misconceptions, can concentrate solely on concrete, isolated, or almost irrelevant detail and can be exclusively wrapped up in what he could use the word for or do with the word. Then the puppet can be helped by the pupils and teachers to find a broader, more accurate definition. Since staying long enough to think abstractly with a word is desirable, this

* The author is indebted to the experimental teachers of the Children's Thinking Project in the Goleta School District, Goleta, California, for many of these ideas and other ideas throughout the chapter.

technique affords pleasurable concentration. Stick figures or flannel-board or paper-bag characters may be made by pupils for this activity. Examples of words that might be used are "culture," "fiercely," "conformity," "evolution," "deliberate," "relationship," "cast," or "face."

6. Forest and Trees. Another prerequisite to higher mental processes, such as creative problem solving, is the ability to organize spoken material, to "tell the forest from the trees," to distinguish between main idea and detail.

On the right side of the paper let pupils make a general outline of a forest, from an airplane view, and on the other side let them make drawings of isolated trees. As they listen to or read a selection, they can write the main ideas in the forest side, and the details on the trees. Or pupils may draw a tree placing the main ideas on the trunk, subideas on the branches, and details on the leaves. Pupils themselves, can devise stories for this purpose.

7. Sound Pictures. A prerequisite to creative listening may be improvement in sensitivity. To develop a sensitizing period in listening, ask children to close their eyes and listen for (1) sounds they know, (2) sounds they have never heard before, and (3) man-made sounds as opposed to sounds from nature. If, for example, a fire truck goes by, ask pupils to list and use original, descriptive words. (One useful record is "Sound Effects," Audio-Fidelity, DFM 3006.)

Then ask pupils to listen to a poem or story containing a mood, such as the graveyard scene from *Tom Sawyer* (gloom, suspense) or *The Little Match Girl* (sadness, pity). Ask them to notice whether or not anything happened to them as they listened. Examples of questions might be: "How did the scene make you feel?" "Did your feelings change?" "Why do you suppose you felt happy (amused, afraid)?"

Poems with much imagery, such as Cynthia A. Weber's "Come Away,"* might be listened to appreciatively:

> Come away with me to marshmallow fields
> Where dreams go on as high as the sky,
> Where wishes can reach a feathery peach
> Or swim in the clouds that roll by.

* Poems used by permission of the authors.

Come away with me to the deep blue sea
Where seashells play in the foam,
Where seahorses race at a frightening pace
And oysters build forts out of stone.

Come away with me to the green forest world
Where the evening breeze blows in your hair,
Where stars appear to smile away fear
And night sounds envelop the air.

Come away with me to meet fantasy,
A king whose court is your mind.
All the dreams you behold can be yours, I'm told,
With a youth that doesn't know time.

Another example, "Autumn Ecstasy," is found in the poems of Sara Brandon Rickey:

What fun to walk through fallen leaves!
  What crunching, crackling bliss!
How soft and damp beneath the feet
  Where frost has left its kiss!

What joy to kick and toss about
  Or plow through like a ship
And watch them scud before us as
  We make them dance and skip!

To list other activities: As the children enter the room, the teacher might play a record of bird calls. A sensitizing period of listening to poems about color (from Mary O'Neill's [1961] *Hailstones and Halibut Bones*) stimulated one pupil to write, "Green is the freshness of shine in the grass." Pupils could be encouraged to bring equipment for making sounds: a potato peeler, a toy piano, sandpaper, an egg beater. A tape may be made of sounds to be identified. Individual and group vocabulary lists may be built around words that describe sound: mumbling, munching, howling, and sloshing. A problem focus might be: "What new thing did I discover about my sense of hearing today?"

Perhaps a field trip for sound at a quiet corner and for sound at a noisy corner would illustrate for the pupils the balance of nature with respect to quiet and noise.

Activities in the Area of Listening-Speaking

1. Hitchhike Story. This activity demands a hierarchy of skills culminating in creative listening. First, the teacher needs to introduce

the concept of chain stories or "hitchhiking onto" a part of the story. Give children a story-starter or, later, ask a child to begin telling a story orally, while the other children in the group listen attentively. While the pupils are listening to the story, they must use any leftover thinking space in their minds to concoct possibilities for continuing it. But their minds must constantly return to the actual facts of the story as the speaker is presently telling it. If the pupils can handle these two tasks, attention plus invention, they will be ready to continue the story creatively when they get the signal. The teacher can simply raise his hand and point to a child, signifying that it is time to hitchhike. A sample story follows:

> Peter entered the classroom with an odd-looking box that he tried to keep hidden under his coat. How he hoped that the teacher would not ask about it! Maybe she would just think it was his lunch box. But as he started for the cloakroom door, he felt every eye on him.
>
> "Peter," said the teacher, "what is in that box. . ."

You take it from there.

2. Finish the Play. Read the first act of a play to the children. Within the framework of facts, characterization, and style have the children respond by creating and dramatizing the last act. Sources such as the *Play Index* (1953, 1963), available as reference books in most libraries, will be helpful.

3. Unfinished Problem-Stories. Stories constructed with a plot design in which the main character or characters attempt to solve a problem or to reach a goal may be used for this activity. When the story reaches a point where the problem can be inferred, the teacher should stop and elicit discussion.

The discussion may focus on many aspects of problem definition. For example, the teacher may ask directly: "What do you think is the main problem?" "Usually a big problem has many little problems connected with it. Can you think of what the smaller problems in this story are?" "First, try thinking of the details you have noticed about this problem. Second, what does the character do?"

Following these questions, the teacher, who may have been recording these responses on the board, might ask for a more encompassing view of the problem with a question such as the following: "What type of problem would you say this was?" Next, she might attempt to elicit transfer with this question: "Have you ever had a problem such as this one?"

Realizing that further facts in the story may modify ideas as to the main problem, the teacher may continue reading the story. Or the point reached may be appropriate for continuing the discussion. Then the teacher, working for a free flow, could ask questions to elicit ideas (hypotheses) for solving the problem. Other questions might concern procedures, organization in solving the problem, original search strategies, and evaluation of ideas suggested by a criterion of consequences. (See questions used about in motivational or readiness activity no.1: "Taking a Test.")

Appropriate stories for all grade levels may be found in *Reading Ladders for Human Relations,* edited by Crosby (1963). This volume groups problems found in children's literature in six ways: (1) How It Feels to Grow Up, (2) The Individual and the Group, (3) The Search for Values, (4) Feeling at Home, (5) Living with Change, and (6) Living as a Free People.

Another source of material is the set designed by Ojemann and Hawkins (1960). Story-starters frequently appear in the *NEA Journal* and children's magazines. Novels for children, such as Louisa R. Shotwell's (1963) *Roosevelt Grady,* often lend themselves to creative listening and problem-solving discussion.

Teachers can construct their own teacher's guides. These guides may consist of carefully designed and sequenced questions, questions that open up thought to many possibilities, probabilities, and causes. Children can be encouraged to create their own problem-stories to use as a springboard to creative listening and discussion. These materials represent problems with which children can become deeply involved, not trivial problems.

Evaluative Activities for Listening-Speaking

1. Evaluating a Class Discussion. So far, suggestions for the creative teaching-learning act have progressed from motivational or readiness activities intended to build supcapabilities through activities designed to help pupils to think creatively while listening and speaking. Next follow activities to test these operations or to evaluate creative behavior. Techniques for evaluating discussion are not yet fully developed. Evaluation of oral language has been largely neglected in teacher-training institutions. The following system is offered on the basis of recent experimental use.

A SCHEME FOR CODING TAPED DISCUSSION OF CREATIVE PROBLEM SOLVING

I. Problem-solving process (steps)

1 = main problem
2 = smaller problem
3 = definition
4 = type of problem
5 = hypotheses
6 = facts (evidence to solve problem)
7 = grouping and labeling facts
8 = missing data
9 = search strategy
10 = big ideas (may grow out of facts)
11 = application of ideas
12 = evaluation of hypotheses or other aspects (backed up with reasons)

II. Qualitative levels of thinking

o = original (an elaboration, an appreciation, unusualness, infrequency)
a = abstract (breadth as well as accuracy)
f = functional (child action or use in regard to object or situation)
c = concrete (sensory or other isolated detail)
e = error (misinformation—possibly stemming from careless listening, or emotional projection; overgeneralization—"always," "never"; complete irrelevancies; rigidity—a set of attitudes completely inflexible, such as, "This is the only problem, the only answer, the only way to do it")

III. Teaching strategy (discussion techniques)

W = warm up
F = focus (on topic, problem steps, or level of thinking)
RF = refocus (reiteration when pupils lose thought, drift away, do not hear)
CF = change of focus (i.e., to another problem)
CO = control (closing in thought needlessly or prematurely, premature disapproval, causing class to stray, asking too narrow a question, jumping in with the answer too soon)
X = extend ("Can you think of other reasons, Mary, . . . Joan, . . . Ted?")
L = lift (movement to a higher qualitative level of thinking, or to another step in problem solving or to transfer)
TG = teacher gives (a fact, a value-agreement or approval, a bit of information)

IV. T = transfer (to pupil's own problems, to other times, places, content areas)

V. Frequency (fluency, quantity)

On record sheets teachers can list pupils' names allowing space for coding. They can tally (1) pupil responses according to the qualitative levels of thinking above; (2) the number of times each problem step is represented; (3) the frequency of certain teaching functions (it may be illuminating to check the number of times certain strategies occur—especially controlling, refocusing, changing focus, and teacher giving); and (4) the number of times transfer occurs.

As the teacher and pupils listen to a discussion, eventually both can keep records. The teacher or even individual pupils can put a tally mark for each of the symbols in the chart above, or beside certain selected symbols as responses occur. Then the marks can be counted for a total self-evaluation, or even a group-evaluation.

The contents of the chart may be described as follows: The first group of symbols (numbers) represents steps or aspects thought to illustrate the creative problem-solving process. The second group represents certain qualities of thought. The third group designates teaching strategies of special interest for guiding a creative discussion. These strategies have been adapted from a scheme by Hilda Taba (1964). Fourth, transfer to other problems may be coded as it appears during the steps in the process, or as a result of any products or conclusions stemming from the problem-solving discussion. The major concern of this chapter, however, is with the process, not the product. Fifth, the quantity or frequency of expression may be analyzed according to these four divisions.

If desired, segments of discussion may be diagrammed in order to check pacing and sequencing of teaching strategy or questions. If preferred, the discussion can be taped, then typed as a tape-script and coded later. Of even more advantage would be videotaping. Then the full impact of nonverbal gestures and expression could be taken into account. As teachers code their own classroom discussions, they can grasp and improve the creative functions of their questions and of responses from their pupils.

Another scheme for coding class discussion is described in *Procedures for Teaching Critical Reading and Listening* (Lundsteen,

1964a). Or, as an alternative evaluative technique, the teacher may wish to give a test similar to the one described above in motivational or readiness activity no.1: "Taking a Test." However, since it is not desirable to shrink the boundaries of evaluation to testing limits, a teacher may find individual conferences to her advantage. A pupil evaluation committee could help the teacher with conferences. Or an individual activity such as the following one might be used.

2. Use of Leftover Thinking Space. This evaluative activity is especially valuable for the child who does not feel able or secure in participating in discussion. Most children will profit from the kind of note-taking that is a record of their own—not the speaker's—thoughts while listening. Before reading a selection, tell the children that they are to think while listening in the following way and take notes accordingly: "As I am listening, what ideas do I have?"

1. Old Ideas. Ideas that I already had in the past that I could relate to this talk.
2. New Ideas (including elaboration). For example, other topics I would like to investigate.
3. Questions. Questions I would like to ask the speaker.
4. Uses. Ways in which I can use the ideas presented.
5. Feelings. Feelings for and feelings against the materials or speaker.

Pupils may discover that they have trouble listening all the way to the end. They may find that they need to discipline themselves enough so that they can engage in divergent thinking while listening and still: (1) not miss too large a segment, (2) not spend all their thinking space on a parallel or never-meshing train of thought, or (3) not go completely off on an unrelated tangent, never to return to the speaker (adapted from Niles, 1955).

What Research Says to the Teacher about Listening-Speaking

What does research say to the teacher about creative listening and speaking, about creative problem solving? Very little, thus far. There is evidence that general listening ability can be improved (Pratt, 1953; Hogan, 1953; Edgar, 1961, to mention a few). There is some evidence that critical listening ability can be improved (Devine, 1961; Lundsteen, 1963, 1964a, 1964b, 1965; Lundsteen and Michael, 1966). Experimental work conducted by the writer is presently underway within the Children's Thinking Project at the University of California, Santa Barbara, with some encouraging results thus far from taped discussions of creative problem solving in grades three and six.

Much attention has been given here to activities in the areas of listening and speaking because: (1) Normal children learn, sequentially, first to listen, then to speak, next to read, and last to write. Since listening and speaking develop first, they are thought to be the keys and the bases for achievement in reading and writing. (2) Since words are tools of thought, the ability of children to think, to solve their problems creatively, is linked solidly with their development in listening, speaking, reading, and writing. (3) In spite of the fact that listening and speaking are the most frequently used means of communication, they are also the two most neglected in terms of instruction and research. (4) It is almost inevitable that activities designed to stimulate creative listening and speaking will also stimulate, be interrelated with, or transfer to creative reading and writing—especially if the teacher seeks this transfer. Differences, however, do exist between listening and reading. These differences, with methods for maximizing advantages and minimizing disadvantages, are discussed in a recent article (Lundsteen, 1964a).

Activities for Creative Problem Solving in the Area of Reading

Motivational or Readiness Activities to Build Subcapabilities

The activities suggested in the previous section, listening-speaking, can be adapted to reading. Another source of activity to build subcapabilities for creative reading is the little book by Russell and Karp (1951), *Reading Aids through the Grades.* Many of these games will foster appreciations that will enable a child to "come up to you with reading all over his hands and face." Other creative reading activities are suggested in recent articles (Lundsteen, 1964a; Strickland, 1957; Robinson, 1960).

1. Word Recognition as Problem Solving. Whenever children encounter a new word, teachers can help them meet it as a creative problem. Carroll (1964) has suggested that word recognition is a

case of problem solving, especially for young children. The teacher can work for transfer from the concepts in a problem-solving process introduced in listening and speaking to a child's problems in reading. With the tools of problem solving at his command, the child can be helped to attack his reading problems autonomously.

Carroll suggests that the process of learning to read involves the building up in the learner of a "set" to expect not only variety in the kinds of word recognition he will meet, but also ambiguity in the cues available to him. Here is an opportunity. Onc of the marks of a creative person is supposed to be his tolerance for ambiguity. Various word recognition cues are available to the child. Sometimes a cue gives an immediate answer; other times a cue suggests only a series of possibilities. The child must try out the various possibilities until a satisfying fit is made.

Carroll classified cues as follows: (1) letters; (2) letter-sound correspondences (phonic cues); (3) intra-word context cues (commonly occurring syllables, such as "un," "cept," or "ty"; (4) larger-context cues (total message—"He went sailing in a ——.")

But Carroll appears to discuss the problem-solving process in reading solely in terms of word recognition. There is more. The following activity is an example of a teacher and pupil who came to believe that the problem-solving process in reading also meant pupil autonomy in learning method.

2. How Would You Learn? One of the teachers in the Goleta School District gave this anecdote about using the creative problem-solving process with a child in the area of reading. It follows almost verbatim:

> This little boy could not read. He had repeated second grade, and I tried everything that I could. I sweated over him; I dreamed about him. So I decided, I'm just going to level with him, and called him up and said (we'll call him Dick), "Dick, you're not reading."
>
> And he said, "No."
>
> He knew he wasn't reading. I said, "I've tried everything I can to teach you. Here I've been to college, I learned everything, and still can't teach you to read. Now, how do *you* want to learn to read. How about your telling me how to teach you."
>
> He thought for a minute. Then he said, "You know that book you are reading to us, *Charlotte's Web?*"
>
> I said, "Yes, I remember."
>
> He said, "Well, I like that book. If I copy words from that book, will you tell me what they are?"

So I said, "Sure, that's swell!"

He drew the web and copied some words and brought it up to me. He said, "See." And it was just gibberish; half the words were backwards, half the letters were upside down.

I said, "What did Charlotte write in the Web this time."

He said, "I put what Charlotte put. It's in the book, look." And he pointed out the words "some pig." But he had written the phrase backward and upside down, going from right to left, instead of left to right.

Then I said, "Dick, I can read it, because you explained it to me, but the main purpose of writing is so someone else can read it as well as yourself. And we all agreed to go from left to right and write it like this."

"Oh-h-h," he said, like it was the first time he had discovered it.

So I got him a beautiful big eraser, and the rest of the year that was what he did. He would write. Then he would come up to me and say, "Which ones are straight and which ones aren't." I would mark them. He would erase them and turn them around. The paper was sometimes worn thin. But he didn't care; he was reading. Not too well, but he accepted his problem and told me how to teach him. I suppose this gave him status. Now I know he had a dominance problem which we know a great deal more about now. But this case was a departing point for me in thinking about children and reading and learning.

One conclusion that may be drawn from this anecdote is that no matter what the child's problem in reading is, it might well be approached from an attitude of creative problem solving on the part of the pupil. A focus in the language arts on creative problem solving can aid children in defining their problems within the skill areas. Then pupils can hypothesize solutions from among the many probabilities to which they are introduced by their teachers or even by themselves! Then they can plan a procedure to meet their own diagnosed needs (in Dick's case, copying from E. B. White's [1952] *Charlotte's Web*). Lastly, the pupils can help test or evaluate their operations or solutions.

To carry the idea of a set for problem solving further, as a child meets difficult techniques that an author used in writing, such as, flashback or revelation or stream of consciousness, he can rely on some of his problem-solving skills that he has been developing within the language arts. Moreover, as a child meets a personal problem he may more readily go for help to books that deal with the same human problem. Bibliotherapy—or getting the right book to the right child at the right time—may work better within the context of a language arts program focused on problem solving.

Evaluating Activities for Reading

In addition to certain questions or sections in standardized tests, such as those designed for the Ginn Readers (1964-65), and suggestions for activities in Russell's (1961) chapter 14, an excellent pamphlet (McCullough, 1959) has detailed how a very simple story can become creative reading. The author classified and gave examples of different questions that might well be used for evaluative purposes.

What Research Says to the Teacher about Reading

McCullough (1957) found a positive relationship, though not an extremely high one ($r = .47$), between tests of literal reading comprehension and of creative reading (seeing relationships, drawing conclusions, and passing judgments). She concluded that the two types of reading may involve a common factor, probably an ability to get facts. But the relationship between the scores did not justify testing children on only one type of measure.

The present writer (Lundsteen, 1963) found a similar relationship ($r = .58$) between general reading ability, as measured by the test of reading in the *Sequential Tests of Educational Progress: Reading* (Educational Testing Service, 1956-59b), and a test of creative problem solving. But an examination (Lundsteen and Michael, 1966) of the relationship between scores on qualitative levels of thinking within the problem-solving test (abstract, functional, and concrete qualities) and scores on the above measure of reading revealed that the main substance of the relationship came from the abstract quality of thinking ($r = .50$), the relationship with functional modes of thinking was very low ($r = .11$), and children who thought about problems very concretely did not appear to do well in reading ($r = -.49$).

Furthermore, the quality of the reading material for stimulating children's thinking appeared to be of importance. Though caution must be used in generalizing from this one study, it appeared that more abstract thinking was elicited from third grade children when the material was challenging and complex and filled with possibilities for high-level thought, than when the material was less challenging, merely involving definitions of single words.

If the central purpose of American education is to teach children to think, and if reading is thinking, then some reading programs with very limited materials (only words or short, trivial paragraphs) may not be helping teachers to accomplish these purposes. Instead of a narrow purpose, employing a limited number of objectives for each reading activity, teachers might accomplish a great deal more with more adequate materials. As Horace Mann once said, starting reading with letters is like practicing eating without food. In the rush to find a newer, better phonic-linguistic method, there is danger that a hard-won lesson—the most valid concept of reading—may be lost: Reading is thinking and should include all of the higher mental processes.

> Think before reading.
> Think while reading.
> Think after reading.
> Think beyond reading.
> (Russell, 1961, p.112.)

In experimental training studies, Clark (1959), Nardelli (1953), and Neff and Collins (1963) had some success in improving creative reading. In a carefully planned study Wolf and others (1967), using children in grades one through six, improved critical reading abilities. In a recent review of research in bibliotherapy, Witty (1964) mentioned several studies which appeared to indicate some value from using bibliotherapy with children.

Activities for Creative Problem Solving in the Area of Writing

In connection with other areas of the language arts, many activities for creative writing have already been suggested. These earlier activities represent contributions to development of subcapabilities for writing as well as for speaking, listening, and reading. They included games for fluency, for "warming up," for building vocabulary and concepts, for sensitizing, and for organizing. Few children write better than they speak. Teachers should seek transfer to writing from most of the activities already mentioned.

If all the following factors are present: if the child is motivated, if he has the subskills, if the class climate and environmental conditions up to that time are favorable, if he is able to retrieve ideas, images, and memories from storage, and, perhaps of utmost importance, if he feels free to act, free to write on his own, then—creativity. But when any one factor is impoverished, the appearance of creative writing will be doubtful.

Moreover, if the child is helped to see the task of writing creatively as his own problem, then it is likely that he will try to improve specific lacks with greater zeal. He will make it his business to keep a writer's notebook or envelope. He will make it his business to collect sensory words to induce his reader to feel, hear, touch and see, and to make him think and wonder. He will even make it his business to revise. Any treatment of creative writing in isolation from a larger conceptual scheme of aptitudes and development in children is of little significance.

Perhaps, as has been said, creative writing appears when a person with necessary skills has a deep concern with a problem over a period of time. Teachers need to give time to think. Woodfin (1966) found children wanted days, even weeks, to complete her purely voluntary writing tasks. The main concern of this section will be getting children to grasp the problem of thinking as a writer thinks.

Motivational or Readiness Activities to Build Subcapabilities

1. Getting in the Author's Skin. Literature should not be omitted from the lives of elementary school children. Ample thinking time should be devoted to such outstanding expressions of values. As a novel is read and discussed in class, parts of the discussion can turn to certain aspects of writing and to the particular author's style.

For example, the teacher might question, "Does the writer make you see pictures when I read this?" "What?" "How?" "What did you notice that he did?" "How could you do that when you write?"

Again, to use *Roosevelt Grady* as an example, one of the characters in this book makes a story for his class, a story within a story (p.102). The teacher might ask, "Why do you think the children enjoyed the boy's story?" "How did he use the animals that he had 'planted' earlier in the story to solve the main character's problem?" "What else did you notice about the story?" "How could this be done with other stories?" "Let's try to make a story using some of these techniques."

Or the teacher might turn attention to symbolism and question, "What do you think the toy horse that the boy carried around in a kerchief from place to place stood for, actually, in the eyes of the author?" "How might a symbol serve a purpose in a story that you might write?"

In turning attention to theme, the teacher might ask, "If the author could say only one sentence which would take in as much as possible about his book, what might he say?" "About what big idea do you think he was writing even though he never came right out and said it?" "How did he get this idea across to you?" "Let's each think of a big idea that we feel is valuable and try to write about it so that we 'get it across' to each other without flatly saying it."

CAUTION: Note that the suggested questions attempt to lead children to discover elements in a writer's thinking, such as symbolism, imagery, and theme. In teaching for creativity, a teacher would avoid saying, "Children, there are three important concepts to notice in literature; they are (1) symbolism, (2) imagery, (3) analogy." Also, any questioning should usually stop while the children are still interested and eager to discuss.

Children may enjoy writing in the various styles of authors. For example, a child might try writing in the style of Mark Twain, using his conversation techniques with child characters, or his satire on superstition. Then pupils could try writing the same story in the style of a different author. In storing ideas and skills, in developing flexibility, the child is building toward his own writing style.

2. Getting in the Character's Skin. One teacher who had been using Shotwell's book, *Roosevelt Grady*, as a stimulus for creative problem solving through discussion, asked the children to do the following: They were to pretend to be Roosevelt Grady at the very moment he was settling down in the hammock to fall asleep. She asked these questions, "How do you feel? What are your thoughts? What is life like for you?" A pupil's response in writing follows:

> I'm glad. I have a bed of my own. I can roll over, kick my legs and stretch. I can really find out what an attic is. I can go lay on my hammock any time. If I don't want to hit my head on the attic ceiling, I can stoop down and glide around like an Indian. I can run up and down the stairs. It's kind of like the house in Mama's and my secret.
>
> But in a way I'm also sad. When I look out the window, there's the beanfield. No school. Why couldn't we stay longer where we were before? Now I'll probably never find out what happens to the little leftover number. Darn those machines. They started it all. . .
>
> Not done yet.

Activities in the Area of Writing

1. Story Guide. One teacher in the primary grades found this guide useful for stimulating creative writing:

1. Where is your character? (Setting)
2. What does your character look like?

3. What does the character do?
4. What does the character like?
5. What does the character dislike?

   NOTE: What anyone says he likes or dislikes builds a picture of that person. Why he likes or dislikes it adds a motive. Such lists from the class may provide pupils with valuable details for character portrayal.
6. What problem does the character have?
7. If the character is "in a fix," how does he get out of it?

To arouse interest and reduce the load of writing, pupils may contribute the first six aspects in groups, trade until they have most of the story, and then finish the ending, question 7, themselves.

An excellent source of activities designed to motivate creative writing is the book by Applegate (1963). Given adequate development, children will need little stimulation from the teacher other than the provision of time for creative writing. The difficult task is the diagnosing of capabilities and underlying factors and the provision of developmental activities designed for individual pupil needs. From the many evaluative scales of children's writing mentioned in the literature, two appear to be most relevant.

Evaluative Activities for Writing

Two scales which should be useful to the elementary school teacher in evaluating creative compositions are by Carlson (1961) and by Yamamoto (1964). The Carlson Analytical Originality Scoring Scale deals with five categories: story structure, novelty, emotion, individuality, and style of stories. "Story structure" contains 6 items rated on a 0 to 5 point scale, such as novelty of title and unusual ending. "Novelty" contains 14 aspects, such as unusual punctuation, ingenuity in solving situations, and recombination of ideas in unusual relationships. "Emotion" has four items, such as unusual sincerity in expressing personal problems and unusual ability to identify self with problems of others. "Individuality" includes individual facility in beautiful writing as one of three aspects. "Style of stories" has six aspects, which include highly fantastic central idea or theme and fantastic creatures, objects, or persons.

In the Yamamoto measure of imaginative writing, pupils are instructed to write a story in fifteen minutes after they have selected a topic from a list provided or have made up a similar title of their own.

The topics, of an unusual nature, were designed to provoke pupil interest. Seven scores are derived from the stories: Organization, Sensitivity, Originality, Imagination, Psychological Insight, Richness, and a total score.

1. Using Evaluative Scales. Teachers might profit most from examining several scales, such as those just mentioned, and developing their own check list.

2. Developing Evaluative Scales. As pupils and teachers, together, notice various aspects of creative writing in the work of pupils and in the work of skilled authors, they could develop their own standards for taste and for creativity.

What Research Says to the Teacher about Writing

Generally, the picture that research in creative writing gives is somewhat confused. Studies are relatively scarce and many give no clear-cut answers to the questions that they raise, especially when results deal only with total groups. Some important contributions, however, have been made by the following investigators.

Carlson (1961) found that a multi-sensory technique of motivation with a variety of verbal and concrete stimuli provoked more originality and fluency than did a technique which merely provided interesting story titles. Littwin (1935) also found that a method of teaching creative writing in which he emphasized perception through the various senses gave results superior to those emphasizing picture descriptions and using literary models. Torrance (1962) attempted to develop creative thinking through language arts activities. Over a three-month period, he found that the pupils of teachers who used large numbers of his creative activities produced significant growth in creative writing. Clark (1954) reported, after teaching creative writing to sixth grade pupils for a year, that the best technique appeared to be using topics which encouraged children to write about personal experience and feelings. Moe (1956) found success from a method which encouraged pupils to write about problems of human relations.

On the whole, the picture of our current knowledge of teaching for creative endeavor in the language arts resembles the tip of an iceberg with two thirds of the mass not yet even visible. Research has not yet shown the value of providing what kinds of environment, of fostering which kinds of skills, under what sort of attitude, and of using what kind of teaching strategies for what particular type of pupil. Optimistically, however, because estimations are possible, knowing about the tip of an iceberg is better than not knowing anything at all. More research needs to be done, especially on sequencing of skill-building techniques.

Conclusion

In order to help pupils learn to listen, speak, read, and write at ever higher levels of creativity, this chapter has suggested a focus on problem solving, a focus intended to encourage transfer and interrelationships. Without this focus, the language arts were likened to snakes in a barrel. With this focus, teaching for creative endeavor was defined as an emphasis on creative problem solving leading to autonomy in learning on the part of the pupil.

The teaching task implied is a creative problem for the reader. To help out, activities and their rationale were described for improving creativity in each language arts area. Usually these activities were grouped as motivational or readiness activities, process activities, and evaluative activities. Also given were suggestions for possible transfer from one area to another and a sampling of what research says to the teacher.

Many of the activities stressed the neglected area of listening. But for the teacher to know what lies behind the quick nod or head shake, the perceptive twinkle, the eager gleam while listening requires that the child express his ideas. Then occurs the full circle in the language arts from reception—reading and listening—through creative restructuring and problem solving to expression—speaking and writing.

What difference does this focus make? Perhaps this emphasis will not remake the world, will not restructure the "mass society," or will not even improve the nation's educational system. But perhaps the quick nod or shake, the twinkle and the gleam will occur with more frequency if the thinking process of autonomous and creative problem solving threads its way through the "barrel of snakes." Then for the pupil, there they are, the four areas of the language arts—happily interrelated.

CHAPTER 9

English Composition and Literature in the Secondary School

by

WILLIAM GEORGIADES AND
JOAN J. MICHAEL

Professor of Education and chairman of the Department of Secondary Education at the University of Southern California and associate director of the National Association of Secondary School Principals Internship Program, William Georgiades holds the A.B. degree from Upland College in English and the social sciences, the M.A. degree from Claremont Graduate School in curriculum and English, and the Ed.D. degree from UCLA in curriculum. He began his teaching career in Whittier, California, as an English teacher. Other teaching posts have been at Brigham Young University, the University of Hawaii, and the Institute of Child and Youth Study at the University of Maryland. Recently, as a Fulbright scholar and lecturer, Dr. Georgiades worked with problems of secondary education in twenty nations in Europe and Asia. He is a consultant on curriculum innovation and change to numerous school districts, state departments, and county offices throughout the United States.

Joan Michael, who is assistant professor of Psychological Foundations at the San Fernando Valley State College, did undergraduate work at Pomona College and at the University of Southern California, where she received her A.B. degree in psychology with a minor in English. After completing her M.S. degree, she earned her Ph.D. in educational psychology with a specialty in research design and statistics at the University of Southern California. While a graduate student, she consulted with numerous school districts on evaluation problems and also served as assistant editor for the book review section, validity studies section, and the computer and accounting machines section of Educational and Psychological Measurement.

SINCE THE AVERAGE SECONDARY SCHOOL STUDENT is required to take at least three years of English, and since the nature and quality of the English curriculum is reflected in almost all other classes, teaching the composition and literature for creative endeavor would seem to lie at the very heart of all teaching at the secondary level. Unfortunately, however, most of the research on creativity has been laboratory oriented and has had little impact upon actual classroom practice. Occasionally, the secondary school has offered noncreative courses in creative writing, but for the most part creative endeavor in the English classroom appears to have been the exception rather than the rule.

The barriers to teaching English with an emphasis on creative expression have been both external and internal. Externally, the amount of feedback from the lay community relating to the English curriculum has probably been in excess of that found in any other academic area taught by the secondary school. There is always someone prepared to explain precisely why Johnny cannot read, spell, or write a composition. Everyone is an expert on this topic! Internally, the existence of moth-eaten, highly structured lesson plans, which "served me well in 1940, so why should I prepare new ones now?", has further stifled creative expression in English. There appears to have been a comparatively small effort to effect the establishment of conditions in English classrooms which would encourage the emergence of creativity among the students. The focus of this chapter is on the creation of such an environment.

The purpose of this chapter is to define conditions which produce a creative environment for teaching English composition and literature. To make these definitions as clear as possible, specific examples of programs which have been observed or developed by the writers are included.

Since classroom size and structure have received so much emphasis in recent years, specific suggestions have been offered which would apply to three types of classrooms: (1) conventional size classes, (2) assembly groups, and (3) inquiry groups. It is recognized, however, that many of the examples which have been listed under a specific category could be adapted to other classroom situations.

Prerequisite Environmental Conditions

If creative programs are to emerge in the teaching of English, administrative leadership at both the district and the local school levels will need to create an environment in which "freedom to experiment" is a dominant characteristic. If the attitude prevails that "we are presently meeting the creative needs of children in English and no changes need be made," one can hardly expect creative endeavor on the part of teachers.

Probably the most important person in determining such a climate is the building principal. With him lies the responsibility for selecting the chairman and the staff of the English department. Through this act the tone is set. If, on the one hand, he chooses individuals who are both talented and creative and in turn provides incentive for them to exercise their gifts, the results are likely to be positive. If, on the other hand, he does not select such people or does not encourage and support his teachers as they attempt to cultivate the emergence of creativity, negative results can be anticipated. Hence, the writers fully realize that the success or failure of any suggestion which they propose in this chapter is greatly dependent upon the climate for teaching and learning fostered by the respective administrators.

Conventional Size Classes

For many generations class sizes in English have fallen within the broad range of 25 to 35 pupils. Numerous recent recommendations have suggested that smaller classes be developed in the English subject area, but any progress toward such changes will tend to be excruciatingly slow. Consequently, if creative programs in English are to develop, they will need to do so in most schools within the existing conventional class size.

Among the weaknesses characterizing classes of 25 to 35 is the lack of adequate opportunity for in-depth discussion of literary concepts and ideas. There is increasing evidence to support the theory that discussion groups of 10 to 14 provide the best possibilities for involvement of each individual. Thus, the conventional size classroom may be too large. Another common weakness mentioned is the problem of identifying the particular compositional deficiencies of each pupil in classes of 25, 30, to 35. If one accepts the point of view that creativeness must be nurtured and that it is primarily divergent activity rather than convergent, it then becomes essential that the English teacher develop an environment of creativity for each individual in the classroom.

Specific examples of creative work in English in conventional size classroom which the writers have observed include:

Example 1: Grade level: 11; class size: 34; *California Test of Mental Maturity* (*CTMM*) range: 90-140; facilities and materials: conventional; socioeconomic status (SES): middle and upper middle class.

The teacher opened the class by discussing a current international problem that had received prominence in the morning paper and then talked about the ways in which various people might interpret the events of the day. Discussion moved from a concern with international crises to the ways in which people adapt themselves to live in a world which is continually fraught with crises. Such sources of strength as religion, philosophy, and the role of humor were mentioned. The teacher then held up a picture taken from the series in *Life* Magazine entitled "Miscellany." In addition to the laughter which this photograph produced, there was a more serious question of how various people would interpret the circumstances depicted. This discussion of creative photography led to a discussion of creative writing, and the conditions which must exist for such work. It was agreed that one could not be obsessed with structures, grammar, punctuation, and many of the basic rules relating to our written language if one is to write creatively. There was general consensus that an undue awareness of the rules of writing could impede the flow of creative thought. Following the discussion each pupil drew a different picture from a portfolio collected by the teacher over a period of years. Records were used to create a musical background. The pupils were asked to describe the emotion or incident depicted in the picture from which the actual story of the incident had been cut.

An important point to note is that the teacher had spent considerable time creating a climate for creative writing. Moreover, the discussion had started at the point where the pupils were at the moment, at a point of vital current interest. The writers have noted that many times the development of the environment will take more time than the actual creative act itself. The end result of this example was that a number of highly provocative, creative papers were written. Several pupils were eventually identified whose previous work had given no indication of potential for creative writing.

Example 2. Grade level: 10; class size: 40; *CTMM* range: 85-120; facilities and materials: conventional; SES: upper lower class.

At the beginning of the class the teacher circulated mimeographed copies of a poem which had appeared in *Harper's Magazine*. This poem focused upon the assassination of President John F. Kennedy, an event which was very real in the minds of these tenth graders. The teacher wisely sought to involve the peer leader of the group in the reading of the poem. In this way much of the negativism which boys at the adolescent age tend to feel toward poetry was offset. Following the reading, discussion took place about the contemporary meaningfulness of poetry. Many of the pupils were surprised to find that this mode of communication had meaning for their daily lives. It was then suggested that each pupil take an event in his life, such as crossing the street against a red light, bargaining with his or her kid sister to do the dishes, and use the event in the writing of a poem. It was emphasized that the focus for the poem did not have to be a world-shattering event, but rather should be something with meaning and significance for the individual. By the close of the class period the pupils had started to write simple poetry centered around a particular theme in their own life experiences.

As in example 1, the teacher once again had started with a dynamic, traumatic event which the pupils themselves had experienced. Many of the boys and girls in this class, during the poetry unit, not only developed a new attitude toward poetry, but also found to their amazement that, somewhere within, a creative spark existed which enabled them to write poetry.

Example 3. Grade level: 9; class size: 32; *CTMM* range: 80-105; facilities and materials: conventional; SES: lower middle and upper lower classes.

Required reading at the ninth grade level in this suburban high school included *Julius Caesar.* The problems of teaching Shakespeare to adolescents whose reading scores are below average have plagued English teachers for generations. In the initial stages the teacher in this school decided to focus on the use of media other than the printed page. During the first several meetings of the class a film depicting the *Julius Caesar* story was used. Careful planning and discussion preceded and followed the use of the film. Subsequently, Orson Welles' records of *Julius Caesar* were played in class. Discussions took place relating to the social habits and customs of people in the time of Caesar as well as to the means of warfare which were employed by the Roman army. Each pupil assumed a written or craft project. Some chose to write a paper about Shakespeare or about some aspect of Roman life depicted in *Julius Caesar.* Others chose to make small wooden chariots and Roman dolls. Such work required considerable investigation and use of library sources. Many of the girls spent hours reading about Roman dress while the boys frantically sought descriptions of Roman chariots and other Roman artifacts.

After approximately two and one-half weeks of such activity a copy of *Julius Caesar* in printed form was given to each pupil. While there was some vocabulary difficulty, the plot and the story were so well known by this time that no serious problems were encountered in the actual reading of the play. This use of divergent approaches in an attempt to cultivate an appreciation for classical literature appeared to be quite successful in provoking interest on the part of boys and girls who did not have a strong literary background.

Assembly Groups

In recent years many American secondary schools have developed programs in large-group instruction in English. These groups customarily range in size from 70 to 110 pupils. Such large groups make it possible for teachers to function in their areas of specialization within the English curriculum. One of the strengths of the large assembly groups has been that it has enabled a teacher with a specialization in grammar to teach grammar to a large class, while those with certain specializations in literature may do likewise. This more effective utilization of teacher specialization has been one of the results of large-group instruction. A weakness frequently mentioned in the large group is the danger of impersonalization and an unwillingness to recognize individual differences. Other limiting factors with the large group include the necessity for adequate room space and the need for certain pieces of audiovisual equipment. Unless such provisions are made, a high percentage of the pupils may lose contact with the presentation.

Example. Grade level: 9; class size: 106; *CTMM* range: 95-130; facilities and materials: large classroom with a loud speaker, overhead projector, and adjacent small-group discussion rooms; SES: middle and upper middle class.

During the previous assembly meeting the pupils had written one paragraph in reaction to a film presentation of *Oliver Twist.* It was emphasized that this paragraph was later to be analyzed, but that the focus at the moment should be primarily on reaction. Time was then allowed for revision with concentration on form. Consequently, all pupils wrote the paragraph twice, first, with emphasis on their own emotions and feelings and, second, in terms of appropriate form and compositional structure. When the group of 106 assembled, the teacher began to discuss some of the strengths and weaknesses of the paragraphs which had been written. He then proceeded to project on a screen selected compositions written the previous day. Errors in grammar and format were noted and discussed by the teacher by choosing papers which were illustrative of typical problems. In this way 106 people were directly involved in the correction of selected paragraphs. The entire assembly group were able to work directly from their own materials rather than from those which had been prepared by the teacher.

Although in group fashion, this assignment focused attention upon individual student's needs and deficiencies. That the interest level in this class was appreciably higher than might have been anticipated could be partially attributed to the direct use of pupil materials. The level of participation was quite high, since the pupils were occupied with a written experience at their desks and a visual experience through the presentation by the teacher at the front of the room. Following the large-group presentation, the class broke into inquiry groups of 12 to 15 pupils.

Inquiry Groups

Inquiry or small groups have been developing in school systems throughout the United States and particularly in the area of the English curriculum. The development of such groups has tended to accompany assembly or large-group instruction. Larger groups with team teaching create a framework which makes possible the organization of small discussion and production groups. It is in these groups that creative potential can be more readily identified and cultivated.

Example 1. Grade level: 9; class size: 12-15; *CTMM* range: 95-130; facilities and materials: small seminar rooms adjacent to regular classroom; SES: middle and upper middle class.

These inquiry groups had spent the previous period in the large group just described discussing composition problems. The first step which the teacher took in the small group was to have each pupil write a topic sentence around which a paragraph could be structured at a later time. The topic sentences were then discussed by the group of 12 to 15 pupils. Considerable interaction took place as to whether the topic sentences actually communicated the intentions of the writers and as to what various methods could be utilized to develop these sentences into paragraphs. Following the discussion, the pupils were asked to write a paragraph around the topic sentence using two or more of the methods discussed. The teacher circulated among the group and provided direct assistance to each pupil on questions of format and grammar.

Although this may seem to the reader to be standard procedure, the writers believe that creativity will be facilitated if the pupils learn certain conventional procedures around which to structure their work. Once they have learned these basic rules, then they may invest their energies in creative writing. It cannot be stressed too strongly that true creativity will probably be more likely to emerge if some guidance and assistance is afforded by the teacher.

Example 2. Grade level: 12; class size: 15; *CTMM* range: 115-145; facilities and materials: conventional; SES: upper lower and lower middle classes.

This group was a double-period class of culturally deprived, but talented youngsters. Its purpose was to enrich their cultural backgrounds and to assist the pupils in better understanding the relationships between some of the great literary works of our world and the other humanities including music and art. Reading had been taking place concerning the Greek society, both ancient and modern. The pupils were becoming increasingly conversant with *The Republic* as well as with the contemporary poetry of George Sefaris. A former Fulbright grantee to Greece was invited to show slides and to discuss the development of Greek society, sculpture, and art. Following the presentation and discussion, the pupils proceeded to write a paper summarizing their impressions of Greek society based on both their readings and class discussion. They were urged to focus on the threads of influence found in the American society today which might conceivably be traced to ancient Greece. In susequent weeks this particular group selected a theme and wrote a play growing out of their study of ancient and modern Greece.

Lectures were not characteristic of the methodology used with this class. The focus was on the participation of each individual and on interaction rather than on one-way communication. The creative work in English which emerged from this group is all the more spectacular when one is aware of the fact that the homes in the community are in a manufacturing district with the large majority of the parents being employed in unskilled and semiskilled occupations.

Independent Study

Independent study has been a companion development to large assembly groups and small inquiry groups. Unfortunately many programs have interpreted independent study as a conventional study hall. This is not the intent of the independent study concept. Rather, independent study appropriately utilized can provide opportunities for individual creative work. The lack of both adequate resources and working stations has plagued many districts in their attempts to develop such programs. Schools such as Marshall High School in Portland, Oregon, and Troy High School in Fullerton, California, have created laboratories in mathematics, English, the social sciences, and the sciences in an attempt to provide an environment for individual creative work. Such laboratories have customarily included in addition to printed materials, filmstrips, records, tapes, and numerous other materials to be used under the direction of the teacher aide. Since creativity is highly individualistic, it appears to the writers that independent study is an area which needs careful exploration and utilization in English programs, if creativity is to emerge.

Example 1. A ninth grade boy enrolled in freshman English was spending approximately two hours a week in independent study working on a project consisting of an illustrative series taken from ideas received through the reading of Jack London's *Sailor on Horseback*. The objective was a pictorial presentation of the theme of the book. Since no special facilities existed, the studying and illustrating were done in the library. There were ample written references but few materials of an audio or visual type. Since several other pupils were working on projects at the same time, they did occasionally confer and exchange ideas. This particular project had been not only well defined but also thoroughly discussed by the teacher and the student. While the pupil involved fell within the normal range of intelligence, he had special artistic talent which the English teacher permitted him to use as a medium of expression in the interpretation of literature.

Example 2. The project in which this twelfth grade girl was involved focused on literary criticism. This pupil, who was a member of a class in English literature, chose as an area of special interest the works of Dryden. Under the supervision of a teacher aide, who was an English major working toward a teaching credential at a nearby university, this pupil spent one period a week in the English laboratory. During this time she analyzed and criticized various Dryden works from her own viewpoint as well as synthesized various existing critiques of this author's works. Through the use of visual materials and printed resources and under the direction of the aide, a level of understanding and insight was gained which would hardly have been possible if the pupil had been a member of a class of 32.

Example 3. During a study of poetry in a tenth grade English class, a particular pupil developed a keen interest and exhibited some talent in the writing of poetry. Consequently, she chose to spend one hour a week working on the development of her own poetry under the guidance of the classroom teacher and the librarian. The pupil frequently used the listening room in the library to establish a mood for writing poetry. Once she and the teacher had agreed upon a theme, suggestions were made as to the kinds of music and art which might provide appropriate background for writing poetry. By the close of the school year, the pupil had written a small book of poems, several of which received wide circulation through a student publication.

Example 4. Following the discussion of the works of Edgar Allan Poe, an eleventh grade boy of above average intelligence selected independent study time to produce a series of tapes in which he presented extracts from some of the works of Poe and discussed their meaning for contemporary life. These tapes were so prepared as to be of use to other pupils who wanted to know more about Poe than that which was customarily included in the curriculum. This boy did most of his work in an individual study carrel in the library. The taping was done in an adjacent listening-recording room.

Numerous other independent study ideas can and will emerge if the facilities and time are made available to the students and the teachers. The writers wish to stress at this point, however, that the students will not necessarily be creative if they are "relegated to a corner and told to write creative themes or poetry or whatever." Some direction and guidance by the teaher will be required in independent study as well as in group situations.

Evaluation

All efforts of the classroom teacher to cultivate creative programs in English can be virtually negated by a system of evaluation which emphasizes the noncreative facet of English to the exclusion of the creative. Some thoughts on the evaluation of these programs, arising from the writers' experiences, are as follows:

First, unless careful consideration is given in advance to the purpose and type of evaluation needed, creative English programs are likely to flounder for lack of direction.

Second, once specific objectives, stated behaviorally, have been developed, creative lesson plans can be implemented to accomplish these goals.

Third, it is essential that teachers and administrators concur on both objectives and instruments which will be used to assess creative programs.

Fourth, affective as well as cognitive objections must be kept in mind. If creative English programs are measured with a cognitive focus alone, many deep and significant insights and attitudes which accompany such a curriculum may be overlooked.

Fifth, the horizontal as well as the vertical aspects of measurement must also be considered. Creative attempts in English must be viewed over a longer time cycle than one or two semesters. Many changes, especially in the affective domain, cannot really be identified in a short period of time.

Sixth, and probably the most elusive of all to assess, efforts must be made to determine whether the creative potential developed in English spreads to other aspects of the curriculum. For example, if a student's potential for creativity is cultivated and emerges in the English program, will the effects of this emergence be felt in other facets of his school life? Can creativity be contained within departmental lines?

The preceding thoughts for evaluation are somewhat of a departure from the cognitive focus to which our schools are generally committed. Innovative programs demand not only creative teachers and administrators in their initial organization and structuring, but also a high level of creativity in the development of the means of evaluation.

Since creativity is primarily an individual matter, evaluation must focus upon the individual. Group testing of one type or another may be useful, but the real measure of the strength of the creative English program will of necessity be oriented toward the individual. Caution must be exercised in the use of measuring devices based on group behavior; for if the individual is expected to be creative, he may not fall within the framework of the well-defined group mode of writing or interpreting literature. It is highly doubtful that existing standardized tests in composition and literature measure beyond the level of the cognitive domain. While these tests may have some significance for college admissions, they have little merit in identifying the creative individual.

The evaluative examples for composition and literature which follow can be adapted to conventional classes, assembly groups, inquiry groups, or independent study situations.

Composition

A concrete illustration of an attempt to evaluate creative work in composition was observed in a ninth grade English class mentioned earlier. Various pictures from *Life* Magazine had been used with a musical background to establish an environment for creative writing. The evaluative process did not focus on the specifics of sentence structure and grammar, but dealt with the originality of response to specific pictures. The emphasis was upon the ability to create word pictures rather than upon language structure.

Literature

An evaluative program in literature was observed in a ninth grade class studying *Julius Caesar.* The class consisted of ninth graders whose reading scores were two to three years below grade level. The teacher had emphasized the meaning of Shakespeare's writing to the world in which these adolescents found themselves. The teacher selected quotations from *Julius Caesar* and asked the pupils to tell what significance they might have for an ordinary citizen in twentieth-century America. The evaluation focused upon the application of literature rather than upon its history or upon simple memorization of quotations. As contemporary events were discussed throughout the year, references were made to *Julius Caesar.* Frequently, pupils far outperformed their peers in their grasp and understanding of the play as determined by teacher-made tests at the close of the school year. In addition, their attitudes toward Shakespeare, as measured by a teacher-made attitudinal scale, were definitely more positive than were those of their counterparts in other classes.

Another example of evaluation observed by the writers was in the teaching of poetry to a tenth grade class. For the most part these adolescents came from an upper lower class background and had negative predispositions toward poetry. The teacher did not examine this class on the structure of poetry, including meter, rhyme schemes, metaphors, and similes, but rather focused upon the affective significance of the poetry to the individual pupil. Each pupil was asked to select three of five poems and to describe what emotion the poet was trying to convey. They were then asked to give positive or negative reactions toward the poetry selected and to substantiate their feelings with specific reasons generated by the poem itself. No "I don't like it because I don't like poetry" answers were acceptable. The teacher graded these papers on originality, sincerity, and understanding of the meaning or meanings of the poem or poems chosen. Because of the nature of the student population involved, the teacher did not grade the student down if he missed the major significance of the poem provided he made some attempt to delineate the meaning and to explain in a reasonable manner why he liked or disliked the poem.

Since literature has an affective significance which is equally as important as cognitive understandings, creative means must be sought to measure its emotional or affective impact. It is the writers' sincere hope that teachers of English will devote increased attention to this facet of learning and that their evaluation as well as their teaching will recognize the importance of creative endeavor.

What of the Future?

The structure of the English classroom in terms of size and modular pattern will undoubtedly continue to change. Some of the changes will provide additional time for creative planning and thinking and a reduction in many of the nonprofessional duties of English teachers. With the widespread introduction of flexible scheduling and the use of paraprofessional aides, English teachers of the future will spend fewer hours in the classroom and larger amounts of time with individuals and small groups.

There will continue to be a redefinition of English so that the English teacher is no longer asked to be everything from a speech pathologist to a structural linguist. This refinement will make possible a higher level of specialization in teacher assignments. The English teacher of the future is likely to function mainly in one or two of the many areas which now comprise the English curriculum. The generalist English teacher of today will give way to the specialist English teacher of tomorrow. The writers believe that specificity of assignment could encourage a higher level of creative endeavor on the part of English teachers. While our society will continue to demand excellence in English teaching, more and more premium will be placed on divergence in achieving this excellence.

CHAPTER 10

Foreign Languages

by

JESSE O. SAWYER

Of Norwegian descent, Jesse O. Sawyer is a graduate of Leland, Illinois, high school and St. Olaf College. Turning from Scandinavian studies to linguistics, he attended the University of Wisconsin and received his Ph.D. at the University of California, Berkeley. For some time he taught English as a foreign language on the Berkeley campus, where he is now director of the Berkeley Language Laboratory, of which he was the founder, and also lecturer in the Department of Linguistics. His present interests include one or two American Indian languages and some of the languages of Sumatra.

The Place of Tradition

AT FIRST BLUSH, the idea of creativity in learning a language seems slightly incongruous. It has come to be accepted in recent years that speaking a language is a skill and that this skill is acquired by long and not always happy hours of drill and practice. To the extent that this is true, the study of language differs from the disciplines with which it shares the center of the arts and sciences curriculum, and it is probable that the place of language studies in our schools today depends not on the fact that studying a language is a process comparable to studying history or mathematics but on the nonlinguistic, and from this point of view irrelevant, fact that language holds the special place it does in the work of the world.

It is in this problem—the place of teaching a skill in the midst of the arts and sciences—that we find a partial explanation for the perpetual struggle of traditional language teaching to reassert itself. Traditional language teaching oriented around an intellectual examination of the structure of a language and assisted by exercises in translating literary texts into and out of the new language was indeed, and is still, a subject matter appropriate in manner and dignity to the place of esteem language holds in the curriculum, and comparable to those other studies central to liberal education. Another reason for the persistence of the traditional view lies in the fact that most of us were trained in the traditional approach to language. Not until the mid-fifties was it possible for any other view of language to be taught in our primary and secondary schools, and the last teachers to receive some part of their language education in traditional contexts will be retiring around the year 2000.

The first job of the creative language teacher today is to know why he should not lapse into this traditional manner of presenting language, why he must avoid talking about the language he is teaching and instead teach the language. The reasons are largely a matter of history.

The revolution which has taken place in language teaching is now almost a century old, although we still happily label our classroom practice the "new method." No less absurd is the label, the "linguistic method," for linguistics, as an independent discipline, dates from the second quarter of the present century, almost half a century after the methods of language teaching we now consider acceptable were becoming current. The existence of the so-called "linguistic method" comes not from the development of anything particularly new, but from the fact that from the very beginning linguists naturally sided with those teachers who placed emphasis on the language itself rather than upon the artistic creation possible in the language.

The gist of the last century of change in language teaching is that we must teach our students to speak before going on to the pleasantly academic fields of grammar and literature. The contemporary language teacher has been occasionally characterized as being anti-intellectual and opposed to literature. This reaction has been described by Leonard Bloomfield (1944) as a tertiary response to language in his "Secondary and Tertiary Responses to Language." Secondary responses, he finds, are the various common opinions and myths which exist about language. A tertiary response is the angry reaction of a citizen whose opinion about language has been questioned. The nonprofessional critic assumes that if one emphasizes the spoken language, one is opposed to literature and to rhetoric, anti-intellectual; and if a skill to be attained by practice is emphasized, then the proponent of the skill is opposed to a more abstract consideration of the same data. No language teacher has ever seriously taken such a ridiculous position. At worst, what he has said is that the more purely intellectual activities necessarily follow the raw labor of acquiring the forms.

If the obvious fact of the language teaching revolution is the emphasis on teaching speaking, we can inquire into the reasons this position is urged upon us. Perhaps the most important reason is that the spoken language is the central and primary datum in language. Writing may, as in English, represent a dozen times and a great variety of places. Writing does not usually follow the changes in language very faithfully. Some of our spelling does indeed represent Shakespeare more efficiently and truly than it does ourselves. Writing ordinarily fails to indicate large, important areas of phonological structure—for instance, intonation patterns can usually be written only by ingenious and not very standard devices which must often be manufactured on the spur of the moment. In short, we are informed in a variety of ways that the primary set of data that we call language is the sounds we hear and use daily in talking to each other. Writing represents these sounds in a pallid and incomplete way. We can react to the symbols we see only when we already know the sounds they represent. In the realm of secondary responses it is possible to suggest that the student who learns to speak, stays to talk. Undoubtedly, more students acquire a permanent interest in a language in which they have first learned to speak, and then learned to read and write. The tertiary response of the student who has really learned to talk is scorn and anger, or at best indifference, to those who have not learned a second language and who fail to understand the significance of what the learner has done.

Teaching Speaking

An extension of teaching our students to speak is the obvious necessity of teaching in the language being taught. A teacher of languages cannot consider himself competent until his subject matter is also the vehicle of his teaching. It has been common in the past to insist that for the first semester or two English should remain the class language. This is no longer a usual pattern. In more and more language classrooms, English is not used except for occasional one- or two-word definitions of vocabulary new to the student. It is possible from the very first day to eliminate the students' native language from the classroom. Even the teacher who is not himself a native speaker of the language he teaches can almost achieve this goal if suitable mechanical facilities are available to him and if the texts selected are really good texts.

A common practice which may be recommended is to set aside certain hours for lectures in English about the language being taught, its grammar, the culture of its speakers, the appropriate history, and so on. Such arrangements originated in intensive courses, usually in situations in which a variety of lecturers presented their interests to a class. Regardless of origins, such a compartmentation of activities is one of the ways in which the foreign language teacher keeps from being overwhelmed by his subject and keeps the hours devoted to teaching a second language free from extensive excursions into English.

The attention one pays to pronunciation is part of teaching speaking, and success here is more difficult to predict than in most of the teacher's tasks. It appears likely that elements in the student's character which are slightly or not at all affected by language teaching determine whether a student will be good at pronunciation or not. If this is true, one might expect the teacher's function to be only nominal in teaching pronunciation. But this, of course, is impossible, too. Even though the specific product can vary greatly, the teaching must be adequate. For the situation is not that we are accomplishing nothing, but that we have little control over which learners will benefit most or at all. Part of the reason for this unpredictability may lie in the fact that the student's own judgment of his performance in pronunciation may vary so widely. When one uses a wrong word or construction, the error is obvious and inescapable. However, everyone listens to himself and wants to hear himself favorably. While our grammar error is black and white, right or wrong, our errors in pronunciation appear to be arbitrary gradations of sound away from the well-beloved sounds of our own language. Perhaps there is no possible absolutely right or absolutely wrong and there is our desire to judge ourselves favorably—although other elements in our thinking patterns may make us feel either satisfied with ourselves or unhappy with our performance. In this tangled area, the teacher can only step with caution.

A further caution arises from the observation that we cannot explain why a certain correction in pronunciation is made on a particular day at a particular hour. We may assume that our observation is faulty, that we cannot know on which day our student made his three-hundred-seventy-eighth effort to pronounce a sound which he had previously failed in producing three-hundred-seventy-seven times and which he now produces nearly perfectly. Comparison of sound systems allows us to pinpoint sounds which we expect to be difficult and other sounds which are predicted to be easy, but between these two kinds of sounds we have very little idea as to which sounds are persistent problems and which tend to cure themselves fairly quickly. The analysis of student errors which would approach the same question from a practical vantage point is an equally unfruitful source for aid. Such analyses are either undone or in a very small number of cases just begun or exist only in the minds of a number of teachers who can reel off examples in a sequence based on observations of frequency of occurrence.

Given our conclusion that we know neither the psychology behind success or failure in sound production nor the relative difficulty of individual items in any given language, there is a legitimate question as to what we do about our student's work in pronunciation. The habit of various teachers will vary greatly here from those who spend little time to those who seem to spend too much. Perhaps here teachers'-students' choice should be recommended. The teacher in the absence of compelling reasons against it should seek to teach a pronunciation of as detailed excellence as he feels capable. He should adjust the students' load to the amount that satisfies each individual student's desires and compulsions. Some students—perhaps those who are particularly self-critical—can be urged to work a bit more intensively and those students who are satisfied with the skills they have attained fairly early may be allowed to go on to other material upon which they may spend the time they save by doing less work on pronunciation.

Teaching Grammar

If the class spends most of its time speaking the language being learned, the lectures on the grammar are naturally discussions of those elements of the language structure for which the student will have already memorized examples. While a brief description of patterns may be used as part of introducing new material, the more complicated statements about structures—if made at all—must be repeated after the student has memorized examples of the material discussed. A good reason for the second presentation is that a study of structure as first presented is detailed and specific. The student needs to be told how two patterns parallel each other in being different examples of what may be one shared pattern. And all of this takes place—if the course is so oriented—in one class hour in which the discussion is in the student's native language.

A harder question to take sides on is the question whether grammar should be eliminated completely from the elementary language course as the contemporary teacher has, from time to time, been accused of doing. However, the question is probably a pseudo-question. Do you know of any number of popular texts in which such a procedure is followed? Again, we may have a tertiary response here. Those who favor language courses centered around grammar-translation have insisted that teaching grammar is by definition teaching their kind of grammar. The fact is that we have at least two kinds of grammar to teach today and probably several more if we stopped to think about it. First, there is the grammar needed by an individual whose aim is to learn to speak. Second, there is a different, more detailed, grammar which is studied by teachers and research workers whose aim is to learn something more than we already know about a language or languages. The needs for these two grammars are quite different. The person who is learning to speak wants to know that part of the structure of a language that is not obvious to him as he studies and which has immediate results in terms of pointing up correlations he had not observed automatically, but which help to fix the material he must learn in his memory. The other kind of grammar includes correlations in the structure that would not help a person learn to speak either because of their low frequency, or their application to low-frequency structures, or their complexity, or because they contrast structures rather than comparing them.

Teaching Vocabulary

Work on vocabulary is less rewarding than that on pronunciation or structure, since most vocabulary teaching results only in additions to the students' knowledge which affect his performance scarcely at all. This does not mean that vocabulary learning can be abandoned.

However, for most language courses, the presentation of vocabulary is the least adequate of the various compartmentations of the textbook. This roughly represents the state of language studies and reflects recent academic history. Our inadequacy in teaching vocabulary reflects the fact that dogma on which we could reasonably base our teaching does not yet really exist. The phonemic principle which dates back at least to the last decades of the nineteenth century evolved rapidly in the thirties and forties in this century in the research of the linguists. The resulting finesse in handling phonological systems is evident in a variety of texts for a large number of languages. Work in morphemics and syntax led to the production of some texts based on new analyses of the grammar of the languages to be taught. The sixties brought the beginnings of refinements in contrastive analyses applied both to morphosyntactics and to phonology. The relations of morphemes and syntax to meanings of words, to vocabulary, are still in a relatively inchoate state.

Recently, Freeman Twaddell (1965, p.9) pointed out the inadequacy of the frequency counts of vocabulary on which most of us have depended rather blindly. The difficulty is a simple one which can be simply stated: The two-thousandth most frequent word in most languages does not recur very often at all if looked at in terms of the number of pages one must read before a single example occurs. In short, our students need a much larger vocabulary than we have admitted to ourselves. We were forewarned of this fact by estimates of the speech of six-year-olds, which have suggested that the number of minimal meaningful elements in most six-year-olds' vocabularies is not to be measured in thousands, but in tens of thousands of items. It is evident that we would like to reach at least the level of these children in our foreign language teaching, but it is equally evident that we cannot reach so far with two thousand frequent words.

If we were to guess at the strategy of a good vocabulary lesson, we could suppose that it would select from a much wider group of items than was formerly true. We can also suppose that some sort of semantic generality would be achieved by subgrouping into classes of words with partial semantic-morphemic likeness and partial difference; a convenient starting point might be to present such groups as the English words which may take a certain suffix or prefix, to discuss affixation as a process appropriate to vocabulary learning. Here the student concentrating on the differences between items will indeed be learning the properties of the common elements in the collection. Concentrating on the different words ending in -th, such as health, wealth, width, the student learns something about the element they have in common, the -th.

Avoiding Excesses

A difficult problem exists in the practice of depriving the beginning foreign-language student of a printed text until a semester or a year or even more has passed. We tend, once we begin such a plan, to assume that it is a good thing and that more of it is better. Eventually, we may die of our own self-administered poison.

As I see it, the denial of a printed text to the student has been based on our over-enthusiastic approach to audio-lingual teaching. Presumably, "audio-lingual" does not involve a printed text. That is what it seems to say! At the same time, the traditionalists have overemphasized and sometimes distorted the importance of the printed word and the audio-lingual enthusiasts have retorted by dropping the printed word for as long a period as they are able to without losing their students completely.

The truth, as in most such cases, lies somewhere in between. The child can best be taught to read a new language after he has learned to read and write his own. Once the child has learned to read and write the situation gradually changes. He now knows that all languages can be written. Listing and explaining the exceptions to the generalization would not greatly affect matters.

Without assurance from psychology it still seems highly probable that denying the printed word to the language student will not make the learning job any easier, and as the student becomes older, it seems likely that the period during which study without a printed version of the lesson is effective may become very short indeed.

A student gets information as does every normal human being through eyes and ears, through touch and smell, and from the mind itself. Not only do these various paths compete with each other, but the world supplies a variety of information to each sense which may provide ample temptations to shift one's attention or lose it to a new or different sensation, even against one's will. As one becomes more and more accustomed to getting information through his eyes, and as his experience of reading his own language deepens, he becomes less and less able to work effectively without a visual stimulus or, at least, without some object associated with his language lesson on which he can fix his eyes without losing track of what is going on.

Another less common excess (which is only worth noting because it still exists—although not in public schools) is the insistence in a few special courses that the student shall neither hear nor use his own language during the foreign-language-class session at all. This insistence is based upon and usually supported with the argument that one learns a second language just as a child does. The fact, of course, is that the adolescent or young adult is not a child and probably does not learn a language just as a child does. While there may be parallels, there is an overwhelming likelihood that second-language learning is different from the first language learning of the child in a number of important respects. While a child takes several years, the young adult may spend only two or three years in learning a language. While the child practices to learn a set of sounds, the second-language learner must replace his native sounds with a rather different set. While the child makes errors by analogy, the second-language learner has also to deal with mistakes he creates by borrowing from his first language. At the same time, the adult can be told what a pattern is, and his learning can be speeded by explanations in his native language. And finally, the student of a foreign language does not have to refine his knowledge of the concept for truth or heat or health at the same time he is learning the word for the concept. He does, of course, have the problem that concepts do not always neatly match from language to language.

Our final position then becomes this: While the students' native language should not be used very extensively in foreign-language instruction, and if used should be isolated to a certain hour, and to brief two- or three-word definitions or comments, it cannot be eliminated completely without abandoning the few advantages a student does have in learning his second language. Eliminating the native language completely makes many activities burdensome and slow which might otherwise have proceeded quickly and easily.

Correcting Errors

One of the problems of the language teacher is managing his function as a corrector of errors in any sensible and efficient way. It is necessary to consider this skill because it represents about half of the activity of a teacher. Lesson material is presented, and then a considerable amount of time is spent correcting the variety of errors which result as the student gradually moves out on his own. It is obvious that in the most elementary classes, detailed correction of even a majority of the errors would result in the use of so much time that very little else could be done. The teacher must decide when to correct and when not to. If we were to examine the performance of good teachers, we should probably find that they operate on certain general principles which we can abstract and recognize as our own practice, albeit not planned. The ordinary procedure is to correct errors in the material upon which we are focusing class attention. Usually we correct only those sorts of errors which are the particular aim of the part of the textbook we are working with. The skillful teacher offers his help and asks for revisions of his students' activities not randomly, but following a plan as highly sophisticated as is his presentation of the work to be done. While any random correction will do, if the purpose is only—as sometimes in a laboratory—to make the student aware that he is being judged, such a random correction can be destructive in some contexts. Most students study best when the teacher is working with them, or when they are working with the teacher. A correction of pronunciation during a drill in which the student is expending all of his effort in organizing a complex sequence of words may lead the student to believe that the teacher is not properly aware of the problem he is working on. Even when the drill worked on is a pronunciation drill, and a pronunciation error is corrected, the teacher may have corrected an item on which the student was not concentrating, and of which he was relatively unaware.

Whether we are conscious of it or not, we deal with different kinds of language skills at different times and in different ways, and for good reasons. In most language programs and in most texts, pronunciation practice, memorization, and practice with structural patterns are extremely different types of activity, presented in different ways, and requiring quite different approaches by the student and the teacher. If the teacher corrects a grammatical sequence in a student's recitation of a pronunciation drill, he does so at the expense of diverting and discouraging the class from the subject at hand.

The decision to limit certain times to certain activities is so important that it is possible to extend this device even beyond the regimen we usually consider normal. Individual students may do better jobs if they are assigned limited goals for the duration of a course. Specific details of pronunciation or of structure may be assigned on an individual basis as areas in which absolute perfection is to be sought. In reaching these limited goals the student may learn how to deal with all of his problems in a more fruitful way. The assignment of such jobs serves to divert the learner from the total complexity of his ultimate task of learning a new language. Again, the instructor in assigning limited goals has promised that he will concentrate his corrections in these areas on an individual basis. The device is destroyed if corrections are not channeled in the direction of the chosen problems.

A further general principle is the relative usefulness of different corrections that can be made. By assiduous and repeated practice with correction a student manages to eliminate one problem in pronunciation. The achievement will likely be reflected in almost every utterance he will make in the language. Or let us suppose we learn one grammatical pattern. Basic patterns recur with great frequency. Again, the learning has affected the speech of the student in a major way. The addition of one new vocabulary item, however, can have no very obvious effect on the overall capabilities of the student. Besides this, as the student becomes more advanced, differences in vocabulary from student to student become greater. Correcting nuances in vocabulary control is likely to be of little usefulness to all of the students and offers a strong temptation to the teacher to lapse into long explanations in the students' native language.

The Language Laboratory

This discussion began with an examination of the traditional approach to language learning and the place of the language teacher vis-à-vis traditionalism. It is inevitable that as we approach a conclusion we must turn to the language laboratories which have come to represent for most teachers an ultimate expression of the present times in language teaching. Beginning, we looked briefly into the past; and now we consider the future.

The most impressive aspect of most audiovisual aids is their cost. To the language teacher who has depended on his wits for many generations, the thought of the cost of these new tools is staggering. And the cost has its effect on teachers. The day in which a new text could be purchased each year is now rapidly disappearing. The investment in tape-recorded lessons, discs, slides, and filmstrips, is great enough that every school administration must consider carefully before abandoning one investment in order to make another. Regrettably, the day when a teacher could write his own texts is also almost past. The basic language texts today are usually the effort of a group of people, each contributing his special skill. The resulting books and their associated visual and audio aids are expensive, but they are also worth the price we pay.

In choosing the new materials for language students we are offered both pictures and sound. The language laboratories have come to be used widely for the simple reason that sound is central to learning to speak a language. While filmstrips and moving pictures or television are now available, pictures are not so widely used as tape-recorded sound tracks because they are more expensive and because there is some question as to their real usefulness at some levels of instruction. While sound accompanied by a picture may be ideal for the young child, it seems possible that sound alone may serve quite well for an older student, accompanied by a printed text of some kind.

Some teachers claim to have had excellent results introducing a foreign language with slides and a sound track or teacher-drill master. These experiments are interesting in that they attempt to remove the students' native language from its role as a possible, almost unconscious, mediator in the stages of language study before the student can think in his new language. There is no real evidence, though, that this kind of teaching-learning is more efficient than the more usual textbook and tape combination. It may very well be, but there is no convincing proof. Consequently, the extra cost of visual aids becomes the controlling factor in two directions, that fewer schools make use of visually oriented materials, and that the number and quality of those available is less than the number of good courses for which sound tracks are on sale. By default the language laboratories have become our main additional tool in language teaching.

But there are a number of features of language laboratories that badly need explanation. First of all, what does a laboratory do? Its function can best be described as supplying spoken materials for those students and teachers who wish to augment their work in such a way. If our aim is to teach a student to speak, then the laboratory supplies a variety of models for student imitation which cannot usually be provided in any other way. The laboratory functions for the language student just as the library does for students in other courses.

A great deal of effort has gone into trying to prove that students learn more in courses including tape-recorded materials than they have done in others. This argument has usually aligned traditional teachers against other teachers who are considered to be more up to date. The more up-to-date teachers favor language laboratories. We have mercifully outgrown this distressing attitude. The traditional position as opposed to a progressive one usually means a difference in subject matter. The student who learns to speak does not ordinarily read quite so well or know so much about the structure of the language he is studying. On the other hand, the student who has concentrated on reading and grammar usually does not speak so well. I must admit my bias in favor of learning to speak before learning reading and structure. It has always seemed to me that the student who learns to speak first, albeit this does not mean that he is denied a printed script of what he is hearing, is likely to develop a permanent interest that will more rarely develop in the student who starts out translating and studying grammar.

A second fact about laboratories which needs negation is the conviction that they are necessarily complex and expensive. The teacher with a tape recorder in a classroom is accomplishing most of the work that the most complex audiovisual installation can accomplish. It does not matter how the student increases his exposure to good models of the language he is studying so long as he does get such experience. Almost all of the other gadgetry of the language laboratory is excess which in many cases cannot be justified.

For instance, the teacher has been told over and over again, usually by commercial organizations with a product to sell, that the student must be allowed to record and listen to his own performance. This means that each student must have his own tape recorder or have access to one frequently. While on the surface this appears to be a good thing, we have no really conclusive evidence that all students are helped by hearing themselves. Supplying such recording facilities can double the cost of a laboratory without any assurance that student achievement is really greatly enhanced.

Finally, the teacher must give up writing extensive lesson materials. Many teachers spend endless hours creating indifferent language lessons because they are unwilling to work with the existing texts. Almost every new set of lessons one finds is created to fill a crying need not satisfactorily taken care of by anyone or anything else. Such singly created texts are no longer good enough. Such creation is equally bad in recorded lesson material. Nevertheless, many schools purchase language laboratories without making adequate allowance for the purchase of lesson materials to use in the laboratory. Certainly no mechanical device is any better than the lessons we put into it. Another hazard for the laboratory appears in the recorded lessons of the teacher who was a native speaker twenty years ago and does not realize that his language has gone on growing and changing. His version of it has not. The teacher must realize that in the laboratory the student deserves a good program and the voice of a real native speaker.

Creativity in Language Teaching

In spite of all of the old that is still good, and there is a great deal, there is one area of special import to the teacher of language which is both a little old, but largely new. It is in this new trend that the real horizons of our effort may lie. Oddly enough we can label it creativity, although this seems a very broad and all-inclusive rubric. More and more teachers are coming to realize that a matter-of-fact schoolroom atmosphere is not conducive to learning. The student learns best when his teacher, his books, and his work generally transport him from his workaday world into a new and different and exciting place in which the unadorned fact is abandoned for a different reality. There are two ways I know of in which this creative reality is coming into our classrooms. First, in texts. The old language textbooks were written in a special kind of prose which existed nowhere in the world except in the classroom. In the best of the new textbooks, reality comes back into the classroom in the form of vivid prose which, without boring the student, still carries with it an air of absolute reality. The student can study here with some assurance that he is not learning the very special pen-of-my-aunt dialect which is not long gone and still fondly remembered. The special nature of such new materials lies in their success in overcoming the great difficulty text writers have had in producing lessons which bear repetition. Most material with reasonably interesting content does not stand frequent repetition without arousing feelings of antagonism in the student. How the fine edge of interest without annoyance is achieved is the special trade secret of the successful writer.

The other feature of creativity which is part and parcel of the new reality lies in the ways the teacher and the text writer combine to involve the student in the realities of his lessons. I have been told by one textbook writer that he attempts to involve his students in their language lessons by subtly creating psychological pressures that serve to keep the student immersed in the lesson. The lesson says something that he agrees with in a very positive way, or it hints at restrictions which annoy him or arouse his feelings in one way or another. We can see how this is done, although perhaps only clearly enough to be able to sense that one language book is good and another bad.

Returning again and finally to traditionalism, it seems reasonable to say that the new reemphasis on learning to speak languages will be successful, and that the teachers and writers will finally recognize that the new reality, the new creativity, was the value sought for by the original tradition. It is the value which seemed for a while to be lost.

CHAPTER 11

Elementary Social Studies

by

MARY JO WOODFIN

Currently assistant professor of Education at California State College, Long Beach, Mary Jo Woodfin earned her B.S. degree at Pepperdine College, her M.A. at Long Beach State College, and her Ed.D. at the University of Southern California. After teaching for three years in the Long Beach Unified School District, she then served as a vice principal in that district for eight years. In addition to being supervisor of student teachers at the University of California, Santa Barbara, Dr. Woodfin worked as elementary curriculum consultant in the Goleta Union School District for three years.

THE CONTENT, THE METHODOLOGY, AND THE PRODUCTS associated with elementary social studies are particularly well suited to promoting creative learning and teaching. In the process of studying about man's relationship to his environment, the processes of finding out about man's social development, the study of how social problems have been solved, the inquiry into one's own social problems and into intelligent ways of solving them, or the study of group interaction processes—whichever way a teacher chooses to begin the study of social studies—he will find abundant opportunities for helping children to develop their creative faculties and processes. The chances for children to pursue creative problem-solving techniques are almost endless. They may exist, simply, in the discovery of the problem, or they may involve the gathering of pertinent data, the making and checking of hypotheses, or the evaluation of the process or product. They may involve the discovery that there are many possible answers to many questions; conversely, that there are many possible questions to an answer. The social studies curriculum offers a wealth of opportunities for trial-and-error behavior, which is perhaps the usual pattern of creative effort.

The teacher can set the stage for creative learning in the social studies in a number of ways: (1) by careful diagnosis of class behavior; (2) by designing social studies activities around the characteristics of the class as a whole and of each individual child, as revealed by behavior; and (3) by interrelating content, process, and product into a unified approach to creative problem solving. Each of these phases is discussed in detail in this chapter, together with some suggestions on the implementation of a unified approach to creative endeavor in the social studies.

Relating Content, Process, and Product into a Unified Problem-Solving Approach

Guilford (1956, 1959) developed a theory of the intellect that has great implications for relating content, process, and product into a unified problem-solving approach to social studies. In essence, he theorized three dimensions to the intellect, which were further defined as follows:

1. Contents: the kinds of information received
   a. Figural: concrete in form, often involving visual and spatial objects
   b. Symbolic: denotative signs, such as letters, numbers, codes, when meanings and forms are not considered important
   c. Semantic: meanings to which words, pictures, or notations have become attached
   d. Behavior: social aspects of intelligence; information essentially nonverbal regarding behavior of ourselves and others
2. Operations: how the information is processed
   a. Cognition: simple recognition, comprehension, or understanding
   b. Memory: retention or storage of information in same form it was committed with retrieval potentiality existing to some degree
   c. Convergent Production: output of a single answer in terms of conventionally accepted expectations
   d. Divergent Production: output of many and qualitatively different answers from same source of information

e. Evaluation: making judgments and decisions in terms of criteria considered correct, suitable, desirable, or adequate

3. Products: results

a. Units: segregated items of information having such unique characteristics as digits, letters, dots, or words

b. Class: a set of units involving a conception associated with the common elements, such as words with a similar meaning or with plural endings

c. Relation: an association between units or classes as in word or figure analogies

d. System: an organization or structuring of items, classes, or relationships often involving discovery of rule required, as in a letter or number series task

e. Transformation: change, permutation, or redefinition of existing information or its use as in coming up with clever uses of bricks or new interpretations of stories or poems

f. Implication: formation of extrapolations as in making inferences or predictions or in suggesting antecedents of observed events or in anticipating consequences

Guilford's theory furnishes several implications for creative endeavor in the social studies:

1. The theory implies that content, process, and product are more interrelated than was previously thought to be true. Process is modified by content and the type of output planned. Content is modified by process and output. Output is modified by content and process. All this interrelatedness takes place in a dynamic, quick-changing, constantly cross-transferring process among the three dimensions of intelligence. This interrelation transfers readily to a concept of problem solving in the social studies in which content, process, and product are inextricably interwoven; where content helps to determine process and product; where process forces changes in content and product; and where the demands of the product force changes in content and product in individual children.

2. Guilford's theory implies that there are no moral connotations to levels of content, process, or product, other than those imposed by the objectives of the group or individual. Sometimes the learning of single facts is important in relationship to certain processes or prod-

ucts; sometimes non-verbal learnings are important; sometimes other content acquisitions are necessary. Similarly, under certain conditions each process can be useful individually, and none should be either omitted or overly stressed.

3. Guilford's model implies that product may refer to any of a great variety of things. It may be, variously, a written word, an expressed attitude, a stated generalization, or a tangible thing, such as a painting, among many other possibilities.

4. Guilford implies that the lines between content, process, and product become less clear as the perception of their interdependence becomes more apparent.

5. The Guilford concept implies that all of these abilities are capable of being trained through school activities.

6. It also challenges teachers to provide experiences which will help children to develop in all these areas.

7. It implies that content, process, and product are all important to intellectual or creative growth, and that none of the three may be omitted without damaging this growth.

Dimensions for Diagnosis

Areas for Diagnosis

Reactions of children to certain teaching procedures provide clues for ways in which teachers can design classroom activities. In the social studies, activities can be planned which help the teacher to learn more about each child. The teacher can observe his children at work to find the answers to many questions. Information can be recorded for each child at the beginning and at several points during the school year. Each dimension for diagnosis should be viewed as a continuum and not as a dichotomy. Hence, on each dimension children can be expected to fall between the extremes.

The teacher needs to know:

1. Which children prefer to work alone; which in groups? Which children actually work better alone, in terms of products or behavior; which work better in groups? Subsidiary questions can be asked about which children work better with which combination of chil-

dren; and what size of group is best so far as participation, behavior, or work pattern is concerned?

2. Which children work best under short-time or long-time conditions? Some children work best when working under no time limits.

3. Which children work best when permitted to respond orally; which when allowed to write, draw, act, or use other non-oral methods of response?

4. Which children work best under relatively close teacher direction; which under self-direction?

5. Which children are adept at which levels of thinking? No matter which method of categorizing thinking the teacher may use of the many currently available methods discussed in the literature, he will find that most include some type of recall of facts, some type of putting information together to make systems or categories, some type of evaluative thinking, some type of creative thinking resulting in new concepts, as well as other categories linking those mentioned. Without assigning moral values to the "goodness" of any of these types of thinking, the teacher can observe his class at work and determine which of these approaches each individual child can do, or prefers to do, or chooses to do.

6. Which children question readily; which accept facts, procedures, or circumstances easily?

7. Which children prefer a warm-up before starting classroom activities; which do better by plunging right in?

8. Which children do better when activities are planned carefully in advance (by either the child or by the teacher); which children prefer to jump excitedly into an activity and modify behavior along the way to meet problems as they arise?

9. Which children prefer to operate at a high emotional pitch; which operate best in their own emotionally calm style?

10. Which children work better when participating in actual, concrete experiences; which prefer vicarious experiences?

11. Which children work best when they do their own self-evaluation; which work best under teacher evaluation; which work best under peer evaluation? If a child works better under the evaluation of others, does he respond best to praise, to criticism, or to more stoical methods of evaluation?

12. Which children work better under whole-to-part learning conditions; which children work better under part-to-whole learning situations?

13. Which children work better under conditions which allow unlimited length of response (in written work, oral work, art work); which work better when response length is limited?

14. Which children work better under quiet conditions; which prefer noisy environments?

15. Which children have a high level of oral participation; which a low level of oral involvement?

16. Which children prefer to work on several things at once; which on one thing until it is completed?

17. Which children work better if they (or others) evaluate their work as they go along; which work better if evaluation is done at the end of work?

Conditions for Diagnosis

As the teacher diagnoses the areas listed above, he may find that he needs to add condition dimensions to his observations because of differences of individual responses under differing conditions. Some of the conditions he may wish to study in the social studies, in conjunction with his diagnostic procedures, are the following:

1. Are there differences in these responses of individual children when studying various topics, interest areas, or units?

2. Do the characteristics of learning behavior of individual children occur several times in a row, or are these behaviors a one-time phenomenon?

3. Do these behaviors continue over a long period of time, or do they change with time?

4. Are there differences in these behaviors in a formal group situation and in less formal situations?

Utilization of the Diagnosis

Once the teacher is able to diagnose classroom behaviors without assigning moral judgments regarding how children should react, once the teacher really decides that a child who prefers to work at one end of a behavior continuum (be it social-individual behavior, or differing levels of thinking) is no better and no worse than a child who works at the other extreme, then the teacher is free to use this diagnosis in any of a variety of ways. He may use it as a means of checking what is going on in the classroom; as a way to improve classroom learning and teaching; as a way to select appropriate classroom experiences for his children; and as a means of evaluating changes in his classroom.

By knowing the characteristic learning or behavior patterns in the classroom, the teacher can provide alternatives which will enable children to choose more comfortable ways of learning. At the same time, alternatives imply that other choices can be made attractive enough to help shake children out of one pattern and into others. In this way they may be freed from the tyranny of being dependent on one mode of activity. Moreover, the teacher is assured of a more rounded social studies program which does not rely upon some behaviors which penalize children who perform better at other ends of the scale.

Some type of formal or informal records of the characteristic responses of each child, jotted down at intervals during the school year, will provide the teacher with a means of evaluating behavorial changes in each child, and in the group as a whole.

Diagnosis of Teacher Preference

As a teacher diagnoses behavioral preferences of children by providing various types of activities at both ends of many behavioral continua, he may find that he prefers to teach to certain of these patterns more than to others. For example, he may prefer lessons in which there is little teacher direction to activities in which there is more, or he may find himself more comfortable directing rather than permitting children to go ahead on their own. In the same way that he observes and uses children's preferences in learning styles of behavior, so the teacher may observe his own preferences in teaching styles and play to his own strengths and weaknesses without robbing the children of alternatives. Periodically he may check himself to see whether he continues to limit himself to a single end of a behavioral continuum, and, on the basis of this self-evaluation, may be able to plan activities which will add new dimensions to his skill as a teacher.

Suggestions for Implementation

In the social studies, the teacher will find many opportunities for helping children to become more adept at creative thinking. The broad scope of the term allows ample room for multidimensional learning, thinking, and behavior—always necessary concomitants of creative behavior.

Interrelate Content, Process, and Product

As suggested earlier, content, process, and product occur as a unified whole and can be learned as a unified whole. As an example, one teacher and class decided to study about an imaginary planet. One specific problem was to decide what was needed to make this planet a desirable place in which to live. Committees were chosen to inquire into possible foods, climates, liquids, shelter, ways to communicate, transportation, recreation, and education. Very soon it became clear that characteristics of the inhabitants would have to be decided upon before any of the other areas could be probed in depth. This necessitated a study of our own characteristics, and decisions made as to whether the inhabitants would have the same physical, emotional, and social needs as the inhabitants of the earth. Similarly, developing a new language was difficult until some of the characteristics of earth languages were explored, and the possibilities of rejecting or keeping familiar ways of communication were explored.

Improve Question Asking

The teacher should ask questions and encourage children to ask questions which promote creative thinking and problem solving. Questions similar to the following encourage thinking of alternative solutions or processes:

1. How many ways can you think of to:
   a. Use some object?
   b. Solve this problem?
   c. Learn these facts?
   d. Evaluate this procedure?
2. What can we do to find out about . . . ?
3. Is there anything else we can do to . . . ?
4. Did everyone see the same thing when . . . ?
5. How do you know . . . is true?
6. How do you feel about . . . ? Does everyone feel the same? Should everyone feel the same?

Recognize the Value of Varying Answers

When children are encouraged to think in multidimensions about a problem, many solutions may occur that seem bizarre or threatening or ridiculous or impractical or smart-alecky to teachers or to other children. Resisting the impulse to evaluate too quickly or to stifle further response is necessary at this point. Unworkable solutions will soon enough be discovered by children as they try them out in relation to their objectives, and some of the more ridiculous answers many serve as springboards for more unusual solutions; they may even provide an opening in the thinking process of another child.

Do Not Seek Closure Too Soon

Holding discussions open as long as possible without the necessity of coming to a conclusion or generalization or solution may encourage greater freedom in children's thinking. Trying to jump too fast into a generalization may cut off further solutions on which children may be working; it may even anger some children who may then continue working alone on the problem, without the teacher's knowledge.

Provide Alternatives

Activities which challenge one child may very well discourage others. Provide alternatives in social studies activities, in learning content, in production processes, and in varying kinds of products.

Encourage Both Creative Producers and Creative Consumers

Children will alternate between creating and reacting to the creations of others. The teacher can help children to become more proficient producers, and more sensitive consumers.

Devise Ways for the Child To Teach Himself

Not enough has been done in elementary schools to help children to become more proficient at teaching themselves. A problem demanding a creative solution could very well be the following: How can an individual child teach himself content, or certain processes? Some ways in which this might be done would be:

1. Ask a child to pretend he is a computer. He has to store certain ideas and when someone presses the proper button, he has to be able to repeat them. How could he do this?
2. Ask a child what is preventing him from learning some process.
3. Ask what ways could be invented to see whether he really knows some process.
4. Ask where he could work that would help him learn faster.

5. Ask what conditions he needs to help him work better.

6. Provide opportunities for free time for thinking, free from teacher demands.

Involve Children in Evaluation Procedures

Teachers need to involve children in evaluation procedures concerning how learning can be planned, carried through, and checked. If testing of any sort seems necessary (for content, for particular solutions, for differing processes), children can contribute much to evaluation procedures and techniques. Indeed, creative activities call for self-evaluation as an integral part of the creative process.

Try To Overcome Some Sex-Role Handicaps to Learning

In the social studies, some sex-role definitions may prove harmful to good learning. Girls may not feel that studying about airplanes is feminine; boys may not wish to participate in some esthetic experiences. But sex-role definitions may be as helpful to learning as they are harmful. (The fact that girls are supposed to be quiet in the classroom helps them in some types of learning but definitely discourages them in others. Boys, too, may be inhibited in some types of learning but may quickly be given other learnings.) Sex differences should not (and could not) be eradicated. But teachers do have an obligation to try to remove those that inhibit creativity in individual children by shutting them off from some experiences and emphasizing others that promise to widen their creative potential.

Provide Time for Individual Study Projects

The study of man and his environment provides opportunities for children to become excited about certain ideas and to want to pursue them further and in depth. Some children will do this in extracurricular, non-teacher-motivated activities. Opportunities should be provided for individual children to have time and materials during school time, as well, to explore an interesting idea further and in depth. It is not necessary that the problem be of interest to the other children in the class. Whether the problem that fascinates the child is an idea, a people, a mountain range, a scientific puzzle, or an era, he should be turned loose to work on it. Nor do these individual interests necessarily need to be reported in detail to the rest of the class. Teacher-child conferences may be all the reporting needed.

Provide Practice and Help in Group Process

Some social studies projects can be carried on well in groups. Not only is the particular learning or process facilitated by the group, but learning how groups work together to obtain creative solutions is a skill of value in itself. The teacher may accomplish this in a variety of ways:

1. Vary the composition of groups to include a diversity of backgrounds and abilities. The more the variance, the greater the possibilities of creative solution. However, it would be wise to include at least two children who possess similar characteristics, that is, it would be better to include at least two girls on a committee of boys, rather than only one.
2. Vary the size of the group according to how easily children participate. For certain children, smaller groups may be more beneficial than large ones.
3. Have many grouping formations going on at the same time during any one period so that each child will be involved successively in several different groups and experiences.
4. Have both highly chosen children and rejected children in each group. Do not restrict one group to the isolates or one group to leaders.
5. Have groups, both large and small, engage in creative problem-solving processes, including brainstorming, as another way of implementing creative processes.

Some Specific Approaches

There are numerous additional ways in which creative endeavor can be realized in the elementary social studies. Since the reader may feel that this chapter is already too long, only a few representative examples of virtually limitless opportunities will be enumerated: (1) the use of map construction, (2) the building of dioramas, (3) the employment by both pupil and teacher of specially devised audio-visual aids, (4) the application of sociometric devices, role playing, and problem-solving techniques in social situations that are associated with living together in the classroom, (5) the integration of social studies with creative endeavors in visual art work, dramatic presentations, and music activities, and (6) the participation of pupils in elementary research activities on which they give oral reports to the class.

Conclusion

Increasing the potential creative behavior of children is a legitimate goal for a social studies program. Social studies activities lend themselves to helping children to become more familiar with techniques of creative problem solving, to realize the rightness of many different solutions to social problems, to see how varying research tools can provide help in learning about man, to learn more about themselves in relation to the way they solve problems, and to become adept at observing and appreciating the problem-solving activities of others.

Similarly, for the teacher, social studies activities provide the data for diagnosing individual and class behavior; for devising alternative activities that capitalize on the characteristic behaviors of the group; for helping children to become more able to use a wider variety of behaviors in problem solving, rather than being limited to a few; and for trying out new teaching strategies which broaden the teacher's own creative problem-solving ability.

CHAPTER 12

Secondary Social Studies

by

DALE L. BRUBAKER

Dale L. Brubaker, assistant professor of Education at the University of California, Santa Barbara, received a B.A. degree in humanities from Albion College and the M.A. and Ph.D. from Michigan State University. His graduate work was in the social foundations of education with special emphasis in the areas of social science education and international studies in education.

Dr. Brubaker is the author of Alternative Directions for the Social Studies, *contrasting citizenship education and social science inquiry with a comparison of the Soviet–U.S. position on social studies. He is also the editor of and a contributor to a recently published book on innovation in the social studies.*

WHETHER OR NOT the student, teacher, and administrator in a secondary school think and act in what we call a creative manner depends on the total school as a social system and on the various subsystems within it. It is important to recognize this, for many of our future teachers, who are presently in our colleges and universities, think their future happiness as a teacher will depend solely on their classroom teaching. It is natural for them to think this because the college or university setting and even student teaching give them but part of the total picture. If the teacher's classroom relationship vis-à-vis the students were the only relationship on which success is based, there would be fewer teachers leaving the field each year. Noisy assemblies, disrespectful students, fights in the halls, pressure from parents and community groups: these are some of the things which "box the teacher in" so that his classroom teaching is impaired. At the same time, activities outside the classroom may be very rewarding for the classroom teacher. Evidence the delight which may come from seminars, coaching, and even chaperoning a Saturday night party.

In sum, the success of a secondary social studies program depends in large part on activities outside the classroom; likewise, the success of the secondary social studies teacher depends on how he relates to students outside the classroom.

Background: The Present Status of Secondary Social Studies

The social studies curriculum is another part of the environment which fosters or stifles creative expression by students, teachers, and administrators. As a point of information it might be well to specify the common secondary social studies curriculum (Rand McNally, 1965):

Grade Seven:	The Old World–Eastern Hemisphere Geography and History or World Geography
Grade Eight:	United States History
Grade Nine:	Civics
Grade Ten:	World History
Grade Eleven:	United States History
Grade Twelve:	Problems of Democracy or Government and Economics

It is obvious that the main orientation of secondary social studies courses, if course titles are representative, is in history and political science. How much history and social science, especially behavioral science, is understood by students is an open question. The one thing which is sure is that social scientists are dissatisfied with present treatment of their individual disciplines and are therefore doing their best to wedge their way into the curriculum.

History and the Social Sciences: Innovation in Progress

Most historians would probably agree with the statement that "history is not a science, and the historian is not a scientist" (Commager, 1965, pp. 64-65). History, then, is more an art than a science, according to most historians. History departments are frequently part of the humanities and apart from the social sciences. Does this mean that history lends itself more to creativity than do the social sciences? Many would argue in the affirmative by saying that the historian's biases and normative judgments provide history with its spice, its élan vital. Relativism and subjectivism are the heart of creativity, the argument continues, so that whether or not the student's ideas are accurate is less important than the fact that the student perceives his work to be accurate and enjoys writing his account of the past. The individual's personal discovery is all important; the question of the validity of his findings is incidental. It is the opinion of the writer that many secondary social studies teachers subscribe to the aforementioned view in theory, if not in practice. If the matter of validation of results is overlooked in favor of a "good feeling" for the students, the teacher has a relatively easy time with his students: rapport is enhanced, for "anything goes" in the name of creativity; and if the teacher does not have an adequate background in history and the social sciences, no one is the wiser.

It is because social scientists think social studies classes have consisted of normative judgments at the expense of the social sciences that they want to "clean house." At the minimal level social scientists want secondary social studies teachers to differentiate between description (what is) and prescription (what should be). For example, the teacher's attempt to teach values should be differentiated from an analysis of values; students should likewise be cognizant of this distinction. The more aggressive social scientists, usually identified as positivists, feel that social studies teachers should deal only with the descriptive; normative value judgments are for preachers, not teachers, it is contended. It might be noted in passing that the very existence of positivism depends on a society which will tolerate this detached analytical viewpoint. It is also interesting to note that the *UNESCO Dictionary of the Social Sciences* (1964) does not define the word creativity.

The crucial question is, can social science inquiry be considered creative? It can, in the writer's opinion, if its method(s) of inquiry always remain(s) open to criticism and revision. The main enemy of the social scientist is the absolute or definitive solution to any problem; how ironic it is if he adopts an absolute method of inquiry, for example, *the* scientific method. A closed method of inquiry is no substitute for closed results in the form of normative value judgments.

What will the secondary student be like if he understands social science and history? He will be free to discover, and he will be informed as to the methodologies of the various social sciences and history. He will understand the operational frameworks in which social scientists and historians operate. He may or may not agree with Orwell's Napoleon ("all animals are equal but some are more equal than others") but he will know how results are validated in the various social science disciplines and how some written history is better than others. It is hoped that administrators will join teachers and students in a fruitful dialogue based in large part on an understanding of the social sciences and history. In short, secondary social studies students will be inquisitive, informed, and responsible for their decisions.

Those who feel that the creative person is one who primarily deals with abstractions will find the social scientist's preoccupation with specifics and their interrelationships to be something less than creative. It would, however, be a mistake to think that only those in the humanities are involved in creative enterprises.

Your School and Creativity in Secondary Social Studies

There are a number of ways in which one may approach the subject of creativity in secondary social studies. One may attempt to identify the characteristics of the creative person. A second approach is to deal with the kind and quality of psychological processes by which creative solutions to problems are reached. A third approach is to deal with the qualities which identify creative products, that is, the expressions of creative activities. A final approach is to study the creative situation so as to discover that which helps and that which hinders creativity (MacKinnon, 1961). It is the latter consideration which is the major focus of this chapter, although the first three approaches are dealt with incidentally. Because secondary social studies is more than the classroom situation this discussion will be divided into two parts: creativity in the secondary social studies classroom and creativity in related areas outside the classroom.

The Classroom

If you were to construct an "ideal" classroom setting in which creativity could be developed, what would you choose as the ingredients of this classroom? The answer is relatively easy to give:

ideal students (that is, students eager to learn), an ideal teacher, and ideal curriculum materials. This utopian paradigm is of little value except to identify the principal actors and/or ingredients of the creative classroom situation.

Many educators, the writer included, believe that much of what the students learn is caught rather than taught. The teacher's example as a creative person is more important than his deliberate attempt to foster creativity in his students. If the teacher is a key variable in the classroom, it naturally follows that administrators should hire the most creative persons available. If the teacher expects his students to understand history and the social sciences, he had better understand history and the social sciences himself. But are administrators prepared to ask the prospective teacher questions which will indicate whether or not the teacher knows what he is talking about? Another way to ask this question is, how much history and social science do those people know who interview prospective teachers? The writer's experience in being interviewed as a prospective teacher was most disheartening. Whether or not the applicant knew anything about his subject was incidental. The main question asked time and time again was, what is your philosophy of education?

How can this problem be solved? If the school believes that its social studies teachers should understand historiography and the methodologies of the various social sciences (that is, these understandings are necessary for the teacher to teach creatively in secondary social studies), then it should have an interviewer who knows how to ask questions which will tell him whether or not a candidate should be given an offer to teach in a particular school system. If a school system does not think it is important for its secondary social studies teachers to have a good background in history and the social sciences but is looking for other qualifying criteria, then the interviewer should ask questions which will get at these criteria. The important thing is that the school system be honest with its faculty, students, and community so that all concerned know what the school system considers to be teaching qualities which foster creativity. In short, "the school should know what it is doing, insofar as this is humanly possible, and accept full responsibility for its acts" (Counts, 1932, p. 25).

Now that the teacher has been screened by the school system and has been hired, his position in the classroom may be discussed. One of the first questions the new teacher asks is, what text are you using for social studies class x? The question is a realistic one, for most social studies classes are built around a single textbook. The use of a textbook in particular and curriculum materials in general constitutes an important variable in determining whether or not a classroom atmosphere is conducive to creative work by both the students and their teacher. If the teacher believes in the inductive method, critical thinking, and discovery, the textbook has many limitations. The first is that most textbooks put in the student's hands a predetermined conclusion. How can the teacher advocate the importance of inquiry if he is tied to the textbook? The second limitation is that most textbooks are aimed at the average or below-average student so that the bright student with high reading ability is bored by the book. It was the writer's experience that the average and below-average students also were frequently not interested in the way the material was presented. A third limitation is that the methodologies of the social sciences and history are rarely dealt with in present social studies textbooks. The facts are given without reference to how we know what we know in a particular discipline.

Admittedly, the textbook may be used in many different ways. Some social studies educators say the textbook should be used to point out what poor scholarship—for example, poor writing style and research methods—is like. The writer brought this idea to the attention of a junior high school social studies teacher. Her reaction was as follows: "We may point out that the textbook is poor, but we had better not do this too much or the parents will ask us why we are using the book."

Present administrative policies in many school systems do not allow the teacher to be imaginative in his choice of assigned materials: paperbacks cannot be used or must go through a long screening process; some schools allow as little as ten dollars per teacher for audiovisual materials; and textbooks and curriculum materials are often chosen without regard to the feelings of those teachers who will be using the book or materials. In short, there is little communication between faculty and administration; however, both groups usually fear public censorship of materials and thereby adopt a "play it safe" stance. If a school system has good hiring and screening policies, so that good teachers are employed, why cannot it trust teachers to choose materials which they feel will best fulfill their pedagogical purposes? Lack of funds is an argument frequently used, but if one looks at the price of textbooks he soon realizes that many other curriculum materials may be purchased for the price of textbooks.

In sum, the secondary social studies teacher's competence is not really trusted and he will never be considered a professional until he is trusted. More importantly, it is difficult for the teacher to teach imaginatively and therefore creatively when his ability to choose is not trusted.

Creative teachers, good curriculum materials, and an informed and sympathetic administration all exist so that the student may enjoy and profit from the best learning situation possible. It is primarily for the students that our schools exist. What are our secondary students like? The writer cannot help but venture certain generalizations about secondary social studies students compared to college students: (1) most secondary social studies students have a freshness and lack of intellectual cynicism commonly found in the college student; (2) many secondary school students crave intellectual experiences such as evening seminars, whereas college students find these "old hat"; and (3) secondary school students find the reading of many and diverse materials novel, whereas such reading is common for the college student. In sum, the secondary school student has "an edge on" and wants to be challenged. The old idea that he must wait until college to be intellectually challenged is becoming passé. That social studies as a curriculum area has been or at least has appeared to have been dormant is accepted. At least, at the research level we may say that "everything is up for grabs"; there is no set curriculum, course content, or set of methods. Research must indicate what will happen as different experiments are conducted in secondary social studies.

Does all of this mean that creativity in secondary social studies is confined to an elite group of students? Does the student have to be college bound, in the top ten percent of his class, and a member of the student council to be considered a creative individual? It was the writer's experience that some of the most imaginative, flexible, and responsive social studies students were not in the "in" group in the school; that is, they did not consistently receive good grades, they were not members of the student council (they had to have a high grade average to participate), and they were not considered to be "good Joes." These creative individuals outside the fold had frequently experienced the workaday world. They would often hitchhike rather than ride in the family car; they met all kinds of people from all walks of life. When given a chance to demonstrate their imaginative insights they were superb. It was Steinbeck, Orwell, and Remarque who fired their imaginations—not the textbook. It seems to be a special challenge in this day and age when grades seem to be everything (to university admissions officers and the draft board) to foster the creativity of the "out" group students. Perhaps such programs as the War on Poverty will assist us in this task, but think of the majority of students in our schools whose imaginations we have not tapped. Long-used testing procedures (Torrance, 1964), curriculum materials, teaching methods, and teachers' and administrators' attitudes will have to be altered if we are to meet this challenge.

Outside the Classroom

Students may frequently be reached through social studies activities held outside the classroom. Listen to the following account (Brubaker and Turner, 1966, pp.9,42) of a high school seminar by a student:

> Students of high school age are concerned with many of the problems confronting society, but often, because of a lack of understanding, or a feeling of immaturity, are embarrassed to express their concern in a classroom situation. However, in an informal situation such as that afforded by senior seminars, where interested students come together for the specific purpose of discussing subjects of this nature, the problem of self-consciousness is minimized.
>
> It is extremely valuable to have an interested and sympathetic adult listen to and comment on one's views and to have an opportunity to question and comment on the views of one another.

Perhaps the main thing students learn from social studies activities outside the classroom is that teachers, and adults in general, care enough to spend their time with students. Students feel they have something to contribute and appreciate adults who listen to them rather than "always tell them what to do." Students also appreciate the fact that an adult believes something and acts on the basis of this belief. According to the previously quoted student:

> One of the most interesting seminars was one at which a philosophy professor spoke about humanism as a personal philosophy of life. Being a humanist himself, he was outstanding because he presented his ideas with a great deal of sincerity and insight.

The great "whipping boy" in secondary social studies has been the coach—social studies teacher. There is, however, no evidence that the social studies teacher who coaches is any less competent than the social studies teacher who does not coach. In fact, the coach may well teach a good deal of social studies outside the classroom; certainly if he is liked, he will have established rapport which may be valuable in the classroom and the school as a whole. The writer vividly remembers rides home from freshman basketball games when history was discussed and argued at length. That the coach also taught social studies proved to be an asset rather than a liability.

The reader has probably heard of social studies clubs, mock elections, field trips, and other activities which have been successes or failures. The main point to be made is that the success of social studies activities outside of class depends on their relevance to history and the social sciences and the teacher's ability to listen and learn along with his students. There is no definite stance one should assume toward such activities; however, if the teacher thinks back about his years as a social studies teacher, he will probably think of some students who were reached because of activities outside the classroom.

Examples of Teaching Which Foster Creativity Among Social Studies Students

A short time ago the writer observed a ninth grade class in civics and vocational guidance. The young woman teaching the course had thrown out the traditional approach of one semester of civics and one semester of vocational guidance and in its place had substituted a cross-cultural approach which spanned the entire academic year. Her background in the behavioral sciences, especially sociology, was revealed early in the class period: she not only had a good subject-matter background but she knew the means of inquiry used by the behavioral scientist.

Earlier in the year the students had been introduced to certain key social science terms, for example, culture, status, and role. The first culture studied was that of the Hopi Indians. Then the Eskimo culture was studied. An interesting paperback, *Four Ways of Being Human,* by Gene Lisitzky (1956) was used along with relevant magazines, television programs, books, and movies.

The following summary of a class period gives one an idea how social science concepts were used in cross-cultural analysis.

Teacher: Do all cultures provide for differences in status for their members?

Students: Yes. We can't think of any exception.

Teacher: Different societies determine what will determine status and what will give its members prestige. One's status dictates the role he is supposed to play. Isn't it true that you are expected to play a certain role as a member of your family?

Students: Yes.

Teacher: What is the role and how does it differ according to whether or not you are a boy or girl?

Girl: As a girl I am expected to help my mom with the dishes.

Boy: I'm expected to help my dad with work around the yard.

Teacher: True. And in your homes certain people have more prestige than others. For example, who in your home has the most prestige?

Student: My dad (one boy said, his mother).

Teacher: In our school we all play certain roles and these roles give us certain status and prestige. The teacher, the custodian, the principal, and you students have certain status because of the roles we play. There is a hierarchy of prestige. My status is higher than that of the custodian and the principal's status is higher than mine. What happens when we step out of our roles? What would happen, for example, if I acted in the role of the principal and told other teachers how they should act?

Student: You would be fired.

Student: There would be a lot of conflict.

Teacher: True. We are expected to stay within our roles. This leads me to the next question. What determines status in our society? What gives one prestige?

Student: Money.

Teacher: What else gives one prestige?

Student: Education.

Teacher: What determines status and gives prestige to the Eskimo man?

Student: To be a good hunter.

Student: To be a good fisherman.

Teacher: What determines status and gives prestige to the Eskimo woman?

Student: To have her teeth worn down. This means that she chews her husband's boots well so that they are soft and keep out the water.

Teacher: What do we think in the United States if a woman has wrinkled hands?

Student: Dishpan hands.

Teacher: What do we think in the United States if a woman looks old?

Student: It's bad. Women use dye to keep their hair dark. In the United States it is better to be young than old.

Teacher: I believe that you now understand how status and role are related and how prestige is greater in some roles than in others. An important idea that I want you to write down is that prestige is based on what is valued in a culture and different cultures value different things.

A major point to be made is that the teacher did not encourage the use of the cross-cultural method to any great extent until the students first had a good understanding of the particular culture they were studying. The classroom atmosphere was not at a high emotional pitch but instead the students were using rational analysis in a way which appeared to be both interesting and beneficial to them.

A second class which the writer observed recently was a basic class in world history. The young teacher probably learned more from the students than they learned from him. In fact, the teacher learned to listen and draw from the backgrounds of his students, many of whom could hardly read or write. The students seemed quite shocked that someone would listen to what they knew and considered interesting. The teacher's objective was to get his students to express themselves verbally and on paper. At the end of the week the students were asked to write a half-page description of the life of a narcotics addict. The following are two examples of papers written by boys who had taken little interest or done little work up to the time the class began discussing narcotics. Punctuation, spelling, and word usage have not been changed.

> The life of a narcotic addict is a very lousy life. They don't care about anything. They go around steeling money and goods.
>
> The addict does not like his habbit but he can't help it his body is built up to it and he can't do without it. He doen'st care about him self he only cares about where he is going to get his stuff.
>
> Most of the addicts go to needle park to wait for there pusher. The police hardly every do anything about it but when they can get them with the drugs on them they have got them.
>
> When it is costing the addict to much money he will turn him self into a hospital so when he comes out his habbit wont be so expensive and he wont have to take so much.

The other student wrote:

> It's pretty hard when your a narcotic wondering where your going to get the money to buy stuff who your going to rob or what your going to rob.

> Then you got to worry about getting caught with it on you. When your an addict it's really a sloppy life Because they don't even clean the neddle or take a bath or change cloath.

The following is one of the longer essays received. It was written by one of the girls in the class:

> Well to start off with before they go to bed they have to go out and find some herione for when they wake up in the morning. Its really a terrible life to live and I no that I would never take the stuff and I would try to stop anyone I saw taking it. Well the girl usually becomes a prositiute and the robs and steals and thing he gets his hands, They usually need about 10 to 15 needes. They really are dirty people the girl usually if she hasn't have any she doesn't feel like doing anuthing she doesn't take baths wash her hair but when she has a date going on she gets real slicted up. When they don't have any stuff they go to the hospital go get some and then when they get out they don't need as much money. They all use the same needle and can you emaghen how dirty it is it most carry a lot of germs. They sleep where ever they find a place park benches, brake into cars and sleep there. Then when they get the stuff they dont no if its good or bad and if its bad they lose maybe 10 to 20 dollars. Wll I no I wouldn't give up the life I live for a life like that. you just cantn't believe the things they do. Now days you don't know what this world is coming to.

The teacher encouraged these students in their writing by praising them for the improvement they had made. The students felt that their teacher cared, that he wanted them to improve their reading and writing skills, and that he would work very hard right along with them to achieve what he felt needed to be achieved.

In short, teaching so that students may develop their creative capacities is very individual so that no one style may be prescribed for all teachers. The two examples previously cited, however, should give the reader a flavor of teaching and learning atmospheres in which creativity was fostered.

Conclusion

The total school as a social system fosters or stifles creativity on the part of students, teachers, and administrators. The classroom is but one place where students and teachers relate to each other. This is not to say that the classroom is unimportant, for with imaginative curriculum materials and an imaginative teacher students may be free and informed. It is incumbent on the school and therefore the community to hire those teachers who are themselves creative, for much of what the students learn is caught rather than taught. Secondary social studies activities outside the classroom provide a relaxed but often serious opportunity to express and discuss what one really feels; student-teacher rapport may also be invaluable to a good learning situation in the classroom–a situation which may follow from outside of class activities. A special challenge is presently facing secondary social studies: history and the social sciences must be fully tapped for their information and methodologies. Finally, it is the writer's opinion that all social studies students must be considered capable of creative endeavor, for a basic tenet of our system of education is that each student is a diamond, polished or unpolished.

CHAPTER 13

Visual Arts

by

JEROME J. HAUSMAN

Jerome Hausman came to the teaching of art through an unusual route. He left Pratt Institute, where he was studying advertising design, to enlist in the Navy during World War II, only to be assigned to an academic environment in the Naval V-12 Program. At Cornell University he majored in biology and chemistry (no programs existed for furthering the training of artists). Completing his B.A. degree at Cornell after the war, he worked as a chemist. Since this did not hold the same attraction for him as the arts did, he enrolled at the Art Students League and Columbia University School of General Studies, going on to earn his M.A. and Ed.D. at New York University. He taught in Elizabeth, New Jersey, and then accepted a position in the School of Art at The Ohio State University; he is now its director. He has edited the National Art Education Association Yearbook and Studies in Art Education. Presently he is working on an introductory text in the field of art appreciation.

IN WHAT FOLLOWS, I shall address myself to the problems of teaching art in the elementary school. I shall deal with these problems from what will necessarily be a generalized point of view. First, I shall set forth some of the propositions from which my point of view emerges:

Proposition 1: By "creative," I am referring to those behaviors where a person reflects and realizes a new idea, image, or form of which he was not previously aware. Thus, the simple act of mixing blue and yellow paint and realizing the resultant green for the first time can be said to be creative by this definition. In a similar sense, the youngster who starts with a vague feeling tone about an idea and is then able to realize and clarify the idea in terms of a drawing or painting can be said to be creative.

Proposition 2: By judging an act to be creative, I make no assumptions about its value. Thus, it would be possible for a pupil to be "creative" as he engages in an antisocial or unwarranted act. I do assume, however, that it is the responsibility of the teacher to encourage and foster those creative activities that are directed toward positive values. I take the creation of art forms to be one of those values. The creation of visual art forms is a basic human activity in which young children would engage even if art was not included in the curriculum.

Proposition 3: The characteristics that I would attribute to the child, while engaged in a creative artistic art are as follows: He is deeply involved in what he is doing; he ventures into an unknown area; he risks a simple and available solution for the possibility of new insights and forms; he is open to new possibilities and willing to act in terms of these possibilities; he creates a visual "analogy" or "metaphor" that, for him, transcends anything that he has realized before.

Proposition 4: Any teaching of art must draw its essential content from the very nature of art itself. Merely engaging in manipulative activities (fingerpainting, weaving, cutting and pasting) does not necessarily lead to art. Objects become works of art by virtue of their inherent artistic qualities: the manner in which a work is organized to embody the vividness, intensity, and uniqueness of feelings of an idea. In large part, these qualities are only possible when a person engages in his own exploration of reality—the shaping of ideas and feelings in a medium in relation to particular values and purposes.

Proposition 5: Any definitions of art must account for its open-ended and metaphoric nature. Thus, there is no such thing as an established form of perfection to which all students and artists must strive. Teachers can help students to see how others have given form to particular ideas and feelings—how they have used the elements of form, line, color, texture; how they have drawn upon particular symbols to convey meaning; how they have used tools and materials. In the end, however, each person is faced with finding and embodying his own unique ideas and feelings in a tangible form.

Proposition 6: Philosophers and aestheticians have devoted lifetimes to the question "what is art?" Much as I am tempted to pursue this argument, I will not do so except to assert that making judgments about art is making judgments about quality. "The more insight the history of art gives us into the necessities that form the artist, the more nearly it liberates us from the temptation of formulas, theories, and fashions, because it shows us that these things being subject to perpetual change, are relative and vain. The only permanent thing is quality, which cannot be reduced to a formula or a definition" (Huyghe, 1959, p.438).

Proposition 7: Just as definitions of art must account for its open-ended and metaphoric nature, conceptions of artistic process must recognize the changing relationship between a person and the art form he creates. In the process of a child's forming a painting or piece of sculpture, the emerging object (the evolving qualities of the visual form being shaped) takes on an identity of its own. The artifact suggests its own form and meaning. The object being created can be said to be the expression of an idea; it is also the means by which the creator is shaped by the artifact itself.

Proposition 8: The traditions of art provide the oldest known records of man's thought and activity. From the cave paintings of Altamira to our Pop Culture, there is an infinite variety of visual forms created by men. These forms reveal and reflect particular ideas and values. They can also provide poetic insights into our present and future. The teaching of art, at all levels of our curriculum, should seek out and utilize visual forms as the embodiment of human ideas. The diversity of art reflects the diversity of human beings; the differences in art give emphasis to the differences we seek to encourage in the youngsters we educate. Art thereby provides an important route to humanistic study; it focuses upon uniqueness and insight in men.

Proposition 9: Making judgments about art involves making judgments about qualities to be found in the object itself. In the end, each art object stands in mute testimony for what it is; it forces us to turn to our own standards and values. Two paintings may be the same size; they may have the same subject; yet their differences can be found on a qualitative level. The ability to perceive these differences is a function of being able to make judgments and discriminate among qualities that make up the paintings.

Proposition 10: A key factor in the teaching of art, at any level, involves creating conditions in which pupils can learn the joy and excitement in the search for visual ideas, in the investment of their own ideas and feelings toward realizing new forms. Necessarily, such teaching would have to help children to court mystery, deal with ambiguity, and on occasion suffer the pain and disappointment of failure.

Proposition 11: The problem of identifying what is to be "taught" in our elementary school art programs involves us in different kinds of specifics. Obviously, the specifics of a kindergarten class should be different from those of a fifth grade; the specifics of programs should vary in relation to geography, cultural emphases, and general experiential backgrounds of the students involved. The highly personal and subjective nature of art instruction confronts the teacher with a tremendous challenge and opportunity. The teaching of art necessarily involves a demonstration by the teacher of the very values that are being sought. The willingness to be "involved," to venture into the unknown to seek the poetic and the unusual, to tolerate ambiguity–these are qualities that must pervade the teacher's approach to students.

Where does a teacher start? It would seem to me that the cues for starting must be sought in the students themselves as well as in the ideas and objectives of the teacher. Teaching art in the elementary school involves encouraging that which young children can do naturally–the creation of symbols that give form to their ideas and feelings. Human beings are essentially "symbolic" organisms; they learn to select infomation and "construct" it into a uniquely human world. Children should recognize their own power in giving shape to their ideas and feelings; they need to learn that what they do suggests other possibilities; they need to become aware of the poetry in their vision, of the drama in their lives. Such learning should draw upon ideas and experiences that are part of the child's life–the people he knows, the places he has seen, and the ideas he has. As the student's intellectual and experiential horizons expand, the potential for ideas and forms is thus enlarged.

Through our words, images, sounds, and gestures we seek to communicate ideas and feelings. Indeed, through the manipulation of symbols it is possible to realize new ideas and feelings. From simple and uncomplicated beginnings, a child's repertoire of symbols (signs, words, images) expands as he learns to deal with his environment. This pattern can be clearly seen in the drawings of children. There is, at first, an undifferentiated and uncontrolled "marking" that reveals a developing sense of movement and touch. What begins in a rather haphazard way soon leads to the exercising of physical controls over these "markings"; children's scribbles take on qualities of controlled repetition and clearer definition of form. Of equal importance, children learn to relate their movement and markings to ideas. They become aware of the power of symbolization for projecting and realizing ideas and feelings. Beginning from a simple and uncontrolled motor projection, children move toward image making as a means for invention and communication. As part of their language they develop schematic representations of their reality. For example, the five- or six-year-old seeks the development of simple schema to represent man, sun, house, tree, bird, or other object. The problem for him is the personal task of inventing symbols that convey active meanings from his experience. He becomes deeply involved with the image he creates. When new forms (or schema) are "invented," they are repeated and reinforced until such time as the schema are no longer adequate to embody and reflect active meanings with which the youngster is involved. Children then seek to change and enlarge upon their repertoire of images for the drawings they make. Given the growing complexity of ideas and feelings that they face as well as their increasing mental awareness, the problems attendant to artistic expression become much more complicated. The inner-directed and ego-centered beginnings of visual expression soon are merged with forces external to the youngster. Environmental factors, traditions, and values gradually exert greater pressure upon the growing child. Factors of reinforcement and reward as well as the structure of language and other means of communication impose themselves upon him.

Teachers can help children to recognize their own power in giving shape to their ideas and feelings by the emphasis and directions they foster in the classroom. At the simplest and most obvious level, the activities selected and the task presented must be such as to allow for the shaping of visual forms. Hence, it is easy to see that the "coloring in" of already prepared forms (e.g., turkeys, Christmas trees) does not allow much latitude for personal choice. At the other extreme, a blank piece of paper with a "do whatever you wish" instruction provides little or no help for a child whose thoughts and feelings may not be sufficiently structured for approaching the task of drawing. Teachers must be sensitive to a balance in which there is sufficient "structure" to enable a student's moving ahead with confidence but sufficient latitude for choice to invite and encourage uniqueness of expression.

By "structure" I am referring to the various factors that provide the "givens" as a youngster approaches his art work. For the most part, it is the teacher who creates an "outer structure" by the choices he makes—the medium or media to be used; the breadth and complexity of theme (or themes) for art activity; and the organization of time, space, and materials. This aspect of structure might be said to be the preconditions and the prevailing conditions within which the children work.

There is another sense in which the term "structure" can be used; namely, the "inner structure" created by the student as he engages in art activity. The training, purposes, values, and expectations of a child give direction and emphasis to the activities in which he engages. Effective teaching makes use of these directions and emphases as starting points. Effective teaching also seeks to enlarge and redirect these emphases in terms of standards that the teacher helps to evolve.

Thus, the model that I am projecting involves two matrices: the first, made up of an "outer structure" created by the teacher—the nature of the task or assignment presented to the students; and the second, made up of an "inner structure" provided by the student—his private values and directions as he views the task. The meeting place of these interlocking matrices is in the classroom.

To the extent that teaching is an "art," teachers need to deal with the subtle nuances of form and meaning in the classroom; their teaching involves qualitative decision making. To the extent that teaching is a "science," teachers can understand, control, and communicate about factors involved in such decision making. To be sure, any given teaching act may be the result of simultaneous judgments involving intuitive and felt responses. However, the point of view that I wish to set forth is that a teacher who is knowledgeable and informed of the multiplicity of factors involved in his own decisions and actions is more likely to make a qualitatively better decision.

What, then, are some of the factors that enter the "mix" of teacher decision making in the teaching of art?

1. Teachers must be aware of the medium or media being used. Every medium has its own intrinsic qualities. These qualities dictate its potentials for forming—the resiliency and resistance with which it can be shaped, its permanence as a form. Each medium imposes its own requirements upon its use. For example, working with a water-based clay requires damp storage until the work has been completed; working with plasticene enables continuous reshaping of forms, but no permanency. Working with wire involves certain physical con-

trols; the medium is, by its very nature, linear in quality. Working with cut paper in doing collage affords opportunities for overlapping shapes and planes; working with pen and ink provides opportunities for descriptive detail. Every medium also imposes its own demands in terms of skills and techniques. Generally, more resistant materials can only be changed by actions having a relatively fixed consequence (cutting into wood, stone, or linoleum); more resilient materials can be reshaped and reworked after an initial action (modeling of clay, moving and replacing collage forms, or painting over an already dry tempera form). A more resistant medium (wood, wire, or stone) can lead to frustration on the part of a young child who seeks to change its form or quality without having developed adequate knowledge of technique or insights into the inherent nature of the material.

2. Teachers must be aware of the dynamic relationship between the medium being used and the ideas being formed. All too often a youngster is heard to say, "I had a clear picture in my mind, but I just can't get it on my paper." The "clearly formed image" in one's mind is often the source of frustration when the medium being used does not lend itself to that image. By fixing an image in one's mind (using the forms of imagination) an inexperienced student can set an unattainable goal in terms of his abilities and the nature of the medium being used. Moreover, by setting such a fixed goal, the student robs himself of the discovery and invention that takes place in the process of working. Rather than starting with a fixed image (an already completed picture in one's mind), students should be helped to see and feel their own changing images as their ideas interact with materials. The starting point for art work must be ideas and images that will lend themselves to change and modification. In the process that follows the student's hand and mind engage in interaction with a medium. The evolving form is then the resultant of this interaction. The final image is usually not what may have been envisioned at the start. After all, the image "painted" within one's mind has been created in a different "medium" than is the case when one used paints and brush.

3. Teachers must be aware that creative activity in art (as in any other field) does not involve the creation of a form from "nothing." Creativity in art is not creativity in a mystical or biblical sense. The forms that are created grow out of already existing facts, ideas, and skills. To be sure, each child is unique; to some extent his drawings,

paintings, and sculpture can reflect this uniqueness. However, there is a sense in which the capacity to be "creative" is related to the store of skills, images, and ideas that are provided by others. This is what Pasteur meant when he said, "Fortune favours the prepared mind." Thus, good teaching in art introduces a flux of ideas and images and then helps students to uncover, select, rearrange, combine, and synthesize ideas and images drawn from this flux.

By asserting that children can be helped to recognize their own power in giving shape to their ideas and feelings, I am saying that teachers can help students to recognize that they (the students) can and do respond to their visual world. The nature of this response in the art class has to do with the dramatic and poetic aspects of seeing and forming visual images; it has to do with fostering creative insights in the way that such responses are formed.

Many classroom teachers approach the teaching of art with some hesitancy. Frequently they are heard to say, "I can't draw a straight line; how can I be expected to teach art?" Of course, the classroom teacher cannot be expected to be skilled in all techniques and processes for working with art media; nor can the classroom teacher be informed of the full range of resources for art activities. There is an essential role to be played by an art specialist in every elementary school. More than likely, however, this art specialist also will not be able to "draw a straight line." Moreover, I would assert that the drawing of a "straight line" has nothing to do with the central problems of teaching art in the elementary school. The central problem to be faced in the teaching of art involves attitudes toward adventure and discovery rather than toward technical skills. It is much more an attitude that would allow for the repositioning and restructuring of ideas. Of equal importance, it is an attitude that would allow for activity in terms of these values.

The classroom teacher can do certain basic things in relation to the students in his classroom:

1. He can accept and value his students as being creative. Questions and comments can be directed toward the more personalized and unique aspects of what children do in their art work. An attitude of teacher "acceptance" can give greater psychological freedom and security for the projecting of new ideas and forms.

2. He can consciously relate the inventions of one person to what others are doing. Johnnie's drawing may be of a bizarre animal;

Mary's drawing may dwell upon her doll; yet each may be inventive in the quality of detail or in the manner in which line has been used. By relating the variety of means by which children give shape to their ideas, teachers can give support to the differences as well as to the similarities in visual forms.

3. He can recognize the importance of feedback, invention, and intuition. By helping children to see new possibilities through the emerging forms, by encouraging children to talk about their feelings as they are being realized, and by supporting the willingness to build something different, teachers can set a tone for the exploration of visual forms.

4. He can encourage the making of visual judgments. Much of our communication is based upon verbal and/or mathematical symbols; yet much of our experience is based upon visual symbols. From pictures in textbooks to mass-produced images in our magazines, on our television screens, and on our highways, we are being confronted with powerful and pervasive images. Children need to learn to see the world about them; they need to learn to make visual judgments. They can be helped to talk about what they see—by comparing and noticing differences and similarities, by becoming aware of shapes, textures, and other visual qualities, and, above all, by making judgments as to quality. Judgments of quality are not simple, yes-no, good-bad judgments. Children should be helped to realize their own feelings about what they see; they should be helped to develop and refine their own criteria for the judgments they make.

The task of teaching art in the elementary school need not involve complicated equipment or the introduction of a great variety of techniques. Indeed, my own bias would be directed toward much greater simplification of media and materials being utilized, with much greater emphasis upon depth and quality of ideas. There should be, of course, some variety in the materials utilized in elementary school programs: paint, pastels, crayons, charcoal, clay, wire, wood, and textiles, to name a few. However, teachers should be wary of introducing such variety of media that novelty of materials becomes an end in itself to replace the challenge of ideas and art forms. It is then that children (and teachers) fall prey to "what is new and gimmicky"; that deep and personal quality of art gives way to the impersonal emphases of fad and fashion.

Thus far my discussion has focused upon the processes by which children can be helped to see and create visual forms; how teachers can encourage depth in response; how the process of forming visual ideas can be seen as an adventure in which feelings and materials are fused. The emphasis that I have identified is one that has its basis in the ideas and experiences that are part of the child's life. There is, however, another major dimension that needs to become part of the complex that comprises the elementary school art program—the knowledge and insights about art that are introduced by the teacher. The structure of teaching art, at any level, must be done with a sense for a larger body of knowledge and understanding about art itself. The concept of what constitutes an "artistic" problem—its limitations and possibilities—is central to what is to be taught. What the teacher does, of course, is related to the students in his class; what the teacher does must also draw upon the field of art as a basic resource. What then are the factors that make up "the field of art"? How can these resources be utilized?

Ideas as to what constitutes "art" have changed from period to period. In the Middle Ages, an "art" was a technique or a craft; those persons who engaged in the making of painting or sculpture were seen as engaging in a lower level of mechanical activity. The making of artifacts was not thought of as being particularly challenging; men made "art" because they were born into families that engaged in this kind of activity. Given these circumstances, there could be no interest in the expressiveness of the artifact or in the individuality of the artist. It was not until the Renaissance that the concept of the artist as an individual and the work of art as the result of human sensory, intellectual, and practical faculties appeared. Gradually, artists began their "transformation" from the role of craftsman and artisan to a position more closely aligned to that of the humanist: the poet and scholar. This change had (and continues to have) its impact upon the forms of art and the concept of the artist; it also has had broad implications for the idea of education in art. The change should be seen as part of a larger development involving the growth of individualism and the dramatic forces that developed in the Industrial Revolution. The displacement of artisans by machines and the popularization of ideas of individual freedom characterized a new and powerful stream of cultural change in whose force we still live. As a result, we have been and are now confronted with a changing array of styles and forms in art. Given the fantastic developments in mass media and mechanization, we are now faced with bewildering styles and forms with increased frequency and intensity.

When Walter Smith arrived from England in the 1870's to teach art, the focus was upon the training of skills in drawing and the crafts. A nation involved in the "important business of growing up"—expanding and developing its frontiers and building its industry and agriculture—had little or no time for the fine arts. Education was tied to utilitarian principles; education in the fine arts could only be part of our leisure-time activity or, at best, an activity of moral enlightenment. It was not until the 1920's that John Dewey and the progressive education movement started to formulate a viewpoint of art forms as the resultants of a creative process and the centrality of such process to educational goals. What followed was largely an "activity-centered" concept of teaching art—"art as experience."

From those reappraisals that have taken place in recent years (Hausman, 1965; Hastie, 1965), it is clear that the field of art education will have to address itself to the problem of rethinking and reconciling the child's personal resources for learning about art and the tremendous resources provided by art itself.

The more we look at the traditions of art, the more compelling George Kubler's statement about the limits of art becomes: "Let us suppose that the idea of art can be expanded to embrace the whole range of man-made things, including all tools and writing in addition to the useless, beautiful, and poetic things of the world. By this view the universe of man-made things simply coincides with the history of art" (Kubler, 1962, p.1). It then follows that the elementary school teacher can draw upon an infinity of man-made things as a resource for study and speculation. In the art class, the focus for such study would be understanding those factors that pertain to the aesthetic and artistic qualities inherent in the artifacts.

I cannot think of a single subject or theme for study in the elementary school for which there is not a rich source of related ideas and images to be drawn from the work of artists (to include craftsmen, designers, architects, and planners). Moreover, these images are readily available through publications, slides, photographs, and circulating exhibitions. Children can be shown the many ways that artists have shaped forms dealing with the same or similar themes as their own drawings and paintings; they can become aware of how one artist may have handled a particular subject in different ways.

Artists have dealt with an infinity of themes for their work—man, work, play, life, death, happiness, sorrow, fear. Even the simplest of themes such as "trees" or the "sun" can open tremendous visual and conceptual possibilities when one looks to the forms that artists have created. The trees in a Constable landscape as compared to those in a Van Gogh landscape could become the basis for a rich discussion. Children could look at the trees around their homes. What are the feelings of a tree when seen in a storm? What about the lonely tree surrounded by buildings in a city as compared to the tree in the forest? Trees could also be looked at for their color and structure. My example of "the sun" lends itself to a fantastic array of resources. From the Celtic sun worship remains of Stonehenge to the Egyptian sun-god Ra to the sun-temple of Konarah to modern conceptions of the same subject as seen in the works of Rousseau, Klee, Max Ernst, Miro, and Lippold, the teacher can demonstrate how artists of other times and places have given meaning to the very subject matters that concern the students. Naturally, some geographical areas will have greater advantage than others in the art forms that are available in local museums and galleries; some locations will have a greater concentration of artists and craftsmen. In all cases, however, imaginative teachers can do a great deal in bringing together the available resources to expand upon the student's knowledge and insight about visual forms.

My own bias is that children should be shown original works of art as often as possible. Just as we would want them to develop confidence and skills for shaping their own ideas, we should seek opportunities for children to come to grips with the primary data of art. Seeing and feeling the scale and subtle qualities of the materials used as well as sensing the tangible and real qualities of the artist's work are important to the realization and appreciation of an artifact. Put more simply, children should learn to deal with "real things." All of this is not to say that teachers should not use slides, photographs, and reproductions. Given a sense for the original qualities of art forms, children are better able to deal with "reproduced images" of artifacts. They are better able to place these images in "perspective" in their conceptions of "what is a painting?" or "what is a piece of sculpture?"

It is important that the elementary school provide an environment in which children see some of the rich store of images and forms of art. Placing a painting on a wall or a piece of sculpture in front of the building has educational value in itself. Children can and should learn to look at works of art as part of their normal surroundings. Concepts of art as being "in a museum" have tended to separate the perceiving of art from "what we do every day." The "masterpiece complex" (accompanied by a great deal of publicity as to the cost of a Rembrandt or a Van Gogh or a Picasso) has tended to shift attention from the basic level of experiencing artifacts to a prestige-oriented and commercial-valued point of view.

Works of art can and should be taken out of the realm of the "remote" and the "detached." In whatever way is possible the school should reflect an awareness of visual learning: (1) by exhibiting the art works of children; (2) by exhibiting the original works of artists (paintings, sculpture, ceramics, prints); (3) by arranging for visits to galleries and museums; (4) by arranging for visits from or to artists, craftsmen, architects, and designers.

My contention is that an imaginative classroom teacher, working with an art consultant or supervisor, can do a great deal to bring together the available resources for the teaching of art. This is especially the case when one approaches the problem of defining art to "embrace the whole range of man-made things." Teachers and their students could then set up their own galleries: of paintings, of sculpture, of toys, of musical instruments, of unusual tools, of strange photographs–the list could go on and on. By helping students to talk about the aesthetic qualities of things (helping them to realize their own response to the qualities inherent in the objects), teachers can help children to realize that they can and do respond to their visual environment. By encouraging children to seek out the unusual, subtle, interesting qualities of their own art work and the works of others, they can develop the students' breadth of perception as well as their conscious sense for the relationships between form and meaning. By focusing upon creative insights into the visual forms that children make and the visual forms about them, teachers can give new and enlarged meanings to the students' future.

In a recent article, Robert M. Hutchins posed the question "Are we educating our children for the wrong future?" Hutchins (1965, p.66) observes "The world is new and is getting newer every minute. . . . Almost every 'fact' I was taught from the first grade through law school is no longer a fact. Almost every tendency that was proclaimed has failed to materialize. The 'facts' and tendencies of today are those that nobody foresaw fifty years ago." Given the prospect of a world of even greater change, there are far-reaching and profound questions concerning just what it is that can be "taught" to prepare our youngsters for the future. Hutchins concludes that "what education can and should do is help people become human." I agree. By teaching people to become "human," I would place the theme of this volume as being central: "teaching for creative endeavor." In the visual arts, I would place key emphases upon developing knowledge and insight about the visual symbols and forms about us and the capacity to give visual form to emerging ideas and feelings. Visual symbols have always been critical to man's thought processes. By educating our children to be more sensitive to and knowledgeable about their visual world, we shall provide a key avenue for dealing with the future. The knowledge about art that I am referring to is really knowing art as an activity that is never satisfied with the obvious and the trivial. Knowing art, in the sense that I use the term, requires newly created visions and insights at every moment of living.

CHAPTER 14

Performing Arts

by

JOHN EDWARD BLANKENCHIP

John Edward Blankenchip earned his BFA degree at the Carnegie Institute of Technology and his MFA degree at the Yale Graduate School of Drama. After spending nearly three years in military service, he taught directing, scene and costume design, lighting, and theatre in relation to the community at Sarah Lawrence College. For two years he served as director of dramatic activities at the Boys Club of New York City. Currently, he is professor in the Division of Drama in the School of Performing Arts of the University of Southern California. He is involved in teaching experimental theatre, in directing, and in participating in contemporary theatre as well as in several creative production projects. He has served as producer-director of the USC Festival Theatre. Recently, he was producer-director of the Eugene O'Neill Festival at Stop Gap Theatre on the USC campus.

John Blankenchip's professional experience has been extensive. He has participated in the design of scenery, costumes, and lighting for productions on and off Broadway in New York City; at Tanglewood; at the Guild Opera in Los Angeles; at the La Jolla Summer Playhouse; and at the Sombrero Playhouse in Phoenix. He has also been active in productions at the Ivar and Civic Playhouse in Los Angeles and in the direction and design of production for the Ebony Showcase, Los Angeles.

CREATE. RE-CREATE. RECREATION. Three words. Similar sometimes—sometimes poles apart. They represent three approaches to the performing arts.

Create: (1) To bring into existence; make out of nothing, and for the first time. (2) To produce (as a work of art or a dramatic interpretation) along new or unconventional lines (created a new Hamlet). (3) To design (as a costume or a dress). (4) To make or bring into existence something new (as something of an imaginative or artistic character).

Re-create: (1) To create again. (2) To form anew, especially in the imagination. (3) To recollect and reform in the mind.

Recreation: (1) The art of re-creating or the state of being re-created. (2) A means of diversion or entertainment.

In the performing arts there is usually one who creates for a group who, in turn, re-creates or interprets for the recreation of a still larger body or group.

Work and study in the performing arts could progress more readily if more people would fully realize that the truly creative artist is the person who brings the idea into existence for the first time. In the theatre he is the playwright; in dance, the choreographer; and in music, the composer.

Next is the group who re-creates or interprets the idea: actors, dancers, musicians, directors, designers, and conductors. These are the interpretative artists whose function is to bring the creation of the author, the composer, and the choreographer to life. The better the interpreter the more creative he will be in his endeavor to realize as fully as possible in performance the intent of his role as conceived by the author.

Finally, there is the larger group who witnesses the re-creation for their recreation—the audience.

Creating in the Theatre

Theatre is a performing art. It is dead on the shelf. It lives on the stage; unfortunately, it can die there, too. Theatre is not only a performing art; it is also a collaborative art. The playwright creates the play; his creation is realized through the collaboration of interpreters. Properly understood and applied, this art of collaboration can be one of the theatre's greatest assets. One of the outstanding examples is *West Side Story*. The program states:

A musical (based on a conception of Jerome Robbins)
Book by Arthur Laurents
Music by Leonard Bernstein

Lyrics by Stephen Sondheim
Entire production directed and choreographed by
Jerome Robbins
Scenery designed by Oliver Smith
Costumes designed by Irene Sharaff
Lighting by Jean Rosenthal
Musical direction by Max Soberman
Orchestration by Leonard Bernstein with Sid Ramin
and Irwin Kostal

Jerome Robbins' "conception" was to adapt Shakespeare's *Romeo and Juliet* for the contemporary musical theatre. The unity of style achieved in the dialogue, lyrics, music, movement, and decor confirms the intelligence of his choice of collaborators. Each person, including Robbins, was working at his peak of creativity to interpret Robbins' conception. Each needed the other for full realization in performance. True, all of them were top professionals, as evidenced by their ability to work creatively within Robbins' conception of Shakespeare's play.

Oklahoma revolutionized the musical theatre. But plays had been used before as the "book" for a musical. What was so revolutionary, then? The revolution occurred in terms of the highly selected and motivated integration of the performing arts. The story and much of the dialogue were based on Lynn Riggs' *Green Grow the Lilacs.* Even though the story was not new, the treatment or adaptation was. Dialogue was employed in the usual sense, but when the effect of the words needed to be heightened Oscar Hammerstein II created the lyrics that were wedded to Richard Rodgers' score. The same kind of heightened selectivity occurred in terms of movement. Directorially, Rouben Mamoulian advanced the play to a certain level and then turned it over to the choreographer, Agnes De Mille. Ballets had been used in musicals before, but never had the dance blended so skillfully into the overall structure of the work. Dance is a heightened form of movement, of course, just as singing is a heightened form of speech. Here, as in the more recent *West Side Story,* the collaborators were all in tune.

Each collaborator is vitally concerned with interpretation. Oral interpretation is the concern of the director, acting coach, vocal coach, and actors. Visual interpretation is the concern of the designers (scenery, costumes, lighting), choreographer, director, and actors. Auditory interpretation is the concern of the director, conductor, actors, musicians, and sound men. All areas of interpretation—oral, visual, and auditory—should serve as a solid base for creative endeavor in the performing arts.

The performing arts abound with interpreters and performers but are sadly lacking in creators. Dance is developing many excellent performers. Here, as in the other arts, the technique can be taught. Music teems with performers, both vocal and instrumental; the theatre is full of actors, directors, and designers.

Nurturing Creativity in the Artist

But prime consideration must always be given to nurturing the truly creative artist-author. They are the creative catalysts of the performing arts and are the most difficult to discover and to develop. When one considers how few musicals, operas, or films are originally conceived for their particular media, one begins to have some idea of the problem. Most contemporary musicals and operas are based either on a former play or on a novel. In film credits, one has to search for "original screenplay," while the "based on" or "originally suggested by" flourish. Even composers of the caliber of Richard Rodgers and Oscar Hammerstein II have been most successful with adaptations.

To discover and develop truly creative artists, courses in composition are of vital importance—composition with words, sound, movement, and images. Students with ability must be encouraged to experiment in these areas. Every experiment will not pay off, of course, but a surprising number will, and each attempt will serve to increase the confidence of the student and promote further experimentation. Some elements that might prove stimulating to the student in composition are:

Line: straight, curved, diagonal, broken, regular, irregular
Color: intense, neutralized, light, dark, nonchromatic, polychromatic
Form: shape, predictable, unpredictable
Mass: size, amount, weight
Movement: kind, amount, high, low, contracted, extended, sustained

Sound: intensity, pleasing, disturbing, soothing
Rhythm: regular, irregular, repetitive
Texture: smooth, rough
Clarity: transparent, opaque, translucent
Conflict: kind, cause, contrast

It is essential that the creative work of the young playwright, composer, or choreographer be realized through performance; only in this way will he obtain the collaboration of the creative interpreters as well as the reaction of the intended receiver—the audience.

Selection of Material for Performing Artists

If original material is not available for performance in schools, as is often the case, then the problem of selection of material becomes extremely important. Great care should be taken at all times to produce the best available material. There should be solid reasons for the selection of the material to be presented. It should meet the specific needs of the occasion as well as of the students presenting it. Often, because of various pressures, a play, musical, opera, or orchestral work is put in rehearsal so the students can be working on something instead of working in it and with it.

The following list of questions should aid in the selection of material and in the preparation for performance:

1. Where is the work (play, musical composition, dance) to be performed? By whom? For whom?
2. What is the theme (author's intent) of the work?
3. What is the time of the work? When does it occur? Does the time have historical significance?
4. What part does each character have in the play, dance, or opera in relation to the development of the plot?
5. How is each character to achieve his function, as far as the plot is concerned, most creatively and effectively? What is his characterization?
6. What are five key moments of the work?
7. How and where on stage would you place the characters in each of the key moments to show the emotional content of the scene?
8. How would the placement of entrances and exits enhance the effectiveness of the key moments?

9. How should the performers be dressed?
10. How should the performers move?
11. How should the performers speak or sing?

Obviously, these questions must also be answered by the designers, actors, choreographer, and conductor. This group of creative interpretative artists must be guided by the director to find the particular style which is right for the re-creation of the playwright's creation.

Alternative Interpretations for Creative Performances

Robert Edmund Jones, the first important American scene designer, stated that "designing for the theatre is designing for an occasion." This seemingly simple statement contains the essence for success in all areas of performance: the "occasion" being the particular play, opera, or dance. Each production must be treated as a separate entity. The good collaborative artists—directors, actors, conductors, choreographers, and designers–do this instinctively. How can there be so many successful productions of *Hamlet* by actors of the caliber of Richard Burton, John Gielgud, Laurence Olivier, Christopher Plummer, Paul Scofield, John Barrymore, Maximilian Schell in so many different media—stage, film, television? They all use the same text; the words of the story or plot do not change. It is the individual interpretation of each artist with the aid of his director that distinguishes the performance. Obviously, each performer has carefully analyzed Shakespeare's intent in writing the play as well as the character of Hamlet in relation to the other characters in the play. The productions were not all placed in the same period historically; yet each of them was valid.

The student must become aware of the possibility of numerous right answers to an interpretation of a role or a production. He should be sufficiently motivated to explore approaches before eventually settling on one. Or he may have made his decision and then be shown by the director how a different interpretation would be more effective in the overall conception of the production in relation to the author's intent. So many productions go off the beam in performance because the director or designer or actors become enamored of an approach to a work that is completely foreign to the author's intent.

Developing the Imagination

The dramatic imagination can be stimulated and developed; it cannot be created. Some methods of developing this dramatic imagination are: creative dramatics (proven especially effective with children); mime or pantomime; eurythmics; improvisation, intelligently and thoroughly planned; and Stanislavski's magic "if."

Developing the imagination is involved in the process of freeing it. There must be some ostrich in all of us as evidenced by Halloween merrymaking: Cover one's face with a mask and he feels much freer as though he could not be seen. A similar kind of freeing will take place in actors, singers, and dancers, if one asks them to be something other than a person, that is, an inanimate object or an animal. Coordination and variety of movement are almost immediate. It is so much easier for the person to assume an impersonal identity. Field trips to the zoo for selection and detailed observation of a particular animal will prove beneficial not only in terms of movement but also in terms of emotional response.

Helping the Student to Become Creative

Teachers in English composition, journalism, music, art, dance, drama, and athletics should be aware of the possibilities for contribution and enrichment to the student in the creative field of the performing arts. The creative student with demonstrated ability should be encouraged in writing, composing, or choreographing. Equally important is the recognition and development of the student who is capable of creative interpretation—the good or outstanding performer, designer, or conductor. Both the creative and interpretative artists must develop through performance. The more creative and imaginative the preparation of these students, the closer they will come to the realization of the potential of the performing arts.

CHAPTER 15

The College and University

by

WILLIAM B. MICHAEL

A native of Pasadena, California, William B. Michael received his A.B. degree from UCLA and earned his M.S. in Education, M.A. and Ph.D. in Psychology from the University of Southern California, where he is professor of Education and Psychology. He also has taught at Princeton University, the University of California, Immaculate Heart College, and other colleges. He has served as a research associate at the RAND Corporation and the Educational Testing Service and as a research consultant to numerous colleges, school districts, civil service agencies, industries, and foundations. He has participated in several different editorial assignments for Educational and Psychological Measurement; *worked on the editorial board of the* Journal of Educational Measurement; *served as chairman of the editorial board of the* Review of Educational Research; *acted as co-chairman of a joint committee of the American Psychological Association, the American Educational Research Association, and the National Council on Measurement in Education, and as co-editor of the committee in the preparation of* Standards for Educational and Psychological Tests and Manuals. *The author still finds his greatest satisfaction in teaching, a profession he had hoped and planned to enter from the time he was five years old. Thus, his interest in* Teaching for Creative Endeavor *is a natural outgrowth of his many years of dedication to the teaching profession.*

ALTHOUGH MANY, if not most, of the points that have been made in previous chapters concerning how teaching for creative endeavor in the elementary and secondary school may be realized apply to the college and university setting, certain characteristics in the higher education scene suggest somewhat different emphases regarding how creative outcomes may be attained. What is to follow may well reflect to an excessive degree the perceptions and feelings generated from the writer's nearly twenty-six years of teaching experience in colleges and universities rather than information based upon objective evidence furnished by research studies. However, relatively little if any research has been published regarding the effectiveness of outcomes that have been associated with any systematic teaching efforts directed toward the manifestation of creative behavior on the part of college students.

The use of the word "creativity" in this chapter carries many of the meanings suggested by other contributors to this volume. Viewed as a constellation of primarily problem-solving activities in the learning process, which reflect the utilization of several different and relatively independent abilities such as those proposed by Guilford, creative endeavor represents an effort on the part of a student to generate or to bring about new information, a novel idea, or a unique product previously nonexistent in his conscious experience. Although this definition of creative endeavor is not completely satisfactory and although one must establish differential norms concerning the degree to which productive efforts may be considered creative relative to the level of maturity and experience of the college student, it will serve as an approximate frame of reference within which the contents of this chapter may be considered.

In what is to follow attention will be given to how expression of creative behavior by college and university students may be facilitated in relation to the following five factors in higher education: (1) the selection and placement of students—basically the admissions problem; (2) the curriculum and pattern of course requirements of the environment or climate of the college or university; (3) the social psychological characteristics of the environment or climate of the college or university; (4) the utilization of specific teaching procedures in relation to the learning process; and (5) the evaluation of student performance. Relative to each of these five categories, an attempt will be made to point out existing circumstances which often discourage the realization of creative endeavor on the part of students as well as to suggest steps that would seemingly enhance the likelihood that creative outcomes might be effected.

The Admissions Problem–Selection and Placement of Students

It seems evident to many psychologists and counselors that during the recent and current population explosion in the colleges and universities many promising candidates who have exhibited highly creative and enterprising behaviors during their high school years have been denied admission on the basis of too low a score on a scholastic aptitude or achievement test or on the grounds of too low a grade-point average in the college preparatory program in the high school. Admittedly, colleges must maintain academic standards, require suitable levels of competence in basic skills of language and mathematics, rely on past information gained from validation studies involving use of traditional achievement and ability measures, and reasonably expect a certain minimum level of conformity and responsibility on the part of students who have been given the privilege of studying at institutions of higher learning. Furthermore, academic programs and their standards vary immensely from one collegiate institution to another.

However, it is well known that most tests used for admissions tend to require convergent thinking abilities and conforming patterns of intellectual behavior rather than divergent abilities and other intellectual processes judged to be related to creative thinking. To the extent that the expectations of the faculty members and requirements of the curriculum make demands upon the exercise of convergent production of ideas and necessitate conformity to the frequently narrow range of professors' expectations concerning appropriate academic pursuits, traditional aptitude measures will continue to be important in the admissions process. Nevertheless, the failure of most colleges to introduce, even experimentally, measures related to creative behavior can lead to at least two undesirable consequences: (1) the exclusion of capable students who could make use of special types of abilities not measured by traditional test variables in order to meet even the requirements of a conventionally taught and often somewhat sterile curriculum or (2) the denial of admission to students who would probably be quite successful in an imaginatively planned curriculum creatively taught.

What is clearly needed is a comprehensive research program in a number of carefully chosen colleges and universities—a program in which the subsequent performance of one group of students with high scores on measures of creative ability but with somewhat lower scores in traditional tests of scholastic aptitude and achievement than those usually required are compared with a second group of students admitted on conventional and often rather rigid bases. It certainly seems reasonable to believe that in the fine arts, theater arts, colleges of business administration and accounting, and certain professional schools, such as engineering or dentistry, very special types of creative abilities may be required that are relatively more important to success than they are in traditional liberal arts programs. For example, how many potential painters, ceramicists, sculptors, actors, poets, novelists, dramatists, or musicians are being lost either because of inflexible and mechanical standards for college admission or because of the lack of appropriate or valid indices of their potential aptitudes?

As the writer has pointed out elsewhere (Michael, 1965), the selection of highly creative college students may not be expected to work out too successfully unless (1) allowance is made for differences in creative abilities required in different curricula, (2) efforts are directed toward placing students in faculty and student cultures appropriate to the perceived goals of the prospective freshmen or transfer students, (3) expression of creative behavior is anticipated, encouraged, and rewarded by faculty members, (4) class assignments afford appropriate opportunities for students to engage in creative activities, and (5) evaluation is based on measures of achievement which themselves reflect outcomes associated with creative endeavor. Thus the use of so-called creative ability tests for college admission cannot be expected to reveal high predictive validities unless the evaluation of student progress is based on clearly specified and operationally defined objectives reflecting creative experiences in the college curriculum itself. Thus the development of valid tests for selection and placement of creatively oriented students could seemingly be achieved if committees of faculty members and students could work closely with a professional staff of an office of evaluation or of a testing bureau in coordinated and truly collaborative efforts to devise instruments of evaluation that are clearly anchored to objectives emphasizing divergent production and other creative thinking processes and outcomes.

Curricula and Patterns of Requirements of Colleges and Universities

Although definitive research evidence is lacking, one probable reason for the absence of a greater amount of creative behavior on the part of students—despite the heroic efforts of a noteworthy minority of certain professors—is the almost unbelievably rigid set of patterns of course requirements in many institutions. Well-meaning faculty committees—especially those in general education—are stifling almost any expression of creative behavior by putting virtually every imaginable hurdle in the way of eager students who yearn for even a limited opportunity to study certain areas of keen interest to them in at least a reasonable degree of depth. Large state and even privately endowed municipal universities seem to be particularly guilty of this unfortunate emphasis of having students meet rigidly set unit requirements. How many students in such institutions have ever succeeded in being graduated without at least one petition? Very few!

Even in some graduate schools the problem of inflexibility in the curriculum is almost as serious as it is at the undergraduate level. As in undergraduate programs, not only the required sample of courses supposedly devised to ensure breadth of knowledge, but also the invariant sequence in which they must be taken serves to discourage a student's doing any original work in an intensive and imaginative fashion. How frequently the writer has heard outstanding graduate students who already having published two or three articles say that they have not really had the opportunity to study the sorts of things they need to know for their professional careers! How often these same students who are about to take their qualifying examination for the Ph.D. degree after two full-time years of residence sincerely and rightfully complain that they have had virtually no time to learn anything about the particular field in which they wish to specialize!

Although many colleges and universities take pride in the fact that they supposedly encourage autonomous decision-making behavior and self-reliance on the part of their students, the general education requirements in terms of fixed numbers of units in carefully prescribed courses in the humanities, social sciences, natural sciences, and the arts often leave neither room for electives nor time for the creative student to probe and to study intensively even one area in which he may be highly interested without his taking a substantial risk of suffering a severe drop in his grade point average—a risk which could well mitigate against his securing a scholarship, his retaining the one he already has, or his later being admitted to graduate school.

Perhaps most offensive of all to the creatively oriented student is the college or university with numerous one- and two-unit courses. Students who are simultaneously taking six, seven, or even eight essentially unrelated courses, as often happens in the general education program during the freshman and sophomore years, are spread so thin that they have little or no time to pursue in depth any intellectual hobby or particular field of special interest—to say nothing of their inability to spend even a few hours a week reading the *Saturday Review* or the Book Review section of the *New York Times*—without the risk of losing valuable grade points necessary for them (a) to retain their scholarships, (b) to qualify for one the following semester, or (c) to receive favorable consideration for future admission to graduate school.

Some of the most creative students are willing to take academic risks of earning C's in most of their courses in order to have time to devote their energies to one or two courses that are of considerable interest to them or to certain important school activities such as drama, the debating society, or the school symphony in order to give expression to their creative energies. Although many a student will be able to earn a sufficient number of A's or B's in specialized courses of considerable interest to him, some of the less fortunate ones may receive one or two F's in required courses that cannot be counterbalanced by even two or three A's earned in other courses during one semester. If the creatively oriented student is unusually lucky by being placed on probation, he may still have to face the dreary experience of repeating the same unimaginatively taught courses in general education in order to earn the necessary C's for graduation.

Although systematic research evidence of an extensive nature is lacking, it has often been suggested that there is a negative correlation between the amount or quality of creative endeavor—especially on the part of the student in the fine arts or in applied sciences—and grade-point averages earned in college. Definitive research studies are needed as soon as possible to ascertain to just what extent highly creative students, as judged by their performance on tests of creative abilities or by their products of a unique and novel nature, are dropping out of college or are failing to attain admission to graduate schools because of questionable scholarship.

In particular, for assisting the student who in terms of test data and previous performance has shown promise of being highly creative, several suggestions may be formulated, although it must be emphasized that conclusive research evidence is lacking on which to base their feasibility. As a matter of fact, most if not all of the recommendations apply to students of superior intellectual capabilities whether they be assessed on convergent or divergent dimensions of cognitive functioning. Moreover, one may expect that many of the more timid bright students who have not given evidence of creative expression may have been stifled in their few attempts to do original or independent work or may have been penalized on previous occasions when they have deviated in even slight ways from the inflexible expectations and standards set by certain authoritarian and fear-provoking high school teachers. The following six recommendations with reference to curricular practices would appear to be worthy of consideration in the realization of the expression of creative behavior:

1. In the liberal arts college as well as in the selected professional schools, curricula should be developed in which fewer courses per semester (e.g., three five-unit or five-hour or four four-unit or four-hour subject areas) constitute a full-time load. In addition, an average allowance of at least one contact hour per week should be made for small group meetings (seminars), visitations with professors, independent readings, attendance at cultural events, or participation in other broadening activities. Such a plan, if not burdened with simply more repetitive busy work, should afford most students not only improved opportunities for the development of lasting understandings, for enhancement of problem-solving skills, and for formation of both positive attitudes and enduring appreciations, but also encouragement for the initiation of some highly original work in which each student may be greatly interested.

2. For the highly creative student who is desirous of planning and undertaking his own investigations embodying library or laboratory research, at least one four-hour course should be available each semester on an independent study basis. Even at the freshman and sophomore level such encouragement should be given, especially if a highly creative student has keen interests in special problem areas.

3. To encourage freedom in creative efforts with minimum risk to academic standing as determined by conservative and traditional marking procedures, a grade of "credit" might well be assigned upon completion of courses of independent study. Such a plan would allow the student freedom to develop his own ideas in his own unique

ways rather than in a manner that might be directed or contrived toward pleasing a professor or toward meeting an artificial set of course requirements in disguised form.

4. To stimulate the highly creative and gifted college student, the opportunity to progress as rapidly as his abilities and efforts permit should be allowed through use of a plan of comprehensive examinations much as in the University of Chicago tradition—examinations which represent a challenge to the student to exhibit higher levels of intellectual performance including demonstration of his creative abilities. Graduation in three years or less should frequently be possible and indeed would often be desirable for the student who will be pursuing a long term of graduate work or who will wish to derive practical benefits of working for one year before beginning his graduate studies.

5. Provision should be made for completion of a substantial amount of course work at both the undergraduate and graduate levels on a tutorial basis. The interaction of creative professors with the individual student or with small groups of students would seem to be highly beneficial as evidenced by the frequently heard students' statements that one or two teachers who took a personal interest in working with them exerted a tremendous influence on their professional careers. Two noteworthy examples of such individual attention are to be found in the precept system for undergraduate students at Princeton University and in the tutorial system available to undergraduate students in the honors program at the University of Southern California.

College and University Environments

The college and university environment is a broad term which includes (1) physical facilities such as buildings, classrooms, laboratories, libraries, and residential quarters and (2) the social psychological climate which may be conveniently viewed in Stern's (1963) terms as consisting of (a) a press and (b) needs. "Press" stands for external pressures placed on members of the college community as inferred from actions done to its members, and "needs" represents the important determinants of behavior within the person. Actually, press is a characteristic of the environment which is pertinent to the fulfillment or denial (frustration) of a need. In the college setting, the construct of press is probably most advantageously viewed in terms of how groups of individuals (such as students, faculty members, administrators, or alumni) perceive or interpret their social environment. Thus if the major social groups on a campus perceive that great emphasis is placed on scholarly activities, the social climate would be judged as intellectual. It may be hypothesized that the closer the perceptions of different campus groups are concerning the characteristics of the social environment, the higher will be the degree of harmony and morale of both the students and faculty members of that campus. Therefore, it is reasonable to believe that the realization of creative endeavor in students will flourish when teachers, administrators, and students not only hold similar value systems regarding the importance of opportunities for teaching experiences that foster creative endeavor, but also actively perceive that each group is working toward this common goal.

In advising high school students who either have shown high potentiality for creative endeavor on appropriate ability tests or have performed in a highly creative fashion in their school assignments, counselors might well try to suggest to them those colleges in which it appears that emphasis in the curricula and in teaching procedures is placed upon the attainment of creative problem-solving processes and upon the production of new if not at times bizarre and unconventional ideas. At the present time, objective evidence is lacking concerning what the highly creative individual's perceptions would be of institutions of higher learning in which teaching was undertaken for the encouragement of creative endeavor. However, psychometric devices developed by Pace (1963) and by Stern (1963) afford a means of ascertaining the perceptions that students and faculty members hold of the characteristics in their college and university environments. For example, using the College Characteristics Index (CCI) prepared by Pace and Stern (Pace, 1962), Thistlethwaite (1963) demonstrated sharply differentiated patterns in student cultures and faculty cultures relative to productivity in the natural sciences and to output in the arts, humanities, and social sciences.

It may well be that for each of several curricular areas students with certain patterns of measurable creative abilities hold rather distinctive profiles on environmental measures of what their perceptions concerning the ideal college would resemble. Once necessary normative data can be furnished by different institutions of higher learning for each of several academic areas, such as the natural sciences, the social sciences, or the humanities, it would seem possible to match certain groups of creatively oriented high school students who have one kind of profile pattern in their perceptions of their dimensions of the ideal college environment with a collegiate institution whose students and faculty members both hold patterns of perceptions similar to those of the high school students.

However, if there is a conflict in the perceptions of faculty members and college students regarding the relative standings of their institution on each of several measurable environmental characteristics, the prospective candidate for admission, whether highly creative or not, may be somewhat dissatisfied with the sort of educational program to which he will be exposed. Thus one source of dissatisfaction for the student placing relatively high in one or more creative abilities might well be explained in terms of discrepancies between a student's ideal conception concerning what the standings of a college should be on each of several measurable characteristics and what his actual perceptions are of the position of a given college on these same characteristics.

At the present time attention may be advantageously directed toward one highly useful scale for the assessment of five dimensions of college and university environments—namely, the instrument called CUES (*College and University Environmental Scales*), which was prepared by Pace (1963) and is distributed by the Educational Testing Service. Furnishing scores on five perceived dimensions of (1) community, (2) scholarship, (3) practicality, (4) propriety, and (5) awareness, CUES gives a basis for the comparison of the perceptions of various social groups on the campus as well as of prospective groups of freshmen or transferring students. Although normative data are available concerning the perceptions of student bodies at more than forty colleges throughout the United States (Pace, 1963), what is very much needed is a set of comparative norms for relatively productive groups of high school students in given academic subjects with respect to (a) their idealized perceptions of measurable dimensions of college environments and (b) their differential standings on standardized tests of creative abilities. Perhaps the accumulation of such normative information on high school students would afford a relatively helpful means for counseling those individuals who give promise of being highly creative provided, of course, that comparable data can be made available for college majors at least at a divisional level.

Even for the relatively less creative individual, every opportunity should be afforded for such an evaluation of his potentialities and preferences, as it is quite possible that latent abilities will be developed to a substantial degree provided that the student can be placed in the sort of college environment in which he receives the kind of nurturing which his particular personality structure may require. Admittedly, the practical difficulties facing the implementation of such a counseling procedure are great in view of the still existing gap between the research and developmental phases of tests of creativity and their availability on an operational basis. There is also the risk that matching students with certain creative potentialities to college environments of their choice may possibly induce undesirable patterns of conformity—patterns that might not arise had the students been placed in a somewhat more challenging environment than that dictated by their idealized perceptions. Although numerous problems exist in placing students in the sort of college environment that will bring about the fruition of their creative potentialities, it does appear that under the guidance of competent psychologists and counselors potential measuring instruments and clinical procedures exist or will soon exist for placing students in the types of educational institutions in which they have the maximum possible opportunities for the development of their creative potentialities.

Restraints in the College Environment upon Teaching for Realization of Creative Endeavor

Although much attention has been given concerning the perceptions which both students and faculty members may have regarding the characteristics of the campus environment, one should be aware of the environmental pressures in the university or college which are placed upon many faculty members—pressures which may well interfere with the quality of teaching and eventually influence to a marked degree the perceptions which members of the student body may have concerning the worth of the education which they are receiving. Even though an institution of higher education may be renowned for the reputations of its scholarly professors and for the high general-ability level of its students, the continuation of undue pressure to publish research and the persistence of perhaps unreasonable expectations regarding the performance of professors on the part of college and university administrators may lead to an erosion of teaching effectiveness on the campus.

That there is not greater effort on the part of many college professors to facilitate the expression of creative behavior in their students may in some instances be attributed in large measure to the restraints imposed by the college environment—especially the policies of the administrative staff relative to the system of rewards for professors. Although it is true that there are a few rare professors who can bring out the creative potentialities of students under even the most adverse working conditions, only a handful of college professors can simultaneously be internationally famous scholars, inspiring and resourceful teachers, dedicated committeemen, and self-sacrificing servants in community and government assignments.

Much has been written during the past few years about the "publish or perish" reprint race under which the professor in the relatively more prestigious institution is under increasing pressure to turn out large numbers of highly abstract and theoretical articles in esoteric journals, if he is to be promoted in rank, advanced in salary, or given tenure of employment. (The term "reprint race" is an expression used by many professors who compete with one another in amassing reprints of articles which they have published. For each article a professor usually receives 100 or more reprints which he distributes to his colleagues and superiors to keep them abreast of his work. The professor who generates the greatest number of inches of different reprints—one reprint per article—on his shelf or in the faculty archives wins the race.) It is the writer's impression that there has been some reduction in teacher effectiveness in the light of such pressure. Moreover—and perhaps even more damaging to teaching than the reprint race—has been the excessive amount of administrative committee work (much of it of highly questionable value) in many institutions of higher education—committee activities which have seriously drained the energy of professors from their primary task of teaching.

Seriously, one may ask, what has happened to the activity of teaching in the prestigious college or university? Although much lip service has been given by well-meaning administrators to the importance of teaching, attempts of evaluating its effectiveness have not been too satisfactory. However, for academic and administrative review committees passing upon promotions in salary and rank it is simply too easy to count the number of bibliographic entries on an annually submitted biographical data form or to total up the number of special awards, prizes, editorships, or elective offices held in national professional societies. As human beings who have needs for recognition and security, professors are likely to devote their energies to those activities for which they receive the greatest reinforcement and reward from their administrative officers—mainly publication, at the expense of needed time and effort given to preparation of lectures and examinations, to the teaching process itself, and to conferences with students.

The publish-or-perish reprint race has already reached such ridiculous extremes in some colleges and universities that a fairly well-defined hierarchy has developed regarding the types and qualities of scholarly journals, the required thickness of the covers on a book or monograph if it is to have status as a publication, or the expected length of the bibliographic entries in an article submitted for publication. In some institutions the professor in an academic field or one even in a school of education may be penalized by his peers or his department chairman for preparing manuals containing useful instructional materials, for writing highly readable textbooks for elementary and secondary school students or for even college students, and for writing popularized versions of his discipline, as such efforts do not meet the image surrounding certain obscure criteria concerning the esoteric properties of research productivity and of scholarly enterprise. Needless to say, well-written and stimulating books irrespective of the audience for which they may be intended can do much to spark interest in an academic field—a degree of interest that may well lead to subsequent creative endeavor, innovation of problem-solving approaches, inventive styles of thinking, and lasting attitudes of a highly constructive nature on the part of the readers of these publications.

One rather amusing story was brought to the writer's attention a few years ago concerning an elaborate point system that had been worked out by a chairman for promotion of his staff members in a department of psychology at a large university in the Midwest. Since publication productivity counted for most of the points earned by professors, the system of assigning credits to articles and monographs is perhaps of greatest interest. First, each of several journals was assigned a prestige rating from a scale value of ten to the lowest possible scale value of one. The prestige level was derived from the pooled judgments of a special committee of professors so that the reliability of the prestige score would be relatively high. Next, a standard printed page size of 350 words was chosen as the basic unit for counting, and then elaborate conversion factors were worked out for changing the numbers of words per page to the number of basic pages. Special allowance was made for charts, graphs, tables, and footnotes.

Each year at evaluation time the numbers of basic pages in the written publications of the professors were calculated. For each journal article the converted number of basic pages would be weighted by its prestige value to arrive at a certain score, and the resulting numbers of points for the articles were totaled. In a parallel system of counting, special allowance was given to monograph research. A fairly accurate rule-of-thumb allowance was that one monograph of fifty pages was worth approximately six articles. Once a certain number of points had been accumulated promotion to the next salary step or rank level was virtually automatic.

In order to meet the deadlines for publication evaluation, professors hit on elaborate schemes for scheduling the output of articles such as by paying for early publication or by regulating the pace of publication so that in no one year would there be an appreciable gap in the amount of productivity. Certain professors tried desperately to have themselves appointed to editorial boards so that their manuscripts would be more readily accepted. Because of a discount in the number of points assigned to writers who co-authored articles, professors would solicit the help of graduate students but not list their names in order to avoid losing any points despite the fact that these students had made important contributions. In their enviable position in the power structure, senior professors would tend to involve in their research efforts as many instructors and assistant professors as possible in order to turn out large numbers of articles so that they could win the reprint race by the sheer weight of numbers of points even though they as co-authors were also subject to the usual discount in numbers of points received. Whenever the instructors and assistant professors could effectively resist the pressures of having to co-author articles without the risk of political jeopardy, they would pad their articles as much as possible in order to amass a greater number of credits. Competition became so stiff that individuals of equivalent rank would not talk to one another about their research ideas lest another colleague would rush first into print with the basic idea. In this highly competitive situation ghost-writing facilities of graduate students as well as those of off-campus authors (frequently frustrated housewives of underpaid professors in related departments) were put to a supreme test.

Soon graduate students began to register complaints to the faculty deans for not having received recognition for their research contributions. Undergraduate students who were never able to find their professors during their scheduled office hours began to complain. Even a few disgruntled groups of students circulated petitions asking for the removal of professors whose teaching had reached an all-time low in its quality and stimulus value. One can readily imagine how teaching performance must have deteriorated under such pressures and especially how efforts of these teachers to stimulate creative endeavor on the part of their students must have suffered. As a consequence of the anxiety underlying the almost prohibitive tension to accumulate points for the reprint race, many a professor manifested soured dispositions and negative attitudes toward teaching. Any semblance of a happy atmosphere in the classroom or seminar soon evaporated, and any attempt to spark creative work or interest in students quickly disappeared.

It would seem that the mature college or university administrators would make allowance for individual differences in the strengths and weaknesses of their faculty members with respect to each of the four commonly applied criteria for promotion: (1) publication of research in scholarly journals, (2) teaching effectiveness, (3) committee participation, and (4) community services. Great strength in one area or moderate strength in three out of the four areas should suffice for promotion at a reasonable rate, and great strengths in two or more areas should lead to accelerated promotion. For example, it should be possible for a member of the instructional staff who is an outstanding committee worker, a reasonably good teacher, a somewhat inferior research worker, and an average contributor in his service to the community to realize relatively frequent salary increments and regular promotion in rank. Although there is no demonstrable evidence that individuals who are outstanding in research productivity are necessarily the most capable teachers, one could hope that participation in research activities should invigorate and improve teaching, if professors are not pushed too hard. It also appears equally reasonable to believe that relief from the anxiety to publish at a rapid rate should be associated with superior teaching, relatively greater amounts of attention devoted to the individual student, and a generally relaxed atmosphere in which creative endeavor on the part of students would be not only encouraged but also achieved. In the long run, the production of a higher quality of research on the part of professors might well result.

Teaching Procedures Conducive to Realization of Creative Endeavor

In several of the previous chapters numerous suggestions have been made regarding ways in which elementary and secondary school teachers may facilitate the expression of creative endeavor on the part of their pupils. Many of the points set forth are quite applicable in the college setting. As the writer has indicated elsewhere (Michael, 1964), the optimal opportunity for realization of creative behavior of college students rests upon a flexible style of teaching in the classroom situation—a style that requires (a) a broad but sensitive plan lending itself to quick modification and involving the judicious arrangement of curricular experiences in terms of the level of intellectual and affective readiness of students, (b) the provision for an appropriate set of incentives and motivational devices that reward creative endeavor and thus enhance its continual expression, (c) the encouragement of open communication in a non-threatening atmosphere that allows for a high degree of feedback and interaction for both students and teachers, (d) the planning and development of exciting, meaningful, and worthwhile assignments, special projects, and examinations that in avoiding trivial and repetitive busy work provide a means for the periodic assessment and further encouragement of creative behavior around broadly but carefully developed behavioral objectives underlying the processes of creative learning. With respect to these four requirements, it probably goes without saying that considerable leeway should be given to individual differences in creative abilities, interests, and any highly specialized talents. Moreover, the thoughtful reader, who may wish to find theoretical support for the four requirements just suggested, can probably find some degree of confirmation in the theoretically oriented presentation in chapter 2 by Guilford and Tenopyr. There appear to be many implications in the model posed by Guilford and Tenopyr concerning the nature of creative thinking that afford practical insights regarding ways in which the teaching-learning process can be directed or modified to effect the expression of creative endeavor by college students.

At a more concrete level than that immediately suggested by Guilford and Tenopyr are certain practical suggestions that the writer has prepared on the basis of his experience with a number of college students who have specifically listed patterns of teaching behavior which they have observed in their college professors. In particular, interest is centered on what students have judged to be behavioral manifestations of the professor who stifles creative activities. Although not exhaustive, the following list of behaviors constitutes a syndrome that partially describes the college professor who does not teach for the realization or facilitation of creative endeavor:

1. Takes roll at each class meeting and/or uses a seating chart.

2. Gives highly repetitious and frequently pointless assignments consisting of almost endless busy work.

3. Requires memorization of petty facts, names, dates, formulas, and other trivia.

4. Fails to outline or to state clearly at the beginning of the semester what the schedule of specific requirements in paper or laboratory assignments or in examinations will be so that the creatively oriented student can carefully plan for the effective use of his time. Often assigns extra papers with short due dates or announces examinations for times when important school activities conflict.

5. Frequently exhibits punitive behaviors in a number of petty ways, as in reprimanding students for being late, locking the door to the classroom after class starting time (in violation of all reasonable fire regulations), scheduling examinations on the Monday after homecoming weekend, shortening previously announced due dates for term papers, withholding answers indefinitely to problems in mathematics and science courses, forgetting to give back examination papers for many weeks, promptly returning papers to have all the "i's" dotted, or lowering a student's final mark when work is turned in slightly late for perfectly valid reasons.

6. Gives the impression or frequently expresses concern that students are trying to put something over on him if they are given a chance to do so. (Students are assumed to be guilty of trying to avoid work or scholarly obligations unless they are first proved to be innocent.)

7. Keeps class in constant state of jitters by putting students on

the spot in an emotionally threatening way, by giving unannounced examinations, by losing emotional control, or by making inconsistent, punitive, and generally unfair demands on certain students whom he singles out for one reason or another.

8. Shows a virtually complete lack of sense of humor in his lectures or during discussions in the classroom. Since he almost never smiles or laughs, he gives the impression of being apathetic, indifferent, or even hostile to his students.

9. Conveys an exaggerated sense of his own importance by behaving in a pompous fashion, by deliberately trying to confuse students with a pedantic display of his esoteric knowledge, by reminding them of their stupidity, intellectual deficiencies, or inferior positions, or by belittling their well-intentioned efforts.

10. Displays a lack of emotional maturity or control by trying to cover up when asked a question to which he does not know the answer, by becoming highly defensive if not outraged when challenged by students on a controversial issue, by being rude or sarcastic when students have difficulties with their assignments or examinations, or by even losing his temper and sense of propriety in speech when students fail to understand him.

11. Talks in an almost endless monotone with almost no appreciable change in inflection or emphasis. Such deadly lectures often occur when professors read dog-eared lecture notes yellow with age.

12. Discourages students from asking questions either through his punitive and hostile manner or through his failure to provide time for a question-and-answer session or for a discussion period.

13. Fails to give much needed overview of what will be or has been discussed or explained in class so that students can grasp the main points and interrelationships (the Gestalt) and not become lost in a myriad of detail.

14. Either poses no stimulating questions in his lectures or asks questions that fail to bring about any creatively oriented discussion. Occasionally may pose thoughtful questions but does not permit the students time to answer.

15. Spends large portions of class time in trying to make up his mind—to make even the simplest decisions may take thirty to forty minutes—concerning whether to give or not to give an examination next week, to require or not to require an extra paper, to discuss one topic or another at the next class meeting, to give or not to give make-up examinations, to waive one requirement or to substitute one

requirement for another when a student seeks admission to a class, or to give or not to give a homework assignment over the Christmas recess. Frequently so confined and rigid in his conceptions that he cannot make decisions about circumstances that do not neatly fit his previously conceived and rigidly formulated set of operational rules.

16. Provides no system of rewards for creative endeavor. Often penalizes students for an original or novel rendition of an assignment or an examination even when his directions to its completion are highly ambiguous, contradictory, and confusing.

17. Arbitrarily assigns marks or grades on the basis of a normal curve or some other equally ridiculous statistical model that is totally inconsistent, irrelevant, and unrealistic in relation to the ability level of the class or to the process of selective admissions of college students. Rarely makes any allowance for raising grades of students who have completed their assignments in unorthodox but highly imaginative and creative ways. Year after year uses the same standards for assigning grades even though the general ability level of classes is systematically on the upswing because of improved admissions procedures.

18. Gives examinations the resemblance of which to the content of the course or to the stated objectives of the lectures, reading assignments, discussions, laboratory or project assignments is purely coincidental.

19. Administers examinations with such short time limits that the highly creative student has no opportunity to organize his presentation or to develop an exposition of his novel ideas or new insights.

20. Fails to include in his examinations test questions that evaluate creative endeavor but tends to incorporate either objective or essay items that restrict the student's thinking to memorization and recall of isolated and unrelated bits of information about which any student after graduation could care less.

Evaluation of Student Performance

In the previous sections there has been frequent reference to the evaluation of the creative performance of students. It has been implied that without the presence of a certain degree of continuity and coordination in the admissions process, in the planning of the curricula, and in the evaluation of student work in terms of carefully defined objectives with a curriculum planned for the manifestation of creative behavior, one cannot expect a high degree of predictive validity for measures of creative abilities or a high degree of content validity in the achievement tests to which students will be exposed in their courses.

The evaluation of the attainment of operationally defined objectives in a curriculum emphasizing the realization of creative behavior depends upon the use of a variety of criterion measures. College professors must go considerably beyond the construction of multiple-choice test items which all too frequently tend to encourage the development and enhancement of only convergent thinking abilities. Important and useful as objective tests are, there is probably a practical limitation concerning the degree to which objective test items can be prepared and modified for the evaluation of creative abilities in most curricula. What appears very much to be needed is the continued, if not expanded, use of tests with simple completion items in which students are granted considerable freedom in their generation of relatively novel and imaginative answers. At a somewhat higher level of evaluation of creative abilities, carefully designed essay examinations probably afford one of the best means for the assessment of creative endeavor provided that faculty members can be given sufficient guidance in improving the reliability of their scoring procedures. As mentioned previously a college testing bureau or center for evaluation can be most helpful in providing service to professors who need aid in constructing, scoring, and marking examinations provided that the professors do not feel that their academic freedom is in any way being threatened. Joint committees involving professionally trained specialists in measurement and evaluation, academic professors, and students themselves could be most helpful in evolving participation of faculty members in evaluation processes that embody the use of examinations designed to assess creative endeavor.

A special word should be spoken for the open-book examination which may be written during an extended class period or even outside of class if students feel that they need additional time. Most professors—even the conservative ones—must admit in all frankness that existing examination procedures are highly artificial when viewed in the light of the sort of creative working experiences which students will face after graduation. Whenever a student has a challenging problem to face as a member of the adult community, he will rarely be denied access to the books, reference volumes, articles in professional journals, or other library sources which he will need to consult. It is high time that professors cut down on the amount of sheer rote memorization which they require of students on examinations. Stringent time limits upon examinations also constitute another artificial restriction imposed upon the student who may simply need more time to show his talents for creative productivity.

Perhaps even more important than the use of examinations to assess creative endeavor are such other criterion measures as scales for the evaluation of products in the arts or check lists concerning the adequacy of research papers in the natural sciences and the social sciences. The involvement of students in the humanities in such important learning experiences as preparing book reviews embodying literary criticism or in writing short stories, essays, poems, plays, expository articles, or even novels furnishes additional means of generating products that panels of judges can evaluate for their creative merits. Given encouragement to submit such creative works for publication, students may feel a new license of freedom in their course work. Not to be overlooked as another form of creative experience open to evaluation is participation in colloquia, seminars, and professional meetings by outstanding upper division students and graduate students. In short, there are many ways for evaluating creative endeavor—approaches which many professors have probably felt hesitant in trying, perhaps in fear of being criticized by their colleagues or even of being outmaneuvered by their students.

The need for diversification in evaluation procedures is underscored by the frequent observation that examination procedures have been so artificial and so unrealistically contrived that they serve only to encourage students to find ways to outwit the professors. In a highly competitive situation involving a tremendous amount of memorization of unrelated and trivial facts, students are encouraged to use somewhat unorthodox procedures—less politely known as cribbing—in achieving a reasonably satisfactory standing in class. Although the problems of formulating reliable and valid decisions regarding the extent to which students attain a level of achievement commensurate with the level of expectations of their professors are indeed difficult, an exciting challenge is posed to the academic community for the evaluation of creative endeavor, especially if all the hard work spent during the past twenty years in research on creativity is to bear any meaningful and practical rewards in the future education of both undergraduate and graduate students.

Summary and Conclusion

The realization of creative endeavor on the part of college and university students has been shown to be dependent on at least five interrelated factors. First to be considered has been the need for a flexible admissions process in which allowances are made for the selection of a reasonable proportion of students who either have shown high standing on measures of certain creative and divergent thinking abilities and/or have demonstrated their creative potentialities during their high school years. Even though some students may exhibit relatively low performance on conventional tests of scholastic aptitude and achievement, which usually tend to stress convergent rather than divergent thinking abilities, an opportunity for admission to college should be extended to those students who appear to be gifted or near gifted in one or more kinds of special talents.

Second, modifications in the curricula and in patterns of course requirements were suggested as ways in which creative endeavor could be substantially stimulated. Specifically, it was recommended that (1) fewer courses carrying large numbers of credit hours make up the college curriculum so that students in not being spread too thin with numerous one-, two-, and three-hour courses can explore academic areas in considerable depth, (2) provision should be made each semester either for at least one independent study course involving library, laboratory, or field research or for tutorial courses along with possible assignment of marks of credit or pass for such courses, (3) a plan for acceleration of the truly gifted and creative student to the extent that his abilities and interests allow.

Third, attention has been given to the desirability that creatively oriented students be placed in college and university environments or climates in which both faculty members and administrators anticipate, encourage, and reward the expression of creative behavior. Through use of existing scales which furnish measures of the perceived dimensions of college environments, the potential degree of satisfaction which the creatively endowed applicants for college admission may realize in subsequent college experiences can be enhanced to a considerable degree. Specifically, the creatively oriented applicants whose idealized perceptions of the measurable dimensions of the college environment resemble the actual perceptions of well-satisfied and creatively productive students at certain colleges should be encouraged to attend these colleges. It was also suggested that rewarding professors for teaching competence and relieving them of mandatory pressure to publish could also aid in the formation of a college environment conducive to fostering creative endeavor on the part of both students and professors.

In the fourth major area of concern, suggestions were made concerning ways in which teaching procedures could be adapted to facilitate the manifestation of creative behavior in students. Specifically, emphasis was placed upon (a) flexible and dynamic planning of curricular experiences that can be quickly modified by perceptive professors who are sensitive to the cognitive and affective readiness of students, (b) the use of appropriate incentives for rewarding and encouraging the continued expression of creative endeavor, (c) the provision for ease of communication between professors and students in a non-threatening atmosphere, and (d) the involvement of students in challenging assignments, in novel projects requiring independent study, and in meaningful examinations that emphasize divergent outcomes and minimize inconsequential, repetitious, and deadening busy work. Specifically, a list of 20 behaviors of the professor who stifles the expression of creative behavior by students was set forth.

The fifth and final broad area considered was that of the evaluation of outcomes of student behavior. Stress was placed on the need for use of a variety of criterion measures developed around operationally stated objectives. Specific suggestions were made concerning the (a) greater use of open-book tests, (b) inclusion of substantial numbers of simple completion items and provocative essay questions with a possibly slight reduction in the numbers of multiple-choice and matching items, (c) development of scales for the evaluation of certain kinds of projects as in the arts, humanities, and the applied sciences, (d) preparation of check lists which may be used by panels for appraisal of research papers, book reviews, inventions, and other contributions of creatively oriented students. It was also stressed that any evaluation procedure to be effective must rest upon a coordination of teaching procedures and curriculum planning throughout the entire period of college attendance. It was also mentioned that tests for selection and placement of creatively oriented students could not be expected to show very high predictive validities unless the content and process objectives of these measures were coordinate with the objectives in the curriculum within a particular institutional context.

Although college faculties and administrations can do much to facilitate the expression of the creative potentialities of their students, the ultimate responsibility for creative behavior rests upon the student himself. Given the freedom and encouragement necessary for achieving creative outcomes the student must assume a commensurate share of responsibility in disciplining himself to carry out the hard but rewarding work of creative learning. In short, he has the obligation of showing his professors that he does indeed deserve the opportunities for creative endeavor that have been afforded him and that he merits the confidence which his high school teachers have placed in him.

PART III

HOW SUPERVISORS, ADMINISTRATORS, AND COUNSELORS CAN FACILITATE EXPRESSION OF CREATIVE BEHAVIOR

Overview

In addition to the central role of the teacher in fostering creative endeavor are the essential activities of other professional personnel—supervisors, administrators (principals and vice-principals), and counselors—who also can be highly instrumental in achieving this goal. With the possible exception of the counselor, most professional staff members in the public school setting have had at least a minimum amount of teaching experience which should aid them in grasping some of the dynamics in the teaching-learning process, even though their previous activities may have tended to be somewhat rigid and noncreative. The active support of teachers who dare to try out new ideas and who want to introduce innovations can frequently mean the difference between merely a mediocre educational program or one that is judged to be outstanding in the realization of creative endeavor. Such needed support can be effectively furnished by certain special members of the school setting—namely, the supervisor, administrator, and counselor.

How supervisory personnel can facilitate teaching for creative endeavor is the subject of Chapter 16 by Woodfin—her second important contribution to this volume. Prior to helping teachers in the process of their own creative efforts (a process which in Woodfin's view is often prerequisite to the fulfillment of the creative potentialities of the learner), the supervisor needs to examine his own beliefs. Woodfin poses twelve soul-searching questions which many a supervisor needs to answer as honestly as possible if he is indeed to facilitate creative teaching. Emphasizing the need for supervisors to be cognizant of individual differences in teaching styles, she urges that they (1) not try to find a solution to every problem posed by a teacher, (2) show a willingness to progress at the teacher's rate of speed in promoting creative potentialities in children, (3) allow teachers to make some mistakes in their experimental approaches in the classroom, (4) accept small changes in the behavior of some teachers commensurate with their state of psychological readiness, (5) respect teachers who may not wish to change their instructional styles when they feel that they have already been quite successful in meeting the objectives of the school program, (6) prepare himself for the same kind of emotional buffeting that the teachers themselves take and give in their efforts to provide a classroom atmosphere for creative endeavor, (7) accept inconsistencies within himself in the suggestions he has made in his consultative capacity, and (8) honestly ask himself whether he is willing to encourage the teachers to be innovative in their activities at the expense of a change in the comforts and conveniences of the existing conservative order.

Specifically, Woodfin urges that supervisory personnel should help teachers to take a new look at children in terms of a number of different criteria most of which are suggested in twenty-nine additional questions she has posed. To be effective in promoting creative endeavor, supervisory personnel should (1) help provide an atmosphere conductive to creative expression, (2) furnish emotional support for teachers during periods of change, and (3) aid teachers in trying out new techniques. With respect to the last-mentioned point, Woodfin includes sixteen suggestions of possible actions that supervisors could encourage teachers to try.

In the closing section, the author describes how supervisory personnel can help student teachers to foster creative enterprise largely through helping them to be perceptive of certain kinds of behaviors in the classroom, giving them emotional support in their innovative efforts, and offering them a climate in which they feel free to experiment. Although both teachers and students have been creative in restrictive atmospheres, Woodfin believes that both groups can function more productively, more readily, and more happily when their unique contributions are recognized, valued, and encouraged than when they are given only tacit recognition or indifferent treatment.

Reiterating independently several of the issues raised by Woodfin,

Hophan and Peters reveal in Chapter 17 how the school administrator can help facilitate the teaching for creative endeavor. Putting great emphasis on the importance of the administrator's providing an open channel of communication among the major groups of school personnel—the central office staff including the superintendent and his assistants and curriculum consultants and directors, the parents and members of the immediate community surrounding the school, and the teachers who are directly involved with children—the authors contend that the school administrator who is secure and creative in his own personality can help set the climate which ultimately may encourage or discourage the expression of creative potentialities of children. Specifically, the administrator can initiate and maintain this climate by (1) recognizing that teachers are different and work differently, (2) allowing them opportunities to vary their approaches relative to differences in subject-matter requirements, (3) permitting them to work at solving the problems involved in teaching for creative outcomes, (4) refraining from giving direct guidance but offering instead encouragement and appropriate opportunities for innovation, and (5) refraining from criticism when teaching approaches to bring about creative expression have been ineffective as judged by cooperative evaluation procedures.

For the administrator in the elementary school, Hophan and Peters describe ways of planning for the creatively designed curriculum that is dynamically oriented to the learner and his potentialities. They discuss current emphases in instruction important to curricular planning and consider patterns of classroom and school organization in relation to the design of the curriculum. To implement a curriculum planned to evoke creative efforts, the administrator encourages practices that free the teacher and children in the learning process. More than thirty specific suggestions are set forth. In his leadership role, the administrator can provide the environment for each child to develop freely his present potential in being a self-directing, self-confident individual who is willing and eager to learn, to discover, and to create.

After pointing out that little has been written concerning how the professional guidance worker can serve as a forceful and constructive factor in assisting the learner to attain his full creative potentialities, Bonsall and Neumann propose at the outset of their presentation in Chapter 18 that the counselor may direct his efforts to three overlapping tasks: (1) identifying which creative abilities each child has as well as the relative extent to which he possesses them, (2) fostering and developing creative potentialities by becoming aware of the needs of creative persons, by developing an understanding of their characteristics, and by manipulating the school environment to allow for maximum adjustment and effort—a demanding task achieved through the counselor's interacting with the student, the teacher, the administrator, the parent, and others in the community, and (3) evaluating how successful he as a counselor has been in identifying and fostering creative efforts in students relative to a number of varied criteria.

With respect to the first task, the writers briefly discuss their view of the nature of the creative process, furnish a helpful list of relatively well-established tests and scales that are available to guidance workers by author, title, use, and developmental level, and include a useful bibliography concerned with these measuring devices.

For the second task of fostering and developing creativity, nine hypothesized needs of creative students are enumerated, and nearly a score of traits are listed to aid the counselor's understanding of the creative individual. To facilitate creative expression in the school environment over which the professional guidance worker can exert some influence, he may advantageously give consideration to four courses of action: (1) offering freedom from encumbrances that might mitigate against a student's maintaining an effective level of adjustment as well as against the demonstration of his abilities, (2) affording to whatever extent he can a positive learning atmosphere that is exciting to students, (3) furnishing necessary material and emotional support to meet the student's need for achievement, and (4) placing emphasis upon learning for creative outcomes for their own sake. Counseling the creative learner embodies four key principles: (1) an acceptance of the student where he now is in his development, not where the counselor hopes or wants him to be, (2) a recognition of the customary constraints placed upon the student who is creative, (3) an awareness of the importance of solitude for a creative person, and (4) a tolerance for the presence of feminine patterns of interest in creative boys and of masculine patterns of interest in creative girls.

To assist the counselor, the writers provide a chart that not only indicates several of the characteristics of the creative individual but also includes samples of the sorts of classroom problems that may arise in conjunction with the traits cited. In addition, several suggestions are made regarding how the counselor may help the teacher who is working with the creative learner. Specifically, it is urged that the counselor encourage the teacher to remove the emphasis from the student and to put it instead on the product of creative learning. Brief consideration is also given to how the counselor may communicate the needs of the creative learner to the administrator, to what kinds of activities oriented toward creative outcomes he may encourage and arrange so that the community at large will be involved, and to what varied types of approaches he may use with parents in encouraging them to foster creative behavior in their children.

To determine how successfully he has attained the objectives of the first and second tasks, the counselor is faced with the problem of evaluation. Eight points of departure for the evaluation process are offered. Specific mention is made of the promise that self-initiated student activities afford for evaluation. Comprehensive information gained from the evaluation phase will furnish the necessary basis for the validation of the procedures employed in the identification of the creative learner and will suggest ways in which the counseling process and the numerous activities related to it in the counselor's interaction with the administrator, the teacher, the supervisor, the parent, and the school community may be modified and redirected to achieve even greater levels of success in the fulfillment of the learner's creative potentialities.

CHAPTER 16

Supervisory Personnel

by

MARY JO WOODFIN

IN SCHOOLS, change is often facilitated best by encouragement from personnel in higher ranking positions. Although some teachers may wish to try out new ideas, they may hesitate or may do so secretly unless supervisors, consultants, principals, or other supervisory personnel openly approve of change. Therefore, in order to encourage more creativity in teachers and children, supervisory personnel need to make teachers feel that creative endeavor is valued and wanted.

Among ways for supervisory personnel to encourage changes toward more creative teaching practices are the following:

1. Projecting of attitudes which reassure the teacher that creative teaching is important and desired.
2. Helping teachers identify creative behaviors.
3. Providing emotional support during the process of change.
4. Establishing an atmosphere in which teachers and children feel free to try creative processes.
5. Suggesting ways to approach creativity, whenever these suggestions seem pertinent and appropriate.

Supervisory Personnel Should Examine Their Own Beliefs

Supervisory personnel should examine their own beliefs, prejudices, and inclinations as honestly as possible before attempting to help teachers teach more creatively. In the same way that perfection cannot be supplied on demand by others, neither can perfection be supplied on demand by self. Knowing about one's own approach to education can help one be more effective in the role of consultant to teachers who may be attempting to break the habits of long years (or short months for that matter, since pattern sets can be established quickly) of practice of techniques or methods.

1. What are your own feelings about techniques and methods that are or are not "good"? Have you feelings about certain "unforgivable methods" that you cannot help but label poor teaching? Perhaps the teacher who uses the dramatic play-construction approach or the teacher who does not use the dramatic play-construction approach to social studies is automatically classified in the good guy list. Perhaps teachers who display bulletin board materials above the chalk board, teachers who have children line up, teachers who do not have children line up, or teachers who do or do not write lesson plans are the bane of your educational existence. Knowing these things about yourself may make it a little easier when a teacher says to you, as one undoubtedly will when you ask her to think of new ways to work with children, that she is tired of construction, or lesson plans, or group reading, or individualized reading, or any of your pet categorizing tools for evaluating teacher competence, and wants to try to develop a new approach. You did ask her to take a new look at her teaching, didn't you?

2. Can you accept the idea that every problem posed to you is not for you to solve? When a teacher comes to you with a problem, it is almost more temptation than a consultant can withstand to start telling the teacher how it should be solved. Helping people often means helping them to help themselves, as we all often say, but we still overwhelm teachers with advice, pages of reading material, and lists or prescriptions of ways to proceed. It is difficult to know when a question is an attempt to clarify for oneself and when it is a call for specific help.

3. Do you know some definite techniques you can suggest to teachers to help them begin to teach more creatively? If you suggest to a group of teachers that they should try to promote divergent thinking in children, some teachers will be able to translate this immediately into practical procedures, others will need additional suggestions from you, and still others will not have the least idea of what you have in mind. Even the most independent teacher can be confused by earnest urgings on your part to "be more open, help children think for themselves, or give children freedom to explore." Keeping a balance between giving out recipes on how to teach

creatively and giving out vague, bland exhortations that teachers should help children find themselves creatively is not easy.

4. Are you willing to go at the teacher's rate of speed? For some teachers, trying to promote creativity in children is seen as a complete break with their former methods of teaching. No matter how a consultant works with them, they feel that the consultant wants them to change. Since a need to change is often seen by a teacher as indicating that something was wrong with his teaching, teachers react to suggestions that they should provide more opportunities for creative thinking in their classrooms in a variety of ways. Some adopt the "mea culpa" pattern of behavior, where they talk constantly about how bad they were before, but how now they have seen the light and all is creative. Some hide behind a screen of talk and little action. Others vacillate between trying new techniques and retreating to familiar methods of working with children. The consultant needs to understand that all these behaviors and many others are legitimate, he needs to accept many different patterns of teacher behavior, he needs to know that such behaviors reflect honest reactions, and he needs to remember that a teacher is not more or less professional for having such reactions.

5. Can you let teachers make mistakes? No one really knows how to help children be more creative. Some general principles seem to be emerging from research in the field of creativity, and more general principles seem to be in the process of general acceptance as a result of opinion and prejudice unsubstantiated by any research. Teachers who attempt the difficult job of either making their teaching more creative and/or helping children be more creative (unfortunately, the two are not synonymous) will make mistakes. Here, the job of the consultant becomes one of balancing too much help with too little. Because many conscientious teachers will have guilt feelings whenever they make an error, the consultant needs to be able to help the teacher past this stage as gently as possible. For the most part, teachers need no lecture on what went wrong; they need understanding that we can learn from our mistakes, that no one knows the best way to help children be more creative, that the teacher did the best he could, and that now he should try another approach.

6. Can you be content with small changes? Any attempt to help teachers change behaviors results in some teachers completely revising their teaching styles and in others moving scarcely at all. For some teachers, the willingness to try a different type of reading

seatwork is as important and as hard a decision to make as the decision to do away with all formal content areas would be for others. The consultant needs to know that a slight movement may require more courage for some than a revolutionary change would for other teachers.

7. Can you respect teachers who do not want to change their style of teaching? Some teachers are quite content with their methods of teaching. They feel that they are promoting creative behavior, even though the consultant may disagree, and they refuse to take a new look at method. The consultant needs to be able to accept this decision and still retain his respect for the teacher. It is, after all, for the teacher to decide how much or how little change he is able to handle at a given time. Currently, not enough is known about the effects of teaching style on children's learning to justify any demands for a change from one style of teaching to another or to justify beliefs that one method of approach is superior for all children.

8. Do you believe in individual differences for teachers? Teachers need encouragement as they attempt to develop a teaching style of their own. The consultant should not urge teachers into one teaching pattern, but should help teachers use their own individual assets.

9. Do you value creative teachers more than non-creative ones? In education, there is a tendency to value "good" teachers more than "poor" or "average" teachers, as though how well one teaches is some measure of how good a person one is. This is not necessarily true. Being a good teacher is not the same as being a good person. All of us have met fine, well-integrated personalities who could never in this world teach well.

10. Can you withstand the emotional buffeting teachers take (and give) whenever they attempt to make their classroom atmosphere more creative? The emotional energy called into play by a teacher who wants to become more creative or one who wants to help release children's creativity more effectively can be frightening both for the teacher and for the consultant who is attempting to guide him. There is something about the thought of and the practice of creativity that can be emotionally exhausting for both children and teachers. The consultant needs to be prepared for the cycle of feelings of elation and depression that teachers and children experience in the creative process and be ready to encourage, to listen, or to make suggestions that will move teachers along toward their goal.

11. Can you accept inconsistencies in yourself? As you work to

help teachers provide an atmosphere in their classrooms more conducive to creative behavior, you will find yourself trapped into seemingly inconsistent behavior. You will urge one teacher to try group process, another to concentrate on individual teaching. You will be counseling one teacher to go faster and another to slow down. One day you will think you know the best way for a class to proceed in reading, and the next day you will not be so sure. You will need to be as tolerant of inconsistencies within yourself as you will be of inconsistencies in others.

12. Do you really want teachers to be more creative in their teaching? Creative teachers are apt to be troublesome in any school organization. They want supplies that are not available in the supply room, they want to rearrange the bell system or ignore it entirely, they want to extend the curriculum boundaries beyond the currently acceptable framework, they are apt to inspire envy in other teachers, they may pay more attention to teaching than to clerical duties, and they may never obtain a high rating on teacher evaluation forms for neatness, or teacher-staff relations. Do you as a consultant really want to encourage these teachers to change the existing order? When answering this, remember that you are part of the existing order.

Supervisory Personnel Should Help Teachers Take a New Look at Children

One way to help teachers encourage more creative behavior is to help teachers identify children who are likely to have more creative ability than others. The check list below describes behaviors which may be indicative of creative talent. Some of the behaviors will contradict others. However, since creative talent is not restricted to a single skill, talent, discipline, or process, it is probable that traits associated with some creative endeavors may be different from traits associated with others.

1. Which children do you like the least? Several research studies indicate that teachers are apt to reject the more creative child and value the more conventional child.

2. Which children are over-achieving by scoring higher in daily work and on achievement tests than their scores on intelligence tests would indicate they should? This is often a characteristic of more creative children.

3. Who is persistent about work, assignment, complaints, ideas? The child who persists in working on an idea when discouraged, when a solution seems impossible, or when he has passed the point of logical expectations may be so wrapped up in his problem that he must work it out. This child may have above average creative talent.

4. Which children carry on projects outside the school requiring diligence and persistence? Neither the teacher nor the parents may be aware of these projects, and may discover them only accidentally.

5. Who is reading all the books available on a given subject without outside motivation? The school or city librarian may give teachers valuable information concerning children who, on their own, are reading all the material available on their particular interest.

6. Who has a great deal of knowledge about one topic or subject that he learned on his own?

7. Who daydreams more than he should? This may indicate emotional disturbance, or it may indicate preoccupation with a problem demanding creative ability.

8. Who sits and scribbles or sits and stares whenever a problem is presented, works on the problem to the exclusion of all else until it is completed, and then exhibits feelings of depression and unworthiness after the problem is solved? Many of our best authors describe their working process in just this manner.

9. Who does more than is required? Who turns in twice or three times the amount of work required?

10. Who challenges the teacher openly? Subtly? The challenge may be on subject matter, organization, rules, or attitudes. The challenge may take the form of direct confrontations in front of the entire class, subtle opposition in which another child does the challenging at the instigation of the creative child without being aware of being used, balking the teacher's wishes through slowdown tactics, or presenting so subtle a challenge that only the teacher is aware that the child is fighting him. In the latter case, the child may never say anything that can be termed provoking, but the teacher is in a constant state of unease.

11. Who resists majority opinion down to the last vote, and then continues to resist? Children who are less subject to pressure by peers often may be among the most creative.

12. Who is the perfectionist? Who could not care less? Both extremes may contain children who are so absorbed in a problem that they are unable to concentrate on another.

13. Who works best alone or with one co-choice? Creative children

often have trouble with committee work. They may find a reinforcer who recognizes their ability and serves as a buffer between them and other children.

14. Who works best with distraction such as music, noise, or television in the background? Such minor distractions may serve to release the more creative child to be free to do dull, unchallenging work. For more creative work, background noise may serve to distract the conscious mind and allow the unconscious to work more freely.

15. Who is readily distracted from classroom work by the slightest sensory interruption? Noise, unusual colors, smells, interruptions may cause some creative children to turn their attention to solving the distraction rather than to the classroom assignment.

16. Who goes into a trancelike state during work? Trancelike states sometimes occur when a child becomes intensely involved in any problem.

17. Who does not conform to group goals and who conforms too much? This lack of conformity is not rebellion or attention seeking. This failure to conform would be characterized by disinterest in group goals. Conversely, the child who recognizes this lack of interest in group goals in himself and overconforms in an attempt to belong may very well be more creative than average.

18. Who is the observer—of you, of the class, of himself? Writers and artists often find themselves observers rather than participants in group actions.

19. Who really does not care about the opinion of the teachers? He may not necessarily fight the teacher, but his own opinion is more important to him.

20. Who in the class is from a low socioeconomic background and has an I.Q. of 110 or over? Such children may have had to improvise games, problem solutions, and the necessities all their lives and may have had more practice in finding unusual solutions to problems than middle and upper class children who have had many more material comforts and have been more protected from having to make decisions for themselves.

21. Who has to feel or manipulate objects in the course of problem solving? More creative children tend to do this.

22. Who can think of many different responses to a question?

23. Who thrives on disorder? Who either does not see disorder or tries to organize it into a meaningful whole?

24. Who is compulsively neat?

25. Whose drawings are complex, asymmetrical, vital, and dynamic?

26. Who is painfully truthful to himself and to others?

27. Against whom does the group impose sanctions? Groups often penalize more creative children by isolating, attacking, or ignoring them or by making them secretary or chairman of a group.

28. Who causes feelings of unease? Oftentimes, more creative children cause feelings of unease in others.

29. Who provides the ideas, yet often receives no credit for them? More creative children frequently offer ideas which are elaborated upon by more verbal or socially adept children. The group may forget who originated the idea and give credit to the other child.

Each of the behaviors listed above may be systematic of creative behavior or they may result from other causes. The teacher should draw conclusions with care.

Supervisory Personnel Should Help Provide an Atmosphere Conducive to Creative Endeavor

Supervisory personnel can facilitate teaching for creative endeavor by providing an environment in which creative teaching is encouraged.

1. Supervisory personnel should take a new look at organizational routines and procedures that have evolved into sacred cows over the years to see whether these routines and procedures are inhibiting creative teaching. Must the supplies be ordered only on Tuesday? Is the only possible use of a supervisor the canned observation-conference routine? Do faculty meetings have to follow a certain pattern? And on and on. If the answer to any of these questions is yes, then how may these inhibitors be changed to avoid stifling teachers by needless routines. Could teachers' aides, parent volunteers, sixth grade girls, or secretaries fill out the Tuesday supply order, for example? Could teachers be involved more creatively in the solving of organizational details?

2. Supervisory personnel should not be trapped into the standard observation-conference routine either by their own planning or by that of the district or the building administrator. Group conferences,

time for informal talking, chances for supervisory personnel to become acquainted with teachers in situations in which the supervisor or consultant is not telling and the teacher listening are all possibilities. The teacher should participate in his own personal in-service program, and he should be able to say to the consultant that he wants help, ideas, or a chance to fight issues or to talk over various approaches, rather than having the supervisor, consultant, or principal initiate all contacts of a supervisory nature.

3. Time schedules should be flexible. Some administrative arrangements could be made for the occasional situations where the school bell interrupts a teacher in the middle of a creative session with her class, where the lesson should be allowed to develop with interruption, and where the teacher is supposed to be on yard duty for this particular recess. Creative endeavors take time to plan, to develop, and to evaluate. Rigid time allotments and bell schedules should not be allowed to interfere with this need for time.

4. The use of the physical environment of the school should be subjected to study for the purpose of finding new ways to use it. Are certain activities confined by custom to the auditorium? Why? In what possible ways could the auditorium be used? Is all art work done in the classroom? Why? Why not outside? Why not in the auditorium? How else might the lunch benches be used other than for one hour at noon and for sinners who have to be "sat" at recess time?

Supervisory Personnel Should Provide Emotional Support for Teachers During Periods of Change

Supervisory personnel can aid teachers through the emotional hurdles of teaching in more creative ways and of helping children be more creative. As the teacher tries out new ideas, looks at his own teaching in a different way, and encourages children to strike out into various thinking processes, he will often encounter certain emotional and philosophic pitfalls. The supervisor or consultant can help the teacher through these periods by knowing about the possibilities of their occurrence, by helping the teacher to anticipate emotional ups and downs, and by providing whatever emotional support the teacher will accept (and the supervisor is comfortable in giving).

1. Help the teacher to experience failure. Teachers, perhaps even more than most people, do not like to fail with children or with methods. Much of creative problem solving is a trial-and-error process. Trial and error is by definition learning by mistakes. Even though the teacher is intellectually aware that failure is a good teaching device, he may not be prepared for the feelings he generates within himself as a result of seeing his work or a child's work fail.

2. Help the teacher who is attempting new techniques feel a part of the faculty. This teacher may secede from the faculty both because of his own feelings and because of the unease he causes the rest of the staff. He may tend to see himself as fighting the monolithic organization alone, as being the only one who has "got the word," or as causing others to reject him. Other teachers may tend to regard this teacher as a threat, a boat rocker, an isolate. Other teachers may feel that this teacher is judging them unfairly. Anyone in a supervisory position has to help the staff and the teacher reach an accommodation which benefits both.

3. Help the teacher meet the depression that sometimes follows success. More than most successes, a success in creative endeavor tends to be a highly emotionally charged moment for both children and teachers. This elation often is followed by a period of depression in which the teacher may feel that what happened was an accident or cannot possibly happen again. Sometimes emotional exhaustion is not seen as being a result of previous elation but is seen as failure, as inadequacy of self, or as the fault of someone else. Of course, it might be one or some or all of these things or might be for other reasons.

4. Help the teacher down gently from emotional peaks. At the height of elation during the creative process, teachers may need help to bring themselves down gently to everyday affairs. Providing the teacher with the opportunity to talk, emphasizing less emotionally laden subjects, and planning quiet periods in the school calendar are all ways to accomplish this.

5. Help the teacher through the conformity vs. creativity stage. Many times, teachers who are discovering new ways to teach creatively will pass through a stage in which they see conformity of any sort as a threat to creativity. Other teachers will pass through a period in which they feel that creativity is a threat to conformity. It is the

responsibility of the consultant to help teachers see that creativity and conformity are neither mutually exclusive nor antagonistic.

6. Help the teacher through the "anything goes" stage. Occasionally, teachers who are interested in helping students be more creative will pass through a period in which they feel that children can be creative if only they are left alone. To overstate the case, somewhat, teachers may feel that classroom organization of any sort, standards for classroom behavior, teacher direction, the learning of skill subjects, or any outside direction will prevent children from being creative. To help the teacher work through his feelings about balances between teacher and pupil responsibilities is another supervisory responsibility.

7. Help the teacher to retreat to safe ground occasionally. Trying out new ground is exciting, satisfying, exhausting, and frustrating. Supervisory personnel have an obligation to help teachers retreat to safe ground at times. No life should be lived constantly at top emotional speed. Teachers should be able to withdraw into staid, fairly unimaginative teaching from time to time. Any in-service program which has as its goal increasing creativity in teaching should plan for slack or regrouping periods in which teachers should be allowed and encouraged to drift for awhile and to catch up with themselves emotionally.

8. Help teachers retain an appreciation for the less creative child. Educators sometimes are guilty of allowing the enthusiasms of the moment to become so important that other ideas are momentarily forgotten or shunted aside. Thus, in an era that emphasizes creative children, gifted children, culturally deprived children, or socially adept children, children who do not fit into the more popular theories of the time may be slighted. A child who is highly creative is no more nor no less valuable than a child who is less creative. Both types of children deserve gifted, creative teachers.

9. Help teachers overcome the feeling that there is a best way to teach creatively. Teachers who use inquiry techniques, language approach to reading, analogy procedures or other so-called creative methods may be no more creative than teachers who use textbooks. The use of analogies may be stilted and sterile, while the use of one textbook for every child in a classroom could conceivably be done imaginatively.

10. Help teachers understand that techniques are not necessarily

gimmicks. There is a danger that teachers who are looking for ways to facilitate creative endeavor will regard techniques as gimmicks, label them as such, and sit at dead center in their approach to creative teaching because they do not wish to be considered gimmicky. They would rather do nothing than run the risk of being considered superficial. Helping teachers see that any attempt to teach creatively runs the risk of being gimmicky but that most approaches can be made meaningful and challenging is not an easy task for the consultant.

11. Help teachers understand that openness does not benefit all children. As with all people, teachers have a tendency to forget that children are individuals. A current phrase popular in creativity circles today is that teachers should provide an open system in which children can learn. This may give the impression that children who are uncomfortable without some direction or teacher guidance could not possibly be creative since they do not respond well to the highly prized openness. Supervisory personnel need to help teachers understand that under an open system, teachers are free to vary approaches so that children who work best under minimal direction and those who work best under tighter boundaries are given opportunities to learn under both. To complicate the problem further, children may be able to respond to little direction in some areas and need much direction in others. Furthermore, the needs of the same child for direction may vary from day to day. Responding to these needs in a style which recognizes individual differences is true openness.

12. Help teachers resolve the process vs. product fight. In the literature concerning creativity, a current battle involves the relative importance of product and process. Process supporters are often seen by product partisans as hiding behind talk because of an inability to turn out a creative product, and product people may be seen by process people as limiting the scope of creativity to narrow boundaries. Teachers need to see the value in both process and product. It is virtually impossible to tell the difference between the two, as any product evolves as a result of creative process and is modified constantly by that process. Similarly, creative process is modified by the demands of a particular product. It is not enough to talk of a good creativity session, after all. In the end, something will have to result, if not in a concrete sense, at least in attitudes, values, or way of life. These last three items are certainly products as well as processes.

Supervisory Personnel Should Help Teachers Try New Techniques

When teachers ask for specific suggestions for making their teaching more creative, supervisory personnel might suggest some of the following ideas:

1. Provide for unscheduled times during the day when children are encouraged to work on self-initiated projects.
2. Find out about and encourage self-initiated projects children carry on outside class.
3. Provide plenty of time for thinking. Some of this time may be relatively free, other times would be for thinking about specific problems.
4. Use many projective techniques which encourage children to project themselves into a problem. Examples of this approach would be questions which ask children to think how they would feel or react in similar circumstances to those described in books, to those encountered by classmates, or to those met by historical figures.
5. Provide for both individual and group activities which will give children oriented best toward either type of learning a chance to participate.
6. Plan alternate periods of freedom and direction during the day. Children need experience in both situations.
7. Use time wisely. Plan both short-time and long-time activities. Children need the experience of working on extended projects which take several hours, several days, or even several weeks to complete. They also need to be able to work quickly to completion. Do not restrict the selection to either short- or long-time periods, however. Plan some lessons in which children who finish quickly may do so and those who need more time may take it.
8. Plan activities which encourage divergent thinking. Use open-end questions, questions which ask for more than one answer. Help children see more than one way to solve problems.
9. Encourage self-evaluation.
10. Do not leave out evaluation. Evaluation is usually listed in writings concerning creativity as one of the steps in the creative process. It should not be left out of creative activities, either academic, aesthetic, or social. For some children, delaying evaluation until after all ideas are explored is valuable. For others, an interaction

of evaluation and product is necessary as the creative problem-solving process proceeds.

11. Do not praise or criticize indiscriminately. Both assume a superiority on the part of the teacher which may not be justified. Help the child to understand that everything he does is acceptable but that he needs to test solutions, products, or processes to find whether they work, whether other people can understand, use, or duplicate them, or whether he wants to improve them in some way.

12. Occasionally give children problems for which the teacher has no answer.

13. Try variations of the more guided techniques for group and individual problem solving, including analogies, brainstorming, attribute listing, analysis of opposites, or inquiry methods.

14. Let the children plan the daily program occasionally.

15. Break out of a set schedule pattern from time to time. Neither lockstep schedules nor constantly freewheeling time allotments should be used on a permanent basis. There are times when children (and teachers) need a fixed schedule. There are other times when more flexibility is desirable.

16. Arrange to exchange papers or art work with another teacher occasionally for evaluation purposes. Certain criteria for creative products may vary from one teacher to another. Some teachers may like sparse prose; others may like more adjectives. Some may enjoy non-representative paintings; others may see value in highly literal drawings. When teachers look at the work done by classes other than their own, children in their own classes receive the benefit of other viewpoints as well as the benefits of not having their work stimulate the same kinds of reactions day after day.

Encouraging Student Teachers in Creative Endeavor

In addition to the usual hazards experienced by teachers who attempt to help children be more creative, student or cadet teachers may meet special problems.

1. They may not be familiar with the usual responses of children to stimuli.

2. There is always the risk of competition for children's favor between master and student teacher.

3. The class, after all, belongs to the master teacher. This restricts substantially what a student teacher may do.

4. The master teacher may not be in accord with some of the goals of creative teaching.

5. The student teacher may mistake mischief for creativity, noise for purposeful activity, or insolence for critical inquiry.

6. The student teacher may not be able to see the behavior of all children in the room. The stress of teaching may narrow his field of vision to the first row or two; and he may not observe children at the back of the room, children who cause no trouble, or children who withdraw. This lowers his effectiveness in helping children to be more creative.

Some of the weaknesses of student teachers may prove to be assets, however, because lack of experience may cause them to approach a learning difficulty in a new way or to make an accidental discovery about method that experience would never allow a veteran teacher to make.

Teachers, principals, or college supervisory personnel can help student teachers be more creative in their teaching by helping them be more proficient in observing children's behavior, by providing the same sort of emotional support classroom teachers need when trying to be more creative, and by providing a climate in which student teachers are free to experiment.

Using questions wisely during conference periods to promote more divergent teaching may help student teachers be more creative in their approach to teaching. Some examples of questions which might cause student teachers to look for more than one way to teach are:

1. What kinds of experiences do the children need after the last lesson? How many ways can you think of to provide these experiences?

2. What ways other than books could you think of to provide research activities?

3. Where else in the room could a reading circle be held?

4. What other means except book reports could you use for sharing books?

5. How could you plan so that more than four could paint?

6. How many ways can you think of to motivate such activities as watercolor work or creative writing?

7. Who participated in the discussion today? Who did not? Do you want more or less participation? How many ways can you think of to encourage either?

8. What did Mary do during clay time? What techniques could you encourage her to try?

Conclusion

No one can say with assurance that certain environments stifle more creative teachers or children. Creative teachers have in the past worked well in non-supportive atmospheres. Creative children have produced under unsympathetic teachers. It seems certain, however, that both groups function more easily, happily, and productively under conditions in which their unique contributions are valued, recognized, and encouraged. Supervisory personnel have the obligation of helping provide such an atmosphere.

CHAPTER 17

The School Administrator

by

IRENE S. HOPHAN AND
MARY M. PETERS

A graduate of Wisconsin State University, River Falls, and Claremont Graduate School and University Center, Claremont, California, Irene Hophan is now principal of Berlyn Avenue Elementary School, Ontario, California, and is on the teaching staff at La Verne College, La Verne, California. Berlyn Avenue School staff is participating in a Cooperative Teaching project which has as one of its prime objectives, the releasing of teachers to explore—through various educational innovations—learning experiences that will foster a more creative teaching and learning effort.

Mary M. Peters, who holds a B.A. and M.A. from the University of California at Los Angeles, has been in the employ of the Ontario-Montclair school district for over forty years as a teacher, a supervisor, director of Elementary Education, and presently assistant superintendent, Instruction. The growth of the school district from six to thirty elementary schools during this time has challenged the creative talents of the central office staff, which includes the school administrators. The community is close to many colleges offering teacher-training, internship, and in-service programs, and Miss Peters has worked with their administrative staffs to coordinate the district programs with those sponsored by the colleges in the area.

WE MUST BEGIN with the hypothesis that every individual is capable of divergent ideation. It is a bold hypothesis but an essential one for a school administrator if there is to be any teaching for creative endeavor on the part of teachers working in the school. It is essential for the administrator and all those with whom he works to understand fully the precise meaning of creative endeavor and its implications for those who read it, say it, or practice it. As expressed in this chapter, creative endeavor is that effort which enables an individual to bring into being something from his own thought or imagination which is new, unique, original, not existent before.

With the acceptance of this concept of creative endeavor one may readily distinguish between the process of discovery, which involves learning something already in existence, and creativity, which encourages the mind to manipulate and experiment with knowledge that will serve as a springboard for new ideas. Creation is a completely personal matter. Teaching for creative endeavor is an attitude, a basic set of values—a way of life. Some teachers find it easier than others to accept these values. If teachers can accept the premise that all individuals are creative, then administrators can assist teachers to accept those principles which lead to the cultivation of creativity and creative teaching.

Philosophy

Great benefits accrue within a school when the administrator genuinely has the creative spirit or is the creative spirit. Provision for use of the imaginative faculties converts the conforming, compliant team into effervescent, spontaneous individuals seeking originality, inventiveness, and creative expression whenever possible. This in no way is to say that there is no place for conformity, but rather a need for an atmosphere that will provide for a freedom to think, to do, to discipline, and to direct oneself toward ever more creative individuals using their human potentialities to the greatest extent.

An environment—an orientation to life—conducive to creative endeavor may be thought of as an attitude toward self and toward the world in general that is willing to accept the unique, the new, the different, the sometimes almost bizarre as unexplored experience, as a challenge rather than a threat. Fromm (1959) describes the conditions essential for the creative attitude as the capacity to be puzzled, the ability to concentrate, the sense of "I" as the true center of my world—the originator of my acts—and the ability to accept conflict.

The educational implications of this conceptualization of creativity are significant for everyone concerned. It negates the idea of either-or, the haves or the have-nots, for it recognizes creative ability in all individuals. It challenges leadership to release what may be suppressed potential and develops the creative personality. The administrator needs to ask: How much is left? How much can be recovered? How can I assist in the development of this potential?

School Personnel Relations

School personnel as used in this chapter refers to three rather well-defined groups: the central office staff, which includes the superintendent and his assistants and curriculum consultants and directors; the parents and members of the immediate community which is affected by the school as a community center; and the teachers who work directly with the children. The school administrator has the absorbing and personally rewarding opportunity to provide for this complex of personalities an environment which will facilitate teaching for creative endeavor.

The climate is set by the school administrator in the district. His faith in people, to the extent that he is eager for new ideas and secure enough to permit freedom to try these ideas, will determine the environment that will encourage creative expression.

Central Office Staff

The most important facility which a school administrator can use in any aspect of his work is that of communication. The sensitive school administrator will never permit a channel to remain closed. He must subscribe to a philosophy which cultivates and appreciates creative behavior and must be willing to support this concept in all professional relationships. Central office staff must be continuously kept aware of the aims and objectives of the environment through continuous open channels of communications. Sharing of experiences, invitations to visit the building and observe and participate in the coffee-break discussions as well as the classroom activities, and a continuous review of purpose and progress through consultation will assist in keeping everyone informed and interested in the advance of creative education.

Parents and Immediate Members of the School Community

The massive growth in performing activity has not been matched by growth of artistic and creative maturity. School personnel are trapped by the pressures of public performance and of community and student tasks that produce the technician, the follower, or the teammate. In order that a school community prize creativity, originality, and individualism, the school administrator must continuously involve all appropriate groups in an organization that shares in the creation of ideas as well as in dissemination of information, and participates in appropriate ways in various phases of the program. The school organization that provides for frequent and constructive communication between parents and teachers is more likely to provide a creative learning environment for children.

The administrator and the school community who work cooperatively as a group often can reduce the number of restricting routines. The school as an institution both supports and limits the teacher's activities. The influence of the community reaches into every school activity, and the organized life of the community, its values, and its lines of prestige are reflected in the school and in teachers' attitudes toward their teaching; therefore, it is of supreme importance that the administrator provide every possible means for parent-teacher-community participation in understanding the educational philosophy of the school.

What environment must a school administrator attempt to create which will facilitate effective school-community communication and participation? There must be genuine respect for and confidence in all persons involved. The administrator must place his professional knowledge, information, insight, and experience at the service of the parents and the community. He must keep in mind that one of the most important benefits of creativity is that it provides a means of utilizing information and skills in a functional and meaningful way. The parents must be psychologically ready to work and share in an atmosphere for which they care because they have given of themselves to promote the process and to share in the product. The administrator must demonstrate a willing and uncritical acceptance of a parent's contribution whenever possible. He must try to find some use for it, some value in it. Once suggestions are ventured, ideas begin to flow. True, there will be situations where mistakes are made, displeasure or disapproval incurred. This is all the more reason to encourage further learning situations, where the free relaxed atmosphere of experimentation can be fostered. To make a mistake is part of being creative. The administrator must patiently and sympathetically establish a climate for creating. As the parents and school-community live in this atmosphere, they become more perceptive and appreciative of a school environment which fosters faith, originality, individualism, and the unique contribution of each individual.

The opportunities afforded a school administrator for providing an emotional climate where unique human beings are valued is unlimited. The worth of school-parent organizations to creative endeavor is immense and tangible. It is an excellent means to insure participation with a purpose, through which school, parents, and community can contribute fairly and fully to the task at hand.

The astute school administrator will heed the experience and wisdom of the publicity experts and will use school publications to further greater understanding of the school. The principal's newsletter is a means of keeping in constant touch with the community. Special handbooks and brochures give a more specialized or comprehensive account of the schools' program than is possible in a general publication. A common school publication, a means frequently underestimated and undeveloped as a vehicle to create parental insights, is the school newspaper or magazine which is composed, written, and published by the children. This is an excellent means to give attention to unique format and design, to publish original stories, poems, plays and news reports of the school's activities.

Parent study groups, which begin where the parents' concerns are, can contribute materially to parents' understanding of the role of creativity in the life of the child. Through this group, parents can become active participants in school programs.

Educational leaders overlook a real opportunity if they neglect the child study programs. Parent-teacher conferences and Parent-Teachers Associations have long been a potent force in developing positive attitudes toward the school and its educational program. The school administrator has an unequaled resource in the utilization of the creative talents of the parents in the community to spur and initiate new interests in the school. This is an invaluable source of stimulation to the children as well as to the parent who can make this contribution.

These formal aspects and procedures of school-community relations are fine; however in order that they be successful they must be undergirded by a successful human relationship. Parents are interested in the general welfare of all children, but primarily they are interested in their own children. Success of the individual child impresses the parents most. The child who regularly returns home from a satisfying day at school and gives a glowing report of the activities of the day provides the greatest support for the school and its program. The emphasis which creative educational leaders place on the human contact and relationship between teachers and the general public will clearly establish the effective working climate in which goals for children are clearly understood and generally accepted. Unique and creative proposals may well be forthcoming from this environment.

The Teacher

Teaching for creative endeavor demands a complete understanding on the part of the administrator of what the teacher himself experiences during the teaching act. Personal satisfaction in teaching can only be realized when this identification with the teacher's experiences is accepted and encouraged by the administrator. When a teacher can burst into the office of the administrator or the staff room with an exclamation of excitement over a teaching experience that has been "just right," the administrator can feel secure and good about the instructional activity taking place in the classroom. Teachers react wholeheartedly and sensitively to good teaching situations which meet their needs. When they transmit their deeply felt emotions and enthusiasm to the administrator and others on the staff, this energy and enthusiastic behavior are extended and expanded.

When a teacher speaks in an intelligent and articulate manner concerning his perceptive reflections on the nature of the creative endeavor he has witnessed in his classroom, the administrator can also appreciate what may be experienced by all teachers through purposeful teaching. Through the serious account of the teacher's feelings about his teaching experience, the administrator can know the dynamic quality of the teacher's involvement in truly creative activities. There is an encouraging message for everyone in his remarks. The whole secret is the feeling.

Administrative Practices

A Creative Climate

The quality of creativeness and inventiveness that pervades the school program is dependent upon the environment in which the teacher works. Since it is believed that the administrator sets the emotional climate of the school, his personality is an important element in implementing creativity. He must be free to encourage teachers to establish in their classrooms an emotional climate conducive to creativity—a climate which will foster exploration, curiosity, varied approaches to problems—and above all, trial-and-error experiences.

How can the administrator initiate and maintain this climate?

1. The administrator must recognize that all teachers are different and work differently. One of the most obvious ways of securing conditions for teaching for creative endeavor is to develop a curriculum with many opportunities for creative achievement. It can be done by emphasizing how information is sought and processed as well as by what information is learned. Attention to responses and perceptions—how information is stored and used to produce something new—permits teachers to try many approaches to learning.

2. The administrator should feel free to permit varying approaches by his teachers to the subject-matter content. Taylor (1960) has found that it is quite possible that many things can be learned creatively more economically and effectively than by authority. Textbooks and teachers, however, tend to focus on what is known far more than on what is not known. Creative teaching personalities are in the making and the qualities that creative teaching encourages are developed as teachers respond to an atmosphere which awakens their aspirations and involves their wholehearted endeavor. Developing these qualities in teachers is an experience that transforms the tasks and routines of teaching into creative opportunities in human de-

velopment. This in no way sanctions an escape from teaching responsibilities, but rather proposes a higher level of intelligent concern about these responsibilities and a forward adjustment in the approaches and procedures used to implement the curriculum to a fuller concern for creative values.

3. The administrator must permit teachers to struggle with a problem, to try different resources and tentative solutions or conclusions, and to experience the final exhilaration of solution themselves. This is a creative experience in itself. An unpleasantness may prevail and frustrations occur on the part of the individual teacher, but bringing facts into new relationships on their own leads to feelings of security and to further exploring and satisfying of curiosity. Throughout the experience the administrator must support and encourage, but leave hands off.

4. The administrator must refrain from giving direct guidance, but rather encourage and suggest several approaches or trial possibilities. Teachers must have freedom to explore a situation and to try tentative solutions. Freedom to learn through experimentation does not limit them to the "right way," but rather provides experiences necessary to productive creative thinking. The lockstep method of keeping everyone on the "right way" stifles creativity and creative endeavor on the part of the student who is guided by this teacher.

5. The administrator must refrain from criticism in any form for an attempted ineffective approach to a situation. Ineffective or inappropriate endeavor, of course, cannot be permitted to continue without accountability; however, the administrator must not permit emotional rejection on the part of the teacher because of his attitude. Intelligent reexamination of the problem with new solutions evolving provides a positive approach. Freedom from the anxiety of being wrong leads to further attempts to solve the problem effectively. A positive working relationship between administrator and teacher provides a climate which will foster this same relationship between student and teacher and nourishes creative endeavor on the part of the student.

The administrator provides for a time when evaluative procedures are brought into focus. He must keep in mind that the evaluative procedure must be commensurate with the process being evaluated. Application of self to a new problem, the procedures used, and the security with which the teacher approaches the evaluation device must be the test of the ability to respond creatively and to transfer this feeling to those with whom he works.

If teachers are to appreciate and foster creative endeavor on the part of their students, the administrator must provide many opportunities for practice in a school organization where the climate is emotionally supportive rather than punitive. Give each teacher freedom to learn for himself, with supportive guidance from the administrator, and more than likely the teacher will provide a classroom environment in which children will think for and create by themselves.

Planning the Creatively Designed Curriculum

The administrator of the modern elementary school views the curriculum as the totality of the child's experiences for which his school is responsible. He subscribes to certain basic principles in planning the curriculum:

1. The elementary school has a valid statement of curricular objectives and purposes which should be reconsidered as conditions change. Curriculum development is a dynamic process and cannot be static.
2. In determining the aims and objectives of the curriculum, an active and vital part is taken by the children, the teaching staff, the parents, and resource people in the community.
3. The elementary school curriculum is designed by sensitive, inventive classroom teachers with an understanding of child growth and development, learning theory, and skills and knowledges in the various areas of the curriculum.
4. The elementary school curriculum takes into consideration the social setting of the children in that school. Provisions are made for children to understand themselves as individuals and as members of the societal group.
5. The curriculum includes experiences that help children understand, appreciate, and use sound principles of mental and physical health.
6. The elementary school curriculum is based on the interests, abilities, and needs of children, with the needs interpreted in terms of the democratic ideals of our society.
7. The curriculum has its roots in the physical, cultural, and social

aspects of the community and in such contemporary problems as children are able to understand.

8. Included in the curriculum are functional knowledges and skills which children need in solving their problems. These skills are taught so that their need is clearly understood by the pupils and their use is provided for in the problems which children are called upon to solve.

9. Physical facilities, equipment, and instructional supplies should be adequate for and adapted to the type of instructional program carried on in the school.

10. Provision is made for creative activities and creative expressions in the modern curriculum.

11. The elementary school curriculum provides opportunities for children to develop interests, appreciations, and skills which will broaden and enrich their lives.

12. The curriculum provides for a continuity in the learning experiences of children. It disregards rigid grade content.

13. The elementary school curriculum is organized primarily around group experiences, always with provision for variation in the experiences and needs of the learner. The child learns best when the learnings are based on situations that are problematical to him. For most effective learning the child must assume the responsibility for learning and be committed to the task at hand.

14. Administrators plan evaluative procedures to test the effectiveness of the curriculum.

The administrator is often perplexed by the never-ending task of curriculum planning and development. He need not be if he keeps his focus on children and their potential, on teaching and ways of making it exciting and real.

McNeil (1965) states that because of the increasing interest in curriculum and instruction, administrators are concerning themselves with the three current emphases which are important to good curricular planning. The first implies that the ways pupils learn have a bearing on what they learn. This emphasis relates to discovery learning, inquiry training, problem-solving, and the process goals of the curriculum. The second emphasis concerns programmed instruction. Programmed learning has many aspects which the creative administrator will assess in planning the curriculum. Evidence from research studies has been most favorable to the effectiveness of programmed learning in comparison to learning under conventional instructions. The third emphasis deals with organized knowledge. The implication of this emphasis in curriculum planning forces the administrator to consider the differences between what the school should teach and what it can teach.

The many patterns of class and school organization determine to some extent the overall plan of the curriculum. The nongraded school, team teaching, the individualized reading program, cross grouping, back-to-back teaching, the self-contained classroom, all have implications for curriculum planning. No organizational plan in itself will improve instruction, but some of the newer schemes do show some potential for facilitating learning.

The administrator will plan so that curriculum development will evolve from actual teaching situations and will be related to classroom experiences. Many administrators advocate action research—described as carefully planned and controlled research in the classroom, the best laboratory for the discovery of better ways to improve instruction. The administrator can use the research approach as an intelligent means of freeing teachers to study, question, analyze, explore, and plan. As teachers engage in research activities, their teaching tends to improve. There is excitement in inquiry, enthusiasm when one explores, stimulation in sharing and planning, satisfaction in being able to interpret data. As the school staff engages in research all the aspects of creativity are apparent. Making choices, discovering new possibilities, seeing new relationships, trying something different, reconstructing experiences, and finding new alternatives, all are ingredients of the creative act but are also important research components needed to creatively design the elementary school curriculum.

Implementing the Creatively Designed Curriculum

The elementary school administrator has a strategic role in curriculum development. Innovations, changes, and new approaches can be instituted, tested, retained, or rejected. School faculties can be engaged in study groups and can seek to better understand the structure of subject matter, the development of concepts, and the taxonomy of educational objectives.

The creative administrator is a self-starter. How well he implements the curriculum is dependent upon his resourcefulness, his initiative, and his ability to translate goals and objectives into action.

With the basic underlying principles of elementary education in mind, the administrator implements the curriculum with practices which free the teachers and the children to be creative. He will think through all the implications of a program designed to meet the needs of children in their individual development toward their greatest potential:

1. Children have a wide variety of worthwhile mental, social, emotional, and physical activities.

2. Provision is made for individual differences of children within each age group.

3. Children are helped to develop a realistic concept of themselves by having opportunities to pursue their own interests and use their own special abilities with all types of materials.

4. Children are helped to accept themselves and their abilities by having individualized goals and objectives.

5. An effort is made to discover, expand, and utilize the wide range of children's interests.

6. The curriculum includes activities which satisfy a child's desire for adventure, for the mysterious, for drama, for artistic expressions, for sports, and for other interests which develop at different age levels.

7. The curriculum is broad enough to include activities which meet the psychological, social, emotional, and intellectual needs of children.

8. The accomplishments of each child are evaluated in terms of his own abilities and potentials.

9. In developing teaching and learning units, materials are drawn from whatever subject-matter areas are appropriate. Teachers cut across traditional subject boundaries in helping children select content appropriate for solving problems.

10. The sources drawn upon for content materials include first-hand experiences as well as books, reference materials, audiovisual materials and equipment.

11. Children have an active part in developing study units, in planning procedures for developing the unit, and for evaluating the results.

12. The curriculum is developed from the problems that arise in

the daily experiences of children as they work together in a rich school environment.

13. The immediate environment is used in developing the curriculum.

14. Children are given opportunities to engage in community enterprises which they can engage in effectively.

15. Current events which are interesting to children and appropriate to their general maturity are included in the curriculum.

16. Experiences are provided which develop understanding for people of other races, faiths, and customs.

17. People in the community with special abilities and experiences are invited into the school when they are able to contribute to the educational program.

18. Parents are involved in assisting the teacher with extending the learning experiences of children. They can offer tutorial services, assist with enrichment, act as voluntary teacher aides in the many learning activities in progress.

19. Children are encouraged to bring into the school materials which enrich the curriculum.

20. Children are taken on study trips.

21. Attention is given to the structure of the subject to be taught.

22. The skills associated with collecting information, evaluating ideas, using references, guiding discussions, and working in groups are being taught.

23. Skills are developed to the level of proficiency at which normal use will maintain them.

24. Opportunity is given for children to secure expression first and then time is allowed for them to discover the need for better skill.

25. Children are acquiring the skills of learning. They are being helped to learn how to learn.

26. Children are encouraged to do independent, creative, and critical thinking in many types of situations.

27. Children are encouraged to express themselves creatively through writing, graphic arts, music, drama, and bodily rhythms.

28. Children are having opportunities for recreating the art forms created by others by singing, dramatic presentation, playing in an orchestra, and the like.

29. Children are given opportunities to read good literature.

30. Opportunities are given to children to develop appreciations for models and art forms created by others through hearing good

music, classical and popular; seeing examples of good work in the fine and applied arts; seeing good dramatic productions; seeing good expressions of the dance.

31. Children are given opportunities to develop hobbies and other interests along lines which provide for self-discovery and worthy use of leisure.

32. Children are given opportunities to be both participants and spectators in games and athletic events.

The administrator can provide the leadership in setting the goals and procedures for improving the curriculum in his school. He can give guidance to teachers in finding ways to accomplish their plans. His staff will know that the one important criterion with which he is concerned is that each child has developed close to his present potential in becoming a self-directing, self-confident individual. If teachers and children have concerns, interests, and understandings of themselves and their world and are willing and eager to continue to learn, to discover, to create, then the quality of education will also improve in the elementary school and the school administrator's role becomes one of providing the environment in which creativity can flourish.

CHAPTER 18

Counseling and Creativity

by

MARCELLA R. BONSALL AND
ERNEST F. NEUMANN

Marcella R. Bonsall, who received her Ed.D. from the University of Southern California, leads a full and varied private and professional life. She has traveled widely with her husband and has been a teacher of the gifted, an administrator and a supervisor for the Los Angeles City Schools. For seven years Dr. Bonsall was attached to the Division of Research and Guidance in the Los Angeles County Schools, acting as consultant on the education of gifted children and youth. She has taught at the University of Southern California, Oregon State University, and Immaculate Heart College. At present, Dr. Bonsall is in private practice as an educational consultant, and is doing work for the RAND Corporation, individual school districts, and state departments of education. Recently, Dr. Bonsall was awarded a "Citation of Merit" by the National Association for Gifted Children. She has produced films entitled "Rafe: Developing Giftedness in the Educationally Disadvantaged," and "Steve Petchanek: Self-Discovery Through Developmental Guidance."

The father of three highly creative but, in his words, "somewhat demanding" boys, Ernest F. Neumann began his teaching career and his interest in the process of creativity at the same time. He has taught every grade from the ninth through the thirteenth and every ability level from the gifted to the mentally retarded. In addition to being president of a California corporation in the publishing business, he is a counselor at Pasadena City College, which allows him to work closely with the educationally disadvantaged and with those students who are beginning to explore their creative capabilities. Mr. Neumann's past experiences include newspaper work, advertising, free-lance writing, industrial sales, and public information, when on active duty with the Navy.

MUCH HAS BEEN WRITTEN in the past few years about creativity but thus far little has revolved around the professional school guidance worker and what he can achieve as a forceful and positive factor in helping students reach their full creative potentialities. And because the traditional emphasis in the schools has not been centered upon the unique problems of the creative student, the counselor must be such a factor if the needs of the creative are to be successfully met. By the very nature of his training the guidance worker is in a more favorable position to understand the value of the creative individual and to establish a harmonious and intimate relationship with him than is the classroom instructor whose time must be divided among many students.

Historically, the nation's elementary teachers have been a great influence in working with the creative and have compiled a significant record of close teacher-student relationships. For this reason guidance workers have not played a major role at this level. The junior high schools, the high schools, and, to some extent, the colleges have had ongoing, structured guidance programs for some time with clearly delineated role responsibilities. It is at these three levels that the majority of work has been done by trained counselors.

Guidance personnel will be the first to concur in the statement, however, that the bulk of their time is not devoted to the needs of the highly creative student. Instead, it is spent with students whose problems are more common, in the countless number of chores that somehow find their way into job descriptions, and, in many schools, with those pupils who have been identified as necessary recipients of some kind of punitive consideration. But if the recent research is correct, there is little doubt that the creative student is just as numerous as the retarded, or the underachiever, or the honors student. The problems of the creative student are nonetheless as important and as real as those of the minority child who is made fun of on the playground or of the culturally deprived student who drops out of school.

Specifically, the guidance worker can expect to direct his efforts in three overlapping tasks if he wishes to help creative students. First, he must identify, then he must foster and develop, and lastly, he must evaluate that which has occurred as a result of the first two stages. In discussing these stages an eclectic viewpoint of the counseling process has been adopted.

The Task of Identification

The first step the counselor must consider in helping students to realize their creative potential is to learn to identify creativity when he sees it. There are numerous definitions of creativity, but one that serves well is J. E. Drevdahl's (1956), which reads in part, it is "the capacity of persons to produce compositions, products, or ideas of any sort which are essentially new or novel, and previously unknown to the producer." The significant section of this definition is "previously unknown to the producer." The counselor must remember that the creative act is universal to most of mankind.

Creativity, then, occurs when a retarded child discovers, while joyfully painting, that blues and yellows not only are pleasant to see but also produce green when mixed. It can happen to a beginning algebra student learning how to apply an equation satisfactorily when building a ship model. It exists when an honors student applies a principle of a complex economic system to his daily life. The end product is new or novel to each student.

Creativity does not have racial, cultural, or economic barriers. The Negro on the south side of Chicago, ostracized by an affluent white society, is in his own world as creative as any other student. The child of foreign-born parents, with culturally different values, discovers newness and novelty in as many situations as other creative children. The migratory worker's child, lacking continuity in school attendance, can be creative, too. The counselor who fails to realize the universality of creativity, or forgets it in the counseling interview, fails to serve the needs of these students as much as if he fails to prevent an underachiever from dropping out of school. Guidance workers must accept the creative individual as he is, not as they would like him to be.

The creative process is complex. It evokes in varying degrees of strength and at specific times on a continuum a multitude of human functions. The interactions of intellectual, emotional, and physical aspects in the process do not reveal themselves in a clear-cut manner but must be arbitrarily dissected, with boundaries established, for measurement. Measures of need achievement, of academic achievement, the assessing of personality characteristics and the degrees of motivation, the determining of values and of aspirations—all have bearing in identifying and predicting creativity.

Among the basic tools available to counselors in the process of identification are creativity tests. But while creativity tests have been polished and smoothed over the last few years, there is still much work to be done. In the meantime, the use of these measures can help counselors identify creativity more objectively than relying solely on subjective observation and joint opinions.

Most of the measures listed here are concerned with variables considered important to divergent thinking. The items in these measures do not demand a "one and only one right answer." Instead, the elicited answers depend upon the student's own judgment of "goodness of fit." This approach permits the student to be independent in thought and to have freedom of choice. The list is by no means comprehensive. However, the measures included cover a wide chronological age range. These measures also have the following advantages:

1. Each test was specifically developed, or adapted, to measure one or more variables believed necessary for creativity.
2. Each instrument was used in more than one research survey.
3. A numerical score can be obtained on each measure.
4. For each measure printed materials are available on how to administer, to score, and to interpret obtained results.
5. Written references to previous studies, or reprints, are available on each measure.

The Task of Fostering and Developing

Once the creative spark has been identified, what can the guidance worker do to help foster and develop it? He can do many things. The first step is to remember what has already been said about creativity

CREATIVITY TESTS AND MEASURES AVAILABLE TO GUIDANCE WORKERS

Author	*Title*	*Use*	*Preschool*	*Elementary*	*Secondary*	*College & Young Adults*
Mary Aschner and James Gallagher, University of Illinois	Aschner-Gallagher Classification System (4)	Classifies thought processes in classroom interaction		x	x	
Frank Barron, University of California, Berkeley	Barron-Welsh Art Scales (1)	Predicts artistic discrimination			x	x
Frank Barron	Complexity-Simplicity Scale (1)	Self-explanatory			x	x
Frank Barron	Independence of Judgment Scale (1)	Self-explanatory			x	x
Kenneth Beittel, Pennsylvania State University	Combined Art Strategy Criteria (2)	Identifies, measures gains in visual arts				x
Robert Burkhart, Pennsylvania State University	Identification of Spontaneous and Deliberate Groups: Art Process and Products (3)	Self-explanatory			x	x

(continued) CREATIVITY TESTS AND MEASURES AVAILABLE TO GUIDANCE WORKERS

E. E. Ghiselli, University of California, Berkeley	Self-Descriptive Inventory (11)	Measures initiative and self-assurance		x	x
Harrison Gough, University of California, Berkeley	Differential Reaction Scale (1)	Predicts originality		x	x
J. P. Guilford, University of Southern California	Divergent Production (5 and 6)	Measures fluency, flexibility, originality, elaboration, and curiosity through such subtests as Word and Ideational Fluency, Utility, Alternate Uses Test, Associational Fluency, Making Objects, Possible Jobs, Match Problems II, Consequences (both obvious and remote), and Decorations	x	x	x
John Holland, National Merit Scholarship Corporation	Creative Activities Scale (11)	Measures creative achievement		x	x
Esin Kaya, New York University	Kaya Puzzles Test (9)	Measures flexibility, synthesis, originality, and problem solving	x		
Wallace and Ethel Maw, University of Delaware	The You Test (7)	Measures curiosity	x		

Author	*Title*	*Use*	*Preschool*	*Elementary*	*Secondary*	*College & Young Adults*
A. Sarnoff and Martha Mednick, University of Michigan	The Remote Associates Test (11)	Measures creative thinking processes		x	x	x
Rodney Skager and Charles Schultz, Educational Testing Service	The Independent Activities Questionnaire (8)	Measures self-initiative accomplishment			x	x
Elizabeth Stark-weather, Oklahoma State University	Measurement of Conformity (10)	Self-explanatory	x			
	Measurement of Curiosity (10)	Self-explanatory	x			
	Measurement of Originality (10)	Self-explanatory	x			
Calvin Taylor, University of Utah	Biographical Inventory (11)	Predicts creative performance in science			x	x

(continued) CREATIVITY TESTS AND MEASURES AVAILABLE TO GUIDANCE WORKERS

E. Paul Torrance, University of Minnesota (now at the University of Georgia)	Minnesota Tests of Creative Thinking (12)	Measures originality, flexibility, fluency, spontaneity, sensitivity to problems, elaboration, adequacy and inventiveness through such verbal and nonverbal tests as Incomplete Figures Task, Picture Construction Task, Circles and Squares Task, Product Improvement Task, Impossibilities Task, Situations Task, Ask and Guess Test, Unusual Uses, Consequences, Just Suppose, Common Problems, Imaginative Stories, Things Done on Your Own, Creative Activities Check List	x	x
Robert Wilson, University of California, Berkeley	Parent Opinion Scales (contact author)	Measures parental attitudes associated with creativity in students	x	x

Note: Permission to alter tests is required from the authors.
Numbers in parentheses following the titles refer to the numbers in the Bibliography of Measures.
This list follows the references for Chapter 18 under References and Selected Readings.

being potentially inherent in most people and, further, that creativity is relative. When absorbed into the counseling philosophy, these understandings will provide a strong base upon which to operate in helping youngsters realize their creative potential.

This realization is most likely to occur if the needs of the creative student are met. Obviously, the counselor must be aware of them so that he may work with the student. These needs tend to be:

1. To gain personal mastery over experiences.
2. To resist those who wish him to surrender aspects of his own personal, unique, fundamental nature.
3. To accept and understand objective criticism.
4. To place values on a priority list.
5. To learn how to work within imposed structures.
6. To understand that creative behavior is only one of many behaviors at his command.
7. To understand that creativity tends to evoke negative responses from others.
8. To enjoy looking for novel solutions to problems.
9. To learn to accept his intuition.

In addition, the counselor must understand the traits of a creative person. Many research studies have identified these characteristics as follows:

1. Prefers complexity rather than simplicity, and some degree of imbalance.
2. Displays aptitudes of elaboration, fluency, flexibility, originality with semantic and symbolic materials.
3. Is tough-minded and flexible enough to cope with environmental stimuli in a novel yet acceptable fashion.
4. Displays more independence in judgment, self-assertiveness, and dominance than the less creative.
5. Does not become frustrated or anxiety-ridden when his performances do not meet standards of others.
6. Is more willing to break with custom; has less fear of dissent and contradiction than those less creative.
7. Is less threatened by situations which would affect the noncreative adversely.
8. Is stubborn in the pursuit of an aim; can be markedly preoccupied.

9. Does not accept authority on its own terms but challenges the ideas of authority.
10. Is capable of considerable self-discipline.
11. Is particularly observant, intense, and extremely curious.
12. Has a tendency to seek alternate possibilities in the solution of problems.
13. Makes shrewd guesses.
14. Respects his intuition.
15. Possesses risk-taking tendencies.
16. Self-initiates learning.
17. Has perseverance and low distractibility.
18. Has high aspirations for future achievements.
19. Is eager to tell others about his discoveries.

With these needs and traits well in mind, the counselor will find his task centering around the student. And he must not overlook all avenues of effort. The counselor is justly concerned with the following areas of influence: the environment, the counseling relationship, the teacher, the administrator, the community, and the parent.

The Environment

If the counselor sees as a legitimate function of his job the manipulation of student environment to allow for maximum adjustment and effort, he has at his disposal a powerful weapon to use in the fostering of creativity. Indeed, a student who is emotionally comfortable in a class is secure in what it offers and is going to be more able to use his abilities than is a youngster who is not so placed. The counselor, then, should not feel hesitant about recommending a change of teacher in the manipulation of his environment.

Likewise, the creative student who is placed in a stimulating classroom where there is much open-ended discussion is more likely to use his talents than the student in a lecture-oriented class. The perimeter of student creativity is the intellectual and attitudinal surroundings of a class.

When the guidance worker considers the environment he should view it from the following criteria:

1. It should be free of any encumbrances that would negate student adjustment and student ability.
2. It should be positive to the point that students are excited by it.

3. It should provide the necessary ingredients for satisfying the student's need for achievement.

4. It should place emphasis upon learning and creativity in an intrinsic sense.

Singularly, on the elementary level counselors work with teachers approximately one third of their working day. In so doing they can take a positive step by helping teachers to arrange pupil groupings. Suggestions can be offered that the creative child be frequently placed with those who are curious about his activities and with those who take a positive attitude toward him. Or he can be clustered with three or four other creative children for the major portion of a school day.

Homogeneous grouping is now common on the secondary level. Traditionally, these groupings have been by academic ability, not by creative output. The counselor might well exercise every shred of influence at his command to organize a class with a "CO" as a base, disregarding academic ability as a sole criterion.

The organization of extracurricular activities for the creative student is an important objective in the counseling function. Far too infrequently do counselors direct their attentions toward enrichment programs outside of the classroom. This is particularly true in the elementary schools. Habitually, after-school sessions at this level have been recreation periods. While undoubtedly needed, these do not provide the challenging kinds of situations the creative child needs. Realistic offerings blending the needs for physical fitness, manual art skills, and creative fitness should be considered a basic of every school district's extracurricular program.

At the secondary level the need has been partially met with extracurricular seminars in science, English, foreign languages, and the social studies. In such cases the teaching methods have tended to stress more openness and divergence of viewpoint than the usual structured classroom situation. Counselors should urge that such programs be offered in their schools and, further, should encourage the creative to take advantage of them.

The Counseling Relationship

What the counselor knows about human development and sensitivity, combined with an additional knowledge of current research in creativity, makes him probably the only person on a school campus to whom the creative student can turn for sustained help.

There are four points worth mentioning about the counseling relationship and creativity. The first of these is really an extra stress upon a basic principle in guidance: acceptance of a student where he now is, not where the counselor thinks he should be or where he wishes him to be in the future. This total acceptance of a student's beliefs and values is an essential in the establishment of a strong positive student self-concept, which, in turn, is one of the foundations for creativity.

Secondly, the counselor should recognize that it is quite common today to place constraints on the creative. We seem intentionally to place unnecessary barriers in the path of creative individuals, out of a deeply imbedded fear of these "people" who act differently because they think differently. A counselor's inability to accept this as normal for the creative student can only mean ineffectualness in the counseling interview.

A third point for the counselor to realize is that, for the most part, the creative product is born in solitude. It thrives on aloneness. For this reason, some creative persons may suffer from an anxiety of separateness. In many cases the guidance worker will not have to concern himself with this because the creative person likes to be alone. Others, however, still value gregariousness and need more contact with other humans. When this occurs the counselor must be on the alert to the two-headed master the student is trying to serve—that of creative production and that of wide acquaintanceship.

Still another point to remember is that research now indicates that creative men rank higher on tests of femininity and creative women rank higher on tests of masculinity than those less creative. The experienced counselor will instantly recognize the potential problems involved when creative students become aware of this peculiarity and then are faced with having to adjust to it.

To capsulize, a counselor will find helpful support when he can master the qualities of acceptance and understanding. A counselor must be willing to accept and allow the student to be different. Anything short of this attitude will in all probability destroy the rapport necessary to understanding the second attitude.

The types of special problems which highly creative students have are in many ways the same as those of any other student. To this extent the guidance worker is concerned with the students' problems of socialization, personality development, and academics. But, because the creative tend to have certain identifiable traits, some kinds of behavior become more prevalent.

Frequently, students who have trouble with classroom adjustment are referred to the counselor by the teacher. The following chart indicates some of the traits of the creative person and samples of the kinds of resultant problems:

THE CREATIVE PERSON IS LIKELY TO BE	THUS CAUSING SUCH CLASSROOM PROBLEMS AS
Theoretical and abstract	Ignoring stressed data in assignments; handing in unneat work.
Independent, inventive, and ideationally nonconforming	Resisting teacher-chosen assignment in favor of own topic interest; isolating himself from group work.
Complex and involved	Becoming physically tired; concentrating on some assignments far beyond requirements to the exclusion of others.
Sensitive	Having personality withdrawal because of strong goal orientation, or peer-group criticism and rejection.
Alert, eager	Resenting periods of classroom inactivity.
Intuitive	Seeing conclusions without displaying knowledge of sequential concepts.
Daydreaming (concentrated periods of thinking)	Being inattentive to teacher's or classmates' comments and class discussions.
Aesthetically oriented	Resisting participation in active team sports.

While the emphasis thus far has been with the one-to-one relationship between the counselor and the student, no discussion of counseling techniques would be complete without mention of group counseling. Largely eclectic, this approach is a natural for the creative student. An unstructured discussion about the nature of the creative process and the participant's personal feelings about it—and why—pays dividends in the development of the self-concept and in the release of creative energy.

To be truly effective, however, the counselor must feel competent in this technique and, as in the more intimate counselor-client relationship, fully at ease with groups. Guidance workers can expect the creative student to have both the perception and the ability to discuss his values, though, and these traits make "leading" not only unnecessary but unwise.

The Teacher

If creativity is to be fostered and nurtured by the counselor, he must work closely with the teacher. In this regard, the counselor lends support to the teacher, provides whatever services the teacher needs for greater understanding of her pupils, and when asked to do so lends advice. The counselor does not, however, attempt to evaluate the teacher at any time. To do so is to operate in opposition to the role of counseling.

At all educational levels counselors, as they work with teachers, can help them in several ways:

1. They can help them to know what to look for when observing creative youngsters.
2. They can help teachers realize that youngsters cannot be creative unless opportunities are provided for creative traits to emerge.
3. They can help teachers understand the differences between problem solving and creativity.
4. They can help teachers understand why creativity often evokes negative reactions toward the creator.

The counselor can do much by suggesting, organizing, and conducting in-service training sessions with teachers. He can spell out the nature of the creative process and help describe its importance in the curricula. He can summarize and draw implications for education from recent research, and, most of all, he can describe the nature, the problems, and the values of the creative student. Furthermore, the counselor can recommend that teachers take the emphasis off the student and place it on the product.

The Administrator

As with teachers, administrators frequently fail to see the concern over creativity. Only recently in education have school districts formalized attention toward the gifted. Similarly, few districts attempt to organize ongoing programs for the slow. Certainly most of these programs are not designed to develop the creative potentialities within these students.

Administrators have a direct responsibility for all phases of the curriculum. They must be sensitive to the needs of all groups of students and their individual differences. It is the counselor's responsibility, in turn, to call attention to the needs of the creative student and to enlist the aid of the administration for the support of such plans and programs to promote the solving of these needs. By suggesting in-service training programs for teachers, parent education, group guidance for creative students, community reports, and the like, the counselor can materially add to his school solidarity.

The Community

For any organized program for the creative student to succeed, community support is a must. And practicality demands the support of the local governing boards, as the purse strings and policies are knotted here.

The counselor may well consider the following list of suggested activities for gaining the support of governing boards in his district and the community-at-large:

1. Periodic reports about creativity programs to the governing boards.
2. Plays by groups of students for the community.
3. Art displays at fairs or in lobbies of public buildings.
4. Community forums by students on current topics of interest.
5. Student-conceived and outlined answers to such community problems as water usage or juvenile delinquency.
6. Student-planned and completed community surveys.
7. Scientific conferences in the evening for students to report original research.
8. Evening musicals, sometimes including original compositions.
9. Combined student and adult authors' meetings.

The purposes of all of these activities, of course, are to call attention to and gain support of programs for the creative. The role the counselor can play in helping to organize such activities spells the difference between whether or not programs for developing creativity succeed.

The Parent

One of the most critical yet one of the most overlooked and ignored areas of influence a professional guidance worker should consider is working with parents. By the use of parent group-counseling sessions, home visits, personal parent conferences in the school, and the like, the counselor can help parents of creative students understand the needs, traits, characteristics, and behaviors of their children. Useful at all levels, this approach can oftentimes be vital to the welfare of the student.

By increasing parent awareness, the counselor can frequently alter unfavorable home patterns, can suggest extracurricular projects for the family which are in line with the student's abilities, and can, in general, recommend those changes which will create more positive home atmospheres.

The Task of Evaluation

Ultimately the counselor must ascertain how well he has done his job in identifying and fostering creativity in students. Since his efforts thus far have been student centered, so should be the evaluation procedure. A starting point in this process is to know what to evaluate. The following are offered:

1. The nature of the creative student.
2. The nature of the creative process.
3. The kinds of creative expression.
4. The quantity and quality of creative acts.
5. The necessary environmental factors.
6. The attitude changes.
7. The counseling techniques used.
8. The adequacy of the evaluative measures in the collection of relevant information.

Another student-centered approach was suggested by Ernest Hilgard (1959), who felt that students should be permitted to initiate inquiries of their own and that the guidance worker could use this as an evaluatory tool. Additionally, he suggested that students be allowed to exhibit and take responsibility for their creative products, even though the items might not be distinguished, and that the students be allowed to move toward greater diversity of talent rather than toward greater conformity.

Regardless of how the guidance worker answers these questions, an evaluatory process has taken place and it remains only to adjust that which is necessary or continue that which has proven successful.

Too, guidance workers have many valuable tools at their command in the evaluatory process. While each tool certainly has its own shortcomings, the counselor, nevertheless, can wisely employ a combination of such tools as anecdotal records, observations, autobiographies, questionnaires, interview records, rating scales, inventories, tape recordings, concrete examples of production, time samplings, standardized tests, and other such measures.

The data gathering should include a combination of formal tests supplemented by a combination of informal measures so that a broader description is obtained of the area being evaluated. In many instances the use of the above combinations not only provides the broader picture required to understand creativity but also acts as a system of double checking the results obtained. Once all the desired information has been accumulated, then, and only then, is it feasible for the counselor to attempt the difficult job of analyzing and interpreting the data. After this professional treatment is completed, the counselor is in a good position to make realistic judgments and to plan wisely for creative students.

The Summary

The counselor can play a vital role in helping students realize their creative potentialities. Professional guidance workers can best do this by focusing attention upon three aspects of creativity: identifying, fostering, and evaluating.

Each area has its own unique problems and challenges, many of which overlap. And while the problems vary to some extent from age level to age level, there is evidence enough to sustain the belief that basic behavior patterns do indeed exist and that, once recognized by the guidance worker, they will allow him to work closely with creative students, to meet their needs, and to help them become contributing members of our changing society.

PART IV

PRACTICE OF MENTAL HEALTH PRINCIPLES AT SCHOOL AND HOME TO FACILITATE CREATIVE ENDEAVOR

Overview

In their consideration of how mental health principles may be related to teaching for creative endeavor, Schwartz and Bonsall in Chapter 19 take a comprehensive view of the school as an institution and organization consisting of individuals arranged in an hierarchical structure who have interdependent roles of both an institutional and extrainstitutional character. Within the framework of this sociological orientation, an analogy is drawn between the choice situation that a child faces in trying to be creative and that which members of an organization encounter in the achievement of institutional goals. Depending upon his particular needs, the child with considerable potentialities for creative activities is faced with the choice either of expending his energy in creative behavior at the risk of losing social acceptance by his peers and even his teachers and parents or of investing his energy in socially rewarding activities at the expense of giving up creatively oriented learning experiences. The authors suggest that although the decision rests primarily with children and their parents, school personnel need to be sophisticated about such conflict situations so that they can advise parents and children of the implications of their decisions. In the instance of the school organization, the energies of its members can be channeled toward institutional goals in a creative manner only to the degree to which their energies are not needed in resolving organizational stresses. When conflict is present, the realization of progress in the development of new school programs aimed at improved institutional functioning is thwarted. With a resolution of stresses and conflicts described, one can anticipate that the creative endeavors of both the child and the school organization will be improved.

How consultants may be of help to teachers, parents, and children on classroom behavior problems that suggest emotional disturbance on the part of the learner is described and illustrated. Consultation may be planned to enhance creative ways in which the teacher may handle classroom difficulties. The writers indicate that the consultant can advantageously give support and encouragement to the consultee (the teacher or a group of teachers) in approaching and solving problems related to mental health concerns, although direct advice is not to be encouraged. In short, the consultant employs a nondirective approach in which he assists the consultee to pose alternative solutions and finally to select a course of action that seems most pragmatic relative to the particular situation encountered.

After furnishing both a brief overview of Guilford's contributions to the understanding of creative abilities and a description of specific types of divergent thinking abilities, Gowan proceeds in the last chapter (Chapter 20) to discuss how parents can help to foster creative behavior in their children. Reiterating in his own words virtually the same conflict hypothesis proposed by Schwartz and Bonsall —the conflict that may arise between a child's being creative and simultaneously being socially accepted, Gowan urges that parents help the creative child to find another child with whom he can comfortably identify. Such identification is judged to be essential for the development of a social conscience that in turn will permit creative endeavor to be constructive rather than destructive to the needs of both the individual and society. Second, by giving encouragement to and spending time with the creative child, parents may advantageously develop a fostering attitude that gives the child sufficient confidence to try new activities. Thus, the creative child may come to view life as an exciting adventure in which he can make reasonable efforts with a reasonable risk of success in controlling a portion of his total environment that is more or less reasonably organized.

In addition, Gowan urges that parents help children to adjust to disappointment and doubt when their creative activities have not been accepted by others and particularly when their own self-evaluation reveals that perhaps nine out of ten times their creative ideas were not so promising as they had initially seemed. By giving praise rather than criticism to creative efforts—no matter how crude such efforts may be—and by being respectful of a child's curiosity and questioning nature, the parents contribute to the child's favorable state of mental health that Gowan views as a facilitating influence upon creative endeavor. Additional steps that parents may take to foster creative behaviors in their children include the following: (1) affording independence and solitude for the self-starting creative child to complete what he has initiated, (2) heightening his sensory awareness by helping him to enjoy sensory experiences without being made to feel guilty or without seeming to be "sissified," (3) valuing his ideas—an activity prerequisite to his valuing his own ideas or those of others and to his developing a value system, and (4) allowing him to discover through home discussions that often more than one answer is possible for a problem situation in real life—a basis for the development of a tolerance for the points of view of other individuals. The writer next examines sex differences in creative children in relation to parental dynamics. Attention is also directed toward the importance of tolerating fantasy and "tall tales" so frequently indulged in by small children.

In short, the creative child needs from his parents not only the freedom and independence to pursue his creative energies but also their encouragement and emotional support at times of both success and failure. A parent's attitude embodying warmth and affection is particularly basic to creative endeavor, as nearly all individuals want to create for those whom they love.

CHAPTER 19

Mental Health Principles at School

by

DONALD A. SCHWARTZ AND
MARCELLA R. BONSALL

Donald Schwartz received his M.D. degree from Western Reserve University. Following an internship, he spent five years in specialty training in psychiatry with the California Department of Mental Hygiene, which included a year at the Langley Porter Neuropsychiatric Institute and two years at the UCLA Neuropsychiatric Institute, plus a year each at a state hospital for general psychiatry and a state hospital for mental retardation. A sixth year was added as chief resident in psychiatry at UCLA. Perhaps even longer than it was broad, this training period gave him the distinction of being the only resident at UCLA who was certified by the American Board of Psychiatry and Neurology while still a resident. He remained at UCLA for three years as chief of the Psychiatric Inpatient Service and assistant professor of Psychiatry. Leaving the full-time faculty to become deputy director of the Los Angeles County Department of Mental Health, he continues to teach at UCLA with the rank of associate clinical professor of Psychiatry.

The School as an Institution and an Organization

THE SCHOOL IS A SOCIAL INSTITUTION in our society, with functions of varying sorts, changing over time, fluctuating in response to other social forces, and often described formally in one way while taking place in quite different ways in real life. The function of the school as an institution is to teach. But this is surely not its only function. The school also is expected to assume responsibility for promotion

NOTE: To simplify wording, the teacher will be referred to as "she" and the child as "he" in this chapter. Appropriate apologies are extended men teachers and girl children.

of maturity, social as well as intellectual, for its children. It is expected to assist them in learning to develop human relationships with other children and with adults. It is expected to assist them in coping with disciplinary experience. It is expected to help to shape their attitudes toward the world, besides teaching them content material about that world. Other than for subject content, these areas are not delineated much in a formal way, nor are they emphasized as primary functions of the school. Depending upon the circumstances, the school may be criticized for interfering in these areas, or it may be castigated for failing to do more with regard to them. As to the "teaching" itself, long arguments are held as to precisely what should be taught and as to how much teaching should concern itself with values and attitudes related to the content material of the curriculum.

Apart from being an institution with these controversial areas of function, the school is an organization made up of people, arranged in a hierarchical structure. The people have lives apart from their roles in the schools, just as do their students, and there is no clean separation of the organizational or extracurricular roles from the institutional ones. As organizations, schools have problems—administrative, personnel, salary, and relationship—among their employees, just as have all other organizations.

Teaching for creativity takes place in this organizational milieu. It is thus dependent on all the institutional and organizational stresses and strains to which the milieu and its inhabitants are subject. In a more specific sense, the relationship between the teacher and the child is determined by the relationships among teacher, child, parents, principal, suprintendent, and others in the community. Some of the more important relationships in this total constellation are illustrated in Figure One.

The teacher's impact upon a child in the school setting is modified by the child's relationships with other children in the class, as well as by his relationships with his parents, siblings, and others important in his life. To be most effective with the child, the teacher needs to have some impact upon these other relationships. To some extent, this is possible. Certainly, the teacher is in a position to have some impact on parents and on other children in the class. Her ability to accomplish her educational goals with the child will depend in part on how well she uses this opportunity, as well as upon how well she works with the child himself. For instance, there is limited value in encouraging a child to be more inquisitive in the school setting while the same child returns each afternoon to a home setting where he is criticized or made fun of for doing just that. There are problems involved in urging a child to develop artistic interests in the classroom when that child is being called a sissy by classmates because of

THE SCHOOL AS AN ORGANIZATION:
THE INTERPERSONAL TREE

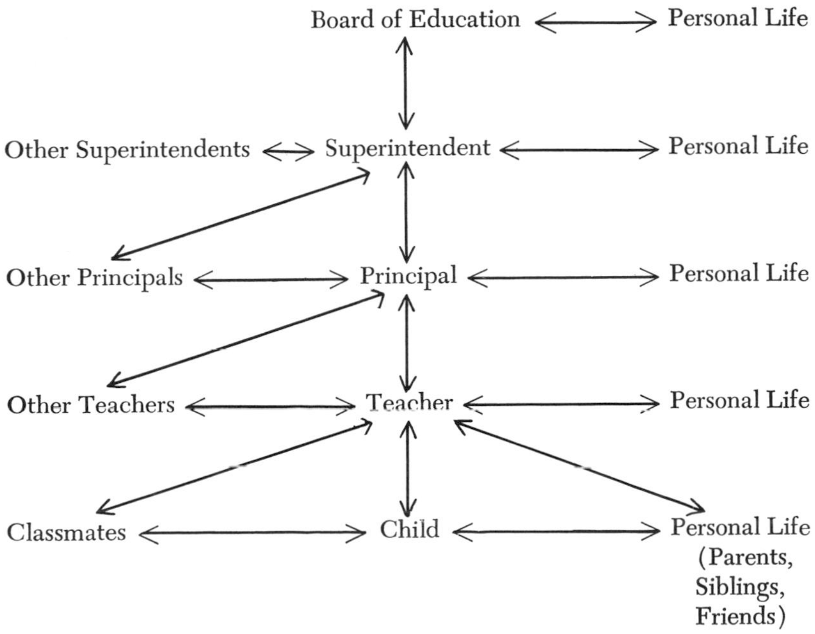

FIGURE ONE

that interest. This is not to imply that the teacher ought not to encourage these attitudes in children just because others react negatively toward them. It is certainly meant to imply, however, that the teacher needs to pay attention to the attitudes of others and to try to exert some influence on them.

The extent to which parents are made aware of what teachers are doing and why they are doing it influences the reactions of the parents to some degree. The wise teacher not only will tell parents about her teaching activity but also will invite the parents to express their own views about it. If the parents refuse to compromise in some view which is at variance with the teacher's goals for the child, this needs to be taken into consideration by the teacher. Otherwise, the child may simply be placed in the middle in a war of giants over his destiny. If a teacher is aware of reactions of classmates which undo what she is trying to accomplish with a child, that knowledge alone may lead her to ways of affecting the attitudes of other children so that there is less of a negative impact on the child in question.

Nor is the teacher herself free of the kinds of influences discussed just above in relation to children. A teacher is influenced by the attitudes of other teachers, as well as by those of the principal and others in the administrative hierarchy of the school. The teacher who would like to develop teaching programs and attitudes which foster creativity may be teaching in a school where the principal's attitudes are much at variance with her own. He may be less interested in fostering creativity than she is, or he may differ with her on how this is to be accomplished.

The attitudes of supervisory personnel influence teachers in different ways. The more submissive teacher may accede to supervisory attitudes or she may express her disagreement in indirect ways rather than by overt opposition. The more rebellious sort of person may be stimulated to greater efforts by opposition. Either kind of interaction occurs in an organizational setting with an existing pattern of relationships and conflicts. And the manner in which the interaction is expressed is influenced by the pre-existing conflicts. For instance, a teacher in conflict with the principal over the manner in which she should work toward creativity with her class may tend to seek support for her point of view among other teachers who are currently at odds with the principal over some other issue. The more submissive teachers will tend to align themselves with the "authority" position and the more rebellious ones on the other side. The outcome may be the development of two opposing camps supposedly in relation to the teaching methods at issue, but where the real bases for the alignment have little to do with the teaching methods or indeed with creativity at all.

From another aspect of this same area of interest, let us suppose that a principal wants to encourage the development of some newer approach to teaching, related to fostering creativity in children. The way in which he introduces the matter determines the outcome of its introduction to a considerable extent. The more authoritatively he does so, the more likely he is to meet opposition from the rebelliously oriented segment of his staff; and this is completely apart from the technical merits or demerits of the proposal. Having done this, he is likely to see his suggestions followed by only a part of his staff. He is then likely to attempt to support those teachers who are following the suggested approach. However, his support for those teachers may further estrange them from their colleagues. This is especially important if there are only a few teachers in the group he is supporting. They may tend to become walled off from the rest of the teaching staff, with the eventual result that severe tensions are created not only in the walled-off group but also throughout the entire organizational structure of the school.

The wise principal is aware of these likelihoods and presents material with mindfulness of the organizational status of his school, as well as of its institutional existence. These patterns apply not only at the level of single schools, but throughout all levels of a school system. The end-product of successful organizational interaction may be a program which enhances the creative behavior of children in the schools; whether it does this or not depends on successful interaction in many different locations. Failures of effective organizational functioning in locations far distant from the classroom may have a negative impact just as serious as failures of effective relationships within the classroom itself.

Creativity

This chapter will proceed on the assumption that creativity is a universal potentiality in children. Intelligence is one element of significance among the determinants of creative potential. For this reason, one will expect more creative potential and more areas of creative potential in the gifted child than in the average child. However, one will also find children in the average range of overall intelligence who will show great creative potential in one or a few areas, and children of below-average intellectual capacity with some area in which they show marked creativity. Perhaps the extreme of this expresses itself in the phenomenon of the idiot savant, whose overall intelligence is in the retarded range but who shows an inexplicable capacity in some single field of thought (usually arithmetic).

This notion of the universality of creative potential is more than an academic point of debate. If we start with this assumption, then teaching for creativity becomes an element of all teaching, of all children, at all school levels. A second assumption of this chapter is that all individuals, teachers and children alike, function substantially below their creative potential. The literature on creativity is replete with comments about personality traits which seem to be seen in especially creative people. The "creative person" is said to be curious, doubting, dissatisfied, driven, and nonconforming in thought (though logical). He is introspective, ruminative rather than exhibitionistic. It is pertinent to point out that all children sometimes show these traits. And one may speculate whether these traits appear in children in accompaniment to more creative periods of thought. Such behavioral expressions may reflect universal concomitants of a sense of dissatisfaction with the way things "are" or "are supposed to be." Such feelings, if accompanied by a willingness to look for alternative conceptions, certainly represent an element of creative thinking.

But the nature of these qualities is quickly seen to be at variance with the kinds of behavior which earn social approval and acceptance in society. It is the accepter, the conformist, the child who shares the values of the group, who is most easily accepted in the social sphere. He is more comfortable to be with than the child who questions, the child who doubts, and the child who rejects the group values. It would seem almost as if there were a choice for the child: to be creative or to be well-adjusted socially. And this appearance of either-or-ness is enhanced by the tendency to conceive of creativeness itself as either-or. If we have the notion that some few children are creative and the rest of them not so, we will inevitably participate in the compartmentalization. We will expect the children who show the "antisociability" to be creative but socially maladjusted, and we will convey this expectation to them. We will expect most children to be socially well-adjusted and convey this to them. One consequence of such adult expectation is that the more creative children will abandon those drives toward social acceptability and turn more exclusively toward their inner preoccupations. Another consequence is that the less creative children will abandon what drives they do have toward creative behavior and see this part of their directedness as "wrong" and unacceptable.

In contrast, to the extent to which we conceive of creativity as a universal potential existing in certain areas in all people, and if our teaching and training encourages the actualization of these creative potentials in all children, we will be making the qualities that correlate with creative expression more broadly acceptable in the social groups in which children exist. In an oversimplified way, if we are able to develop a social climate in which all people are expected and permitted to have areas of doubt, deviance, and nonconformity, then we will have a climate in which the more highly and broadly creative individuals have a greater degree of acceptance and comfort.

Such a prospect may seem like a social utopia, and perhaps its actual existence is. Nevertheless, to the extent to which those of us in education are able to recognize the universal potentiality of creative behavior and to encourage its broader actualization, we will move toward the utopia. In the meantime, we may as well face the fact that children must all too often choose whether to be socially acceptable or creative.

Mental Health and Creativity

The preceding discussion has a number of implications so far as mental health is concerned. Before discussing these, it would be well to take a look at mental health and what is usually meant by that term. It is repeatedly said that mental health does not mean simply the absence of mental illness. However, it is much more difficult to say what mental health is than what it is not. To psychiatrists, as to physicians in general, the concept of health as completely apart from illness is a difficult one. Health is more than the absence of illness, but it is generally thought of as a state in which there is greater, rather than lesser, resistance to illness. Positive qualities which are said to be elements of good health are so described because they are felt to be attributes which enhance resistance to illness. Good nutrition, good muscle tone and development, and physical fitness in general are seen as positive qualities because they represent supposed qualities which decrease the likelihood of occurrence of illness. It is so with mental health also. Good mental health is conceived of as implying possession of those qualities which enhance one's resistance to mental illness. When it comes to saying precisely what those qualities are, we are in somewhat more difficulty. It is often difficult to know precisely what traits of personality or human behavior constitute elements of resistance to mental illness. However, such specifics do not contradict the basic generalization that good mental health implies resistance to illness.

We can go at least one step further than this. The symptoms of mental illness manifest themselves in ways which constitute interferences with relationships with other human beings in one way or another. This leads us to the assumption that mental health implies increased capacity to adapt to the stresses of such human relationships. This does not mean that social adaptability is the sole determinant of mental health. People differ in their need for acceptance within the social group. Some can tolerate a considerable amount of isolation from the dominant social groups of their society. Others can tolerate only a small amount of such estrangement. It is a task of parents and others who must assist children to grow and mature to attend to this area of differential tolerance in children.

In the preceding section, it was mentioned that creative behavior implies a certain degree of idiosyncratic thought processes, and a certain amount of deviation from social norms. Since children vary in the degree to which they can tolerate such deviance, it can be said also that they vary in the degree to which they can tolerate creative expression. It is the task of the teacher, if she wishes to promote the child's mental health as well as his creativity, to consider this fact. It is often seen that creative children tend to be excluded from the dominant social groups of their peers. Tests of personality traits have shown that the more creative child may also appear moody, aloof, emotionally cold or detached, and otherwise seemingly unhappy. These may imply that there is an inevitable negative correlation between social adaptiveness and creativity. It is certainly not clear, however, that this is so. The most creative children may appear socially detached for reasons other than that they are maladapted in a social sense. Creativity implies some preoccupation with inner stimuli: thoughts, reflections, and ideas. One cannot be simultaneously attentive to these inner stimuli and to external, social stimuli. Thus what appears to be social maladaptation may be largely a matter of attention set.

On the other hand, such an internalized attention set will, by its simple existence, tend to separate the child from the social group. He may be perceived as snobbish, critical, or "strange" to other children who are more externally directed. Moreover, adults (parents and teachers) may see creativity as socially unacceptable, and thus convey nonverbally or even verbally to the child that he is different from the others he relates to on a peer level. They may imply to him that he ought to be socially estranged from them. Or they may encourage him to devalue social relationships to an undue degree so as to rely almost exclusively on the inner intellectual stimuli with which he may already be becoming more comfortable.

Thus, what starts as a misassumption may become a self-fulfilling prophecy, as the child is stimulated by others to value his creative potentials while devaluing his social adaptability. If both qualities can be kept in some perspective, it will be more possible to assess the potentials of each child in both spheres, and to be of more help to all children in terms of the balance of drives within them.

In some cases, hard choices need to be made. In the case of the child with considerable potential for creative behavior, but with great need for social acceptance within his peer group, some sacrifice needs to be made. He must function below his creative potential, or else he must accept a certain degree of mental ill health in the form of painful social estrangement.

It would be tempting to award some primacy to good mental health in making such a choice. Especially for a psychiatrist, it would be most comfortable to say that children should be encouraged toward creativity to the extent that they can maintain good mental health simultaneously, but that the limit in encouragement of creativity is the point where the social estrangement becomes painful or produces symptoms of emotional disorder. For the purposes of this chapter, at least, such an assumption will not be made. Rather, it will be assumed that choices of this sort may have to be made, and that they should be made with as much awareness as possible of the implications of the choices, but that they must be made on an individual basis by children, parents, and educators. In our society, the individual is presumed to be entitled to make his own choices, even if they entail pain or distress for him. In the case of children, the right to such choices lies primarily with the children and their parents, with teachers and other educators needing to accept a secondary role. It is, however, the responsibility of school personnel to be informed and sophisticated about the factors implicit in such choices, so as to be capable of advising children and parents of these implications.

Mental Health Consultation

The increasing sophistication and interest in mental health have been confronting psychiatry with its manpower problems in an increasingly sharp manner. One outgrowth of this awareness of inadequate treatment services for those who cannot afford private care has been the search for alternatives to treatment of mental illness in the traditional ways and by traditional kinds of professionals and facilities. Another outgrowth is the increasing interest in developing ways of preventing mental illness in those who seem to be threatened by it.

In addition to newer techniques of treatment, psychiatric interest has been directed more to certain kinds of nontreatment, one of which is called "mental health consultation." Mental health consultation involves a meeting between a mental health professional (the consultant) and another person (the consultee) who may be a professional or a nonprofessional but who has some kind of helping role with other people; this may be as a teacher, a social worker, a probation officer, a minister, a lawyer, a house parent in a residential facility, or anyone in the many kinds of helping roles. The consultee is seeking mental health consultation because some of the people he is trying to help appear to him to have a mental health problem.

Since our focus is on the school, let us consider mental health consultation from the point of its utility and characteristics in the school setting. Teachers frequently are faced with children who seem to them to be emotionally disturbed to an extent that they are not using the classroom experience effectively. Sometimes these children's parents perceive them as the teacher does, and a parent-teacher conference leads to some resolution of the problem. Other times a counselor, school nurse or physician, or someone else can take the problem off the teacher's hands. But often circumstances may also be such that there is no one who can or will do anything effective about the child, and the problem remains the teacher's. At still other times, the problem will seem to be the kind a teacher should be able to cope with, rather than one which needs to be referred to someone else, but nothing the teacher tries seems to work. In other words, there are times when teachers feel at a loss to cope with some problem which they see as being in the sphere of mental health.

We have used the teacher for illustration here, but problems of this sort confront school nurses, counselors, welfare and attendance workers, and administrators at all levels. It is in situations such as these that mental health consultation is being used increasingly. It rests on the assumption that the consultees may have underestimated their ability to cope with the situation they are seeking help with; the consultant starts with this possibility in mind, and listens to the situation being presented to him from that perspective. His comments may be quite variable in form and content, but they are intended to facilitate the consultee's recognition that he possesses the ability to handle the situation himself, if this is indeed the case.

If it is not quite clear from the preceding discussion, it should be made explicit at this point that mental health consultation is not designed to turn the educator into a junior-grade psychiatrist. Quite the contrary, the kinds of problems which consultees come to be able to solve as a result of mental health consultation most often could not be solved by the mental health consultants themselves. The solutions to problems arising in school are solutions which require educational skills that the consultants usually do not themselves possess.

Mental health consultation, then, rests on an assumption analogous to one made concerning creativity in an earlier section of this chapter. This assumption is that consultees are not using the skills they possess to a maximum in handling the mental health problems of their clients; in another way, we may say that they are not functioning as creatively as they could in dealing with the problems. So consultation in this sense is a process designed to enhance the creative functioning of consultees. As such, the consultation process is characterized by some of the qualities which educators cite as needful in enhancing creativity in children in school. The consultant is concerned not with telling the consultee how to do something, but with helping the consultee to find the best way for him to do something. The consultant tries to make it safe for consultees to explore ideas and techniques; he is willing to let them make mistakes in the process of finding the best answers for themselves. The consultant is permissive, being willing to listen to the ways in which consultees conceptualize the problem at hand, rather than needing to rush in to the discussion with his own ways of looking at it.

Perhaps we can illuminate the process of mental health consultation in the school setting with a fictitious illustration. Consultation may take place in an individual or a group setting. Let us use the group setting for this illustration. The consultees are a group of elementary school teachers who have been meeting once a week for the past month with a mental health consultant. The earlier meetings have clarified for the teachers that the consultant does not have ready-made answers for their problems. Mrs. A., a fourth grade teacher, has come to this meeting prepared to describe a situation which is causing difficulty for her. Bill, a bright but restless and willful nine-year-old boy, has been becoming increasingly disruptive to the class. He ignores directions, is careless with homework assignments, and is not achieving anywhere near his potential capability. As Mrs. A. describes the problem, she reveals also that she tends to become committed to time schedules and lesson plans in a rather rigid way. Several of the examples of rebellion she mentions occurred as direct reactions to her attempting to impose this kind of scheduling on the class. One of the other teachers points this out, and asks why Bill should have to learn at this particular rate. Mrs. A. replies that she has to see that he learns fourth grade material by the time he goes into fifth grade; otherwise he would not be able to handle the fifth grade work. The consultant asks what kind of allowances the teachers make for children who do not fit the standard patterns of learning in one way or another. Mrs. A. cites an example of a child concerning whose failure she was counseled by the principal. Mrs. A. felt blamed for this other child's failure and this accentuates her desire to avoid repetitions of this kind of situation. Another teacher mentions an example of a child with a similar problem whom she had discussed with the principal, and with whom she felt the principal had encouraged her to be more flexible. The implication of this is that the principal may not be so inflexible about schedules and curricula as Mrs. A. had assumed from the experience she had had. The only direct suggestion the consultant makes during the discussion of Bill's problems is that Mrs. A. might want to talk with his parents again to find out what his behavior at home has been like.

Two weeks later, Mrs. A. reports that Bill is doing much better. He is less rebellious and even seeks her help on occasion. He is still learning at his own pace, and she is still concerned that he may fail in some areas, but she is willing to relax her pressure on time schedules and rely on her assessment that he is really capable of learning the material. She still has not talked with his parents, but she did have occasion to bring up the problem informally with the principal over coffee, and felt supported in her decisions.

This illustration, though brief and superficial in nature, is intended to show several aspects of the more common kind of outcome of mental health consultation:

1. The consultant would not have been able, even if he had wanted to do so, to tell the consultee what to do and how to do it.
2. The consultee or other consultees in the group were capable of

redefining the problem so that its solution could be sought within the province of the consultee's professional role.

3. The consultee's change in approach to the client averted a process whereby the consultee was acting to aggravate the client's emotional distress, by adding to whatever other tensions existed. This constitutes a change beneficial to the client's mental health, without the consultee providing "treatment."

The relevance of this discussion of mental health consultation to the central issue of this chapter lies in the fact that such consultation need not be used only for behavior problems or apparently mentally disturbed children. It can also be helpful to educators in assessing the sorts of problems discussed in the preceding section of the chapter: specifically, the problems of evaluating children in general or particular children with regard to their potential for creative behavior and their tolerance of the deviation implicit in such creativity.

Applications to the School as an Organization

The material discussed in regard to creativity and mental health has relevance also to the school as an organization. Teachers have their potentials and their limitations in these areas, as well as do children. Principals and other administrators have potentials for creative behavior, and they have limits to their capacity for creative teaching. The principal who wishes to develop more effective programs for teaching for creativity should consider the needs of his staff as well as the needs of their students. One cannot order a teacher to have some particular outlook on teaching, nor to obtain those traits of personality which would enhance a particular teaching program. Similarly, teachers who are interested in developing some program of teaching need to consider not only their own tolerances for such a program, but also the tolerances of the school for it.

As a generalization, one can make a statement analogous to one made earlier in the chapter regarding a choice between creative behavior and social acceptance. With regard to the school, one can say that the energy of the people who constitute the school-as-an-organization can be directed toward institutional goals only to the extent that it is not required by organizational stresses. When the organizational relationships are smoothly functioning, more energy is available for the achievement of institutional goals. When conflict exists within the organizational structure, and when the energy of the people in the organization is directed toward the resolution of those conflicts (or toward creating them), then that energy is not simultaneously available for the achievement of institutional goals. It is necessary to make choices here, also. If there is conflict around organizational issues, it is of little use to expect that great progress is going to be made in the development of new programs directed toward better institutional functioning. It would be more prudent to attend to the organizational stresses first. When these are reasonably at rest, one can expect more successful institutional functioning.

Summary

If the thesis of this chapter were to be summarized in a brief statement, it could perhaps best be done by saying that the children who are to be taught more creatively and the educators who are to be involved in so teaching them are all people with human needs and limitations related to their mental health or lack of it. One cannot address oneself to the problem of teaching for creativity unless one keeps in mind the capacities and limitations of all the people involved in the venture. And one cannot expect to do the best job possible in teaching for creativity unless one also does an effective job of assessment in these other areas.

CHAPTER 20

How Parents Can Foster Creativity in Their Children

by

JOHN CURTIS GOWAN

Internationally known for his work on creativity, gifted children, teacher evaluation, and measurement, John C. Gowan earned his A.B. and Ed.M. degrees at Harvard University and his Ed.D. in Educational Psychology at the University of California, Los Angeles. He taught high school mathematics and served as a counselor for several years in high schools and colleges before joining the staff at Los Angeles State College as assistant professor of Education. Currently, he is professor of Education, specializing in counseling and guidance, at San Fernando Valley State College. Recently, John Gowan was a Fulbright lecturer at the University of Singapore, where he did research on cross-cultural characteristics of Torrance's tests on creativity.

WHAT IS A CREATIVE CHILD? Our knowledge on the subject is very new—so new, in fact, that if you look under "creativity" in Webster's dictionary you will not find a relevant definition. Creativity, for the purpose of this chapter, is to be thought of from a scientific point of view, and this approach as an area of study has been considered only as recently as 1950. Before that date we had talked about a youngster's "intelligence" and we had looked upon the single I.Q. of the child as though it would determine his fate forever after. The child was either up on the intelligence test or he was down on it. There was only one way in which he could be considered as highly intelligent and that was by getting a high score on this particular test, and there was only one score on the test. What we did not know at that time was that measuring intelligence in terms of the intelligence tests then in vogue was very much like valuing a bridge hand by looking only at the red suits and completely neglecting the high cards that you might hold in the black suits. We now realize that there are many factors of intelligence which are not measured by conventional intelligence testing. We now believe we should measure intelligence by a youngster's performance in many areas of constructive activity, and in some of these areas a "creative" child may be markedly superior to the average child.

Creativity in Relation to Computer Technology

It has become obvious since World War II that there is the need for innovative, creative people—people who can produce new ideas or concrete objects, or new combinations of old ones. This has been due partially to the advent of the computer, which can do some things far better than human brains can do them. A computer can, for example, store information at a simply amazing speed and can retrieve this information much more accurately than human beings. Since we are going to live in a world of computers, it is not quite so important for individuals to be able to store rapidly and retrieve rapidly—it is far more important for them to be able to assemble this material into new forms, to organize it in new ways, and so on.

The problem we face in comparing man's mind with the operation of a computer is a very interesting one. In the first place, we want to keep ahead of the computer, and, in the second place, we want to find in the operation of the computer what it can do which we no longer need to do and thereby free ourselves to do that which the computer cannot do so well. All this, of course, has placed a tremendous premium on the areas of creative intelligence where the computer cannot keep up with human capacity. For this reason we have been very much interested in fostering high creativity in our youngsters, assuming that fostering this in children will lead to adult creative production.

Guilford's Research on Creativity

Let us look briefly at some of the research in this new field. Pioneering work has come from the laboratories of the University of Southern California where Professor J. P. Guilford has established, during the last thirteen years, a virtual periodic table of many factors of intelligence. Guilford's model of the intellectual abilities of man resembles very much what the Russian scientist D. I. Mendeleev did with the periodic tables of the elements in chemistry 50 to 75 years ago. Mendeleev constructed a periodic table in which he predicted elements that were then unknown, and Guilford has done exactly the same thing with what he calls the "Factors of Intellect." Guilford has been able to isolate, identify, and analyze some 75 or 80 different factors of intelligence in families.

One of the most important of these families of abilities, according to Guilford (1956), is "Divergent Production," or the divergent aspects of thinking ability. Perhaps it would be helpful in explanation of this to give an example of the opposite or convergent aspects of thinking ability. If you are asked to solve the problem, "What is 73 × 110?", there is only one answer, "8,030." The answer is an example of convergent thinking—you converge on a single correct answer. Many of the problems presented to young people in school are of this kind, and much of our schooling has had to do with the stimulation of convergent thinking ability, the only kind formerly recognized. In contrast, Guilford has pointed out that there are other kinds of abilities, often found in creative people, which have to do with the production of many answers to a problem—divergent thinking.

These divergent aspects of thinking ability are somewhat easily recognized when they appear in a symbolic context, such as in mathematics, or when they can be seen or heard, as in art or music, or even when applied to the behavioral areas, in terms of social intelligence, let us say. However, for this discussion we should like to give examples in the area of verbal production. Let us see how you would find out whether a child has the ability to apply divergent aspects of thinking ability to the area of verbal fluency. Take associational fluency, for example, and ask him to write synonyms for certain words. In the area of ideational fluency ask him to write names of things fitting broad classes, such as the names of European rivers. To "test" for expressional fluency ask him to construct a variety of four-word sentences given four initial letters, such as A T A G ("All taxis are green"; "A teacher ate grapes"), or measure his word fluency by asking him to write words containing a specific letter, such as "Q," and see how many he can think of in a given time, or ask him the question, "How many four-letter words can you think of which begin and end with "R"? Perhaps you are interested in originality which would show up if he were asked to write clever titles for a short story or captions for a cartoon. None of these areas of verbal fluency was measured formerly on the conventional intelligence tests, and all are considerably harder than simply retrieving the answer to a question such as "Who discovered America?"

Fostering Creativity in Children

Many of the specific details to be mentioned in the remainder of this chapter will be true for all children, but the child who is markedly superior to the average child is the one who needs more attention paid to his creative tendencies if we are going to train the kind of talent we will need in the present and future years in our country.

As our children start to grow up and enter what is called by educational psychologists the latency period (between age seven and adolescence), they have to identify with youngsters just like themselves. For the average youngster this is no problem at all, and school is a wonderful place because he meets another child who is just like himself—they are both age seven and both boys, they wear the same kind of pants in the same way, look at the same television shows, and eat the same cereal. If this is your boy we are talking about, you think he has fallen under the evil influence of Billy, the neighbor's child, and the neighbor thinks the same thing about your child. You tell your child to do something and he says, "No, Billy says to do it this way." What is happening is something very good and something very important. Your child has left the family and has begun to find satisfaction with people like himself; he is now identifying with someone else his own age and sex which leads a little later to identifying with people of the opposite sex and of different ages. One problem we have with very creative youngsters is that they never get to meet someone just like themselves, so they never take the first step up this ladder of socialization, which may cause them to become social outcasts.

Parents should help a creative child find another child with whom he can identify in order that he may achieve the social consciousness that is going to be so important in his future and the future of our country. We do not just need scientists, we need scientists with a social awareness; and the parents and school have an obligation in this regard, particularly with very creative children. One of the teachers in an elementary school told me recently of the troubles one of her "bright" students was having because the other youngsters would chant about him, "He's the queer of the year, the goon of the decade, and the nut of the century." In talking with this boy I found him to be an extremely creative child, and it bothered him to have his playmates sing this chant about him. We discussed the need in our society to "get along" with people, even though it might be boring to ones such as himself, and how he would gain nothing from life by acting as obnoxiously as he had toward his playmates. I challenged him to think of ways in which he could gain their respect, and he came up with a number of ingenious ideas; he tried these out and I am glad to report that he has been accepted by his group.

Developing a Fostering Attitude

One of the first things parents should do with all children, though again this chapter is talking specifically about creative children, is to develop a "fostering attitude." A father who is interested in baseball develops a fostering attitude about baseball on behalf of his eight-year-old son by talking to him about baseball, by buying him a bat, glove, and ball, by playing catch with him, and by showing interest when he joins Little League. This combination of expectancy and encouragement gets the boy in the mood to want to play baseball. We need to do the same thing with regard to creative children. We do not start in by setting up an unconscious, unfavorable evaluation which derides any early manifestations of creative function. Creativity is not going to occur in a child unless he feels secure enough to try new things.

Giving the Child Emotional Support

In addition, we always ought to upgrade, rather than to belittle. Some of you will recall a Walt Disney film from way back; it was one of those delightful fairy tales about a little bug that wanted to change into another kind of little bug because he loved a third little bug, or something like that. This bug got halfway through his transformation, and then some other little bug, rather a mean type, sang a nasty little song which went like this, as I remember, "You're nothing but a nothing, you're not a thing at all." So often parents, playmates, teachers, and others say to a child, "You're nothing but a nothing, you're not a thing at all," and the child sees himself as someone who cannot and who does not perform.

Children face constant crises from situations where they do not perform in situations where they see themselves as able to perform. Your son who goes out to play baseball in the vacant lot or with Little League goes out at first unable to catch a fly, but he hopes he will soon be able to catch one; he goes out unable to bat a hit, but he hopes he will soon be able to get a home run. Your little daughter sees herself as not having the proper manners, and she secretly hopes that some day she will get over spilling things and getting dirty and be more like the beautiful Aunt Martha who comes to visit. Childhood and growing up consist of constant changes, and it is very important for parents to help children make these transitions, to help them smooth over some of the hurdles so that youngsters see themselves as able to do things which are reasonable and within their grasp. Then they become youngsters who see life as a reasonable adventure.

Permitting Reasonable Risk-Taking Behavior

Life becomes an adventure in which they can, by making a reasonable effort in a reasonable risk situation in a world which is more or less reasonably organized, bring about a result over which they have control, at least most of the time. This is what we want to instill in creative children, the willingness to risk a little but in a situation where they can expect positive results, where they know they may have an occasional failure, but where they will figure out what happened and try again. The opposite of this mild risk-taking is what we see in juvenile delinquency, the willingness to risk everything in a situation where chances are there will be failure.

Helping Children to Handle Disappointment

In addition, we need to help children handle disappointment and doubt when they have to act alone in some creative endeavor which other people do not understand or where they may encounter some derision and ridicule. A child must be able at that time to reward his ego internally in place of the applause he would like to get; he must give up the childish idea of always wanting to be first and be satisfied with a respectable batting average. The creative child will have ten wild ideas while another child has one, but sometimes only one of those ten ideas will pay off, and if the creative child is going to be knocked down for the nine he is going to end up very poorly. What we have to do as parents is to be willing to let children come out with these ideas, and then to help them do some self-evaluation to realize that a respectable payoff of about one good idea for every ten allows them to be divergent but constructive members of society. It takes ego strength on the part of a child to be able to do this, but we cannot get creative results unless we can get children to operate in this way.

Parents need to make sure that a child's sincere efforts, no matter how poorly executed at the start, bring him enough satisfaction to enable him to want to try again. They should give early rewards for creative behavior. Parents can help by praise rather than criticism, which stops initial creativity, however crude. The child who gets up and volunteers to do something in class, but does not get it right, is not going to be helped by the teacher who says, "No, sit down, that's wrong." The same holds true for parents who need to "disengage" effectively rather than to slap the child down psychologically. The child should be told, "Well, you made a good try, but I think we can add something to that." In other words, we need to give a thought to the child's ego without, however, letting the incident go uncorrected or not adding on to it.

Encouraging Good Mental Health in Children

Also, creating is a tender time. Children cannot create when they are constantly in situations where they are fearful or worried, when they are subjected to undue stress and undue anxiety. These children may learn the cognitive memory types of reactions very well, but there may be almost a complete "wipe-out" of their creative abilities. In order to be creative one must be in reasonably good mental health. There are a few notable exceptions to the contrary. If one has such enormous creative talent, for example, as Van Gogh, the artist, one will continue to be creative for a while, no matter what the mental anguish, but most of us with our lesser talents have to have fairly good mental health, at all times for creativity to shine through.

Showing Respect for Children's Curiosity and Initiative

Further, parents need to be respectful of a child's curiosity and questioning. Very frequently when a child questions you he is going to ask a question which involves a misapprehension. Let us take the case of the four-year-old who asks his mother, "Aren't all those rockets liable to shoot down God?" Here is a child who is thinking, but he is under some kind of a misapprehension. The child with a question like that needs help in rephrasing the question so it will be possible to answer it; also, it is preferable to answer questions in a way which does not block off further questioning. As well as being respectful of a child's curiosity and questioning, we need to help him in naming and classifying things. William James once said that the world appears as a "big, blooming, buzzing confusion" and this applies to children and their world. We need to give them a sense of order.

Creative children are self-starters with lots of energy, a high degree of independence, and a great deal of initiative. These characteristics can be hindered by too much supervision; however, when a child starts on something we should insist that he go through with it. If a child wants to be alone and if he can be on his own, let him go, give him his "head." I have had mothers say to me, "Shall I let him read, he's only three and a half?" Why not? I have had people say, "But he shouldn't take out those adult books from the library." Why shouldn't he? Have you ever been hurt by any book you have read? I have never seen anybody who has ever been willing to admit to me that he has been hurt by a book, though I have had people tell me that other people have been hurt by something they had read.

Heightening Sensory Awareness Without Inducing Guilt Feelings

We need to heighten the sensory awareness of children by helping them to enjoy sensory experiences without guilt. We still have a remnant of feeling that enjoying a beautiful landscape or a beautiful painting of that landscape is something of which to be ashamed.

Pointing out to a child the beauty of the simple things of life—the flowers and trees in the springtime, a snowflake or a grain of sand, a sunset through half-closed eyes—all of these add to the keen enjoyment of living. It is good for fathers to show aesthetic appreciation so that their sons will not feel that it is sissy to do so.

Helping the Creative Child to Develop Sets of Values

A child needs to have his ideas valued before he can value them himself or value others' ideas. Valuing, therefore, is a very important objective in working with creative children. Usually, when visiting in a foreign land, one hires a guide to point out the things of interest and to help one appreciate what is being seen. The child is in the same kind of position with regard to the new experiences in which he constantly finds himself in school and in the world around him, and we have to help him attach value to these experiences.

In the past we have bogged down on this matter of developing values in our educational process because it quickly gets into moral and religious education and then, of course, we are in a morass. Scientists have recently shown us how to get around this situation very nicely. We do so by thinking about the whole concept of values, interests, and attitudes in terms of the levels of what we are now calling the "affective domain of educational objectives." We talk about such things as accepting, responding, valuing, and showing a great deal of attention to something, and then setting the value into its proper perspective. For example, parents can help youngsters value and put in their proper places good television shows over poor ones, good films over poor ones, good comic books over poor ones, and so on. This concept of setting taste and value for youngsters is as easy as that and these examples are good places in which to start. I remember telling my little daughter some years ago that one of the ways she could tell a B-grade movie from an A-grade one was that in a B movie she would know what was going to happen next. This is a very simple kind of awareness, but it is one of the entering wedges in helping a child to look at something and say, "Is this good?" instead of just taking it in as raw experience.

When some new and challenging facts come to children, we need ways in which they can talk about, digest, and process them, so the facts can become concepts out of which they can form some meaningful view of the world. The process of putting meaning into life is the real process of values, and unless we do this we do not get values out of life. The values that creative children have may not be the same as ours and sometimes this disturbs us as parents. But the point is that we should concentrate on building some set of values within the child, and not necessarily ours.

Let the child discover through home discussion that there are many areas of life where there is more than one answer to a particular situation or question and that it is possible for men of good will to differ as to these answers and yet to get along. Children are fortunate who live in a home where parents accept differences, where new ideas are respected and not just tolerated. These children soon find that it is all right to differ with people, that you still respect and love the people with whom you differ, whether they are your playmates, parents, or other adults. In fact, it is good that people are different.

Recognition of Sex Differences in Children

There appear to be important sex differences in the way children respond to parental encouragement. Bayley (1955) reports that the effects of early maternal warmth were more lasting in the case of boys than in the case of girls. She notes that there is persistent negative correlation between girls' I.Q. and early maternal intrusive behavior, but for the most part the genetic determinant of girls' ability is less affected by early environmental conditions than is that of boys. Numerous other studies have shown that the wellsprings of the achievement motive in girls is much more complicated than in boys. Maw and Maw (1963) found parental environment much more productive of curiosity in boys than in girls. Specifically, the fathers of low-curiosity boys scored significantly higher than the fathers of high-curiosity boys on fostering dependency, seclusiveness, harsh punishment, ascendancy of husband, and suppression of sexuality, and they scored lower on the equalitarianism scale. Mothers of low-curiosity boys scored significantly higher than mothers of high-curiosity boys on the subscales: fostering dependency, excluding outside influences, and intrusiveness. By contrast, there were no differences between the parents of the high- and low-curiosity girls.

It may be conjectured that it is the like-sexed parent who inducts the child toward conformity, discipline, and achievement, and the opposite-sexed parent who inveigles him into the byways of curiosity, creativity, and the left-handed talents in general. At any rate, it is obvious that boys and girls are subjected to different influences within the same family, and that parents need to be observant of the relative maternal and paternal influence on both boys and girls. Further research on such differential aspects of child development is certainly to be desired.

High- and Low-Curiosity Children

In addition to sex differences, Maw and Maw found that high-curiosity children when compared with low-curiosity children had a greater level of self-acceptance, more self-sufficiency; tended to feel more secure, to be more creative, flexible, and consistent, to be more dependable; were more often identified as "square shooters"; showed a higher level of group loyalty; exhibited more healthy participation in group activities; were more responsible for group welfare; and showed a better overall social adjustment. These characteristics sound like the result of close and harmonious parental and home relationships. They indicate the opposite of a delinquent or a disadvantaged child—namely, a child who is mature, well-adjusted, responsible, and happy.

We conclude these hints from research by quoting an idea given to the writer by Virginia Kemble. We are all aware of the proclivities of children in the five-year-old range to indulge in "tall stories" and fantasy bordering on what parents may consider a downright lie. To the extent that parents cut this fantasy verbalization off sharply they inhibit the child's future access to these peripheral aspects of consciousness; they narrow his conscious reservoir sharply to the here-and-now or reality. To the extent that these flights of fancy are encouraged and more gently brought into some congruence with reality we extend the availability of marginal preconscious areas by incorporating them into the unrepressed and therefore admissible consciousness of the child. The attitude of the mother who said to her child, "Now, what is the usual color of a dragon?" is a good example. We cannot inculcate creativity from a conformist mold.

Conclusion

Creativity comes in some odd shapes and parents have to be willing to recognize this. Civilization in its desire for conformity tends to put roadblocks in the way of the creative individual, and if we are not careful we tend to class the creative person with the disturber and the delinquent. We need in our society, in order for it to live, a public which can appreciate creativity and will reward it rather than vote it out of existence.

Thus, it would appear that creative children are more like adults than other children; they tend to want more autonomy and more independence. All able people are pretty reasonable about limits and restraints; what no one wants, including creative children, are arbitrary limits. E. Paul Torrance,* one of the great writers in the field of creativity in the country today, once answered the question, "What makes a child more creative?" by "Anything which makes him more free and alive." Without freedom no one can be creative. And creativity is nurtured by warmth and affection. All of us, and especially children, tend to create for those we love.

* Torrance, 1963: personal communication to author.

References and Selected Readings

CHAPTER 1

Anderson, Karl G. "Creativity Is." Paper in Education X327.1, Creative Ways of Teaching, University of California, Berkeley, August 1964.

Binet, Alfred. *Les Idées modernes sur les enfants.* Paris: E. Flammarion, 1909.

Bloom, Benjamin S., and Krathwohl, D. R. *Taxonomy of Educational Objectives: The Classification of Educational Goals.* Book I: Cognitive Domain. New York: David McKay Co., 1956.

Burkhart, R. C., and Bernheim, G. "Object Question Test Manual." Mimeographed. University Park, Pa.: Department of Art Education, Pennsylvania State University, 1963.

Cunnington, B. F., and Torrance, E. Paul. *Sounds and Images.* Boston: Ginn and Co., 1965. (a)

——. *Imagi/Craft Productions.* Eight albums and teacher guides. Boston: Ginn and Co., 1965. (b)

Durrell, D. D., and Chambers, J. R. "Research in Thinking Abilities Related to Reading." *Reading Teacher* 12(1958):89-91.

Enochs, P. D. "An Experimental Study of a Method for Developing Creative Thinking in Fifth Grade Children." Ph.D. dissertation, University of Missouri, 1964.

Guilford, J. P. *Personality.* New York: McGraw-Hill Book Co., 1959.

Hanson, Doris E. "Home Economists in Overseas Work." Ph.D. dissertation, Teachers College, Columbia University, 1964.

Myers, R. E., and Torrance, E. Paul. *Can You Imagine?* Ideabook and teacher's guide. Boston: Ginn and Co., 1965.

Myers, R. E.; Cunnington, B. F.; and Torrance, E. Paul. *Invitation to Thinking and Doing.* Ideabook and teacher's guide. Boston: Ginn and Co., 1965.

Ojemann, R. H. "Research in Planned Learning Programs and the Science of Behavior." *Journal of Educational Research* 42(1948):96-104.

Ojemann, R. H., and Pritchett, Karen. "Piaget and the Role of Guided Experiences in Human Development." *Perceptual and Motor Skills* 17 (1963):927-39.

Rogers, V. R. "History for the Elementary School Child." *Phi Delta Kappan* 44(1962):132-35.

Selye, H. "The Gift of Basic Research," pp.399-408. In *The Gifted Child: The Yearbook of Education,* edited by George Z. F. Bereday and J. A. Lauwerys. New York: Harcourt, Brace & World, Inc., 1962.

Taylor, Calvin W., ed. *Creativity: Progress and Potential.* New York: McGraw-Hill Book Co., 1964. (a)

Taylor, Calvin W. "Developing Creative Characteristics." *The Instructor* 73(1964):5,99-100. (b)

Torrance, E. Paul. *Guiding Creative Talent.* Englewood Cliffs, N.J.: Prentice-Hall, Inc., 1962.

——. *Rewarding Creative Behavior: Experiments in Classroom Creativity.* Englewood Cliffs, N.J.: Prentice-Hall, Inc., 1965. (a)

——. *Gifted Children in the Classroom.* New York: Macmillan Co., 1965. (b)

——. "Creativity in the Classroom." Series of ten articles. *The Instructor* 74(1964-65).

Wallach, M. A., and Kogan, N. *Modes of Thinking in Young Children: A Study of the Creativity-Intelligence Distinction.* New York: Holt, Rinehart & Winston, Inc., 1965.

Will, Patricia P. "A Study of the Effects of Possible Emotional Disturbance on the Creative Behavior of a Group of Delinquent Girls." Research paper, University of Minnesota, 1964.

Chapter 2

Brunelle, Eugene A. "Problem Solving: Intelligence and Creativity." Research paper, California State College at Fullerton, 1964.

Covington, Martin V. "The Effectiveness of Training for Problem Solving Proficiency and Creative Thinking as a Function of Differing Ability Levels among Children." Paper presented at meeting of the Western Psychological Association, Honolulu, Hawaii, 1965.

Covington, Martin V., and Crutchfield, Richard S. "Facilitation of Creative Problem Solving." *Programed Instruction* 4(1965):3-5,10.

Crawford, R. P. *Techniques of Creative Thinking.* Englewood Cliffs, N.J.: Hawthorn Books, Inc., 1954.

Crutchfield, Richard S., and Covington, Martin V. "Programed Instruction and Creativity." *Programed Instruction* 4(1965):1-2,8-10.

Dewey, John. *How We Think.* Boston: D. C. Heath and Co., 1910.

Forehand, Garlie A., and Libby, W. L., Jr. "Effects of Educational Programs and Perceived Organizational Climate upon Changes in Innovative and Administrative Behavior, Sec. V, pp.1-11. In *Innovative Behavior,* edited by Bernard J. James. U.S. Department of Health, Education, and Welfare, Office of Education, Cooperative Research Project, no.975. Chicago: University of Chicago, Center for Programs in Government Administration, 1962.

Getzels, Jacob W., and Jackson, Philip W. *Creativity and Intelligence.* New York: John Wiley & Sons, Inc., 1962.

Guilford, J. P. "Creativity." *American Psychologist* 5(1950):444-54.

——. "Three Faces of Intellect." *American Psychologist* 14(1959):469-79.

——. "Basic Problems in Teaching for Creativity." Paper presented at Conference on Creativity and Teaching Media, La Jolla, Calif., 1964. (a)

——. "Creative Thinking and Problem Solving." *Education Digest* 29 (1964):21-31. (b)

——. "Zero Corrections among Tests of Intellectual Abilities." *Psychological Bulletin* 61(1964):401-4. (c)

——. "Intelligence—1965 Model." Address presented at annual meeting of the American Psychological Association, Chicago, Ill., 1965.

Guilford, J. P., and Hoepfner, Ralph. *Current Summary of Structure-of-Intellect Factors and Suggested Tests.* Reports from the Psychological Laboratory, no.30. Los Angeles: University of Southern California, 1963.

Guthridge, Sue J. *Tom Edison, Boy Inventor.* Indianapolis: Bobbs-Merrill Co., 1959.

Hovland, Carl I., and Weiss, Walter. "Transmission of Information Concerning Concepts through Positive and Negative Instances." *Journal of Experimental Psychology* 45(1953):175-82.

James, William. *The Principles of Psychology.* New York: Henry Holt and Co., 1890.

Johnson, Donald M. *The Psychology of Thought and Judgment.* New York: Harper and Brothers, 1955.

Josephson, Matthew. *Edison.* New York: McGraw-Hill Book Co., 1959.

McNemar, Quinn. "Lost: Our Intelligence? And Why?" *American Psychologist* 19(1964):871-82.

Miller, George A.; Galanter, Eugene H.; and Pribram, Karl H. *Plans and the Structure of Behavior.* New York, Holt, Rinehart & Winston, Inc., 1960.

Osborn, Alex F. *Applied Imagination.* New York: Charles Scribner's Sons, 1963.

Polya, György. *How To Solve It.* Princeton: Princeton University Press, 1945.

Rossman, Joseph. *The Psychology of the Inventor.* Washington, D.C.: Inventors Publishing Co., 1931.

Stein, Morris I., and Meer, Bernard. "Measures of Intelligence and Creativity." *Journal of Psychology* 39(1955):117-26.

Torrance, E. Paul. "Explorations in Creative Thinking in the Early School Years: A Progress Report," pp.173-83. In *Scientific Creativity: Its Recognition and Development,* edited by Calvin W. Taylor and Frank Barron. New York: John Wiley & Sons, Inc., 1963.

Upton, Albert, and Sampson, Richard W. *Creative Analysis.* New York: E. P. Dutton & Co., 1963.

Wallas, Graham. *The Art of Thought.* London: C. A. Watts Co., 1945.

Chapter 3

Association for Childhood Education International. *Told under the Green Umbrella.* One of seven Umbrella books. New York: Macmillan Co., 1962.

Geismer, Barbara P., and Suter, Antoinette B. *Very Young Verses.* Boston: Houghton Mifflin Co., 1945.

Goertzel, Victor, and Goertzel, Mildred George. *Cradles of Eminence.* Boston: Little, Brown and Co., 1962.

Marshall, Sybil. *Experiment in Education.* Cambridge: Cambridge University Press, 1963.

Wilson, John A. R., and Robeck, Mildred C. *Kindergarten Evaluation of Learning Potential.* New York: McGraw-Hill Book Co., 1967.

Chapter 4

Frank, Lawrence K. *The School as Agent for Cultural Renewal.* Cambridge, Mass.: Harvard University Press, 1960.

Stoddard, George D. "Creativity in Education," pp.181-202. In *Creativity and Its Cultivation,* edited by Harold H. Anderson. New York: Harper & Brothers, 1959.

Whitehead, Alfred North. *The Aims of Education.* New York: Macmillan Co., 1929.

Chapter 6

Biological Sciences Curriculum Study. *Biological Science: An Inquiry into Life.* Yellow version. New York: Harcourt, Brace & World, Inc., 1963. (a)

——. *Biological Science: Molecules to Man.* Blue version. Boston: Houghton Mifflin Co., 1963. (b)

——. *High School Biology.* Green version. Chicago: Rand McNally & Co., 1963. (c)

——. *Laboratory Blocks.* Boston: D. C. Heath & Co., 1964.

——. *Biological Science: Interaction of Experiments and Ideas.* BSCS Second Course. Englewood Cliffs, N.J.: Prentice-Hall, Inc., 1965.

Blanc, Sam; Fischler, Abraham S.; and Gardner, Olcott. *Modern Science.* Book 1. New York: Holt, Rinehart & Winston, Inc., 1967.

Cassidy, Harold. *The Sciences and the Arts.* New York: Harper & Brothers, 1962.

Glass, Bentley. "Renascent Biology: A Report on the AIBS Biological Sciences Curriculum Study." *School Review* 70(1962):16-43.

Kuhn, Thomas. *The Structure of Scientific Revolutions.* Foundations of the Unity of Science, vol.2, no.2. Chicago: University of Chicago Press, 1962.

Ripple, Richard, *et al. Piaget Rediscovered.* Ithaca, N.Y.: School of Education, Cornell University, 1964.

Schwab, Joseph J., ed. *Biology Teachers Handbook.* New York: John Wiley & Sons, Inc., 1963.

Schwab, Joseph. "The Structure of the Natural Sciences," pp.31-49. In *The Structure of Knowledge and the Curriculum,* edited by G. W. Ford and Lawrence Pugno. Chicago: Rand McNally & Co., 1964.

Schwab, Joseph J., and Brandwein, Paul. *The Teaching of Science.* Cambridge, Mass.: Harvard University Press, 1962.

Smedslund, Jan. "The Acquisition of Conservation of Substance and Weight in Children. III. Extinction of Conservation of Weight Acquired Normally and by means of Empirical Controls on a Balance." *Scandinavian Journal of Psychology* 2(1961):153-55.

Taylor, Calvin W., and Barron, Frank, eds. *Scientific Creativity: Its Recognition and Development.* New York: John Wiley & Sons, Inc., 1963.

Science Course Improvement Projects

AAAS Commission on Science Education. John R. Mayor (director), American Association for the Advancement of Science, 1515 Massachusetts Ave., N.W., Washington, D.C. 20005

Biological Sciences Curriculum Study. William Mayer (director), University of Colorado, Boulder, Colo. 80302

Chemical Bond Approach Project. Lawrence E. Strong, Department of Chemistry, Earlham College, Richmond, Inc. 47374

Chemical Education Material Study. George Imentel (director), Department of Chemistry, University of California, Berkeley, Calif. 94720

Earth Science Curriculum Project. Robert Heller, P.O. Box 1559, Boulder, Colo. 80302

Elementary School Science Improvement Project. John K. Wood, Department of Physics, Utah State University, Logan, Utah 84321

Elementary School Science Project. J. Myron Atkin, College of Education, and Stanley P. Wyatt, Jr., Department of Astronomy, University of Illinois, Urbana, Ill. 61801

Elementary Science Study. Charles Wolcott, Educational Services, Inc., 164 Main Street, Watertown, Mass. 02172

Junior High School Science Project. Frederick L. Ferris, Jr., Green Hall, Princeton University, Princeton, N.J. 08540

Minnesota Mathematics and Science Teaching Project. P. C. Rosenbloom director), Minnesota School of Mathematics and Science Center, University of Minnesota, Minneapolis, Minn. 55414

Physical Science Study Committee. Jerrold R. Zacharias, Department of Physics, Massachusetts Institute of Technology, Cambridge, Mass. 02139

Physical Science Study Committee—Junior High Physical Science. Uri Haber Schaim, Educational Services, Inc., 165 Main Street, Watertown, Mass. 02172

School Science Curriculum Project. Richard Salinger, College of Education, University of Illinois, Urbana, Ill. 61801

Science Curriculum Improvement Study. Robert Karplus, Department of Physics, University of California, Berkeley, Calif. 94720

Chapter 7

Cass, Betty. *How Long Are God's Shoestrings?* Madison, Wis.: Camden Press, 1965.

Fadiman, Clifton. *Fantasia Mathematica.* New York: Simon and Schuster, Inc., 1958.

Willoughby, Stephen S. "Discovery." *Mathematics Teacher* 55(1963): 22-25.

Chapter 8

Applegate, Mauree. *Easy in English.* New York: Harper & Row, 1963.

Aschner, Mary Jane McCue. "The Analysis of Verbal Interaction in the Classroom," pp.53-78. In *Theory and Research in Teaching,* edited by Arno H. Bellack. New York: Teachers Press, Teachers College, Columbia University, 1963.

Bloom, Benjamin S., ed. *Taxonomy of Educational Objectives: The Classification of Educational Goals.* Book I: Cognitive Domain. New York: David McKay Co., 1956.

Bruner, J. S. *The Process of Education.* Cambridge, Mass.: Harvard University Press, 1960.

Carlson, Ruth Kearney. "Seventeen Qualities of Original Writing." *Elementary English* 38(1961):576-79.

Carroll, John B. "The Analysis of Reading Instruction: Perspectives from Psychology and Linguistics," pp.336-53. In *Theories of Learning and Instruction,* edited by Ernest R. Hilgard. National Society for the Study of Education. 63rd yearbook. Chicago: University of Chicago Press, 1964.

Clark, Charles M. "Teaching Sixth Grade Students To Make Predictions from Reading Materials." Ph.D. dissertation, University of California, Berkeley, 1959.

Clark, Gwyn R. "Writing Situations to which Children Respond." *Elementary English* 31(1954):150-55.

Crosby, Muriel, ed. *Reading Ladders for Human Relations.* 4th ed. Washington, D.C.: American Council on Education, 1963.

Devine, Thomas G. "The Development and Evaluation of a Series of Recordings for Teaching Certain Critical Listening Abilities." Ph.D. dissertation, Boston, University, 1961.

Edgar, Kenneth F. "The Validation of Four Methods of Improving Listening Ability." Ph.D. dissertation, University of Pittsburgh, 1961.

Educational Testing Service, Cooperative Testing Division. *Sequential*

Tests of Educational Progress: Listening. Princeton, N.J.: Educational Testing Service, 1956-59. (a)

——. *Sequential Tests of Educational Progress: Reading*. Princeton, N.J.: Educational Testing Service, 1956-59. (b)

Flanders, N. A. "Intent, Action, and Feedback: A Preparation for Teaching." *Journal of Teacher Education* 14(1963):251-60.

Forbes, Esther. *Johnny Tremain*. Boston: Houghton Mifflin Co., 1943.

Getzels, J. W. "Creative Thinking, Problem Solving, and Instruction," pp. 240-67. In *Theories of Learning and Instruction,* edited by Ernest R. Hilgard. National Society for the Study of Education, 63rd yearbook. Chicago: University of Chicago Press, 1964.

Ginn Basic Readers, revised, edited by D. H. Russell, *et al.* Boston: Ginn and Co., 1964-65.

Guilford, J. P. "Factoral Angles to Psychology." *Psychological Review* 68(1961):1-20.

——. "Creative Thinking and Problem Solving." *Education Digest* 29 (1964):29-31.

Hogan, Ursula. "An Experiment in Improving the Listening Skills of Fifth and Sixth Grade Pupils." Master's seminar study, University of California, Berkeley, 1953.

Littwin, Maxwell F. "Experimental Investigation of the Effect of Method of Presentation upon the Imaginative Quality of Descriptive Writing among Elementary School Pupils." *Journal of Experimental Education* 4(1935):44-49.

Lundsteen, Sara W. "Teaching Abilities in Critical Listening in the Fifth and Sixth Grades." Ph.D. dissertation, University of California, Berkeley, 1963.

——. *Procedures for Teaching Critical Reading and Listening*. Contributions in Reading. no.34. Boston: Ginn and Co., 1964. (a)

——. "Teaching and Testing Critical Listening in the Fifth and Sixth Grades." *Elementary English* 41(1964):743-47. (b)

——. "Critical Listening—Permanency and Transfer of Gains Made during an Experiment in the Fifth and Sixth Grades." *California Journal of Educational Research* 16(1965):210-16.

——. "Teaching and Testing Critical Listening: An Experiment." *Elementary School Journal* 66(1966):311-15.

Lundsteen, Sara W., and Michael, William B. "Validation of Three Tests of Cognitive Style in Verbalization for the Third and Sixth Grades." *Educational and Psychological Measurement* 26(1966):449-61.

McCullough, Constance M. *Creative Reading*. Contributions in Reading, no.15. Boston: Ginn and Co., 1959.

——. "Responses of Elementary School Children to Common Types of Reading Comprehension Questions." *Journal of Educational Research* 51(1957):65-70.

Moe, Sister Mary Loenella. "Teaching Composition in the Seventh Grade." Ph.D. dissertation, Stanford University, 1956.

Nardelli, R. R. "A Study of Some Aspects of Creative Reading." Ph.D. dissertation, University of California, Berkeley, 1953.

Neff, Priscilla, and Collins, Gay. "Children's Literature: An Experiment in Developing Critical Thinking." *Claremont Reading Conference* 27 (1963):153-56.

Niles, Olive S., and Early, Margaret J. "Adjusting to Individual Differences in English." *Journal of Education* 138(1955):2-68.

Ojemann, Ralph H., and Hawkins, Alice S. *A Teaching Program in Human Behavior and Mental Health,* Book V. Iowa City: State University of Iowa, 1960.

O'Neill, Mary. *Hailstones and Halibut Bones: Adventures in Color.* New York: Doubleday & Co., 1961.

Packard, Vance O. *The Hidden Persuaders.* New York: David McKay Co., 1957.

Play Index. Vol.1, compiled by Dorothy H. West and Dorothy M. Reade, 1949-52. Vol.2, edited by Estelle A. Fidell and Dorothy M. Reade, 1953-60. New York: H. W. Wilson Co., 1953,1963.

Pratt, L. E. "The Experimental Evaluation of a Program for the Improvement of Listening in the Elementary School." Ph.D. dissertation, State University of Iowa, 1953.

Robinson, Helen M. "Methods and Materials for Teaching Creative Reading," chapter 9. In *Sequential Development of Reading Abilities,* edited by Helen M. Robinson. Proceedings of the Annual Conference on Reading held at the University of Chicago. Chicago: University of Chicago Press, 1960.

Russell, David H. *Children's Thinking.* Boston: Ginn and Co., 1956.

——. *Children Learn to Read.* Boston: Ginn and Co., 1961.

Russell, David H., and Karp, Etta E. *Reading Aids through the Grades.* Rev. ed. New York: Teachers Press, Teachers College, Columbia University, 1951.

Sorensen, Virginia. *Miracles on Maple Hill.* New York: Harcourt, Brace & World, Inc., 1956.

Shotwell, Louisa P. *Roosevelt Grady.* Cleveland: World Publishing Co., 1963.

Strickland, Ruth G. "Children, Reading, and Creativity." *Elementary English* 34(1957):234-41.

Suchman, J. Richard. *The Elementary School Training Program in Scientific Inquiry.* U.S. Department of Health, Education, and Welfare, Office of Education, Cooperative Research Project, no.216. Urbana: University of Illinois, 1962.

Taba, Hilda. *Thinking in Elementary School Children.* U.S. Department of Health, Education, and Welfare, Office of Education, Cooperative Research Project, no.1574. San Francisco State College, 1964.

Taylor, Calvin W., and Barron, Frank, eds. *Scientific Creativity: Its Recognition and Development.* New York: John Wiley & Sons, Inc., 1963.

Torrance, E. Paul. *Guiding Creative Talent.* Englewood Cliffs, N.J.: Prentice-Hall, Inc., 1962.

——. *Education and the Creative Potential.* Minneapolis, University of Minnesota Press, 1963.

Wallas, Graham. *The Art of Thought.* New York: Harcourt, Brace & Co., 1926.

White, E. B. *Charlotte's Web.* New York: Harper & Brothers, 1952.

Witty, Paul A. "Meeting Developmental Needs through Reading." *Education* 84(1964):451-58.

Wolf, Willavene; Huck, Charlotte S.; and King, Martha L. *Critical Reading Ability of Elementary School Children.* U.S. Department of Health, Education, and Welfare, Office of Education, Cooperative Research Project, no.5-1040. Columbus: The Ohio State University, 1967.

Woodfin, Mary Jo. "Third Grade Children's Written Expression under Short, Intermediate, and Long Time Limits." Ph.D. dissertation, University of California, Los Angeles, 1966.

Yamamoto, Kaoru. *Experimental Scoring Manuals for Minnesota Tests of Creative Thinking and Writing.* Kent, Ohio: Bureau of Educational Research, Kent State University, 1964.

Chapter 10

Bloomfield, Leonard. "Secondary and Tertiary Responses to Language." *Language* 20(1944):45-55.

Twaddell, W. Freeman. "Reading As Skill, Structure, and Communication," pp.97-103. *On Teaching English to Speakers of Other Languages, Series II: Papers Read at the TESOL Conference, San Diego, California, March 12-13, 1965,* edited by Carol J. Kreidler. Champaign, Illinois: National Council of Teachers of English, 1965.

Chapter 11

Guilford, J. P. "The Structure of Intellect." *Psychological Bulletin* 53 (1956):267-93.

——. "Three Faces of Intellect." *American Psychologist* 14(1959):469-79.

Chapter 12

Brubaker, Dale L. *Alternative Directions for the Social Studies.* Scranton, Pa.: International Textbook Co., 1967.

——. ed. *Innovation in the Social Studies: Teachers Speak for Themselves.* New York: Thomas Y. Crowell Co., 1968.

Brubaker, Dale L., and Turner, Georgia. "A New Teacher Seeks a Catalyst." *Michigan Education Journal* 43(1966):15,42.

Commager, Henry Steele. *The Nature and Study of History.* Columbus, Ohio: Charles Merrill Books, Inc., 1965.

Counts, George S. *Dare the School Build a New Social Order?* New York: The John Day Co., 1932.

Cox, C. Benjamin, and Cousins, Jack E. "Teaching Social Studies in Secondary Schools and Colleges," pp.89-120. In *New Challenges in the Social Studies,* edited by Byron G. Massialas and Frederick R. Smith. Belmont, Calif.: Wadsworth Publishing Co., 1965.

Fenton, Edwin, ed. *The New Social Studies.* New York: Holt, Rinehart & Winston, Inc., 1966.

Gilbert, Janet Maude. "Creativity, Critical Thinking, and Performance in Social Studies." Ph.D. dissertation, University of Buffalo, 1961.

Kolb, W. J., and Gould, J., eds. *UNESCO Dictionary of the Social Sciences.* New York: The Free Press, 1964.

Lisitzky, Gene. *Four Ways of Being Human.* Compass book, C128. New York: The Viking Press, Inc., 1956.

MacKinnon, D. W. "The Study of Creativity." Paper presented at Conference on the Creative Person, University of California Alumni Center, Lake Tahoe, Calif., Oct. 1961.

Massialas, Byron G., and Cox, C. Benjamin. *Inquiry in Social Studies.* New York: McGraw-Hill Book Co., 1966.

Mayer, Martin. *Social Studies in American Schools.* New York: Harper & Row, 1963.

Michaelis, John U., and Johnston, A. Montgomery, eds. *The Social Sciences: Foundations of the Social Studies.* Boston: Allyn & Bacon, Inc., 1965.

Orwell, George. *Animal Farm.* New York: Harcourt, Brace & World, Inc., 1954.

Rand McNally & Co. "Grade Placement of Social Studies Topics in the Schools of the United States." Chicago, 1965.

Torrance, E. Paul. "Education and Creativity," pp.52-54. In *Creativity: Progress and Potential,* edited by Calvin W. Taylor. New York: McGraw-Hill Book Co., 1964.

CHAPTER 13

Ackerman, James S., and Carpenter, Rhys. *Art and Archaeology.* Englewood Cliffs, N.J.: Prentice-Hall, Inc., 1963.

Focillon, Henri. *The Life and Forms in Art.* New York: George Wittenborn, Inc., 1958.

Hastie, W. Reid, ed. *Art Education.* National Society for the Study of Education, 64th yearbook, pt.2. Chicago: University of Chicago Press, 1965.

Hausman, Jerome, ed. *Report of the Commission on Art Education.* Washington, D.C.: National Art Education Association, National Education Association, 1965.

Hutchins, Rubert M. "Are We Educating Our Children for the Wrong Future?" *Saturday Review,* Sept. 11, 1965:66-67,83.

Huyghe, René. *Ideas and Images in World Art.* New York: Harry N. Abrams, Inc., 1959.

Kaprow, Allan. "Should the Artist Become a Man of the World?" *Art News* 63, no.6(Oct. 1964):34-37,58-59.

Kepes, Gyorgy. Introduction to *Education of Vision,* edited by Gyorgy Kepes. New York: George Braziller, Inc., 1965.

Kubler, George A. *The Shape of Time: Remarks on the History of Things.* New Haven, Conn.: Yale University Press, 1962.

Moholy-Nagy, Laszlo. *Vision in Motion.* Chicago: Paul Theobald and Co., 1947.

Pelles, Geraldine. *Art, Artists and Society: Origins of a Modern Dilemma.* Englewood Cliffs, N.J.: Prentice-Hall, Inc., 1963.

Perkins, James A. "Should the Artist Come to the Campus?" *Saturday Review,* July 17, 1965:54-56,71.

Reinhardt, Ad. "The Next Revolution in Art." *Art News* 62, no.10(Feb. 1964):48-49.

Rosenberg, Harold. *The Anxious Object: Art in America Today.* New York: Horizon Press, Inc., 1964.

CHAPTER 15

Michael, William B. "The Realization of Reliable and Valid Criterion Measures for Special Undergraduate Programs and Courses Aimed at the Development and Expression of Creative Behavior." *Journal of Educational Measurement* 1(1964):97-102.

——. "Measurement and Prediction in the College Admissions Process: Some Possible Directions for Future Research." *Educational and Psychological Measurement* 25(1965):55-72.

Pace, C. Robert. "Methods of Describing College Cultures." *Teachers College Record* 63(1962):267-77.

——. *CUES: College and University Environment Scales.* Teaching manual. Princeton, N.J.: Educational Testing Service, 1963.

Stern, George G. "Characteristics of the Intellectual Climate in College Environments." *Harvard Educational Review* 33(1963):5-41.

Thistlethwaite, Donald L. "The College Environment as a Determinant of Research Potentiality, pp.265-77. In *Scientific Creativity: Its Recognition and Development,* edited by Calvin W. Taylor and Frank Barron. New York: John Wiley & Sons, Inc., 1963.

CHAPTER 17

Fromm, Erich. "The Creative Attitude," pp.44-54. In *Creativity and Its Cultivation,* edited by Harold H. Anderson. New York: Harper & Brothers, 1959.

McNeil, John D. *Curriculum Administration: Principles and Techniques of Curriculum Development.* New York: Macmillan Co., 1965.

Mearns, Hughes, *Creative Power: The Education of Youth in the Creative Arts.* 2nd rev. ed. New York: Dover Publications, Inc., 1959.

Taylor, Calvin W. "The Creative Individual: A New Portrait in Giftedness." *Educational Leadership* 18(1960):7-12.

Chapter 18

Drevdahl, John E. "Factors of Importance for Creativity." *Journal of Clinical Psychology* 12(1956):21-26.

Hilgard, Ernest R. "Creativity and Problem Solving," pp.162-80. In *Creativity and Its Cultivation,* edited by Harold H. Anderson. New York: Harper & Brothers, 1959.

Bibliography of Measures

1. Barron, Frank. *Creativity and Psychological Health.* Princeton, N.J.: D. Van Nostrand Co., 1963.
2. Beittel, K. R. *Effects of Self-Reflective Training in Art on the Capacity for Creative Action.* Cooperative Research Project, no.1874. Washington, D.C.: U.S. Department of Health, Education and Welfare, Office of Education, 1964.
3. Burkhart, Robert C. *Spontaneous and Deliberate Ways of Learning the Visual Arts.* Scranton, Pa.: International Textbook Co., 1962.
4. Gallagher, James J. *Teaching the Gifted Child.* Boston: Allyn and Bacon, Inc., 1964.
5. Guilford, J. P., and Merrifield, Philip R. *The Structure-of-Intellect Model: Its Uses and Implications.* Reports from the Psychological Laboratory, no.24. Los Angeles: University of Southern California, 1960.
6. Guilford, J. P., and Hoepfner, R. *Current Summary of Structure-of-Intellect Factors and Suggested Tests.* Reports from the Psychological Laboratory, no.30. Los Angeles: University of Southern California, 1963.

NOTE: Tests for Nos. 5 and 6 are available from Sheridan Supply Co., Beverly Hills, Calif. Modifications from Aptitude Research Laboratory, University of Southern California, Los Angeles.

7. Maw, Wallace H., and Maw, Ethel W. *An Exploratory Investigation into the Measurement of Curiosity in Elementary School Children.* Cooperative Research Project, no.801. Washington, D.C.: U.S. Department of Health, Education, and Welfare, Office of Education, 1964.
8. Skager, Rodney W.; Schultz, Charles B.; and Klein, S. P. *Quality and Quantity of Accomplishments as Measures of Creativity.* Research Bulletin 64-31. Princeton, N. J.: Educational Testing Service, 1964.
9. Spaulding, R. L. *Achievement, Creativity and Self-Concept Correlates of Teacher-Pupil Transactions in Elementary Schools.* Cooperative Research Project, no.1352. Washington, D.C.: U.S. Department of Health, Education, and Welfare, Office of Education, 1964.

10. Starkweather, R. L. *Conformity and Non-Conformity as Indicators of Creativity in Preschool Children.* Cooperative Research Project, no.1967. Stillwater, Okla.: Oklahoma State University, 1964.
11. Taylor, Calvin W., ed. *Widening Horizons in Creativity.* New York: John Wiley & Sons, Inc., 1964.
12. Torrance, E. Paul. *Guiding Creative Talent.* Englewood Cliffs, N.J.: Prentice-Hall, Inc., 1962.

Chapter 20

Bayley, Nancy. "The Maintenance of Intellectual Ability in Gifted Adults." *Journal of Gerontology* 10(1955):91-107.

Guilford, J. P. "The Structure of Intellect." *Psychological Bulletin* 53 (1956):267-93.

Maw, W. H., and Maw, Ethel W. "The Difference between the Scores of Children with High Curiosity and Children with Low Curiosity on a Test of General Information." *Journal of Educational Research* 57(1963):78-79.

Index

Ability development, 35-42
Administrator, and central office staff, 284; counselor's influence on, 309-10; curriculum planning by, 290-95; of elementary school, 282-95; encouragement of creative teaching by, 266-95; and English instruction, 164; and parents, 285-87; role in school's creativity, 203-4; and social studies, 207-9; and teachers, 207-9, 287-90; *see also* Supervisory personnel
Admissions, college, 238-40
Aims of Education, The, quoted, 74
American Association for the Advancement of Science, list of science-teaching objectives, 108-9
Anderson, Karl G., quoted, 17
Art, creative vs. interpretative, 230; knowledge of, 225-28; media available to teacher, 221-24; nature of, 217; nurturing creativity in, 233-34; original works of inspirational value to children, 227-28; performing of, 230-36; quality of, 217-18; teaching in elementary school, 216-29; visual judgments based on, 224
Assembly groups, and English teaching, 167-69
Assessment. *See* Evaluation
Attribute listing, 44
Audiovisual aids to foreign language teaching, 186-89
"Autumn Ecstasy," quoted, 146

Behaviors indicating creativity, 270-73
Bibliotherapy, 154, 156
Binet, Alfred, concept of intelligence, 4
Bing, R. H., 125-26
Biological Science Curriculum Study Committee (BSCS), 112-13
Biology, examples of teaching projects in, 109-13
Blankenchip, John Edward, chapter on performing arts, 87, 230-36
Bloomfield, Leonard, 177
Bonsall, Marcella R., chapter on counseling, 296-312; chapter on mental health, 316-39
Brainstorming, 33, 44
Brubaker, Dale L., chapter on secondary social studies, 88, 203-15
BSCS. *See* Biological Science Curriculum Study Committee
Burkhart originality criteria, 10

Carlson Analytical Originality Scoring Scale, 159
Charlotte's Web, 153-54
Children, behaviors indicative of creativity, 270-73; curiosity of, 337; emotional needs of, 334-35; fostering creativity in, 330-41; less creative, 276; mental health of, 336-37; sensory awareness of, 337-38; sex differences and parental influence on, 339-40; socialization by, 321-24, 333-34; very young, creativity in, 55-73; *see also* Students
Children's Thinking Project, 144, 152
Choice period, as classroom aid to creativity, 68
Class size, importance in teaching English, 164-65, 175
Classroom, behaviors diagnosed for social studies activities, 194-97; con-

Classroom—*Cont.*
ditions fostering creativity in, 63-73, 81-82, 206-10; problems of creative student in the, 308; structure's effect on teaching of English, 164-65, 175
Coach, social studies teacher as, 210-11
Coding of class discussions, 148-51
Cognition, defined, 28; training for, 35-42; *see also* Thinking
College Characteristics Index (CCI), 245
College and University Environmental Scales (CUES), 246
Colleges and universities, admissions problem: how to select creative students, 238-40; assessment of, to match creative student to right college, 245-47; course requirements as deterrent to creativity, 240-44; creativity tests for use in, 300-3; curricula to encourage creativity, 240-44; environments conducive to creativity in, 244-52; evaluation of student creativity in, 255-58; faculty promotion and "reprint race," 247-52; grade averages vs. creativity, 242-44; graduate school inflexibility, 241; independent study in, 243; noncreative professor's behavior characteristics listed, 253-55; students compared with secondary, 209; tutorials, 244
"Come Away," quoted, 145-46
Community, counselor's influence on, 310; school administrator's involvement with, 285-87
Composition, teaching for creativity in, 162-75
Computers, emphasize need for creative intelligence, 331
Conformity, and creativity, 56-57, 67-68, 87, 275-76
Consultants, encouragement of creative teaching by, 266-81; mental health, 324-28
Convergent production, college admissions tests for, 239-40; defined, 28; as opposed to divergent, 332; teaching for, 38-39
Counseling, 296-312; creativity tests available for, 300-3; and evaluation, 311-12; fostering and developing creativity by, 299, 304-11; group, 308; and identification of creative student, 298-303; and student, 306-8
Course requirements, college, 240-44
C.Q. (creativity quotient), 117-18
"Creative Analysis," 43
Creativity, assessment of, 18-24, 298-303; can it be developed? 3-6, 18-20; characteristics of, in persons, 304-5; child behavior indicative of, 270-73; and child's enjoyment of, 61-62, 66-67; classroom approaches to, 63-73; and conformity, 56-57, 67-68, 87, 275-76; and the curriculum, 74-89, 240-44, 290-95; defined, 216, 298, 330; educational system as opposed to, 129-30; of elementary school children, 3-24; exists in all, 58-59; and "general intelligence" vs. multi-ability theories, 26-27; and Guilford's research on intelligence factors, 331-33; identification of, 298-305; as information generation, 29; intellectual steps in, 59-61; of interpretative artists in the performing arts, 230-36; and I.Q., 40, 117-18; is it necessary to teach for? 129-30; in language arts, 132-40; is learned, 59-63; as problem solving, 29-34; quotient (C.Q.), 117-18; science projects designed to generate, 109-13; of teacher vs. student, 115-17; tests of, 298-303; and total school as social system, 203-4; universality of, 320; in very young children, 55-73
"Creativity Is," 17
Creativity: Progress and Potential, 4
Critical judgment vs. idea generation, in the classroom, 71-72
CUES. *See* College and University Environmental Scales
Cultures, examples of creative study of, 211-13
Curiosity, child's, 337, 340
Curriculum, administrator's role in planning and implementing, 290-95; college, to encourage creativity, 240-44; to foster creativity, 74-89

Development of creative ability, can it be done? 3-6; in elementary school, 3-24; teaching for, 35-42; in very young children, 55-73
Dewey, John, and art education, 226; problem-solving model, 30; teaching in experimental school of, 123
Discipline, as problem in creative teaching, 129
Discovery by student, mathematical, 122-25
Discrepant events, sequencing of, 102-5, 110
Discrimination training, 41-42
Discussion, evaluation of class, 148-50; groups in English, 165; pupil, ways to encourage, 143
Divergent production, defined, 28; encouragement of, 65-66; Guilford research on, 332; teaching for, 39-40; tests of, 299; and verbalization, 332-33
Drama. *See* Theatre
Drevdahl, J. E., definition of creativity, 298
Dropouts, creative, 130

Elaboration, as creative ability, 11-13
Elementary school, administrator's role in encouraging creativity in, 282-95; creativity tests for use in, 300-3; development of creative ability in, 3-24; language arts in, 131-61; math and science teaching in, 90-100, 105-12; social studies in, 191-202; very young children in, 55-73; visual arts in, 216-29
Elementary School Science Project, 111
Elementary Science Study of Educational Services, Inc. (ESS), 111-12
English in secondary schools, 162-75; class size and, 164-65; evaluation problems of, 172-75; examples of creative work in, 165-72; future possibilities of, 175; and independent study, 170-72; inquiry-group instruction in, 169-70; large-group instruction in, 167-69; specialization of teacher assignments in, 175
ESS. *See* Elementary Science Study
Eurich, Alvin, 116n
Evaluation, of class discussions, 148-50; of college students' creative performance, 255-58; by counselor, 311-12; of creative abilities, 18-24; defined, 28; of English programs, 172-75; new techniques of, 278-79; by observing school activities, 20-22; scales for writing, 159-60; tests of creativity, 22-24, 247, 300-3; training for, 41; and unevaluated time, 13
Examinations, comprehensive college, 244; open-book, 256-57; *see also* Tests
Experience, role in developing creativity, 14-15; role in science, 105-6
Experiments, and development of creativity, 18
Extracurricular activities, for the creative student, 306; of teachers, 203-4

Faculty. *See* Teachers
Fischler, Abraham S., chapter on teaching natural sciences, 88, 101-14
Foreign language teaching, 176-90; audiovisual aids to, 186-89; creativity in, 189-90; in the elementary school, 45; grammar, 180-81; language laboratories, 186-89; speaking, 178-80; texts denied to students, 183-84; traditional vs. linguistic approach to, 176-78; vocabulary, 181-83
"Forest and trees" game, 145
Fostering creativity. *See* Development of creative ability
Four Ways of Being Human, 211
Frank, Lawrence, quoted, 78-79
Free time, and creativity, 68

Georgiades, William, chapter on secondary school English, 86, 162-75
Goleta School District, Calif., 144, 153
Gowan, John Curtis, chapter on parents and creativity, 330-41
Grading. *See* Evaluation
Graduate schools, inflexibility in, 241; mathematics teaching in, 125-26
Grammar, teaching of foreign, 180-81
Group counseling, 308

Group size, in English teaching, 164-65, 175
Guidance workers. *See* Counseling
Guilford, J. P., chapter on structure-of-intellect model, 25-45; intellect theory of, 192-93; 331-33; model's applicability to college teaching, 252-53; theories on problem solving, 134

Hamlet, varying interpretations of, 235
Hausman, Jerome J., chapter on the visual arts, 85-87, 216-29
Hibbs, Albert R., chapter on teaching math and science in elementary school, 87, 90-100
High schools. *See* Secondary schools
Hilgard, Ernest, 311
Historiography, role in developing creativity, 15-17
History and the social studies, is creativity possible in? 204-6
Hophan, Irene S., chapter on school administrator, 282-95
Hutchins, Robert M., quoted, 228-29

Idea generation, in the classroom, 70-72
Identification of creativity, 298-303
Imagination, development of, 236
Incomplete Figures Test, 10, 12
Independence, encouragement of student's, 119-22
Independent study, at college level, 243; and English curriculum, 170-72; and social studies, 200
Inquiry, scientific, nature of, 102-5; use as a teaching method, 75-78
Inquiry groups, and English curriculum, 169-70
Intelligence, Binet's concept of, 4; creative, vs. I.Q., 330-31; factors not measured by tests, 330-31; Guilford's theory of, 192-93; Guilford's research on factors involved in, 331-33; model of structure-of-intellect, 25-45; multi-ability theory of, 26-27; Piaget's four factors in, 105; quotient distinct from creativity quotient, 117; relationship to creative abilities, 40
Interpretative artist, role in performing arts, 230-36

James, William, discrimination concept of, 41-42; quoted, 337
Jones, Robert Edmond, 235
Julius Caesar, examples of teaching of, 167, 174
Junior high schools. *See* Secondary schools

Karplus, Robert, 110
KELP. *See Kindergarten Evaluation of Learning Potential*
Kemble, Virginia, 340
Kettering, Charles, quoted, 89
Kindergarten Evaluation of Learning Potential (KELP), 58, 65, 69, 70
Kindergartens, creativity development in, 55-73
Knowledge, current reorganization of, 78-79
Kubler, George, quoted, 226

Laboratories, language, 186-89
Language arts, in elementary school, 131-61; English, 162-75; foreign, creative teaching of, 176-90; interrelationships of, 135-37; listening-speaking, 140-52; reading, 152-56; in secondary schools, 162-73; speaking, 140-52; teaching for creative endeavor in, 132-40; and writing, 156-61
Learning-motivation model, 59
Learning theory, and science teaching, 107
Leonardo da Vinci, 97
Life Magazine, use in creative English teaching, 164-65
Lindbergh, Charles A., as creative dropout, 130
Linguistics, and language teaching, 177
Listening and speaking, teaching for creativity in, 140-52
Literature, secondary school teaching of, 162-75
Lundsteen, Sara W., chapter on language arts, 87, 131-61

Mann, Horace, on reading, 156

Marshall High School (Portland, Ore.), 171
Mathematics, algebra problem solving, 118-19; as basic tool for science thinking, 94; creativity vs. docility in, 118-19; graduate school teaching of, 125-26; student independence in, 119-22; teaching for creativity in, 115-30
Maturation, role in learning science, 105-9
Mayer, William, 112
Measures of creativity, listed, 300-3
Memory, defined, 28; *see also* Recall
Mendeleev, D. I., 332
Mental health, consultations in, 324-28; difficulty of defining, 322; and school organization, 316-29; parents' encouragement of child's, 336-37
Michael, Joan J., chapter on secondary school English, 162-75
Michael, William B., chapter on creativity in colleges and universities, 86, 237-60
Models, applicability to college teaching, 252-53; of learning motivation in creativity, 59; problem-solving, 30-34; structure-of-intellect, 25-45
Moore, R. L., 125-26
Motivational sequence in creativity, 61-63
Murray, Henry, 81, 89

Narcotics, student papers on, 213-14
National Science Foundation, projects to generate creativity among science students, 109-13
Natural science, teaching of, 101-14
Neumann, Ernest F., chapter on counseling, 296-312

Office staff, administrator's communications with, 284
Oklahoma, 232
O'Konski, Chester, 111
"Open system" of teaching, 277
Open-book exams, 256-57
Originality, classroom encouragement of, 69-70; of math pupils, 119-22; of science pupils, 114; workshop in recognizing and valuing, 10-11; *see also* Convergent production; Divergent production
Overlearning, 36

Parents, administrator's cooperation with, 285-87; counselor's influence on, 310-11; fostering of child's creativity by, 330-41; sex differences and influence on children, 339-40
Pasteur, Louis, quoted, 223
Performing arts, and creativity, 230-36, collaboration of creative and interpretative artists in, 231-33; alternative interpretations of the same work, 235-36; and imagination developmental material selection in, 234-35; nurturing artist's creativity, 233-34
Personnel, supervisory. *See* Administrator; Supervisory personnel
Peters, Mary M., chapter on school administrator, 282-95
Piaget factors, 105
Poetry, creative teaching of, 174-75; teaching for creativity in, 166-67; use in sensitivity teaching, 145-46
Preschool children, creativity development in, 55-73; measurements of creativity for, 300-3
"Press" in college environment, 244
Primary schools, creativity development in, 55-73; *see also* Elementary schools
Princeton University, 244
Principal. *See* Administrator
Problem solving, creativity as, 29-34, 133-38; and development of basic abilities, 35-42; education for, 34-45; and language arts creativity, 132-40; models for, 30-34; and social studies, 192-94
Process vs. product controversy, 277
Professors. *See* Teachers
Programmed instruction for creative performance, 42-44
Pronunciation of foreign languages, teaching of, 179-80
Publications, school, 286
"Publish or perish" race, 248-49
Pupils. *See* Students

Puppets, use in encouraging verbalization, 144-45

Questions, encouragement of child's creative, 337; evaluation criteria for, 10; provocative, to be asked by classroom teacher, 9-10, 198; teacher must respect pupil's, 6-8

Reading, as creative problem solving, 152-56; creatively, development of, 13-14; elaborative thinking in, 12-13; evaluation of, 155; research on, 155-56; and science teaching in elementary grades, 94; teaching for creativity in, 152-56; as thinking, 155-56; and work recognition, 152-53
Reading Aids through the Grades, 152
Reading Ladders for Human Relations, 148
Recall, development of for problem solving, 36-42; memory defined, 28; non-transfer, 36; transfer, 36-39
Relaxation, role in creativity, 37
"Reprint race," 248-49
Rewarding Creative Behavior, 4, 8
Rewards, for creativity in classroom, 4, 8, 58
Rickey, Sara Brandon, quoted, 146
Robbins, Jerome, 232
Robeck, Mildred C., chapter on very young children by, 55-73
Roosevelt Grady, 148, 157-58
Rubin, Louis J., chapter on creativity and the curriculum, 74-89

Sawyer, Jesse O., chapter on teaching foreign languages, 176-90
Scales, evaluative for writing, 159-60; for measuring creativity, listed, 300-3; *see also* Evaluation; Tests
School, administration of, 282-95; creativity determined by total environment of, 203-4; organization and mental health principles, 316-29; *see also* Elementary schools; Secondary schools
Schwartz, Donald A., chapter on mental health, 316-29
Science, behaviorally stated objectives in teaching of, 108-9; dynamic nature of enterprise and inquiry in, 102-5; elementary school teaching of, 90-100, 105-13; high school education in, 113; natural, teaching of, 101-14; original thinking by pupils in, 114; projects for generating creativity in, examples of, 109-13; sequencing of discrepant events in, 110; student's learning process in, 105-9
Science Curriculum Improvement Study (SCIS), 110
Scientists, attitudes toward teaching science in elementary grades, 91-93; dynamic process of inquiry by, 102-5; education of, 101-2; *see also* Science
Secondary schools, creativity tests for use in, 300-3; English in, 162-75; mathematics teaching in, 115-30; science teaching in, 112-13; social studies in, 203-15; students compared with college, 209
Selye, Hans, 11
Seminars, for high school students, 210
Sensitivity, encouragement of pupil's, 145-46
Sensory awareness, and creativity, 64-65; heightening a child's, 337-38
"Set," psychological, 84-85
Sex, differentiation and creative student, 307; differences and parental encouragement, 339-40; role definitions and social studies, 200
Shaw, Bernard, 136
SI model, 25-45
SIPS model, 30-34
Size of class. *See* Class size
Smedslund, Jan, 106
Smith, Walter, 226
Social studies, activities outside the classroom, 210-11; administration's effect on, 206-10; coach-teacher, 210-11; and diagnosis of pupils at work, 194-97; in elementary school, 191-202; examples of creative teaching in, 211-14; and history, 204-6; ideal classroom for creativity in, 206-

10; present status of, 204; in secondary schools, 203-15; seminars in, 210; sex-role handicaps to, 200; and student attitudes, 209-10; suggestions for creative thinking in, 197-202; textbooks as inadequate, 208; unified problem-solving approach to, 192-94
Socialization of creative child, 321-24, 333-34
Socratic method of teaching, 122-23
Sound pictures, 145-46
Sounds and Images, 23
Speaking, of a foreign language, 178-80; and listening, teaching for creativity in, 178-80; specialized teachers for, 175
Stebbins, Robert, 111
Stoddard, George, quoted, 83
Stories, use in encouraging creative listening-speaking, 146-48
Structure-of-intellect model, 25-45
Student teachers, supervisor's encouragement of, 279-81
Students, behavior indicative of creativity in, 270-73; capable of independent math thought, 119-22; characteristics associated with creative, 304-6; classroom problems of creative, 308; college admission of: how to select the creative, 238-40; counseling of, 296-312; evaluation of, 311-12; identification of the creative, 298-303; "out" group as sometimes creative, 209-10; resistant to creativity, 129; secondary compared with college, 209; sex differentiation of, 200, 307; *see also* Children
Study groups, parent, 286
Supervisory personnel, counselor, 296-312; elementary school administrator, 282-95; encouragement of creativity by, 203-4, 207-9, 266-81; and English instruction, 164; identification of creative children by, 270-73; and mental health in school organization, 319-20, 328-29; new techniques encouraged by, 278-79; student teachers aided by, 207-9, 279-81, 287-90; teachers provided with emotional support by, 274-77
Symbols, art defined as creation of, 219-20; visual, 229

Taba, Hilda, 150
Taxonomy of Educational Objectives, 9
Teachers, administrative restraints on, 247-52; administrator's role in encouraging, 207-9, 282-95; of art, 223-25; authority-oriented vs. creative, 4-6; children as own, 199-200; as coaches, 210-11; college, 247-55; counselor's aid to, 309; creativity development by, 4-6, 63-73, 115-17; differences in styles of, 268-69; emotional aspects of creativity by, 269, 274-77; of English, specialization of, 168, 175; extra-curricular activities of, 203-4; hiring of, 207, 215; inquiry method used by, 75-78; of language arts, 136-39; noncreative, problems posed by, 127-28; poor, and creativity, 115-17; problems of creative, 126-29; professor's noncreative behavior characteristics listed, 253-55; student, 279-81; supervisor's role in encouraging, 266-81; total school as social system determines creativity of, 203-4; workshops for, 6-18
Tenopyr, Mary L., chapter on structure-of-intellect model, 25-45; model's applicability to teaching, 252-53
Tests, for college admission, 239-40; college exams, 244, 256-57; of creativity, 20-24, 247, 300-3; of intelligence as not measuring all factors, 330-31; research needed on, 247; *see also* Evaluation
Textbooks, for foreign language teaching, 183, 189-90; for social studies, shortcomings of, 208
Theatre, creative artist in, 230-36
Thinking, cognition defined, 28; convergent vs. divergent, 28, 38-40, 239-40, 332; creative, 133; instruction on nature of, 43-44; reading as, 155-56
Thoreau, Henry David, quoted, 82
Time, role in learning, 106-7

Time schedules, flexible, 274
Tom Sawyer, 140-42
Torrance, E. Paul, chapter on developing creativity, 3-24; experiment on thinking instruction, 44; quoted on child's creativity, 341; writing research by, 160
TOTE model, 32
Transfer recall, 36-39
Troy High School (Fullerton, Calif.), 171
Truth, search for, and development of creativity, 15-18; in science, 105
Tutorial system, 244
Twaddell, Freeman, 182

UNESCO Dictionary of the Social Sciences, 205
Uniqueness, value of, 66
Universities. *See* Colleges and universities
University of Chicago, 244
University of Southern California, 244

Value development, 338-39
Verbalization, and divergent thinking, 332-33; encouragement of, 143-45
Visual arts in elementary school, 216-29
Vocabulary, foreign, 181-83; ways to encourage building of, 143-45

Weber, Cynthia A., quoted, 145
West Side Story, 231-32
Whitehead, Alfred North, quoted, 74, 78
Willoughby, Stephen S., chapter on teaching mathematics, 86-87, 115-30
Wilson, John A. R., chapter on very young children, 55-73
Woodfin, Mary Jo, chapter on social studies, 89, 191-202; chapter on supervisory personnel, 266-81
Word recognition, as problem solving, 152-53
Workshops for training teachers to develop pupil's creativity, 6-18
Wright, Frank Lloyd, as creative dropout, 130
Writing, evaluative scales for, 159-60; research on, 160-61; teaching for creativity in, 156-61